Trayhon

The Czech Revolution of 1848

Stanley Z. Pech

The Czech Revolution
of 1848

The University of North Carolina Press
Chapel Hill

To Vera

Preface

The events of the year 1848 have always attracted the attention of Czech and Slovak historians, who have produced many excellent specialized monographs on various aspects and personalities of that year. Thus far, however, there exists no scholarly monograph in any language covering the whole revolutionary period from March, 1848, to the spring of 1849. The great pioneer work is Kazbunda's *České hnutí roku 1848* (Prague, 1929). Based largely on archival sources made available only after 1918, this volume brings to light many new facts, but unfortunately the author suspends his account with August, 1848, thus restricting it to only half of the revolutionary period. Other accounts of the fateful year are addressed to a wide audience and dispense with the *apparatus criticus*. The most outstanding of these is Roubík's *Český rok 1848* (Prague, 1931; 2nd ed., 1948), an engaging treatment by a historian who illumined the year 1848 with many scholarly articles published over a period of four decades. The most authoritative Marxist account may be found in the survey *Přehled československých dějin*, Vol. II/1 (Prague, 1960).

The work I am placing before the reader covers the entire revolutionary period, and in this sense may claim to fill the gap left by previous works. There is, however, no doubt whatsoever in my mind that the real experts on the Czech Revolution of 1848 are—and have always been—among those closest to the sources, the historians of Czechoslovakia, and that no historian laboring abroad can hope to equal their command of the subject. Yet the very distance that handicaps a historian in North America seeking to grapple with the problems of Czechoslovak history provides at least one compensation: it shields him from the emotions and biases to which a Czechoslovak historian (or any other historian writing about his own country) may be subject and makes it possible for him to offer less partisan views and interpretations. I have endeavored to take advantage of this distance and of the benefits it confers, but others will have to be the judges of the success or the lack of it with which I have accomplished this objective.

For the Czechs, although the year 1848 was one of achievement, it also brought some failures. The Czech leadership in particular has often been subjected to criticism. Among the most severe critics was Thomas G. Masaryk. In his *Karel Havlíček,* which is in effect a critical account of the Czech policy of 1848, Masaryk castigates "our official policy of the year 1848" and labels it "government opportunism" (3rd ed., Prague, 1920, p. v). He accuses the Czech liberal leaders of "irresolution and vacillation" (p. 86) but is equally severe with the radicals, whom he takes to task for their "phrase-making radicalism" (p. 82). These are harsh words indeed; the following pages will attempt to show to what extent the harshness of Masaryk's judgment appears justified today.

A word of explanation is in order regarding the organization of the material. Confronted with a staggering output of historical literature in recent years, very few historians and students can afford the luxury of reading such a specialized monograph as this one from cover to cover. Most will consult only those chapters or sections in which they are particularly interested or to which they are guided by the index, and the volume is organized to serve primarily this type of reader. Except for the final chapter containing the concluding reflections, an attempt has been made to give each chapter a topical unity. Chapters 1-9 are the core chapters, dealing with the revolutionary era from March, 1848, to May, 1849; the chapters follow each other in chronological order, but each chapter is at the same time built around a unifying theme. Chapters 10-14 constitute an added feature designed to explore the roles of five groups during the 1848-49 era.

Chapter 10 deals with the Slovaks. Since Czechoslovakia is today a partnership of Czechs and Slovaks, no historian need offer apologies for being concerned with the interplay between Czechs and Slovaks in 1848. But this chapter does not deal with the Slovak movement as such; it is only concerned with the relationship between that movement and the Czech movement during the 1848-49 period.

Chapters 11, 12, 13, and 14 are devoted respectively to peasants, workers, students, and women. Since there is currently a heightened interest in the historical role of these groups, it seemed appropriate to discuss them separately, in addition to dealing with them in the main body of the volume. The fact that historians are now turning increasingly to comparative studies only underscores the need for according these groups a separate treatment. A West European specialist interested in the role of Czech peasants in 1848 for comparative purposes, for example, will have a special chapter available for his perusal; he will not have to scan the whole volume for the relevant material. Each chapter on a group brings together, in abridged form, for each group, the material scattered throughout the core chapters, but adds some new facts and reflections. A certain amount of repetition was, under the circumstances, unavoidable.

The decision to include a chapter on Czech women, who became politically active for the first time in 1848, is in line with the most recent trends in historiography. The American Historical Association, at its 1966 Annual Meeting, devoted a discussion to the women's movement in the United States; and a leading Soviet periodical recently published a study of the women's movement in Poland in the 1840's (*Sovetskoe Slavianovedenie*, No. 2 [1966]).

I wish to express my gratitude to the Social Science Research Council of Canada, to the Canada Council, and to the following Czechoslovak institutions, all in Prague: the Historical Institute of the Czechoslovak Academy of Sciences, the Czechoslovak Center of the International Exchange of Publications, and the State Central Archives. This work has been published with the help of a grant from the Social Science Research Council of Canada, using funds provided by the Canada Council. The Historical Institute, the Czechoslovak Center, and the State Central Archives supplied me with photocopies of complete runs of Czech newspapers for 1848-49 and of other sources not available on this continent.

My thanks are also due to the members of the staff, too numerous to mention, of the University of British Columbia Library for their cooperation in the acquisition and processing of books and journals. I would further like to thank Frederick G. Heymann of the University of Calgary most warmly for taking the time to read the manuscript and for offering valuable suggestions for improvement. I would also like to thank the staff of The University of North Carolina Press for its assistance and support in seeing the manuscript through to publication.

Finally, I wish to acknowledge a most profound debt of gratitude to my wife Vera, whose critical reading of the entire manuscript brought about some important revisions, and whose careful checking of the diacritics in the footnotes and bibliography was indispensable to me in my preparation of the manuscript for publication. It is only just that this book be dedicated to her.

Stanley Z. Pech

The University of British Columbia

Contents

Abbreviations of Works
Frequently Cited

The following abbreviations of periodicals and other sources frequently cited are used throughout the footnotes and bibliography:

AÖG	*Archiv für Österreichische Geschichte*
AUC	*Acta Universitatis Carolinae*
AUPO-H	*Acta Universitatis Palackianae Olomucensis; Facultas Philosophica; Historica*
CBB	*Constitutionelles Blatt aus Böhmen*
ČČH	*Český Časopis Historický*
ČČM	*Časopis Českého Museum*
ČDV	*Časopis pro Dějiny Venkova*
ČMM	*Časopis Matice Moravské*
ČSČH	*Československý Časopis Historický*
HČ	*Historický Časopis*
JCEA	*Journal of Central European Affairs*
LANM	*Literární Archiv Národního Musea v Praze*
MIÖG	*Mitteilungen des Instituts für Österreichische Geschichtsforschung*
MÖSA	*Mitteilungen des Österreichischen Staatsarchivs*
MVGDB	*Mitteilungen des Vereins für Geschichte der Deutschen in Böhmen*
NLS	*Noviny Lípy Slovanské*
NN	*Národní Noviny*
NNM	*Naše Národní Minulost v Dokumentech*
ÖO	*Österreichische Osthefte*
PHS	*Právněhistorické Studie*
PVL	*Pražský Večerní List*
Rozpravy ČSAV—SV	*Rozpravy Československé Akademie Věd—Řada Společenských Věd*
SAMV	*Sborník Archivu Ministerstva Vnitra v Praze*
SAP	*Sborník Archivních Prací*
SEER	*Slavonic and East European Review*
SH	*Sborník Historický*
SÚA	*Státní Ústřední Archiv v Praze*
SVŠPO—H	*Sborník Vysoké Školy Pedagogické v Olomouci— Oddělení Historie*
ZfG	*Zeitschrift für Geschichtswissenschaft*
ZfO	*Zeitschrift für Ostforschung*

The Czech Revolution of 1848

Prologue

In the second half of February, 1848, Prague was in an impatient mood. Denied a political outlet, the mood found poignant expression in the popularity bestowed by the people on the song "The French before Nizza," a march from an opera by a little-known Bohemian composer which had just had its première on February 19. The libretto, by Richard Wagner, the product of his early liberal days, was set against the background of French revolutionary wars and presented the French army in a sympathetic light. The première with its implied revolutionary message was an instant success. The reception given the opera was on a scale "unheard of" in Prague;[1] the tuneful marching song in particular caught the imagination of the public and soon echoed through the streets and cafés of the city. Within ten days of the première, the people were confronted with another French theme, this time a real-life drama for which Paris herself was a stage and which set in motion a chain of revolutionary movements throughout Central and Eastern Europe.

On February 29 (this was leap year) a great masquerade ball was held in Prague, under the auspices of a leading art and literary society. The society comprised both Czechs and Germans, and the ball was a major event of the season. As expected, the cream of writers, artists, and composers turned out for the occasion. The galleries were packed, and, responding to the mood of the merrymakers, the military band played the march from *The French before Nizza,* earning a thundering applause. It was on this same evening that the Paris mail arrived bearing the fateful tidings: on February 24–25, 1848, the French king had abdicated and the monarchy had collapsed. The news was contained in letters from Paris addressed to certain individuals who happened to be attending the ball; they were delivered to the addressees while the ball was in progress. It was after midnight, and the word spread quickly, though quietly. There were, of course, no open demonstrations of sympathy for the French; only hushed whispers could have betrayed to a close observer that

1. *Bohemia,* February 22, 1848. The opera, like the marching song, was entitled *The French before Nizza* (full title in the German original: *Bianca und Giuseppe oder die Franzosen vor Nizza*). The composer was J. F. Kittl. The opera has since been largely forgotten.

something exciting was happening.[2] Interestingly enough, though police agents were present, they detected nothing unusual.[3]

One of the participants at the ball later recalled his own reaction. The news from France seemed to him so stunning that he had to reassure himself repeatedly that this was no idle prank, that the republic had really been proclaimed in Paris, and that the tide of change would at last sweep into the Habsburg realm. At the conclusion of the ball, with the police out of the way, he relates, he joined with two friends in making a fervent toast to freedom and to the republic.[4] For there was little doubt in the minds of those present that the fall of the monarchy in France spelled the collapse of absolutism in the Czech Lands and in the Habsburg Monarchy. No one quite knew yet how this collapse would occur but there was certainty that it would come.

2. For a description of the ball, see A. Meissner, *Geschichte meines Lebens* (Vienna, 1884), I, 6 ff; *CBB,* April 2, 1848. See also J. V. Frič, *Paměti,* ed. K. Cvejn (Prague, 1957-63), I, 343-44.

3. K. Kazbunda, *České hnutí roku 1848* (Prague, 1929), p. 29.

4. Meissner, *Geschichte meines Lebens,* I, 15.

Part One

The Course of Events

Chapter 1

The Pre-March Years

On the eve of 1848, the Czech (Bohemian) Lands, which consisted of the provinces of Bohemia and Moravia, formed part of the multinational Habsburg Monarchy.[1] Formally Bohemia was a kingdom and Moravia a margravate; in 1846, the last census year before 1848, Bohemia's population was 4.3 million and Moravia's, 2.2 million. Together the two provinces constituted a territorial complex called "Lands of the Czech (Bohemian) Crown." The capital of Bohemia was Prague, with a population of over 115,000; that of Moravia, Brno, with a population of 45,000.[2] Ethnically, the population of Bohemia and Moravia con-

1. Unless otherwise noted, the term "Moravia" includes also Austrian Silesia.

For the pre-March period, see: F. Kutnar, *Přehled dějin Československa v epoše feudalismu*, Vol. IV (Prague, 1963) ; F. Roubík, *Český rok 1848* (2nd ed., Prague, 1948), chap. i; and E. Bass, *Čtení o roce osmačtyřicátém*, Vol. I (Prague, 1940).

2. *Uebersichts-Tafeln zur Statistik der österreichischen Monarchie*, Besonderer Abdruck des X. and XI. Heftes der "Statistischen Mittheilungen" (Vienna, 1850), pp. 1, 3.

The total population of the Habsburg Monarchy was thirty-seven million. Administratively it was divided into three parts: (1) The Lands of the Hungarian Crown (Hungary), including Croatia; (2) the non-Hungarian provinces, including Bohemia and Moravia, for which no single official name existed; (3) the Military Border, which was territorially part of the Lands of the Hungarian Crown but was at this time under a special administrative regime. The population of the Hungarian Lands was thirteen million, that of the remaining provinces almost twenty-four million. The non-Hungarian administrative complex consisted of the following political divisions: Lower Austria, Upper Austria (with Salzburg), Styria, Carinthia and Carniola, the Littoral, Tyrol and Voralberg, Bohemia, Moravia, Galicia and Bucovina, Dalmatia, Lombardy, and Venetia. The non-Hungarian provinces were separated from the Hungarian Lands by the river Leitha, and during the years 1867-1918 (by this time Lombardy and Venetia had broken away from the monarchy) were referred to conveniently though unofficially as "Cisleithania"; the corresponding term for the Hungarian Lands was "Transleithania." For the sake of convenience, the term "Cisleithania" will be occasionally used in the following pages.

The Czechs were the largest Slavic group in the monarchy. Many Slavic and some non-Slavic spokesmen claimed at the time that the Slavs as a whole

sisted of Czechs and Germans, with the former having a clear majority in both provinces.[3] The Germans inhabited a continuous strip of land just inside the Bohemian-Moravian border in the North, West, and South (the later Sudeten Germans); outside this strip they could be found in varying numbers in the cities.

The Habsburg Monarchy was a centralist and absolutist state, ruled, on the eve of 1848, by Habsburg Emperor Ferdinand I, with Chancellor Metternich as his chief minister. Like most other provinces of the empire, Bohemia and Moravia were each administered by a governor, appointed by the emperor. The office over which the governor presided and the territory over which his jurisdiction extended were both officially called *gubernium*. The governor was in no sense a representative of the province, but merely an instrument through which the central government in Vienna exercised authority in that province. Bohemia and Moravia were each divided into administrative divisions called "regions," of which there were sixteen in the former and eight in the latter. Each region was headed by a region prefect.[4]

The monarchy knew no central diet or parliament common to the whole state, but only provincial diets. The diet was a symbol, but no more than a symbol, of legislative power in each province. By

were in a majority in the monarchy. This was not correct. Their proportion was under 50 per cent (see J. Heidler, *Čechy a Rakousko v politických brožurách predbřeznových* [Prague, 1920], p. 145). All nationality statistics for this period must be regarded as approximations at best.

3. Šafařík estimates that in about 1840 Bohemia's population consisted of 3 million Czechs, 1.1 million Germans, and 66,000 Jews; and Moravia's, 1.3 million Czechs, .6 million Germans, 192,000 Poles, and 38,000 Jews. See P. J. Šafařík, *Slovanský Národopis* (4th ed., Prague, 1955), pp. 94-95; this work was first published in 1842. For an estimate from the German side, see J. Springer, *Statistik des österreichischen Kaiserstaates* (Vienna, 1840), I, 86, 136, 138. Springer's figure for the Slav-speaking population of Bohemia is 2.5 million (out of a total of 4 million), for Moravia, 1.5 million (out of 2 million).

4. For "region," the Czech and German terms were, respectively, *kraj* and *Kreis;* for "region prefect," *krajský hejtman* and *Kreishauptmann*. Names of regions were derived from the name of the city in which the region head office was located, with the following exceptions: In Bohemia, the regions of Kouřim and Beroun were each administered from a separate office in Prague; the seat of the Bydžov region was Jičín; of Prácheň (Prachin) region, Písek; of Rakovník (Rakonitz) region, Slaný (Schlan). In Moravia, the Přerov region office was located in Hranice (Mährisch-Weisskirchen).

For a map of the regions, see *Atlas československých dějin* (Prague, 1965), p. 18, a, b.

1840, the powers of the Bohemian and Moravian diets, as well as of other provincial diets, had been reduced to the point where they could be viewed as no more than rubber stamps summoned occasionally for the purpose of humbly registering their approval of the imperial will. Each diet consisted of four estates: the prelates, the lords, the knights, and the cities. Of the four estates, that of the prelates occupied the highest rank. Among the members of the estate of prelates in Bohemia was the Archbishop of Prague, the formal head of this estate, which also included all bishops as well as the abbots of the leading monasteries and a few other high ecclesiastical dignitaries.

The combined membership of the estates of the prelates, lords, and knights numbered more than two hundred[5] in Bohemia and about seventy[6] in Moravia, while the membership of the estate of the cities consisted of only four in Bohemia and seven in Moravia. In both the Bohemian and Moravian diets, however, the cities held collectively only one vote, whereas each member of the other estates held an individual vote. Even had the cities enjoyed a greater representation, their status would not have been much improved, since it was the practice for the cities to be represented by their officials, who were government appointees rather than elected deputies. The peasantry was, of course, wholly without a political voice. (In the Habsburg Monarchy, only in Tyrol and Vorarlberg did the peasantry have deputies in the provincial diet.) In both the Bohemian and Moravian diets, the influence of the knights was limited; controlling influence was in the hands of the lords. In the early 1840's, after decades of apathy, the Bohemian diet began to assert itself and demand from the emperor a restoration of its former privilege of participating in the legislative process (see below).

The absolutist state was distrustful of new ideas and of all forms of dissent, and in checking the manifestations of dissent it relied heavily on the police and on censorship. Since 1801, the police and censorship had been jointly administered at the highest level by the Police and Censorship Court Bureau (*Polizei–und–Censur–Hofstelle*)

5. According to an official handbook for 1846, 14 prelates, 151 lords, and 43 knights were privileged to attend the diet. See J. Čelakovský, "Stav městský na sněmě českém od léta 1794-1847," Part IV, *ČČM*, XLIV (1870), 30.

6. Springer, *Statistik*, I, 260. The University of Prague was represented by its rector, a member of the estate of prelates; after much controversy this representation was recognized in the mid-forties.

headed by Count Sedlnitzky (1817-48), who is, next to Metternich, the best-known symbol of pre-1848 absolutism in the Habsburg Monarchy. Each provincial capital had its own police bureau, headed by a police president who was subordinate to both the Police Court Bureau in Vienna and the governor of the province. At the regional level police authority was exercised by region prefects, but since local police were virtually nonexistent, region prefects had to rely on the army to maintain order. A regular feature of police activity was the censorship of letters from abroad, for which purpose a number of special posts were established throughout the monarchy, usually in the capital city and in cities located close to the border or frequented by foreign guests. In Bohemia, there were four such special posts, Prague among them.[7]

Although the Habsburg police apparatus was not nearly as well-developed as, for example, the one in contemporary France, it maintained a fairly extensive system of surveillance of groups and individuals politically suspect. There were secret agents or informants who received regular pay for their work and whose identity can often be established today from surviving archives. On special occasions, the most celebrated being the Congress of Vienna in 1814-15, a veritable army of spies was impressed into the service of the police; among those recruited were especially those who had easy or frequent contacts with the guests or who were in a position, because of their jobs, to penetrate the privacy of the mind or the dwelling: janitors, housemaids, priests, women of easy virtue. Apart from paid agents, there were always zealous volunteer informants—in fact, the whole system encouraged a proliferation of informants, one of the most damning features of Metternich's regime. Everyone of importance was spied upon: professors, government officials high and low, leaders of cultural organizations, even members of the Habsburg family. Professors were not permitted in their lectures to depart from approved texts and, according to a decree of 1821, public libraries were required to report the titles of books they were borrowing.[8]

Censorship of printed matter was most elaborate. Archival materials accessible today yield lists of books compiled by the Censorship Court Bureau that were either banned outright or variously restricted in circulation. An observer unaware of the purpose of such a list,

7. M. Novák, "Rakouská policie a politický vývoj v Čechách před r. 1848," *SAP*, III, Nos. 1-2 (1953), 52.
8. Heidler, *Čechy a Rakousko*, p. 35.

or "index," as it was called, might be pardoned for assuming it to be a catalogue of masterpieces of European literature. Among the authors gracing the Index for the period 1835-48 are famous historians (Ranke, Droysen), philosophers (Fichte, Rousseau, Spinoza), and poets (Heine, Lessing, Goethe, Schiller), each represented by a few (but not all) of his works. For this period the Index lists no less than five thousand titles.[9] It has been estimated that about 5 per cent of the contemporary output of German literature was included in this Index—not a high percentage in itself but significant when judged according to the quality of the works banned and in conjunction with other aspects of censorship, particularly the almost total ban on foreign newspapers and the heavy censorship of the domestic press. A separate list existed for works in Slavic languages, forbidden specifically in Bohemia.[10] Sometimes a book was not forbidden outright but restricted in some special way: for example, press reviews of it might be banned.

The position of editors of newspapers and magazines was an awkward one. A copy of every publication had to be submitted in advance to a censor who was not likely to approve any politically newsworthy item from abroad or even from within the monarchy. Any serious discussion of controversial political issues was nonexistent. Even as he deleted articles from galley proofs, the censor insisted that the space be filled with other material before the publication was released; this only made the editors more reluctant than ever to consider publishing anything that might even remotely arouse a censor's ire. After the collapse of absolutism one newspaper described the vagaries and follies of the censorship to which a periodical or magazine was subjected during the absolutist era. A manuscript had to be submitted to a "revision" office, from which it was forwarded to a censor. The censor then sent it back to the revision office, from which it went to the Police and Censorship Bureau. Having studied it, the Bureau officials were required to return it to the revision office. Not infrequently a magazine article traveled back and forth among the various censorship offices in manuscript form for two to three months, sometimes for as long as half a year. And even after all approval had been obtained for the manuscript, the

9. J. Marx, "Die ämtlichen Verbotslisten," *MÖSA,* IX (1956), 151-85, *passim.*

10. Reproduced in Z. Tobolka, *Počátky konstitučního života v Čechách* (Prague, 1898), Appendix I.

galley proofs still had to be submitted to the censor for final approval.[11] Such witless bureaucracy produced predictable results: newspapers and magazines were colorless, dull, and unenlightening. Important events either went completely unreported or their coverage was deliberately delayed until the news item lost so much of its current flavor that it was no longer excitable. Curiously, a few (too few) censors were men of high intellectual caliber; it was their thankless task to pass on scholarly works, subject, of course, to a higher decision. Among such censors was P. J. Šafařík, the distinguished scholar of Slovak origin who became associated with the Czech national movement.

The author of a magazine article waited months for the processing of his manuscript; the author of a book waited sometimes years. The procedure may have appealed to the censor's sense of pride and self-importance, but it exasperated the writer and scholar to the limit of his endurance. A scholar who had spent many painful years writing a book was often compelled to watch more years go by as his manuscript went from one censor-bureaucrat to another. It sometimes took as many as three years for the bureaucracy to make up its collective mind concerning whether the book was subversive of public confidence or not.

One of the worst features of the pre-1848 regime was its bureaucratic procrastination and its stifling inertia, which caused vital decisions to be deferred until, when made, they had become meaningless or no longer relevant. It sometimes took years for a request addressed to the government to be answered, if it was ever answered. Thus, in 1832, a memorandum submitted to the government by an established Czech cultural organization concerning the use of the Czech language in schools was answered three years later—in the negative.[12] When established groups had to wait years for official action, one may well imagine what chance an individual stood in dealing with the bureaucratic octopus. The zeal of the lesser bureaucrats was, of course, sensibly diminished by the inadequate pay they received[13] and also by the general contempt for the public that

11. *Bohemia,* April 11, 1848.

12. O. Kádner, "Školství v Republice československé," in *Československá Vlastivěda* (Prague, 1931), X, 29.

13. See the report of the Prague acting police director on the low morale of the lesser bureaucrats caused by poor pay (*SÚA* [Prague, April 12, 1848], PG 1846-49, 15 c/3, No. 2938).

permeated the whole bureaucratic apparatus. In the real sense of the word, the bureaucrat of the monarchy viewed himself as the master, not the servant, of the public. The public existed for the greater glory of the official, not vice versa. It had to be kept at arm's length and constantly reminded of its duty to be patient and grateful and obedient. In dealing with the lower social classes in particular, the bureaucrat came into his own. This applied especially to the landlords' officials, whose arrogance in dealing with the peasantry was proverbial.

On the eve of 1848, the Czech Lands were still overwhelmingly agricultural and the peasantry represented the largest social class. What were the conditions of this class? The peasant was not yet wholly emancipated, although the first steps in that direction had already been taken. The first fundamental step on the road to emancipation was taken by Emperor Joseph II in his now-famous decree of November 1, 1781, restoring to the peasant his freedom of movement.[14] Henceforth, the peasant could leave the domain of his lord, move to the city, learn a trade, pursue higher forms of education, and contract matrimonial arrangements—all without permission from his lord. This decree, which applied to Bohemia, Moravia, and Silesia, wiped out a number of restrictions that made up the complex of social relationships usually known as serfdom. The decision to issue it was hastened by a revolt that had taken place in Bohemia in 1775—the greatest peasant rebellion in the history of that province.

In a decade marked by the most prodigious reform effort in the history of the Czech Lands, Joseph issued a number of other decrees relating to the peasantry, the objective of which was to circumscribe the power of the lords over their subjects, to bring the subjects into more direct contact with the central government, and to extend the peasant's rights to his holding. Of course, certain ingredients of serfdom survived Joseph's reign: the peasant continued to render to his lord a number of services and payments, in labor, in money, and in kind; and those peasants who had not left their land—and they were a large majority—continued to be the legal subjects of their lords, who exercised over them patrimonial jurisdiction, albeit a jurisdiction that was substantially reduced as a result of the reform legislation.[15]   Nevertheless, there is no gainsaying the significance of

14. Text in Czech and German in *Archiv Český,* XXV (1910), 25-28.

15. Emperor Joseph also commuted the *robot* into money payments and introduced a major tax reform calculated to equalize the tax burden, both

Joseph's reforms. The dependence of the peasant upon his lord had been loosened to a considerable extent. The decree concerning freedom of movement made it possible for the peasant to live in the city, thus nourishing the growth of cities and of industry. Since the cities were either predominantly German or at least governed by the German element, and since, conversely, the majority of the rural population was Czech, the migration from rural into urban areas altered the ethnic balance in the cities in favor of the Czechs, with the consequent growth of a Czech intelligentsia and of a Czech national movement. Of course, the effect of this alteration was not to be felt for some time, since for some decades opportunities in the cities were few and the flow of the rural population into them was very limited.

No further substantial improvement took place during the decades following Joseph's reign. Some attempts were made by Joseph's successors in this direction, but none of them attacked the problem in a decisive manner. Steeped in a morass of bureaucratic procedures, loath to introduce any changes as long as there was the faintest glimmer of hope that the cumbersome and outdated social edifice could survive without change, court circles and government authorities followed a dilatory strategy that, in retrospect, could only be viewed as an invitation to disaster and revolution. Not even the terrible uprising of Polish peasants in Galicia in 1846, which sent shudders of horror throughout the higher strata of the population, could shake the authorities out of their lethargy sufficiently to cause them to introduce more than token or highly ineffective measures for improvement. The bureaucratic procrastinations and half-measures continued to be the order of the day, with the result that by the beginning of 1848, a final solution of the peasant question was nowhere in sight and an exasperated peasantry was in the throes of serious unrest.

Traditionally, the obligation most hated by the peasant was the labor service (the Slavic term for this service is *robota,* the German modification, *robot*), which, where it existed, cut deeply into the time required by the peasant to cultivate his holding. Despite the fact that it was the most hated of all obligations, the *robot* was not

by decrees issued on February 10, 1789 (text in *Archiv Český,* XXV [1910], 186 ff.). The nobility objected strenuously to both measures, however, and the decrees were repealed by his successor, Leopold II. See W. E. Wright, "Initiation of Robota Abolition in Bohemia," *JCEA,* XVII (1958), 239-53.

the most widespread; by 1848, it had been commuted, it appears, to monetary payments in most of the estates in Moravia, though it was somewhat more widespread in Bohemia.[16] Besides the *robot,* there was a variety of payments, in money and in kind, not counting payments and obligations to the state and to the church. This simple statement, however, conceals a truly bewildering maze of feudal obligations, some in writing and others only sanctified by custom. The obligations varied not only from province to province, but also from district to district, and were frequently ununiform even within a village. A complete catalogue, if such could be drawn up, would include literally hundreds of different types of obligations throughout Bohemia and Moravia. The rationale for the obligations was that they compensated the lord for his permission for the peasant to use his land, for his exercise of administrative and judicial duties over his subjects, and for his offer of protection to his subjects. However, what the peasant largely needed by 1848 was protection against, not by, the lord, and his chance of receiving it was limited, although it had increased as a consequence of the reforms of Joseph and his empress-mother, Maria Theresa.

The peasant himself was increasingly resentful of his handicapped position vis-à-vis the lord; but in his book of villains it was the administrative or economic official of the estate who more than the lord himself inspired the most bitter hatred. Officials tended to be high-handed in the performance of their duties, and arbitrary and venal in the bestowal of the few favors the subject could expect. There were certainly officials who treated their subjects well, but it is equally certain that the majority did not—and this is one of the few generalizations concerning the peasant question that can confidently be made. When addressing the lord or his official, the subject was expected to clothe his remarks in terms of self-deprecation, and failure to abide by this procedure was not accepted lightly. In the

16. There is no systematic and detailed study of the extent of the various peasant obligations at this time. As for the *robot,* K. Grünberg, in *Die Bauernbefreiung und die Auflösung des gutsherrlich-bäuerlichen Verhältnisses in Böhmen, Mähren und Schlesien* (Leipzig, 1894), I, 368, holds that it was "by far the most prevalent rule till 1848." In contrast, some writers claim that in Moravia, at least, the *robot* survived in a minority of cases (see, for example, J. Radimský and M. Wurmová [eds.], *Petice moravského lidu k sněmu z roku 1848* [Prague, 1955], pp. 8-9; see also A. Klíma, "Ein Beitrag zur Agrarfrage in der Revolution von 1848 in Böhmen," in *Studien zur Geschichte der österreichisch-ungarischen Monarchie* [Budapest, 1961], pp. 15-26).

eighteenth century it was common for a subject to kneel before an official (and also the sovereign) and kiss his hand. Impatient with such ritualistic display of the servility of one human being before another, Joseph II forbade it by a special decree in 1787,[17] but much of the litany of self-humiliation survived and indeed was one of the hallmarks of the pre-1848 regime, scarring social relationships well into the second half of the nineteenth century and beyond. As late as August, 1848, it was possible for an official to scold a peasant for not addressing him as "gracious lord" (*jemnost pane*),[18] and toward the end of the revolutionary era 1848-49 the daily press was replete with complaints about officials whose insolence was again growing with the drift into reaction after a short respite of freedom.[19]

Corporal punishment was far from exceptional, the box on the ear administered to a "recalcitrant" peasant by an arrogant official being among the least painful, if not the least humiliating, of disciplinary measures. Beating with a cane was legally permitted, although, theoretically at least, a decree of 1793 required the approval of a district government official for this form of punishment.[20] It is doubtful if the lords and their officials took this stricture too seriously; in any event, no dispensation was required for the less elaborate forms of punishment. It is safe to say that any official bent upon applying corporal punishment found himself little hampered by the existing legal barriers in pursuing his objective to his utmost satisfaction.[21] The arrogance of the official was perhaps only exceeded by the servility he himself exhibited toward the noble.

Although the Czech Lands were, on the eve of 1848, primarily an agricultural region, with the peasantry constituting the largest social class, an urban and industrial working class had begun to appear. Until the end of the eighteenth century industry in the Czech Lands remained largely within the framework of "domestic industries," manufactories, and handicrafts. The nineteenth century ushered in a new trend: a systematic introduction of machinery into the manufacturing process, particularly in the manufacture of textiles, the most important branch of Bohemian-Moravian industry. This

17. Text in *Archiv Český,* XXV (1910), 155.
18. *PVL,* September 9, 1848.
19. See, for example, *NN,* April 27, 1849.
20. Text in *Archiv Český,* XXV (1910), 350.
21. For examples, see F. Roubík (ed.), *Petice venkovského lidu z Čech k Národnímu výboru z roku 1848* (Prague, 1954), p. 519.

"industrial revolution" led to a decline of artisans and craftsmen and to a growth of urban and industrial workers. It is estimated that from 1780 to 1840 the number of independent artisans in Bohemia was cut in half.[22] A similar crisis was afflicting the workers in the domestic industries, of whom the largest group was the spinners and the weavers. The domestic workers lacked the characteristics of the modern proletariat. They were scattered throughout the countryside; in Bohemia and Moravia most of them were found in the border regions. Many still owned or cultivated a plot of land, and thus were part peasants, part workers. The spinners and the weavers were in a chronic economic crisis throughout the pre-1848 period; forced by machines out of their jobs, they were compelled to move into the city where they joined the swelling ranks of the working class. Yet in the cities the working class, even as it expanded, was again subjected to the pressures exerted by the inexorable pace of technology. The first half of the nineteenth century produced the first major economic crises, with workers exposed to periods of unemployment resulting from the introduction of machinery. At the same time, a special economic pressure in the Czech Lands was generated by the competition from the superior English textiles that were making inroads into markets hitherto controlled by Bohemian and Moravian manufacturers.

By the beginning of the 1840's the two largest concentrations of workers were in Prague and Brno. Of the two cities, Brno possessed the more highly developed industrial complex and is believed to have employed about ten thousand workers at that time, the large majority of whom were engaged in the textile industry.[23] This was a sizable proportion in a city with a population of forty-five thousand. By comparison, Prague, with a population of over a hundred thousand had a working class not in excess of four or five thousand.[24] Of the latter, the largest single group was composed of textile workers, specifically cotton-printers, numbering between eight hundred and

22. K. Hoch, "Sociálně-politické poměry v Čechách před r. 1848," ČČH, XXXVIII (1932), 113-25.

23. B. Šindelář, "O úloze lidových mas v revolučním dění roku 1848 na Moravě a ve Slezsku," ČSČH, IV (1956), 215. Some contemporary estimates, probably exaggerated, place the number much higher; thus K. Havlíček, in NN, November 4, 1848, puts the figure for 1848 at fifteen thousand.

24. A statement issued on April 18, 1848, on behalf of Prague workers and published in NN, April 25, 1848, claims to speak for "four thousand workers."

one thousand.[25] The third largest working-class center was Liberec (Reichenberg) in northern Bohemia, where the workers were predominantly German. On the eve of 1848, the workers were far from representing a homogeneous class and were barely on the threshold of political consciousness. In appraising their attitudes, one must take cognizance of their social origin, nationality, type of skill (or the lack of it), age group, degree of concentration in a given geographical area, and other important factors. A majority were still domestic workers, with ties to the land. In certain branches of production—for example, in the Vítkovice ironworks in the Ostrava region in northern Moravia—there was a considerable percentage of foreign workers (some 20 per cent), including some from England.[26] Most full-time industrial and urban workers in the Czech Lands still came from peasant families; only a small minority were sons of workers and thus at least one generation removed from the peasant class. Under such circumstances, any crystallization of social consciousness among the workers was not possible. Many of them were uprooted individuals, without a sense of loyalty to any set of traditions, which presumably contributed to the widespread alcoholism that constituted a serious problem of the working class.

The combination of expanding numbers and severe unemployment produced the first serious unrest among workers, in Brno in 1843 and in Prague in 1844.[27] In both cases violence occurred on a major scale extending over a period of days. According to an official inquiry, in Brno, by 1843, unemployment had risen to the point where it affected one-third of the textile workers. Yet even as employers laid off textile workers for whom factory work was the only means of earning a livelihood, they hired domestic work-

25. Z. Šolle, "K počátkům dělnického hnutí v Praze," *ČSČH,* V (1957), 668, 687.

26. M. Myška, *Počátky vytváření dělnické třídy v železárnách na Ostravsku* (Ostrava, 1962), p. 81.

27. For Brno, see J. Radimský, "Dělnické bouře v Brně roku 1843," *Český Lid,* XXXVI (1949), 9-13. For Prague, see E. Wolfgramm, "Der böhmische Vormärz, im besonderen die böhmischen Arbeitsunruhen des Jahres 1844 in ihren sozialen und politischen Zusammenhängen," in *Aus 500 Jahren deutsch-tschechoslowakischer Geschichte,* ed. K. Obermann and J. Polišenský (Berlin, 1958); and Z. Tobolka, "Počátky dělnického hnutí v Čechách," *Obzor Národohospodářský,* VIII (1903), 17, 57-62, 113-21, 159-68, 208-19. For background, see also J. Marx, *Die wirtschaftlichen Ursachen der Revolution von 1848 in Österreich* (Graz-Köln, 1965), p. 111 ff.

ers who lived in adjacent rural communities and cultivated small plots of land. Employers preferred this type of worker because his small plot assured him a minimum means of subsistence, which allowed him to work for a lower wage. The regular factory workers, who saw the domestic workers rather than the employers as their enemies, vented their fury on them, the wave of violence reaching its climax at the end of May and the beginning of June, 1843. This was the essence of the Brno riots: they were not a struggle between workers and employers but between workers and workers.

The next year, in 1844, the Prague workers, unlike their Brno brethren, chose their target with better accuracy. The workers involved were the cotton-printers, who had been subjected to layoffs occasioned by the introduction of machines. The immediate cause was a wage dispute; the workers in one plant found their pay reduced without prior notice. The result was a strike and an outbreak of violence of the kind the Czech Lands had never seen before. The workers demanded a wage adjustment and above all protested the systematic introduction of machines. In the course of the rioting in the latter part of June, they attacked and proceeded to destroy the machines, the hated symbol of their plight. The disturbances, which lasted a week, were finally brought under control by General Alfred Windischgrätz and his troops. An interesting fact about these events is that they took place only a few days after the well-known uprising of Silesian weavers, immortalized by the German dramatist Hauptmann. There was no apparent direct connection between the two events, however. It should be added that virtually all the textile manufacturers in Prague involved in the dispute were German-Jewish, and that the rioting was accompanied by outbreaks of anti-Semitism and occasional attacks on the Jews. Similar riots of textile workers took place in two or three other cities in Bohemia during this period, notably in Liberec. In Prague, at the beginning of July, the unrest of the cotton-printers was followed by the rioting of a group of railroad workers in a Prague suburb, in protest against wage reductions and layoffs. Once again, the efficient General Windischgrätz had to move in with his grenadiers in order to bring the uprising under control.[28]

The movement in Prague in 1844 was of great significance in the history of the Prague and Bohemian-Moravian labor movement.

28. *Přehled československých dějin* (Prague, 1958), I, 668-69.

This is true especially of the cotton-printers' movement. Unlike the elemental movement of the railroad workers, the cotton-printers acted in a reasonably organized manner. They used their existing mutual-aid societies as a basis for their action, and throughout the strike, they conducted negotiations with their employers and the authorities through their chosen spokesmen. Though still very vague, there was a certain feeling of a community of interests—yet hardly a full-fledged class consciousness—that bound them together and separated them from their employers. An important consequence of the 1844 disturbances was that they instilled in the other segments of the population a fear of the working class. The latter was increasingly viewed as a dark and menacing force threatening to sap the very foundations of civilization. As the forties drew on, the working class was being referred to more and more as "proletarian"—a term that usually had a pejorative connotation. At the same time the term "Communist" came into use to describe the working-class movement. Thus, the Prussian Ambassador in Vienna noted in a report of the 1844 disturbances that "the Bohemian and Silesian disturbances are being described as movements of communism," but was prudent enough to add that "to me this rests on a misunderstanding."[29] A Czech observer noted that "a fear of the proletariat" had begun to grip the public.[30]

The worker enjoyed no protection against the employer. The only institution that could have offered him some protection was the state, but it was disinterested. Dominated by the laissez-faire philosophy, the state remained aloof from the worker-employer relationship on the ground that both sides must retain the "freedom" to shape their relationship as their needs required. In practice, of course, this left the worker at the mercy of the employer, and before 1848, little was done to regulate the relationship. Only child labor was regulated, when its abuses could no longer be ignored, not even by a laissez-faire state. The most important piece of child-labor legislation was the decree of June 11, 1842, which permitted the hiring of children for regular factory work only from the age of twelve, or, in exceptional circumstances, from the age of nine. The decree also restricted the workday of nine- to twelve-year-olds to ten hours and that of twelve- to sixteen-year-olds to twelve hours. Additionally,

29. Report dated 21.IX.1844; quoted in Wolfgramm, "Der böhmische Vormärz," p. 218.

30. J. Malý, *Naše Znovuzrození* (Prague, 1880-84), II, 11.

the work period was to be interrupted by at least one hour of rest, and night work (after 9:00 p.m.) was prohibited for children under sixteen.[31] Employers were not noted for a scrupulous observance of this law, however, and as late as 1848 a contemporary observer complained that in Prague a thirteen- to fourteen-hour day for children was not uncommon.[32] After such an exhausting day, the child was supposed to receive his education; the instruction took place sometimes as late as 8:00 to 10:00 at night, with the result that the pupils, who could hardly keep awake, profited little from their schooling. Nevertheless, for all the hardship it created, child labor in the Czech Lands never became as widespread as it did in England and other parts of Western Europe. The industrial revolution did not reach its zenith until the second half of the nineteenth century, and when it did, public opinion, which could no longer tolerate the mass exploitation of children, forced the state to give them more vigorous protection.

Although the Czechs constituted a majority of the population of the Czech Lands, they were not the masters of their own fate. In practically all realms of human endeavor, their destiny was in the hands of the Germans. The Czechs of all classes were controlled by the Germanizing centralism of Vienna and by its instrument, the German officialdom in Bohemia and Moravia. Czech peasants were dominated by German landlords; Czech workers labored for German or German-Jewish entrepreneurs; Czech Catholics were led by a German Catholic hierarchy; Czech artisans and small businessmen depended upon or competed with the German *haute bourgeoisie* and German capital.

It was to lead the Czechs out of this desert that the Czech national movement was born—a child of many parents. The roots of the movement reached into the eighteenth century; its decisive period was the first half of the nineteenth. It drew upon the rationalism of the eighteenth century for its scholarly impetus, and on the romanticism of the early nineteenth for its tendency to stress the glories of the past. It was inspired by the egalitarian and democratic ideas of the West and by the consciousness of an ethnic affinity with

31. L. Winter, "Dělnické zákonodárství rakouské," *Česká Politika,* ed. Z. Tobolka (Prague, 1911), IV, 843. There is an official report on child labor in Bohemia (1840) in *NNM,* II (1962), 251-53, and another description in *NN,* April 9, 1848.

32. *NN,* April 9, 1848.

the Slavic nations of the East. It was nourished by advances in the production of material goods as well as of ideas. It was strengthened by patriotism and by a hatred of the nation's oppressor. In it, the conflict between nationalities reinforced, and was reinforced by, the conflict between social groups.

The leading role in the Czech national movement was played by the middle and lower strata of the bourgeoisie: the artisans, the small businessmen, but mainly the intellectuals.[33] The *haute bourgeoisie* was at that time almost solidly German and could not lead a Czech movement; there were probably no more than half a dozen nationally conscious Czech entrepreneurs in Prague[34] approaching the status of *haute bourgeoisie*. Among the pioneers of the Czech national movement, social and economic self-interest went hand in hand with a sincere devotion to one's country.[35] The businessman's concern for his economic future was wedded to his concern for his nation's future. The intellectual's aspiration for a secure post in the civil service[36] blended with his aspiration to win for his people an honorable place in the European community of nations. At all social levels the struggle was both national and economic, and Czech success benefited both the nation and the particular individual involved.

The Czechs had had to contend with a powerful German influence —political, cultural, and economic—from the very beginning of their recorded history. For many centuries, the Germans had made great

33. Some writers hold that the Czech "middle class" at this stage was too weak to constitute a class, and that a middle class, properly speaking, was formed only in the second half of the nineteenth century. See J. Pešková, "Ideologická emancipace společenských tříd v buržoazní revoluci," *AUC, Philosophica et Historica*, No. 2 (1963), 157-85; and M. Hroch, "K problematice formování buržoazního národa v Evropě," *ČSČH*, IX (1961), 374-95.

34. Among these exceptions was the Czech lumber merchant F. Dittrich (1801-75).

35. A fitting illustration of this blend of motives is the article by J. E. Vocel, "Budoucnost české národnosti," *ČČM*, XXI (1847), as reprinted in *NNM*, II (1962), 329-32. Vocel argues for a Czech economic expansion in Eastern Europe as a way of strengthening the nation politically and culturally.

36. This was a Central European characteristic. Before 1848, the students entering the polytechnic were asked to indicate during registration the career they expected to follow. The majority were undecided, but of those who gave opinions almost all hoped for a job in the civil service; only a few wanted jobs in industry—this despite the fact that their training was supposed to prepare them primarily for industry! If such aspirations were common among polytechnic students, one may imagine how much more common they were among the students of the social sciences and the humanities.

positive contributions to the development of the Czechs in the sphere of both material and spiritual culture, but their influence and domination had an adverse effect upon the growth of the Czech people as a nationality. In 1526, the Czech Lands became part of the Habsburg Monarchy. The Habsburgs began to whittle down the institutions of self-government and after the Battle of the White Mountain during the Thirty Years War, in 1620, all but obliterated them. Czech national life then declined rapidly, and the decline reached its nadir in the middle of the eighteenth century, a period known in Czech popular parlance as "darkness" (temno). By this time, the Czechs, who had almost entirely lost their own governing class, had been reduced to a nation of peasants ruled by German officials and nobles. The "enlightened absolutism" of Maria Theresa and Joseph II in the latter half of the eighteenth century brought many beneficial social and political reforms, but its Germanizing and centralizing legislation seemed only to confirm the doom of the Czech language and political individuality. The Germanizing laws were not a reflection of a nationalist antagonism against the Czechs and against other non-German nationalities, but of a rationalist desire on the part of Maria Theresa and Joseph II to create a well-trained bureaucracy united by a knowledge of the German language; this desire in turn was wedded to the objective of creating an efficient modern state.

Yet if the period of the two sovereigns signified the nadir of Czech fortunes, it also brought the first impetus, not intended by Joseph II and Maria Theresa, to a Czech national awakening. This impetus was supplied by progressive educational reforms which stimulated the development of education in general and provided a spark for a Czech cultural awakening. For the next few decades among the strongest intellectual influences that inspired the Czech movement was German Romanticism and German philosophy. It was to be one of the great paradoxes of the German-Czech relationship that German thought exercised a fundamental and positive influence upon a movement that was to become basically anti-German. The Czech awakening could not have taken place without the existence of a mass of Czech population, the peasantry, the last and major repository of the spoken Czech language. It could also not have taken place without the conscious striving of a small (at first) band of enthusiastic intellectuals who drew upon the treasury lying dormant in the countryside and molded and developed it into a vibrant national organism.

Neither the intellectual nor the peasant could have accomplished alone
what they accomplished in partnership.

The most active period of national awakening was the first half
of the nineteenth century.[37] The task confronting the national awakeners, as the nationally active Czech intellectuals of this period are
called, was a truly forbidding one. By 1800 the Czech language had
almost ceased to exist as a language of culture. Everywhere the
German tongue reigned supreme. Before the awakeners could re-
build Czech national life, they had to revive its main pillar, the
Czech language. It was necessary to restore the use of the language
as a medium capable of conveying the finest thoughts of culture and
science. Since this task could be performed only by scholars and
students of the language, it was to this group that the first awakeners
belonged. Though these individuals were ardent admirers of the Czech
language, they usually wrote about the language in German. This
was the seeming paradox of the early stages of the Czech national
movement as well as that of the national movements of many other
East European nations: the first works were written in a foreign
tongue, since the native tongue had not yet become, or had ceased to
be, a vehicle suited to scholarly expression. Nor had the first awakeners themselves yet acquired sufficient skill in its use as a written
medium; although they came from Czech families, they were compelled, for lack of opportunities, to acquire higher education at institutions in which classes were conducted in a foreign-language, usually
German. At the end of this educational process they often emerged
with a better knowledge of German than Czech; at any rate, we
know that the spoken Czech of some of the first awakeners was less
than flawless.[38] It should further be noted that it was to the advantage of the Czech cause that it be propagated, at this stage, in a
major European language, and German was a convenient medium of
communication for any educated Czech desirous of reaching a large
audience with his message.

The first great figure of the Czech national awakening was
Josef Dobrovský (1753-1829), an ex-Jesuit priest, a brilliant scholar
of many disciplines, and the "father" of Slavic philology. Typically,
Dobrovský wrote almost entirely in German. His scholarship provided the foundation for a reform of orthography, and guideposts for

37. For a recent treatment of the period of national awakening, see J. Koči,
Naše národní obrození (Prague, 1960).

38. Bass, *Čtení o roce*, p. 208.

some other developments that left a permanent mark on the Czech literary language. His *Geschichte der böhmischen Sprache und Literatur*[39] (*History of the Czech Language and Literature*) is regarded today as the founding work of Czech literary science. Though deeply devoted to the study of the Czech language, Dobrovský was still far from convinced of the future of that language as a cultural medium. Given the discouraging state of the language at the time, however, he could perhaps be pardoned for such moments of weakness and doubt.

Dobrovský's immediate successors, their confidence fortified by the progress of the language, were able to suppress their doubts; they could even afford the luxury of formulating a program for a systematic revival of the language. The chief architect of that program, and the second towering figure of the Czech national awakening was Josef Jungmann (1773-1847), also a linguistic scholar, and an indefatigable compiler of the first monumental dictionary of the Czech language.[40] Jungmann's translations into Czech of some of the masterpieces of foreign literature proved the ability of the language to express the loftiest of thoughts, especially his translation of Milton's *Paradise Lost,* which constituted a landmark and created a literary sensation in the Czech community. After Jungmann's feat, no one need be ashamed of the language. Jungmann's own contagious enthusiasm helped attract many followers. In this Jungmann differed from Dobrovský. The latter's temperament did not and could not take him beyond a narrow band of disciples, but Jungmann's enthusiasm and confidence produced a multitude of followers. It was a measure of the progress of the Czech awakening that Jungmann's death in 1847 was mourned as a national loss by the Czech community. His obsequies, attended by thousands, represented the first great Czech national manifestation.[41]

Two other awakeners, both scholars in the finest sense of the term, complete the galaxy: František Palacký (1798-1876) and Pavel Josef Šafařík (1795-1861). Palacký, the founder of modern Czech historiography, gave his people their first monumental and scholarly history, the *Dějiny národu českého* (*History of the Czech*

39. First published in 1791 in the Proceedings of the Royal Bohemian Society, later (1792) in book form. See *Dějiny české literatury,* ed. F. Vodička (Prague, 1960), II, 106.

40. *Slowník česko-německý* (Prague, 1835-39).

41. J. V. Frič, *Paměti,* ed. K. Cvejn (Prague, 1957-63), I, 330.

Nation). The first volume appeared in 1836, and although it was written in German, it exerted a vast influence on the Czechs.[42] In it Palacký lifted, as it were, the Czech past from oblivion. He resurrected for the benefit of his readers some of the past glories of their nation, notably the heroic Hussite period. He emphasized the historic conflict between Czechs and Germans, an emphasis well-attuned to his readers' expectations, experiences, and sentiments. He boosted the pride of the Czechs in their past, a pride that could and did easily nourish ambitions for the present and the future. No one could insult the Czechs any longer by telling them that they were a people without a past, and thus, by implication, without a future. Palacký had given his compatriots an argument and an instrument, the usefulness of which was not to be exhausted for generations to come. A Czech nursed on Palacký's history would never again be content to see his nation die by default or vegetate without purpose.

Šafařík was a Slovak by birth who became associated in his later life with the Czech national movement. His *magnum opus,* entitled *Slovanské starožitnosti* (*Slavic Antiquities*), published in 1837, was the first scholarly work on the earliest centuries of Slavic history. It provided the Slavs with a respectable family tree, thereby legitimizing them as ancient and honorable participants in the unfolding of European culture. Besides being influential at home, Šafařík's work served as an inspiration to the entire Slavic world and through translations into foreign languages vindicated the Slavic cause in the eyes of other nations.

Of course, the doubters and the sneerers were still legion. Drawn from a motley assortment of Germans, Germanized Czechs, indifferent Czechs, snobs, bigots, and the like, they all shared a distrust of, or a contempt for, the Czech language. For two or more centuries the Czech language had been the more or less exclusive domain of peasants, housemaids, cooks, farmhands, and servant personnel of all descriptions; it was therefore exasperatingly difficult for the awakeners to break down the barriers of snobbery and win for their language a position of respectability in the higher social circles. The most important instrument by which Czech patriots could influence the

42. *Geschichte von Böhmen* (Prague, 1836-67). The Czech version appeared under the title *Dějiny národu českého v Čechách a na Moravě* (Prague, 1848-67). Several editions have appeared since then. See J. F. Zacek, "Palacký and His History of the Czech Nation," *JCEA*, XXII (1964), 412-23, and "Palacký and the Marxists," *Slavic Review*, XXIV (1965), 297-306.

Czech-speaking, but not yet nationally conscious, masses of the population was the theater.[43] The first productions were usually translations of foreign, mostly German, plays, but native drama soon made its appearance. In its early stages, its quality lagged considerably behind its value as a medium for awakening Czech national feeling, but in the latter role it was of supreme importance. The dominant figure in the theater was Josef Kajetán Tyl (1808-56), a versatile figure who combined the gifts of a dramatist, actor, producer, and director in one person. Characteristically, it was from the womb of the theater that the tender song, "Where Is My Homeland?" destined to become a Czech national anthem, was born. The lyrics issued from Tyl's pen, and the song was first heard on stage in Prague on December 21, 1834, as part of a light and unpretentious comedy written by Tyl.[44] The song soon became popular all over the country and gradually acquired the character of a national symbol.

A milestone in confirming the Czech national cause as socially respectable was the first Czech ball held in Prague on February 5, 1840. Hitherto, any social event of this kind was held under strictly German auspices and with German as the language of social intercourse; no self-respecting citizen would have demeaned himself by speaking Czech on such an occasion, even if it were his mother-tongue. This is what the ball set out to correct. As the author of a Czech magazine article wrote after the ball, "Our tongue must ring publicly—in churches and theaters, in schools and walks, in gardens and at parties."[45] The two leading organizers were Josef Kajetán Tyl and František Ladislav Rieger, the latter soon to become famous as one of the Czech spokesmen during the events of 1848. The snobs and the doubters looked askance at the preparations, but the success of the ball exceeded all expectations. It attracted bureaucrats, officers, merchants, artisans, professors, and artists, all savoring for the first time the thrill of speaking the Czech language on such a glittering occasion. When the merrymakers dispersed in the early hours of the morning the barriers had been broken and the cause of Czech nationalism given a mighty thrust forward. Other balls followed, both in

43. The network of theaters is shown in *Atlas československých dějin*, p. 19, j.

44. The title of the comedy was *Fidlovačka*. The music for the song was composed by F. Škroup.

45. From a description of the ball published in *Květy* and reproduced in *NNM*, II (1962), 249-51.

Prague and in other communities, and became an accepted social outlet in Czech society.

During the thirties and forties, the Czechs gained other outlets,
platforms, and bases for the pursuit of their national objectives.
Among these was the Czech Foundation (*Matice česká*), organized
in 1831, with Palacký as the principal initiator. Its purpose was to
collect funds in order to promote Czech culture and facilitate the publication of Czech books.[46] This was the first truly Czech organization
of any kind; it was under its auspices and with its support that Jungmann's dictionary and Šafařík's *Slovanské starožitnosti* were published. It had to endure official chicanery, but that was to be expected.
The phenomenal growth of the Czech cause is reflected in the membership of the Czech Foundation. There were only 35 members in 1831;
a year later the number rose to 190, and by 1847, there were 2,329
members.[47]

Another important organizational outlet for the Czechs was the
Society for the Promotion of Industry in Bohemia,[48] founded in 1833
by the Bohemian nobility as a German body. A reform of its charter
in 1843[49] permitted the members of the middle classes to join; although this reform had been forced upon the Society by German
businessmen and entrepreneurs, it also naturally benefited the Czechs,
who took advantage of the new opportunities and began to participate
actively in the Society. Rieger joined in 1843 and soon many other
Czech patriots followed, with the result that something like a Czech
section of the Society came into being. The Czechs used it as a forum
to press their demands for national equality—for example, for the
publication of the Society's journal in both the German and Czech
languages and for the establishment of a Czech industrial school—
and in this manner the Society became a testing and training ground
for future leaders of the Czech national cause. Another organization
was the Citizens Club (*Měšťanská Beseda*) in Prague. After first

46. What may be regarded as the founding document of the Czech Foundation is reprinted in *NNM*, II (1962), 191-93.

47. Anyone who contributed a sum of fifty florins became a founding
member. See *Přehled československých dějin*, I, 688. Also *Atlas československých dějin*, p. 19, j.

48. See the proclamation of the directorate of the society to the public in
1833, in *NNM*, II (1962), 207-8. The Czech name of the society was *Jednota
k povzbuzení průmyslu v Čechách*.

49. Text of the revised charter in K. Havlíček, *Politické spisy*, ed. Z.
Tobolka (Prague, 1900-3), I, 187-91.

rejecting an application for the formation of such an association, the authorities relented and issued the necessary permit in 1845.[50] Though ostensibly only a social club for the Czech-speaking bourgeoisie in Prague, the Citizens Club was to be in effect another vehicle for the strengthening of the Czech element and in that sense possessed political overtones. It reflected the progress of the Czech middle class, now ready to strike out on its own to form organizations and formulate policies independently of the German middle class. There was, of course, no question as yet of the lower social classes' belonging to this group. Only the "burghers," that is, those holding property or possessing comparable qualifications for being registered formally as "citizens," were eligible; the Czech worker was not yet part of the Czech "nation."

In this connection, it is worth emphasizing that the national awakening was one of the great historic contributions of the Czech intelligentsia to their nation. The achievements of the awakeners are the more remarkable because they were compelled to make their struggle on two fronts: against absolutism, which, of course, weighed heavily on all nationalities, and against the specifically German and Germanizing tendencies and pressures of the absolutist regime. It is also pertinent to point out that the Czech national movement in Moravia lagged greatly behind that in Bohemia; the Moravian movement had no center comparable to Prague, and its activity and scope could not compare with the movement in Bohemia.

What was the attitude of the nobility to the Czech national movement? After 1620, a large segment of the native Czech nobility had been exiled, punished, persecuted, and its land confiscated. Its place was taken by foreign nobility, largely German, and within a few decades the Bohemian and Moravian nobility became Germanized or at least lost its clear national identity. It was destined to retain that character and to remain forever aloof from the mainstream of national life. This is not to say that a number of individual nobles did not exhibit sympathies for the Czech cause and did not strive to win for the Czech language and the Czech people a position of respect and improved status. But such efforts were always limited to a few outstanding individuals; they never reflected the sentiment of the class as a whole. The persons involved usually spoke the German

50. See Havlíček's article on the occasion of the founding of the club, *ibid.,* I, 253-55.

language as a mother tongue, as was inevitable under the circumstances, but they often acquired a more than perfunctory interest in and knowledge of the Czech language. Nevertheless, this group of nobles was seldom able to rise above a "Bohemian" or territorial patriotism, that is, a patriotism toward Bohemia (or Moravia) as a whole.

The noble family most conspicuous in its support of Czech national efforts during the pre-1848 period was the Thun family. Although J. M. Thun wrote, "I am neither a Czech nor a German, but only a Bohemian,"[51] he warmly supported the cultivation of the Czech language and the cause of Czech nationality, within the limits of Bohemian patriotism. His cousin, Leo Thun, later, in 1848, the governor of Bohemia, also took up the pen in defense of the Czech culture and, more startlingly, in defense of the Slovaks.[52] But because their views remained within the confines of Bohemian patriotism, aristocratically flavored, these nobles could not satisfy a Czech national movement composed primarily of commoners for whom the Czech nationality was an object of a very special affection. Yet in spite of its limitations the movement of the nobility contributed in no small measure to the Czech cause. In particular, the nobility founded the two bodies that were to play a leading role in Czech scholarship: the Royal Bohemian Society of Sciences, in 1774, and the Bohemian Museum, in 1818.

The Royal Bohemian Society of Sciences was founded as the Private Society of Sciences (*Soukromá společnost nauk*), was granted the status of a public corporation in 1784, and in 1790 was permitted by the emperor to assume the name of Royal Bohemian Society of Sciences (*Královská česká společnost nauk*), which it permanently retained. The founders and sponsors of this first great learned society in the Czech Lands were some of Bohemia's leading nobles. The Society was the organizational core of scientific research in Bohemia and Moravia, in both the physical sciences and in the humanities (chiefly history and philology), and from 1775 issued its own journal, the German *Abhandlungen*. At first the physical scientists predominated but in time the historians and philologists captured the leadership, largely as a result of the influence of Dobrovský. Guided by a

51. *Der Slawismus in Böhmen* (Prague, 1845), p. 17.
52. *Über den gegenwärtigen Stand der böhmischen Literatur und ihre Bedeutung* (Prague, 1842); *Die Stellung der Slovaken in Ungarn* (Prague, 1843). Neither work was available to me.

progressive spirit, the Society successfully defended the principle of independence of scholarship even in the face of the absolutist state. Its significance for Czech science in its early stages can hardly be overestimated. Much of the Czech scientific output before the mid-nineteenth century appeared in the *Abhandlungen,* including the works of the early Czech awakeners, such as Dobrovský and Palacký.

It may be added that Dobrovský and Palacký each enjoyed the patronage of a distinguished Bohemian noble family. Dobrovský became a private tutor in the family of Count Nostic, a patron of learning who made it possible for his employee to devote much of his time to scientific work. Similarly, Palacký was befriended by the noble family of Sternberk, whose support helped him to become influential and made it possible for him to develop his potential as a scholar. It was through these connections that Palacký was appointed official historiographer of Bohemia.

It was a member of the Sternberk family who supplied the leadership in founding the other great institution important to Czech scholarship: the Bohemian Museum. Founded in 1818 for the housing of scientific collections, the Museum at first had no explicit Czech national purpose, since it was dominated by the spirit of "Bohemian patriotism." It was left to young Palacký, after his arrival in Prague in 1823, to use his influence in transforming the Museum into a vehicle of the Czech national movement. In 1827, at Palacký's initiative and under his direction, the Museum began publishing two journals, one German, another Czech. The German journal attained a high level of scholarship but died in 1831 for lack of readers. In contrast the Czech journal, called since 1831 *Časopis Českého Museum (Journal of the Bohemian Museum)*, proved its vitality, and in the hands of Palacký became a great organ of the Czech national movement. Its continued success was an indication of the growth of the movement. Palacký and others also used the Museum as a basis for launching the Czech Foundation, already mentioned.[53]

In spite of the impressive progress the Czech language made in the first half of the nineteenth century, on the eve of 1848 it was still a Cinderella as far as its official use was concerned. The strictly academic subjects at the Universities of Prague and Olomouc were taught in German, except for a few theological subjects that were

53. *Dějiny české literatury,* II, 30-31, 148 ff.

taught in Latin. In Prague the Czech language was employed, in
addition to German, only in practical exercises in pastoral theology
and, also alongside German, in courses for midwives offered by the
Faculty of Medicine. Curiously, lectures in the Czech language and
literature—the chair of which had been founded in 1793—were also
conducted in German (after an interlude of Czech) by a Czech
scholar,[54] in the same manner as French and Italian; in other words,
the Czech language was regarded as having no more right of domicile
than the languages of foreign peoples. Similarly, at the polytechnic
only the German language was used. In all secondary schools German
was the only medium of instruction. Czech was not even a regular
teaching subject in any curriculum; a few secondary schools offered
it, but only as an optional subject. As a medium of instruction, the
Czech language maintained itself, of necessity, only in rural primary
(trivial) schools, and in the first grade of primary (so-called principal)
schools in certain cities; in the second grade in these cities, the
teaching was either in Czech or in German, depending on the language most familiar to the majority of children, and from the third
grade it was only in German. All in all, there were in Bohemia 2,821
trivial schools in 1847 in which the Czech language prevailed as the
medium of instruction.[55] All efforts of Czech patriots to obtain an
official blessing for an expansion of the language into the secondary
schools were rebuffed by the authorities—this despite the fact that a
few influential nobles, some of whom were top administrators, had
begun to view with favor the progress of the Czech language and to
support the Czech patriots. This official indifference the Czechs began
to answer with a kind of "resistance movement" calculated to continuously expand the use of the language. Friends constantly reminded
each other to speak Czech wherever possible, and in the 1840's some
Czech patriotic groups levied a fine upon any member caught using
German at a meeting.[56]

   Although the officials never contemplated making the Czech and
German languages equal, the government did at times issue laws and
decrees designed to ensure that government functionaries in Czech-
or mixed-language districts possessed a knowledge of Czech. The
best-known decree was one issued in 1816 stating that district sec-

54. J. Goll, *Rozdělení pražské university* (Prague, 1903), pp. 2-3.
   55. J. Šafránek, *Školy české* (Prague, 1913-18), I, 266.
   56. K. Slavíček, *Tajná politická společnost Český Repeal v roce 1848*
(Prague, 1947), p. 111.

ondary-school (gymnasium-type) prefects and certain categories of teachers in such districts should be conversant with Czech (a knowledge of German was assumed), and that in these districts students speaking Czech should be given Czech-language exercises. The reason for this official concern, according to the decree, was the shortage of officials conversant with both languages.[57] It must have become clear to the government that this situation made it impossible for officials in Czech districts to perform their functions properly. A few other decrees of a similar nature were issued during the next few years. Thus a decree of 1833 stated that persons recommended for the post of region prefect and region commissioner should be "thoroughly" familiar with the language of the region in which they were to serve.[58]

It goes without saying that this decree and other similar ones were never activated, for it was not their intention to elevate the Czech langauge to a position of equality with German. To the contrary, it was the spirit of legislation, since Joseph II, that the German language was to be the official one, with the other languages to be used only as an auxiliary tool in dealing with the lower social classes. In the administration of justice, there was no law or decree guaranteeing the use of the language a litigant would understand—an omission that was bound to penalize the Czech, not the German, litigant. An interpreter might or might not be provided, depending presumably on the good will of the judge. In fact, judicial procedures were dominated at all levels almost entirely by the German language. As late as 1847, a Czech-written complaint submitted to a high Prague court by a barrister on behalf of a Czech client was rejected on the ground that the use of the language was "contrary to court procedure"; and in Moravia as late as 1843 a high court in Olomouc ruled that the keeping of court protocols in Czech and the use of this language in written submissions and court decisions was a violation of court procedure.[59]

Thus the public use of Czech was limited to a very few channels. Apart from the few Czech cultural works permitted by the censor, there were only a few magazines or newspapers. No Czech-language newspaper existed at all in Moravia, and in Bohemia, a complete list-

57. A. Fischel, *Das österreichische Sprachenrecht: Eine Quellensammlung* (2nd. ed., Brünn, 1910), p. 54.
58. *Ibid.,* p. 62.
59. *Ibid.,* p. lii.

ing of newspapers in 1847 yields eight items, of which only one was Czech, the *Pražské Noviny,* edited by Karel Havlíček since 1846. Havlíček used his paper skillfully, within the narrow limits imposed by censorship, to further the Czech cause. *Pražské Noviny* appeared twice a week, and had a supplement, *Česká Včela,* also edited by Havlíček. Of the thirty-seven magazines in 1847, twelve were Czech, and of the ninety-four serials of various types, only four were Czech.[60] In Moravia there appeared in the forties a Czech magazine for the rural population, but it died after a short time. The first Moravian Czech newspaper, *Týdenník,* began publication on January 6, 1848, just before the collapse of absolutism.[61] One of the most popular magazines among Czech readers was *Květy,* founded in 1834 and published in Prague; its emphasis was on Czech literature.

What were the objectives of the Czech national movement during the pre-March period? The first objective was to win for the language—that most precious possession and symbol—a greater place in the school system, and then in other walks of life. The language goal had at this stage the advantage of directness and simplicity. (Of course, the future was to show that in the tangled ethnic structure of the Habsburg Monarchy nothing was simple, and that the task of defining the equality of languages was a very thorny one.) The Czech language could be understood by everyone, from scholar to peasant. It lay at the very root of the nation's life, and the national movement acquitted itself well in pressing for this objective. In the thirties and forties Czech patriots continued to focus attention on the language issue, to present memoranda to the government, to write articles, and to hold their objective before the Czech community. That concrete successes were few was attributable to the exasperating inertia of the political system, not to any lack of determination on the part of the Czech leaders.

There was more than inertia. There was official sabotage of the national movement and its efforts from the very moment it showed signs of consolidating itself. How well the work of consolidation was proceeding, in the face of official displeasure, may be seen in an article written by Palacký in 1837 on the new tasks of Czech science and culture. Surveying the past decade or so, Palacký found reason

60. M. Laiske, *Časopisectví v Čechách 1650-1847,* Bibliografický katalog ČSR—České knihy, 1959, Spec. No. 6 (Prague, 1959), p. 162.

61. H. Traub, "Moravské časopisectvo v letech 1848-49," *ČČM,* XCIV (1920), 105.

for satisfaction with the progress achieved. A few years ago, he wrote, the fate of the Czech language hung in the balance, but currently the survival of the language was no longer in doubt. "What do we want now?" asked the historian. "We should like to advance further. Thus far language considerations have overshadowed others in our work." But now the Czechs faced new tasks. They must start competing, he said, with other nations for the laurels of "true culture, scientific, aesthetic, and industrial."[62]

Thus the ambitions of the Czech leaders moved onto a higher stage. And though their goals were still being described as cultural— otherwise they could not have been discussed publicly—they increasingly acquired political implications. Indeed, the whole striving of the supporters of the national movement during the late thirties and forties was quasi-political in character. The lesson of Palacký's *Dějiny,* the message of Šafařík's *Slovanské starožitnosti,* the meaning of Havlíček's columns was that the Czechs and other Slavs were equal to other European nationalities; once this had been established, it was impossible to avoid demanding the ultimate: some form of political transformation that would express this equality.

The political and constitutional question differed from the language question, however. First, it could not be discussed legally and openly. Under conditions of tight censorship, with political dialogue nonexistent, there was little opportunity to formulate, let alone advocate, a political program. And yet a well-conceived program could only result from a full and open discussion. This is not to say that discussion was completely absent. But insofar as it did exist, it was limited to extralegal channels, to cafés, social gatherings in private homes, secret and semisecret societies, "contraband" literature, and the like. The political program had been driven underground.

Second, the formulation of a mature and informed political program presupposed a knowledge of both native political traditions of the past and political practices abroad, particularly those of Western Europe, where constitutionalism had had a longer and more vital history. But censorship had closed almost all of the channels through which a knowledge of the latter could be acquired. The only foreign daily newspaper the government permitted was the *Augsburger Allgemeine Zeitung,* the main source from which Palacký and other Czech leaders obtained their information concerning current conditions abroad.[63]

62. Text in *NNM,* II (1962), 229-32.
63. See, for example, Frič, *Paměti,* I, 306.

That this situation seriously restricted the range of knowledge even an educated man could acquire about Western Europe stands to reason. It is, however, more chilling to realize that there was almost total ignorance of the political history of the Czech Lands. The universities offered no courses in the history of constitutional law for fear they might lead students' minds into subversive channels. The censor minimized any printed allusions to such topics. The Proceedings of the Bohemian and Moravian diets could not be published, and members of the diets themselves were ignorant of the rights of the august bodies to which they belonged. Nothing illustrates the woeful state of affairs more clearly than the fact that in 1843 Palacký had to be summoned by the Bohemian estates in order to lecture to them on their own past traditions and privileges;[64] even some of the elementary rules of procedure in the conduct of the meetings of the diet were far from commonly known to those who were supposed to participate in such meetings.

Another reason for the difficulties inherent in formulating a program was the complex ethnic and administrative structure of the monarchy. For the Czechs there were a number of questions for which answers were difficult to find or for which no precedent existed. Should Bohemia and Moravia be united? What should be the relationship of these two lands to each other? of the Czech Lands to other lands of "Cisleithania"? of the Czech Lands to the Habsburg Monarchy as a whole? What should be done about the Slovaks, who were struggling for their survival across the river Leitha and were separated by administrative barriers from the Czechs? What about the relationship of the Czechs to the other Slavs of the monarchy and to the Slavs outside the monarchy? What about their relationship to the Germans of Bohemia and Moravia, and to the Germans of the German Confederation? How could Western constitutional practices be applied to the radically different political problems of the Habsburg Monarchy?

With all these handicaps, it is no wonder the Czech leadership did not evolve a clear-cut political program in the pre-March era. Among the proposals of a political nature that appeared during the pre-March period was one by which the union of Bohemia and Moravia was envisioned. First put forward in an anonymous pamphlet entitled *Slaven, Russen, Germanen,* published in 1843, it re-

64. A. Okáč, *Český sněm a vláda před březnem 1848* (Prague, 1947), p. 78 ff.

appeared in a confused form in another pamphlet two years later.[65]
There is also evidence that shortly before the downfall of absolutism
a meeting took place in Prague in 1847 of Czech patriots from Bohemia
and Moravia at which the same issue was discussed.[66] As for demanding complete independence for the Czechs, no such proposal ever
appeared, and if it had, it would have been pure fantasy. The Czechs
were too small a nation and still too weak to contemplate a course
for which there was no precedent.

Painfully aware of their own precarious position as a tiny island
in the midst of a German sea, and conscious of the difficulty of facing
the future alone, the Czechs began to cast about for allies, who were
found in the great and comforting world of Slavdom. The most
powerful impetus to this quest was supplied by the Slovak poet Jan
Kollár (1793-1852). His poem *Slávy Dcera* (*Daughter of Sláva,*
first published in 1824), which glorified the Slavic past and predicted
for the Slavs a rosy future, fired the Slavic intellectuals with an almost mystic faith in the virtues and the messianic destiny of Slavdom.
Later Kollár gave a more prosaic expression to his vision in a treatise
on literary reciprocity among the Slavs.[67] Though he disclaimed any
political objectives, sooner or later his advocacy of a close cultural
cooperation between the Slavic peoples was nevertheless bound to
raise the question of political cooperation, and also the delicate question of the role of Russia in the Slavic world.

It was at this point that the serious limitations of any Slavic or
Pan-Slavic ideal began to manifest themselves to Czech spokesmen.
Russia may have been predominantly a Slavic country, but it insisted
on isolating itself from the rest of Europe, and lagged behind it in
most respects. Its social order hardly inspired confidence; the
autocracy of the Romanovs was more relentless than that of the
Habsburgs, and its treatment of Poles and Ukrainians, who were
Slavs, could only encourage skepticism regarding its possible role as
a liberating midwife to the Slavs. The condition of Russia and the
practical considerations of day-to-day policy dictated a modification
of the concept of Slavic cooperation. The notion of Slavic reciprocity

65. Heidler, *Čechy a Rakousko,* pp. 152, 156. The author of the first pamphlet
is now believed to have been the Czech Jan Erazim Vocel.

66. B. Rieger, "O snaze spojiti země koruny české v r. 1848," *Osvěta,* XXVII
(1898), 863.

67. First appeared under the title *O literární vzájemnosti mezi kmeny a
nářečími slovanskými* in 1835-36.

was never abandoned, but in the sphere of practical politics a more workable scheme had to be devised: this led to the emergence of Austro-Slavism, a concept that may be defined as cooperation among those Slavic groups constituting part of the Habsburg Monarchy.

Austro-Slavism was foreshadowed by certain eighteenth-century thinkers, South Slavic and Czech,[68] and crystallized in the first half of the nineteenth century. It became an avowed policy of the Czech national movement and was formulated clearly by Havlíček in a series of articles entitled "Slav and Czech" published in 1846 in *Pražské Noviny*.[69] The Austro-Slavists held that the small Slavic nations of Central Europe were in danger of being engulfed by the two great powers, Russia and Germany. A multinational state, such as the Habsburg Monarchy, in which a number of small nations existed under one roof and reinforced each other's strength, offered the only realistic alternative to their being swallowed up by the two unfriendly and aggressive giants. As Havlíček put it: "The Austrian Monarchy is the best guarantee of the preservation of our and Illyrian nationality, and the more the power of the Austrian Empire grows, the more securely do our nationalities stand."[70] Havlíček's article was written under the fresh impact of a recent trip to Russia and Poland which had caused him to become disillusioned with both countries. Given the weakness of the Czechs and of other small Slavic nations, the retarded and oppressive character of the Russian regime, and the dangers arising from a possible unification of Germany, Austro-Slavism seemed a plausible enough answer to the difficulties confronting the Czechs. The success of Austro-Slavism was, of course, predicated on the ability of the Habsburg Slavs to bend the monarchy to their aspirations. Only the future could show whether they were collectively strong enough to accomplish this objective.

The pre-March period was not devoid of accomplishments and progress. Sometimes enterprising individuals or groups succeeded in convincing the ruling circles of the utility of certain progressive measures. In Bohemia, Count Chotek, in his capacity as governor (1826-43), initiated and inspired many public projects designed to stimulate the economy and improve public welfare. The legacy of

68. J. Šidak, "Austroslavizam i slavenski kongres u Pragu 1848," *Historijski Pregled*, VI (1960), 204-5. See also M. Novák, "Austroslavismus: Příspěvek k jeho pojetí v době předbřeznové," *SAP*, VI, No. 1 (1956), 26-51.
    69. Havlíček, *Politické spisy*, I, 28-70. Title in Czech: "Slovan a Čech."
    70. *Ibid.*, p. 69.

his administration included public buildings, canals, recreation areas, regulated rivers, roads, bridges, welfare institutions, and cultural organizations.[71] The first railways were built in the early forties; in August, 1845, the people of Prague were treated to the sight of the first locomotive, arriving in the capital on a run from Olomouc. To achieve as much as he did, Count Chotek had to struggle with the bureaucracy in Vienna, which was distrustful of all innovations. It is symptomatic that it was in the field of communications that the best progress was made, with the blessing of the government: communications were useful to the military, and a government that may have failed to grasp arguments in favor of social progress could at least understand the simple fact that a company of soldiers moved more swiftly over good roads than over bad ones, and that a railway would dramatically increase an army's mobility.

In most areas of human endavor, however, the hostility of the governing circles to change was so tenacious as to be—as one can say in retrospect—suicidal. Important and urgent projects and proposals waited years to be dealt with—and rejected. Bureaucrats became accustomed to mountains of paper gathering on their desks into a backlog of years. Given the highly centralized system, local authorities were almost powerless to make decisions concerning any matter of consequence. As a result, many official acts had to pass through all the channels of decision-making, from the local ones to the highest levels in Vienna. Many quite uncomplicated matters traveled as long as ten years through the bureaucratic jungle before a decision concerning them was made.[72]

The situation was serious enough under Emperor Francis I (1792-1835, as Holy Roman emperor, Francis II), who, according to a high Austrian official, "handles matters like a borer that penetrates more and more deeply until it suddenly comes out unexpectedly somewhere without having done any more than bore a hole through the document."[73] Under the new emperor, Ferdinand (1835-48), the situation could only deteriorate; though a good-natured monarch, Ferdinand was mentally retarded and the process of decision-making became more unpredictable and more arbitrary. On occasion Metternich toyed with plans for mild reform, but he lacked the courage and

71. Roubík, Český rok, pp. 16-17.
72. Heidler, Čechy a Rakousko, p. 31.
73. C. F. Kübeck, Tagebücher (Vienna, 1909), I/2, 659.

the determination to carry them out. And almost literally to the last minute, to the very eve of the March, 1848, Days, he resisted the moderate demands of the Bohemian nobility for the restoration of some of their ancient privileges, as exercised through the Bohemian diet. Indeed, had Metternich and the governing circles carefully planned their self-destruction, they could not have done a better job than they actually did. For by the eve of the March Days there was not a group or a class in the monarchy that did not harbor serious doubts about a regime that resisted change in the face of all omens pointing to the need for it.

In the last analysis, the monarchy's cumbersome edifice had become corroded by a mounting crisis of confidence, a crisis affecting, to some degree, all social classes. Confidence in the status quo was being undermined by specific abuses of the regime; but at the more fundamental level it was also being undermined by the spread of rationalist and skeptical philosophies. In this connection, the most influential—and one of the most appealing—figures in the pre-March political awakening was a Bohemian German and Roman Catholic scholar named Bernard Bolzano. Bolzano was a mathematician of international distinction, but to the public at large he was best known as a gentle philosopher who exerted a deep and lasting influence upon a generation of disciples, both German and Czech, from his Chair of Religious Philosophy at the University of Prague, to which he had been appointed in 1805. The government and the police watched uneasily as Bolzano attracted a wide circle of admirers in whom he instilled a respect for reason and morality, even when it conflicted with official theology. Finally, in 1829, he was removed from his chair (he died in 1848). Though a German who never learned to speak Czech, and a "Bohemian" rather than Czech patriot, he was sympathetic to the Czech national strivings.

The growing disaffection was nourished by the awareness, however dim and vague, that in Western Europe, particularly in Great Britain and France, the flow of ideas was freer, the governments more responsive to the popular will, the individual more than a mindless robot required to obey the powers that be. Western Europe, which exercised a considerable attraction for the educated liberal classes in the monarchy, offered a wide spectrum of ideas and practices calculated to suit every taste, every interest group, every type of discontent. The liberal nobles were not unimpressed by the fact that,

in a unique way, Great Britain had succeeded somehow in accommodating within one framework the privileges of an aristocracy and a
modicum of popular will, giving rise to a system that seemed to
produce a considerable amount of stability. The liberal middle classes
were impressed by the strong influence of their class on the political
processes of Western Europe. The radically minded were drawn,
still very vaguely and hesitantly, to the socialist movements of Western Europe. The public also could not fail to see that Western Europe
was the harbinger of technological progress. Basic technological
changes in Bohemian and Moravian industry, and in the industry
of other provinces of the monarchy, were as a rule introduced from
the West, usually directly by Western entrepreneurs and with im-
ported skilled labor; England was one of the main sources of this
development. It was no accident that absolutism's collapse, when it
came in 1848, was triggered directly by the revolutionary events in
Western Europe.

The efforts of censors and informants did not succeed in checking
the flow of ideas from the West. Every time a revolutionary upheaval
rocked the capitals of Western Europe, there were repercussions in
the Habsburg Monarchy. And with every upheaval, the revolutionary
wave was getting closer to the borders of the monarchy. In 1830
revolutions swept France (the July revolution), Belgium, Poland
(the November revolution), and a number of German states, including Saxony. Of these, the Polish Revolution created the greatest
stir, partly because Poland was a neighbor of the Czechs and partly
because it was a Slavic country whose fate was close to the heart of
the Czechs. The impact of the events in Saxony was second only to
that of Poland. The Polish Revolution awakened great sympathies
among the educated classes, the dominant opinion being in favor of
the venture. At the time of the revolution František August Brauner,
who was to emerge into prominence in 1848, helped smuggle refugees
out of Poland and was persecuted by the Austrian police. In the years
following the Polish Revolution, Rieger participated in the smuggling
of contraband literature from Western Europe into Polish territories
and in 1842 was arrested as a suspect; in him, the Czechs produced
the first political prisoner in their modern history.[74] Under the impact of the revolutionary wave, even the most ardent champions of
the status quo appeared to be losing heart and yielding to doubt con-

74. V. Žáček, *Čechové a Poláci roku 1848* (Prague, 1947-48), I, 112, 172.

cerning the future of the monarchy. It was after the 1830-31 wave, in February, 1832, that Karl Friedrich von Kübeck, one of the highest officials in Vienna, purporting to see dangerous symptoms in Bohemia, lamented in his diary that the government, which held the nations of the monarchy in a bond that was becoming "steadily looser" was "sinking in its own weakness . . . the monarchy resembles a mosaic whose paste has become soft and which needs only a push to fall apart." Later in the same month, Kübeck recorded a conversation with another high official, the substance of which was that the political upheavals "are only symptoms of greater, deeper revolution in society itself. The revolution is against the nobility of birth . . . it is irresistible, invincible, and certain of its success."[75]

The terrible and elemental revolt of Polish peasants in Galicia in 1846 only confirmed the worst fears. Yet in response to the revolt nothing more than half-hearted measures could be devised. Instead of inciting the government to take final action against serfdom, the revolt seemed to induce only a more overwhelming paralysis of will. Symptoms of discontent, instead of encouraging the government to remove the underlying malignancies, only rendered it the more stubborn in its determination not to tamper with the status quo. The classic example was the attitude of Francis II after the upheavals of 1830-31. The rebellion caused him to abandon even those projected reforms, the usefulness of which he recognized, simply because he had developed a morbid fear of change. As he told one of his officials in June, 1831: "This is no time for reforms. The peoples are as if seriously wounded. One must avoid exciting them by touching and pressing their scars. You see, the new tax law you are proposing to me may be a sound one; true, I had approved it, but will not have it promulgated in order not to provoke excitement."[76] This remained in essence the philosophy of the Vienna ruling circles until 1848. The government had thus reached a fatal impasse: in times of prosperity reform was unnecessary; in times of crisis, it was dangerous. It would be difficult to devise a formula more unfailingly calculated to bring ruin upon the monarchy.

And yet there was no dearth of advice by men most well-meaning and most desirous of preserving as much of the old as was consistent with coming to terms with the new. The advice came in the form of

75. Kübeck, *Tagebücher*, I/2, 549-50.
76. *Ibid.*, p. 439.

political brochures and pamphlets, mostly anonymous, although the authorship of many has since been established, that began to reach the Habsburg Monarchy in a veritable avalanche in the thirties and forties.[77] Most were written in German, but some were in Czech and other languages of the monarchy, depending on the audience. Virtually all were printed in Germany, in states having more liberal regimes, chiefly in Hamburg and Leipzig. Their authors were usually residents of the monarchy who belonged to the educated classes and who, exasperated by the folly of the regime, took to the pen in order to give vent to their sentiment and suggest measures for political reform. Since they could not have their tracts published at home, they arranged for their printing in Germany, and the publishers in turn arranged for them to be smuggled into the monarchy. Most of the authors belonged to the liberal middle classes, some to the liberal nobility. The pamphlets called for neither revolution nor violence. If anything, they sought to prevent revolution by timely reform. Mainly, they advocated an introduction of some form of constitutional government, somewhat along the lines of the British or French experience. It is significant that the first pamphlet appeared in 1833—clearly the aftereffect of the revolutions of 1830-31. Beginning in 1837, at least one new pamphlet appeared every year to 1848, with several pamphlets appearing in a single year as a rule.

The most influential of all the pamphlets was *Österreich und dessen Zukunft*, published anonymously,[78] but now known to have been written by the Tyrolese noble, Baron Andrian-Werburg. It was symptomatic that Andrian was an official of the central government (Under-Secretary of the Court Chancery) in Vienna. In the pamphlet, he offered a series of moderate proposals for the transformation and modernization of the Habsburg Monarchy, with the nobility still playing a dominant though no longer exclusive role in the political process. Andrian directed the edge of his criticism at the bureaucratic octopus, the vagaries of censorship, the inequities of taxation, the fiction of one Austrian nationality, the dead hand of centralism, the oppressive inertia of the establishment. The effect of the pamphlet was electrifying. No other printed work set in motion such a wave of excitement among the educated classes of the monarchy, chiefly in Bohemia and in the German-speaking provinces. No other single

77. The classic work here is Heidler, *Čechy a Rakousko*.
78. 3rd ed., Hamburg, 1843. (The first edition was published in 1842.)

book or pamphlet matched, not to say exceeded, the effect of Andrian's brochure in crystallizing intellectual resistance to the Habsburg regime during the pre-1848 period.[79] It was as if Andrian had given expression to the unspoken words of thousands, and had destroyed forever the magic of the greatness of the monarchy, of the sanctity of its institutions, of the wisdom of its rulers. Other pamphlet writers had earlier expressed elements of what Andrian stated. But no one before or since put it with such eloquence, pungency, and appeal.

Andrian's brochure helped stiffen the resistance of the opponents of the regime, including the nobility. In Bohemia, it strengthened the estates' opposition, which had begun to gather toward the end of the thirties and took on a more determined tone after 1842. The Bohemian nobility, through the diet, clashed increasingly with the government in Vienna. Inspired by the vigor of the Hungarian nobility, and also by the example of the nobility in German Austria, the Bohemian nobility demanded that the government restore to it the ancient privileges of participating in the political decisions and in the legislative processes affecting the kingdom of Bohemia. A few nobles envisioned a broadening of the diet to give a more equitable representation to the middle classes, but in the main the nobility looked to the past rather than the future. It is true that by its increasing restlessness the diet could and did strengthen the forces of resistance of pre-March absolutism. The significance of its actions, however, was restricted by the fact that it remained too much within the bounds of outworn tradition, that it bore too visible an aristocratic stamp, that it was Bohemian rather than Czech in spirit and thus remained aloof from the mainstream of the Czech national movement. A few nobles spoke truly courageous words in the diet in criticism of the monarchy, but the Proceedings were not permitted to be published and this reduced the impact of such speeches on the public.[80] In Moravia the nobility and the diet were much less active; in Austrian Silesia, there was no comparable forum and as a result no comparable activity.

It was not from the nobility that the impetus to the 1848 revolu-

79. For example, on July 28, 1843, Rieger, in writing to his former tutor about the brochure, stated: "Perhaps you know 'Österreich und seine Zukunft.' It is the most widespread of them." See J. Heidler, *Příspěvky k listáři Dra Frant. Lad. Riegra* (Prague, 1924-26), I, 13.

80. The basic work is Okáč, *Český sněm*.

tion in Bohemia came, but from a radical group known as Repeal. The thirties and forties saw the emergence in Prague of secret and semisecret clubs and discussion groups in which more or less radical objectives were propounded. Most of these clubs were not firmly organized and usually had only an ephemeral existence, but the one called Repeal was destined to play a key role in loosing the forces of revolution in Bohemia in 1848. The name "Repeal" is not an English translation of a Czech equivalent. The English word itself was used to express the sympathy of patriotic Czechs for the Irish cause. The Czechs regarded their own cause and their own position as being similar to that of Ireland, and followed the progress of the Irish independence movement with lively interest. Little is known of the origin of Repeal in Prague. It is first mentioned in 1844,[81] and from that year existed continuously until the March Days of 1848. The majority of its members were Czech, but there were also some Germans. The leading figures were two Czech radicals, František Havlíček (no relation to Karel Havlíček) and Vilém Gauč, both law students. The best-known German radical member was the medical student Ludwig Ruppert. The radicals favored constitutional reform, but went beyond that: they were also interested in social reform, and some of them are known to have maintained connections with the Prague working class.[82] Repeal consisted of many groups only loosely connected. In a fashion typical of the day, the groups met in Prague inns and cafés, often shifting from one to another. In the last weeks before March, 1848, the principal meeting place was the attic of the Inn at the Golden Scale, situated in the center of Prague (now No. 3, Havelská Street).

The general feeling of uncertainty and gloom was deepened, in the last months before the outbreak of the 1848 revolution, by an economic crisis that engulfed all of Europe in 1847—the first crisis on a truly continental scale. In the Habsburg Monarchy the ranks of the unemployed continued to expand. In addition, there was a series of crop failures; a catastrophic potato blight in the mid-forties reduced the harvest in some regions by 50 per cent or more.[83] Prices

81. Slavíček, *Český Repeal*, p. 74. For an engaging description of the Repeal, see Bass, *Čtení o roce*, pp. 516 ff.

82. Frič, *Paměti*, I, 350.

83. See, for example, the appeal for relief funds by a village in northern Bohemia addressed to the regional government office, dated March 16, 1846, reprinted in *NNM*, II (1962). The appeal opens with the statement that "the

of staple food items rose sharply, encouraging the machinations of speculators and inducing further price increases. For the lowest social strata, hovering constantly on the border line separating subsistence from hunger, even a moderate price increase could be disastrous. The workers reacted by sporadic demonstrations throughout 1847 and by attacks on the establishments of Jewish speculators who were in control of the grain trade.[84]

It was amid such conditions that the European revolutionary movement once again began its victorious march. In January and February, 1848, a series of revolutions in various parts of Italy compelled the governments involved to grant constitutions. Soon mysterious hands in Prague began to put up posters on billboards and buildings calling attention to the turbulence in Italy and exhorting the people of Bohemia to follow suit. "Long Live the Sicilians!" one poster proclaimed; "Bohemians, take your example from what a people can do if it wants to."[85] The most thorough investigation failed to uncover the culprits and the police watched uneasily for further revolutionary echoes.

----

potato blight has deprived, as is well known, the mountain population of more than half of the potatoes . . ." (p. 299). See also J. Marx, *Die wirtschaftlichen Ursachen,* pp. 160 ff.

84. *NNM,* II (1962), 318-19.

85. Copy in *SÚA* Prague, PG 1846-49, 15 c/3, No. 994.

Chapter **2**

The Miracle of Revolution:
The March Days

On February 29 Prague received the news of the fall of the monarchy in France, and in the ensuing days tension mounted in the city. In spite of official silence and censorship, it was impossible to keep the news from spreading, as new reports reached the city concerning the outbreak of revolutionary movements in the German states, Lajos Kossuth's daring speech in the Hungarian diet on March 3, and the beginning of the petition movements in Vienna on March 6.

In Prague, political initiative was seized by the radicals associated with the Repeal organization. Among the members of this group the air of expectancy hardened into one of resolution, the attitude of waiting into one of burning desire for immediate action. Sometime during the first week of March, possibly on March 5, the members of Repeal made a decision to issue a call for a public meeting in Prague at which the need for political reform would be discussed and a petition approved for submission to the emperor.[1]

The meeting was to be held—so it was agreed—on March 11, at St. Václav's Baths. The text of the invitation was drafted by two leading Repeal members, Vilém Gauč, a Czech, and Ludwig Ruppert, a Bohemian German, who were responsible, respectively, for the Czech and German versions. The invitations had to be written and copied by hand, and the radicals worked feverishly and clandestinely in order to contact as many individuals as possible before the police could discover their plans. The first invitations were sent out on March 6, and, since only a limited number of people could be reached through individual invitations, placards were placed on street corners on the morning of March 8, inviting the public to the meeting. In the latter move, the radicals had scored a decisive success; after this they could rely on public opinion to force the issue.

1. K. Slavíček, *Tajná politická společnost Český Repeal v roce 1848* (Prague, 1947), pp. 109 ff; J. V. Frič, *Paměti,* ed. K. Cvejn (Prague, 1957-63), I, 358-59. Text of the invitation in J. J. Toužimský, *Na úsvitě nové doby* (Prague, 1898), pp. 51-52.

The document was addressed to "The Citizens of the Capital City." After noting that "the events of Paris awakened the entire Europe from slumber," it urged the people to take an active part in the affairs of the state in order to be in a position "to defend their property against every attack." It appealed to them to discuss their political needs freely, thus awakening national consciousness in all social strata and educating the nation toward morality and patriotism, for a nation so educated would be "worthy of the confidence of the government of which it could be a support." In addition to these general observations, four specific demands were listed: (1) reorganization of public administration; (2) convocation of the diet, with the inclusion of representatives of the royal cities and the peasantry; (3) arming of the people; and (4) abolition of censorship. For a general airing of their views about this program, the people of Prague were asked to attend a public assembly to be held at St. Václav's Baths on March 11 at six o'clock in the evening.

The proclamation was, on the whole, a moderate document. Considering its radical auspices, it was curiously devoid of radicalism, both in tone and substance. Certain individual radicals and Repealists were known to harbor working-class connections and interests, yet not a single word on the subject of workers' rights had crept into the proclamation; indeed, its reassertion of the rights of property played upon a fear of the working class, at least by implication. The rights of the peasants did not receive much fuller treatment. Though their representatives were, according to the document, to sit in the diet, no reference was made to serfdom or related problems.[2] An interesting aspect of the invitation is that it contained no proposal having a specifically Czech (or for that matter German) nationalist flavor. References to "national consciousness" and "nation" are in themselves wholly neutral: they could be construed as applying equally to the Czech and German national consciousness or even to "Bohemian patriotism." This ambiguity was deliberate; in Repeal,

2. I. I. Udaltsov, in his *Aufzeichnungen über die Geschichte des nationalen und politischen Kampfes in Böhmen im Jahre 1848* (Berlin, 1953), is eager to magnify the social-radical character of the proclamation. He succeeds in so doing by reproducing faithfully the whole proclamation, by direct quotation or paraphrase—except for one sentence calling for the defense of private property "against every attack" and for the awakening of national consciousness. This sentence is entirely omitted from his account and no hint is given concerning its contents.

Czech and German radicals worked hand in hand, and they did not want to exacerbate ethnic antagonism by using nationalist symbols and slogans.

The comparative moderation of the proclamation may be explained by the radicals' desire not to antagonize the liberals. The radicals were aware that the liberal middle classes, though deeply dissatisfied with the status quo, were apprehensive about the possibility of radical social outbreaks. Hence the appeal for the defense of property "against every attack"—a phrase clearly designed to assuage the feelings of the liberal middle classes[3]—and hence the homespun phrases concerning "morality" and the incongruous phrase regarding earning "the confidence of the government," which, under the circumstances, would have meant Metternich, if taken at face value. The radicals seemingly hoped that if the liberals were convinced that the whole popular action was designed, at least in part, to protect their property, they might join in and perhaps even march in the streets.[4]

In spite of their comparative moderation, the proclamation and the action surrounding it were without precedent in the Czech Lands. Here was a call for a public assembly, the first in the modern history of the Czechs, and it was to be one to which all men, regardless of social status and wealth, were being summoned. The invitation was conceived and carried out without any permission from the police and the authorities. This in itself was a demonstration of courage, for Metternich was still in power and the police apparatus very intact. The action of the radicals served notice upon the government that the people could no longer be contained or ignored and that they were thrusting themselves forward in order to shape their own destinies.

Meanwhile the edge of the radical thrust was being dulled, from the beginning, by the participation of the liberals. In fact, the very first step, the preparation of the invitations for the assembly, was carried out by the radicals in collaboration with the more moderate elements, as represented by Peter Faster, the popular innkeeper, and his followers. Faster owned the inn at the "Golden Goose," situated in the present St. Václav's Square, and he and his followers, who met there from time to time, were a somewhat less radical version of Repeal. After this, the liberals succeeded, slowly but surely, in reduc-

3. This is corroborated by Frič in *Paměti*, I, 359.

4. In the invitations sent to some individuals the radicals played even more on the fear of the proletariat; for examples, see K. Kazbunda, *České hnutí roku 1848* (Prague, 1929), p. 45.

ing the radicals' influence in the whole undertaking. It must be admitted, however, that the radicals themselves were partly responsible for the success of the liberals. In preparation for the assembly, they drafted a twenty-point petition, but instead of proceeding on their own with it, they approached František August Brauner, a Czech lawyer and a liberal member of the Czech national movement, to edit the draft. Brauner, who had made his name as an outstanding authority on the peasant question, agreed to give the draft a more seasoned form. A comparison of the original draft with Brauner's revised version is most revealing.[5]

Article I of the radicals' draft calls for a "Constitution providing for: a representation of the nobility, the clergy, the burghers, and the peasantry; equal electoral law according to districts; authorization of taxes and legislation; and a diet annually convoked in Prague." Among the recommendations of the other articles are "unlimited" freedom of speech and the press (Article II), public trials and juries (IX), freedom of assembly (XV), and municipal self-government (XVII). Article VIII urges the introduction of the Czech language in schools, and Article X bars foreigners from holding public office. In Article V, the peasantry is favored with a demand for the abolition of feudal labors, patrimonial courts, and certain other obligations, although no mention is made of compensation. The most radical point concerns the workers: Article XVIII provides for "organization of work and wages," a request taken directly from the program of Louis Blanc, a contemporary French socialist and member of the French Provisional Government. This was the first demand of this kind in the history of Bohemia and constituted the first attempt at charging the state with protecting the rights and interests of the Czech working class.

How does the above draft compare with Brauner's version? Brauner published the complete text of his version in Czech and German in the Bohemian press on March 18 (i.e., after the assembly of March 11), appending to each article an explanatory note. Under his pen, the original twenty articles were reduced to twelve. The text, with the comments, reveals Brauner as a man of skill and experience, and cognizant, more than the radicals were, of the ways of the state and of the machinery required to administer it. At the

5. Text of the radicals' draft in Toužimský, *Na úsvitě*, pp. 65-66; Brauner's version in J. M. Černý (ed.), *Boj za právo: Sborník aktů politických u věcech státu a národa českého od roku 1848* (Prague, 1893), pp. 12-17.

same time, he is more conservative, less concerned with social issues, and more preoccupied with national objectives. The edge of protest is dulled. In the midst of change, greater emphasis is laid on the preservation of order than on maintaining the momentum of change.

Gone is the provision relating to the "organization of work and wages." Blanc was a socialist politician deeply involved in the overthrow of the French Monarchy and associated with the radicalism of the working class. The inclusion of a demand originally voiced by Blanc would have frightened both liberals and conservatives, who were already agitated over the specter of a working-class revolution. Brauner omitted the workers entirely from his petition. He and others of like views had as yet displayed no appreciation of the need to deal with the problems arising from the growth of industry and the working-class movements. They adhered fully to the classical laissez-faire concepts of the nineteenth century. In this respect they lagged behind the radicals and showed themselves less sensitive to social change.

Concerning the peasantry, the radicals had asked for the abolition of feudal institutions, without compensation. Brauner modified this point sharply by introducing the principle of compensation to the landlords for the labors and services owed them by the peasants. In Article VI he asked for the abolition of both the *robot* and the subject status.

To be sure, Brauner was not unconcerned with the lot of the lower social classes; he was opposed to the food tax (Article X) because, as he added in his comments, "it bears mostly on the class of the poorer and less prosperous people." At the same time, he was dominated by a fear of the social discontent these classes might manifest. Article VII of Brauner's version asks for communal citizens' guards, which, according to the explanatory note, would ensure the community "against the discontents and associations of paupers [in the German version the expression 'proletariat' is used] . . . without the state's incurring any expense."[6] Brauner and the liberal bourgeoisie viewed the working class as a social substratum whose discontent must be held in check by coercion, not reform. In this respect, it was clearly the radicals rather than the moderates who had the future on their side.

In Brauner's version, the opening article calls for the union of the

6. Černý (ed.), *Boj*, p. 15.

lands belonging to the Czech Crown, i.e., Bohemia and Moravia-Silesia, these lands to be represented in a common diet that would convene annually either in the capital of Bohemia or of Moravia. Article II demands administrative unity of the lands of the Czech Crown, thus supplementing the first article envisioning legislative unity. Josef Václav Frič, usually a caustic critic of the liberals, commended Brauner for a statesmanlike vision in making the unity of Bohemia and Moravia a foremost objective of the national movement;[7] in the decades that followed, this demand remained one of the cornerstones of the Czech national program.

The radicals' plea for "unlimited" freedom of speech and of the press was transformed by Brauner into a "freedom of the press with restrictive laws against abuse." Furthermore, the radicals had called for a representative diet or legislature, with no mention of the existing estates diet, which was comprised almost entirely of the nobility. Brauner posed the same objective, but, more mindful of legal continuity and tradition, made specific reference to the existing "system of the estates," which should be "supplemented" by freely elected representatives of the cities and rural districts. Where the radicals had demanded simply that the Czech language be taught in schools in addition to German, Brauner called for "a complete equality of the Czech nationality with the German in all Czech lands, schools, and offices." The section urging a reduction of the standing army was deleted by Brauner altogether.

By a few strokes of the pen, Brauner succeeded in stripping the original Repeal draft of its social radicalism, thereby depriving the radicals of a program that could serve as a rallying cry for a major radical movement. By March 11, another liberal, Czech government official Alois Pravoslav Trojan had been won over to the revised program formulated by Brauner and had agreed to present it at the meeting. This meant that well before the program reached the public, the liberals had gained an important foothold in the revolutionary movement. Indeed, it may be said that they had taken over the direction of

7. Frič, *Paměti,* I, 360. In asking for an annual meeting of the diet common to the three lands, Brauner demands something that had not, to that extent, existed in the period before the Battle of the White Mountain (1620). During the pre-1620 period, only the diets of individual lands held regular meetings. Diets consisting of representatives of all three lands met only on special occasions and were not regular institutions. See K. Krofta, *Byli jsme za Rakouska . . .* (Prague, 1936), p. 357.

the movement: one of their members had formulated the program while another was to present and read it formally to the public assembly. Nothing illustrates more clearly the weakness of the radicals; they had lost their battle before it began.

If the call for the public assembly provoked excitement and anticipation in some, it provoked fear and even panic in others. The most careful wording of the proclamation could not conceal the fact that here was an unprecedented and daring enterprise, the radical nature of which was being underscored by the failure of the organizers to obtain the blessing of the authorities. The Prague acting police director, Joseph Heyde, noted ruefully in his report that the invitations had been sent "without the foreknowledge" of any of the military or civilian authorities.[8] The second ominous circumstance was the choice of time and place for the meeting. The place was St. Václav's Baths,[9] situated near the district of Podskalí, a predominantly working-class and lower-income area on the right bank of the Vltava, in the southern section of Prague. The time was a Saturday, six o'clock in the evening—a time when the workers, having drawn their weekly pay, were wont to dissipate much of their hard-earned income in alcohol. None of this escaped Heyde, who wrote that he had learned from confidential sources that the organizers of the assembly had chosen "the evening of Saturday" in order to make it possible for "everyone to participate in this assembly because on this day at six o'clock all workers will have begun their hour of leisure."[10]

The situation in Prague appeared alarming enough for Rudolf Stadion, governor of Bohemia, to despatch an urgent note to Vienna in which he commended the "educated middle classes" in Prague for being reserved about the agitation but complained of "ill-willed individuals" who are trying to "arouse the raw mob, which is always capable of excesses, into public demonstrations." Stadion was alarmed at the "unfavorable mood" of the masses, who were expected to turn out in large numbers at the assembly.[11] Neither Heyde nor Stadion knew anything yet about the identity of the organizers of the assembly,

8. *SÚA* Prague, PG 1846-49, 15 c/3, Nos. 1619 and 1629. Report dated March 10, 1848.

9. The original building has since been torn down. The site is now occupied by the Charita Palace, at the corner of Trojan Street and Charles Square.

10. Heyde's report of March 10, 1848, as above.

11. Stadion's letter of March 10, 1848, in *SÚA* Prague, PG 1846-49, 15 c/3, Nos. 1619 and 1629.

and they were not to know until the event took place. Heyde suggested, however, that the originators "were a class of the lesser-known burghers" who probably "stand under the influence of the radically minded Czechs."[12]

It is true that two military barracks were situated not far from St. Václav's Baths and that this fact apparently precluded any possibility of popular violence. But it did not appreciably allay the fear of many Prague inhabitants, who were still haunted by the ghost of the terror of 1844, that the meeting would lead to a rioting of the proletariat. The general fear was magnified by ignorance, which was only too ready to be satisfied by rumors. No one had any concrete information concerning the origins of the campaign for the assembly; no one was sure of the names alleged to be behind the undertaking; no one knew what form a popular assembly might take, for the simple reason that democracy and constitutional government had never existed. There were no precedents, no guidelines for behavior. Many liberal-minded citizens supported the idea of an assembly but were afraid it was being managed by untrustworthy individuals and for that reason viewed the forthcoming event with a sentiment compounded in equal measure of hope and fear.

Josef František Frič, father of the radical, Josef Václav Frič, and one of the most respected figures of the Czech liberal movement in 1848, left an account of his own feelings that is worth mentioning. Frič was in favor of the meeting, at least of the principle involved, but was apprehensive about the outcome since "I have not yet found anyone [i.e., any of the organizers] who would inspire confidence and guarantee a good result." A day before the meeting he instructed his household to observe "utmost caution, to load weapons, to purchase ammunition."[13] Much the same preparation was taking place in other Prague households.

The liberals were confronted by a serious dilemma: even before absolutism was overthrown, their enthusiasm for constitutional government was being checked by their concern for the social excesses that might be unleashed by the collapse of absolutism. With absolutism still in power, the liberals were poising their guns for a possible struggle—yet these guns were not aimed at the bastions of absolutism! Thus the question of the proletariat was casting a long and disturbing

12. Heyde's report, as above.
13. J. Dlouhý, "Dr. Josef Frič," *Osvěta,* VI (1876), 565.

shadow over unfolding events in the very earliest stages of the revolution.

Other prominent liberals viewed the assembly with even greater reservations than Frič. They feared the outbreak of violence, and they were alarmed at the possible spread of socialist ideas of the kind that were sweeping France. It is noteworthy that the two most influential members of the Czech liberal-national movement at the time, the historian František Palacký and the journalist Karel Havlíček, remained aloof from the actions leading to the assembly. Palacký was by nature a conservative endowed with a rigid outlook militating against any involvement of this kind; his ties to the patriotic nobility of Bohemia were not without influence in this respect. Uneasy about the restless mood of Prague, on March 5 Palacký wrote to his wife, "Here in Prague there is by and large joy over the downfall of Louis Philippe . . . it is to be hoped that the national efforts will not abandon a legal road." The calling of an assembly for March 11 presumably did not come under the heading of "legal road." Havlíček was strongly influenced by Palacký; though he was not a friend of the French Monarchy, he greeted its overthrow with reservations for which he was criticized by some of his friends. He too seems to have viewed the plans for the assembly with something less than wholehearted ardor.[14]

The third leading figure of the Czech national-liberal movement, Brauner, also excused himself at the last minute from participation in the assembly, although he had actually drafted the program for it, by pleading illness. Critics accused him at the time of using the plea as a cover-up to enable him to absent himself from the assembly. The illness may indeed have been genuine, but if so, Brauner's conduct throughout the 1848-49 period suggests that he was not one to relish

14. Kazbunda, *České hnutí*, p. 36. Many years later (1872) Palacký explained in his political testament his attitude thus: "I did not take part in the meeting at St. Václav's Baths on March 11, 1848, mainly because Count J. M. Thun, then president of the Bohemian Museum (of which I was secretary) pleaded with me and asked me not to compromise this institution, entrusted to our care, by some hasty action; also I became early convinced that my help was not needed there on that day." See F. Palacký, *Radhost* (Prague, 1873), III, 276.

E. Chalupný, in *Havlíček: Prostředí, osobnost a dílo* (Prague, 1929), p. 312, writes that upon being informed (erroneously), on March 11, that the assembly was not successful, Havlíček exclaimed: "Thank God those good-for-nothings have not brought off the meeting." Chalupný does not give his source.

the prospect of taking part in a popular assembly of this nature and that he must have been relieved to have been saved from fulfilling an embarrassing obligation.[15] The fourth member of the group of great Czech leaders of the year 1848, Rieger, was in Italy at the time of the assembly, recovering from a lung condition, and could not take part; what his attitude would have been had he been in Prague at the time is impossible to determine.

The three men principally responsible for the maintenance of order were Rudolf Stadion, governor of Bohemia; Josef Heyde, acting police director of Prague; and Josef Müller, Prague burgomaster. Had he wished, Stadion, of course, could have banned the meeting outright, but he chose not to risk inflaming public opinion by such *fiat*. However, short of banning the meeting, everything was done to prevent its success and to dissuade the populace from attending. The appearance of the Repeal posters on March 8 was promptly answered on March 9 with bilingual official posters issued by the Prague prefecture (police). The posters warned against disturbances of the peace, but prudently avoided any specific reference to the forthcoming meeting.[16] In every military barracks, a part of the personnel was placed in a state of readiness.[17]

On March 10, the burgomaster enjoined the leading burghers, officers, and commanders of the uniformed burgher corps to help maintain order. This was hardly necessary, since it was the burghers rather than the burgomaster who were pressing for the most extreme measures; they pleaded with him to prevent the meeting and to permit a general arming of the burghers. Evidently the burgomaster was being offered more help than he desired; he had to deny the plea for arms and was compelled to remind the spokesmen that they did not have the authority to speak for the whole body of Prague citizens.[18] Indeed, it appears that the burghers summoned to the burgomaster were very largely the representatives of the highest stratum of the commercial bourgeoisie, who were, from the ethnic point of view, almost wholly German. Their group was popularly and pejoratively known as the

15. Brauner's conduct during 1848-49 contrasts sharply with the radicalism of his youth. In 1831 he was involved in aiding Polish rebels and in 1832, in the face of official charges, defended his conduct with great courage and eloquence.

16. Copies in *SÚA* Prague, PG 1846-49, 15 c/3, Nos. 1619 and 1629.

17. Stadion to Vienna, March 10, 1848, same file.

18. Heyde to Stadion, March 11, in *SÚA* Prague, PG 1846-49, 15 c/3, No. 1668/1848.

"merchant casino," and they represented the most panic-stricken and the most conservative element in the community, completely devoted to the status quo and violently opposed even to the most moderate reform.

A number of other precautions were taken, designed to minimize the expected turnout of the lower social classes. The burgomaster asked the guild masters not to let their apprentices and journeymen out into the streets on Saturday night. Through the existing machinery of pauper administration, the poor were being watched and calmed. Landlords were asked to lock their houses and not allow their tenants and servants to leave the building that night.[19] It was as if the city were readying itself for a battle rather than a political meeting.

On the evening of March 11 there was a great rainstorm in Prague, and it was the considered view of the police that had the weather not interfered, the turnout for the assembly would have been much heavier than it was. Even so, a few thousand people, according to official reports, were streaming toward the appointed place in the early evening hours of Saturday. Some of them were merely curious, a few were hostile, but most were in sympathy with the announced purpose of the meeting. Some eight hundred people were estimated to be inside the hall at the time the meeting was to begin—a "full house." Ushers were posted at the doors to see that only well-dressed and well-behaved guests were allowed in.

The guests consisted "mostly of young people, *litterati*, sons of burghers, and burghers, artisans, indeed even officials, all from the Czech party . . . even peasants were said to be among those assembled."[20] The above observation, from the pen of the governor, is a realistic appraisal of the meeting, corroborated by other sources: the gathering was predominantly attended by young people, especially young intellectuals, and also by the lower-middle-class strata, including the artisans. From the ethnic point of view, the bulk of the audience was Czech, although a number of Germans were also present. There were apparently few proletarians in the audience; nor were many of them likely to be admitted: their poverty did not allow for proper clothing and without respectable attire the ushers would not

19. Kazbunda, *České hnutí*, p. 44.

20. Stadion to Vienna, March 12, 1848, in *SÚA* Prague, PG 1846-49, 15 c/3, No. 1668/1848. See also the special police report on the meeting (March 12) in the same file; it is printed in Kazbunda, *České hnutí*, pp. 362-63.

have admitted them. It is also doubtful whether any large number of them would have been interested in the constitutional and political questions that were to be posed at the meeting. At the opposite end of the social scale, the nobility too, was conspicuous by its absence. The popular character of the assembly did not augur well for the nobility and afforded every expectation that the nobles, with a few individuals excepted, would not be welcome. There were no women in the audience as far as is known. What made the assembly unique was that here had gathered a group of men who enjoyed no noble titles and who, from the legal point of view at least, may be described as the nonprivileged class—the same class that had hitherto been almost completely unrepresented in the Bohemian and Moravian diets and had been thus excluded from exerting any organized political influence upon the state.

The main business of the meeting was to read the text of the petition and get it approved. The reading was done by two Czechs: Faster, the popular innkeeper, and Alois Pravoslav Trojan. The latter was a secretary of the Czech section of the Society for the Promotion of Industry in Bohemia; he was also a government legal official who was willing to jeopardize his official position by taking part in an illegal meeting. The articles were read in both Czech and German, and were based on Brauner's version of the petition. The reading of each article was followed by a thundering applause. From the surviving accounts, one gathers that the organizers were eager to have the petition approved quickly so that the meeting could be terminated before passions could rise. The voting on each article was done by a simple show of hands; no counting was necessary, since the number of hands raised always represented a large majority. The assembly was in a comparatively radical mood; it is not certain whether the original Repeal version was read also, but the radicals did force changes in Brauner's version, evidently by presenting their views from the floor. Thus the assembly voted, at the initiative of the radicals, to include in the petition demands for the organization of work and wages, and for the reduction of armed forces, both of which had been deleted by Brauner from the Repeal original. It also voted, after some discussion, to restore the Repeal version of the demand relating to freedom of speech and of the press. The Repeal version had called for an "unconditional" exercise of these freedoms; Brauner added a clause providing for laws against an abuse of these freedoms, but this clause was now removed. On the whole, the radicals had reason to be satisfied with what had been approved.[21]

The reading and discussion of the petition concluded, the assembly elected a committee charged with the task of editing the definitive text to be presented to the emperor. This committee consisted of more than twenty members,[22] made up largely of the liberal bourgeoisie and intelligentsia. In order to demonstrate good will and tolerance, the assembly included among those chosen a Jewish banker of liberal views and known sympathy for the Czech movement; three nobles, all of whom, quite exceptionally, enjoyed considerable popularity with the people; and several Germans. Of the radicals, two were chosen: Gauč and Ruppert.

After the election of the committee, Trojan announced that the definitive text would be displayed and would be available for signatures during the coming week. Thus far, the meeting had been without incident—indeed, it had been a model of moderation. Eager to keep it that way, Trojan hastily declared it adjourned. This meant that none of the radicals would be allowed to address the meeting. At this point Karel Sabina, one of the most prominent radicals, who had planned to make an address, rushed to the speaker's platform. An argument ensued, with Trojan bent upon preventing Sabina from speaking and Sabina equally determined to be heard. The latter began with the words: "Friends and citizens! With the present day the Czech nation erased from itself that shame which has clung to it since the catastrophe at the White Mountain!"[23] The lights were then turned out and the speaker was not allowed to continue.

At about nine o'clock the meeting ended and the throngs began to disperse. Some went to the inns to discuss the recent experience; no disturbance was reported, and by midnight all was quiet. The burgomaster, the acting police director, and a few other notables had gathered for the evening at the New Town Municipal Hall, not far from St. Václav's Baths, anxiously awaiting the results of the meeting. Police agents, who had gained entrance into the meeting,[24] kept

21. The surviving police report on the meeting is too sketchy. For a detailed eye-witness account, see Frič, *Paměti*, I, 363 ff. See also Z. Tobolka, *Počátky konstitučního života v Čechách* (Prague, 1898), pp. 36 ff.

22. The special police report lists twenty-one names. Kazbunda, in *České hnutí*, p. 47, lists twenty-four names derived from the official records of the committee.

23. Frič, *Paměti*, I, 367.

24. Stadion to Vienna, March 12, 1848, as cited.

the notables informed of the proceedings. Stadion had spent the evening in a private residence, also in the vicinity.

This was the celebrated meeting that ushered in the Revolution of 1848 in the Czech Lands—the first political act of Austrian Slavdom in the revolutionary year. It is interesting to note that most of the well-known Czech national leaders remained aloof from the event. Trojan demonstrated personal courage in taking part; Brauner lent his wisdom and experience to the fashioning of the petition, but at the last minute excused himself from taking part in the assembly, on plea of illness. Conspicuous by their absence were František Palacký and Karel Havlíček, the two most prominent Czechs at the time (see Chapter 1). Responsibility for the initiative and the organization of the assembly rested almost entirely with the radical young intellectuals and with the radically minded tradesmen and shopkeepers.

The following are the names and occupations of some of the leading organizers: František Havlíček, student; Vilém Gauč, student; Ludwig Ruppert, student; Peter Faster, innkeeper; Ferdinand Viták, lawyer; Bernard Banzet, tailor; František Jaroš, roofer; Matěj Vávra, miller; Karel Sabina, writer; Josef Mencl, metal-founder; Antonín Šulc, roofer; Bedřich Peška, writer.[25] The names of these men have since been overshadowed by others who became leaders of the national and political movement during the revolutionary year, but it is to them that chief credit must go for the initiative and for the success of the enterprise. They possessed the courage; they took the risks; they displayed the determination that culminated in the assembly of March 11, a milestone of the history of the Czech Lands. Their valor may be measured by the fact that Metternich was still in power and there was as yet no hint that the merciless current of revolution would sweep him out of office forty-eight hours later.

At the time of the assembly censorship was still in force; the inept silence it imposed was illustrated by the failure of the press to make any mention of this event during the next three days (while censorship lasted), even though it had agitated the whole of Prague. Reporting on a concert given by a noted Belgian cellist on the same evening, a Prague newspaperman observed that the "emptyness" in the concert hall was so "terrible that the performer, it is said, had to pay toward the expenses." The reporter then added succinctly that "in these eventful times people think of other things than concerts."

25. Slavíček, *Český Repeal,* pp. 119 ff.

This is as far as he dared go in hinting about the memorable assembly of March 11.[26]

The authorities in Prague had been happy enough to see March 11 pass without incident. Nevertheless, the election of the committee to prepare the final text of the petition presented them with a dilemma. Here was something entirely new: a political body containing several prominent citizens, popularly elected, yet lacking the stamp of official approval. In the circumstances it did not seem advisable to declare it out of existence by official *fiat*. At first the authorities hoped, not very realistically, that the momentum generated by the assembly would quickly spend itself and that the committee would simply not meet, or, should it meet, that the attendance would be so poor as to deprive it of the aura of popular approval.

This hope was soon dashed, for the committee met the very next day—on a Sunday—to begin its work.[27] At first, it was called the Committee of Prague Citizens, or Citizens' Committee, or Committee of Citizens and Inhabitants of Prague, but within a few days it came to be known as the St. Václav Committee. (Later still, it was reorganized and became the National Committee, a name it retained until its dissolution.) On Sunday, the committee chose from its midst an executive (presidium), with the popular noble Count Vojtěch Ethelbert (or Adalbert) Deym as president (to be distinguished from Count Friedrich Deym). Also, a subcommittee was chosen to prepare the final text of the petition.

This first meeting took place in the Town Hall of the Old Town of Prague. Even before it adjourned, the first indication of the attitude of the authorities came: Burgomaster Müller sent a message that the Town Hall would not be available any more during the coming week for the use of the committee, as it would be required for official business.[28] The conclusion to be drawn from this announcement was clear: until the last moment, the burgomaster had hoped the committee would not meet, but now that it was demonstrating its determination to fulfill the function entrusted to it, he lost no time in

26. *Bohemia,* March 14, 1848.

27. The police director observed, in his report, that the meeting had gathered "against all expectations" and that it had "acquired the status of a representation of the various classes of the population" (March 13, 1848, in *SÚA* Prague, PG 1846-49, 15 c/3, No. 1708/1848).

28. See the above police report, and also Dlouhý, "Dr. Josef Frič," *Osvěta* VI, 566 ff., and Tobolka, *Počátky konstitučního života,* pp. 40 ff.

placing obstacles in its way. If he did not feel strongly enough opposed to it to ban it, he would at least sabotage it. Besides, to have
permitted a popularly elected body the use of official buildings and
facilities would have been revolting to his bureaucratic and autocratic
conscience.

On Monday, March 13, representatives of the St. Václav Committee met with the burgomaster and pleaded with him to reconsider.
But Müller stood pat, and the next meeting, on March 14, had to be
shifted to other premises. On that day, the committee met to discuss
and approve the final text of the petition, as prepared by the subcommittee. As it turned out, this text dulled still further the cutting edge
of the revolutionary program.[29] There were eleven articles. The
demand relating to the unity of Bohemia, Moravia, and Silesia was
toned down as compared with Brauner's version. The latter had called
explicitly for legislative and administrative unity of the three lands
(Articles I and II); and there had been a specific reference to a joint
"parliament" and to joint "political, legal, and financial central offices,"
to be established in Prague. In the final text, which the St. Václav
Committee was now asked to approve, the reference to central offices
in Prague was entirely omitted; there remained only a plea for a
joint meeting of the estates, with the word "parliament" carefully
expunged and the traditional term "estates" employed instead. Any
mention of the abolition of serfdom was completely omitted; all that
remained was a vague request for "thorough reforms of peasant conditions appropriate to the times." It was hardly possible to ask for
less. Also, there was no mention of the organization of work and
wages, and of the reduction of armed forces—this despite the fact
that both had been approved by the assembly. As a general comment,
it may be said that the final text was intensely loyalist in tone; its
wording confined the character of the petition to that of an entreaty in
which the suppliant subjects ask for certain reforms to be granted,
not as a matter of right, but as a matter of grace from the sovereign;
the latter was addressed in the most eulogistic terms, far exceeding the
customary courtesy required on such occasions.

The radicals resisted this diluted version of earlier demands. In
particular, they protested against the vagueness of the article concerning the peasantry, but they also criticized some other articles as
being too mild. While the discussion was in progress, the news was

29. Text in Černý (ed.), *Boj*, pp. 3-6.

brought in of the first bloodshed that had taken place in Vienna on the previous day. Under the impact of this announcement, the final text was hastily approved as it stood, without further discussion. It is an interesting reflection on the outlook of the committee that in a country in which most of the population was peasant, it could not bring itself to ask unequivocally for the removal of the remaining institutions of serfdom. As for the tone in which the petition was written, no one was more pleased than the police director; in his report he lauded the petition's "humble style" and the caution with which it "bypassed the initial absurd propositions."[30]

Among those taking part in the discussion was Palacký. To him, the whole project was too radical, and he demanded that the petition be submitted to the emperor not directly, but through the estates. This was, however, asking too much, and Palacký was overruled: the committee voted to present the petition directly.[31] This was the first time Palacký had taken part in the revolutionary movement of 1848.

Unable to frustrate the work of the St. Václav Committee by denying it the use of official premises and alarmed at the threat to established authority, the burgomaster resorted to another maneuver: he tried to organize a "popular" movement of his own to compete with the St. Václav Committee. Müller's group, which consisted almost entirely of the affluent, German-speaking members of the "merchant casino" already mentioned, was to be armed with an appropriately harmless petition for presentation to the emperor. On March 14, this group was holding its own meeting at the burgomaster's office at the same time that the St. Václav Committee was meeting elsewhere in the city. The latter committee discovered the Burgomaster's "plot" and was scandalized by it. There were now two groups readying a petition to the emperor—a situation that, if permitted to continue, was certain to cause conflicts and delays, and to heighten the impatience of the restless elements in the community. News of the popular outbursts in Vienna had already exercised a sobering effect on the St. Václav Committee. Even as it was meeting on March 14, it was being subjected to a steady flow of rumors indicating that the "mob" was about to invade the premises and force it to complete its work.[32]

The rumors were groundless, but there is no doubt that the

30. Heyde's report, March 15, 1848, in *SÚA* Prague, PG 1846-49, 15 c/3, No. 1784-1848.
31. Dlouhý, "Dr. Josef Frič," *Osvěta*, VI, 569.
32. *Ibid.*, p. 568.

proletariat was beginning to stir; in fact, on that very day, a number
of proletarians (the term is used repeatedly in official police reports)
thronged menacingly in front of bakery shops, complaining of the size
of the loaves of bread being sold to them by the bakers.[33] The Prague
General Command was instructed to institute special precautions in
order to be able to cope with an emergency. Also, the police learned
from "confidential" sources that on March 13 a group of students in
the "College of Engineering" (Polytechnic, *Technika*) were holding
an unauthorized meeting to discuss constitutional reform. Thus,
within three days of the assembly of March 11 the two groups that
were to stand out as a revolutionary force throughout 1848, the
students and the workers, had begun to move. The action of the
Prague students was probably stimulated by contact with the Vienna
students; it is known that a group of Vienna students, meeting
earlier, had specifically suggested that the help of the Prague students be enlisted in a petition action.[34]

With ugly rumors flying about, with signs of unrest becoming
ever more apparent, and with the St. Václav Committee clearly commanding the support of the majority of the Prague population, the
burgomaster and his group were compelled to abandon the idea of
a "counter-petition." Instead, they agreed to join the St. Václav
Committee. On March 14, in a humiliating climax, the burgomaster
himself and a number of his group went to the place where the St.
Václav Committee was meeting, and all of them, including the
burgomaster, affixed their signatures to the petition of the rival
committee! Swallowing his pride, the burgomaster, in a brave display
of the popular spirit, refrained from attaching to his signature his
bureaucratic title *Appellationsrat,* contenting himself with the simple
Burgomaster.[35] Müller's disastrous misjudgment, as well as the
general collapse of absolutism, soon forced his resignation. As for
Governor Stadion, he had, of course, supported the "counter-petition,"
but seeing the consequences to which it might lead, was instrumental
in inducing the burgomaster to back down, and he too, as a symbol of
the absolutist era, resigned in a few weeks. In his report to Vienna,

33. Heyde to Stadion, March 15, 1848, as above.
34. The Vienna police president to Prague, March 12, 1848, in *SÚA*
Prague, PG 1846-49, 15 c/3, No. 1840/1848; Heyde to Stadion, March 14, 1848,
No. 1828/1848. See also Frič, *Paměti,* I, 375 ff.
35. See facsimile of the document in Z. Tobolka, *Politické dějiny československého národa od 1848 až do dnešní doby* (Prague, 1932), I, 40.

the governor refrained from conveying the true picture of the collapse of the "counter-petition" movement, stating only that it proved possible to "unite the two parties in their outlook";[36] considering the fact that the "casino" group signed the petition of the St. Václav Committee and allowed itself to be absorbed by it, not vice versa, this was hardly a correct description of the situation.

Nevertheless, it would be equally incorrect to say that the victory of the St. Václav Committee was an unqualified blessing to the reform movement. The committee, it is true, had attained new stature, and the "merger," in the manner in which it had been carried out, caused it to receive *de facto* official recognition. The fact that a number of German ultraconservatives had now joined the reform movement, however, augured ill for reform, and indicated a continuing shift away from the earlier demands. The St. Václav Committee was indeed strong enough to press its points without the ultraconservatives. But the news of the outbreaks in Vienna and the expectation of similar outbreaks in Prague exercised their effect on the committee as much as it did on the ultraconservatives: it caused it to agree to a dilution of the reform movement by accepting into it a group basically hostile to any kind of reform. One participant wrote later that only the fact that the burgomaster's group joined the committee "preserved order and prevented bloodshed."[37]

March 15 brought a series of startling developments. Providing an appropriately attractive setting, the weather was good, "the heaven clear" (this is one of the rare excursions into weather observation found in a police report).[38] From the morning hours, the petition was displayed for signatures in several places in Prague (soon thousands of copies were to be reprinted and circulated throughout the country). To top the excitement, in mid-afternoon the train from Vienna brought the first news of the downfall of Metternich, the abolition of censorship, and the proclamation of a constitutional era. Rarely had the shame of one man supplied an occasion for the relief

36. Stadion to Vienna, March 15, 1848, No. 1708/1848.
37. Dlouhý, "Dr. Josef Frič," *Osvěta,* VI, 570. Heyde suggests in his report that the final text was the product of late-night, last-minute bargaining (March 14) between the burgomaster's group and the committee (see his report of March 15, cited above). Neither Frič, father, nor Frič, son, knew anything about this, which would indicate that the text had been made final. before the burgomaster's group joined the committee.
38. For this and the following, see Heyde to Stadion, March 16, 1848, in *SÚA* Prague, PG 1846-49, 15 c/3, No. 1828/1848.

and jubilation of so many. The announcements loosed a wave of merriment and wild enthusiasm such as Prague had probably never seen before in its thousand-year history. Thousands milled about in the streets; stranger embraced stranger in public; "champagne flowed in torrents"; countless shouts of "Vivat!" thundered through the city; only the fact that the Lenten season was underway prevented the festivities from reaching more impressive proportions. Metternich's name became a term of scorn on every lip. Torchlight processions were organized at night.[39]

On the following day, people appeared for the first time on the streets wearing cocardes. Within hours, the term "constitution," hitherto proscribed, became a magic word. Merchants cashed in on the mood of the public by marketing products tailored to the political tastes of the moment. Special "constitutional hats," low and wide-brimmed, were introduced and promoted vigorously. One enterprising merchant began to sell "constitutional parasols"; another peddled "constitutional rolls" (crescent-type pastry), acclaimed by one newspaper as one of the most practical innovations of the constitutional era. A composer turned out a "constitutional polka."[40] An innkeeper hoped to attract clientele by naming his establishment the "Inn of the Constitution."[41] Prices of cockades and ribbons doubled in a few days, as the demand for them exhausted the market. Songs were composed, some serious, others frivolous and satirical, the latter having as their target Metternich, the Vienna police, President Sedlnitzky (who had also resigned), and censorship and absolutism in general. There were numerous proposals for the abolition of odius-sounding street names, such as "Jesuit Street"[42] and for the naming of streets after revered historic figures and the building of statutes in their honor, e.g., St. Václav and George of Poděbrady.

Almost overnight newspapers were transformed from dull, tedious media into lively instruments of criticism, with an effect on public opinion that was truly intoxicating. Suddenly the art of the cartoon emerged, having again as its chief target the recently departed personages of the absolutist era. Divine services, public meetings, private

39. *Bohemia,* March 17, 1848.
40. *Bohemia,* March 19, 1848; see also Černý (ed.), pp. 22-23. For a picture of the "constitutional parasol," see M. Novotný, *Letáky z roku 1848* (Prague, 1948), p. 32.
41. *NN,* September 24, 1848.
42. *NN,* April 9, 1848.

parties were held to celebrate the advent of constitutionalism. "One meeting follows another," commented one newspaper.[43] Clubs began to proliferate and new daily newspapers and magazines added color to the landscape of the printed word. Leaflets and pamphlets deluged the streets, seeking converts for a variety of causes, and the selling of leaflets became for a while a full-time occupation.[44] Czechs and Germans fraternized, a situation not destined to last.

Above all, there were rumors: the rumor-mongering never abated and became one of the most typical phenomena of the entire revolutionary period. There were rumors of a German invasion of Bohemia, of a peasant invasion of Prague,[45] of resignations, abdications, new appointments. Most of these rumors proved groundless, but they increased the excitability of minds already greatly excited by the precipitous course of events and by the abrupt removal of the dams of censorship and absolutism. Within three days of the downfall of Metternich, the undue excitement had claimed the first distinguished victim of the Czech national movement: a prominent Czech patriot suffered a nervous breakdown, marked by hallucinations, and had to be taken to a mental hospital. A terse newspaper announcement stated that he was "lying ill with nervous fever—the result of the excitement of the last week."[46]

Although the words "constitution" and "liberty" were on every lip, there was little understanding of their true meaning among the masses. This was to be expected; absolutism had surrounded these words with an aura of taboo, and even at the universities there were no lectures at the Faculty of Law dealing with constitutional law. The people were simply not equipped to come to grips with the whole complex of questions implied in the term "constitution" overnight. To many peasants, "constitution" meant deliverance from the *robot*

43. *NN,* April 20, 1848.

44. For a picture of the leaflet stand in March, 1848, see Novotný, *Letáky,* p. 32.

45. Heyde to Stadion, March 18, 1848, in *SÚA* Prague, PG 1846-49, 15 c/3, No. 1948/1848.

46. Supplement to *Bohemia,* March 20, 1848. The victim was Dr. Frič. See his son's account in Frič, *Paměti,* I, 395-96. Dr. Frič recovered in three weeks and led a most active life until his death in 1876 at the age of seventy-two.

The revolutionary era resulted in many emotional breakdowns. After the Viennese Revolution it was reported that "there occur in Vienna frequently cases of insanity that, according to medical opinion, have their origin in the excitement of the events of our times" (*Bohemia,* December 17, 1848).

and other seigneurial duties. Confidential reports on the public mood filed by the region prefects during this period show numerous instances of peasants simply refusing, in the name of the constitution, to perform their customary duties for the landlords.[47] Half a year later, it was reported that to the comman man, such terms as "democrat," "aristocrat," "reactionary," "despotism," "heirarchy," "sovereignty," "absolute government," "federalist principle," "socialist party" were still causing difficulty.[48]

The university students and other active groups seemed at times to propagate their own peculiar brand of constitutionalism. In one instance, some Prague students demanded free passage by rail to Vienna on the ground that they were members of a student delegation dispatched to visit the Vienna students. Their request having been denied, they calmly boarded the train anyway and proceeded to their destination.[49] Many other deputations rode free trains from Prague to Vienna and from Vienna to Prague.

Soon the concept of popular control was being employed as an excuse to commit acts of revenge or to harass unpopular individuals. Attacks upon Jews were becoming more frequent and merciless. In the rural areas individuals suspected of thievery and other misdemeanors were being dealt with, sometimes brutally, by recourse to "people's justice," which was not deflected from its purpose by any cumbersome sifting of evidence in a court of law. In a few cases, suspects were hauled out of prison and murdered by the raging crowd.[50]

On the lighter and more useful side, it was advocated that the principles of equality implicit in the constitution should make it unnecessary for people to remove their hats while greeting each other on the street; besides being inconvenient, such practice was an outright health hazard "in rain, snowfall, strong wind, and draft."[51]

The very words that evoked so much enthusiasm among the public, however, sent chills down the spines of many officials whose previous careers had been too closely bound with the absolutist re-

47. Reports from region prefects, in *SÚA* Prague, PG 1846-49, 15 c/3, Nos. 2279 (March 29, 1848), 2280 (March 28, 1848), 2292 (March 29, 1848), and others.
48. *NN*, September 27, 1848.
49. *Bohemia*, June 8, 1848.
50. *Bohemia*, April 18 and April 28, 1848.
51. *Bohemia*, March 31, 1848.

gime. Fearing a popular upheaval as a result of the downfall of absolutism, some officials went as far as to conceal from the people the news of recent political developments. In one district in Silesia, local officials were notified of the proclamation of the constitutional era on March 15 but were ordered not to announce the text publicly for the time being.[52] Conversely, the people in the rural areas at times refused to believe the news about the downfall of absolutism because the information had been communicated to them by officials, whom they had learned through hard experience to distrust.[53] There was a widespread distrust of officials among the peasantry in particular. Again, in their reports in March and April the region prefects lamented repeatedly the lack of confidence in officialdom exhibited by the public. One prefect spoke of "government offices which unfortunately so often enjoy only little confidence" and another commented, in an understatement, that "there is appearing a not quite favorable mood toward municipal and economic officials."[54]

The drafts of letters of public officials show how difficult it was for them to become accustomed to dealing respectfully and constitutionally with the public. Overnight they were compelled by circumstances to acquire a whole new terminology and new forms of expression showing some cognizance of public self-esteem. Thus, Governor Stadion, having drafted a letter to Vienna, amended it by inserting into one sentence the words "in a constitutional spirit." In the same letter he had referred to a Czech group somewhat pejoratively as consisting largely of "the lower strata of the Czech people," but upon rereading the phrase decided to omit "lower strata."[55] One may well imagine the suffering of a haughty bureaucrat who suddenly found himself polishing his diction in order not to ruffle the common man's self-respect!

The constitutional era witnessed the emergence of a number of organizations destined to play an influential role throughout the revolutionary era. Among the most important were the National Guard, the Academic Legion, Concord (*Svornost*), *Slavie,* and the Slavic Linden (*Slovanská lípa*). All of these organizations originated during the first days of the constitutional regime.

52. *Týdeník,* No. 94, as quoted in Černý (ed.), *Boj,* p. 23.
53. *NN,* April 13, 1848.
54. *SÚA* Prague, PG 1846-49, 15 c/3, No. 2279 (March 29, 1848), 2292 (March 29, 1848).
55. March 24, 1848, in file No. 2061.

The National Guard was the typical European by-product of a revolutionary upheaval that began with the French Revolution of 1789. National Guards sprang up all over Europe in 1848. The symbol of the free citizenry—of the political emancipation of the "third estate"—they came into being in Bohemia as well as Moravia in March, 1848. Their function was to protect constitutional freedoms and maintain order. They were largely of middle-class composition, and tended to assume a steadily more conservative color with the passage of time. The Academic Legion performed much the same functions, except that it was specifically a student organization. It existed in Prague as well as in other Bohemian and Moravian cities in which institutions of higher learning were located.

Both of the above bodies were of mixed Czech and German character. The desire of the Czechs to have a comparable organization of purely Czech character led to the formation of *Svornost*. Founded on March 18, it was first called the St. Václav Brotherhood,[56] to honor the memory of the patron-saint of Bohemia and also to underscore the fact that it was to serve as an armed appendage of the St. Václav Committee. Subsequently it became the *Svornost*.[57] It was more radical than the National Guard and became one of the great thorns in the flesh of the police and the military. The Czech student organization was *Slavie* (or Slavia), founded as a literary and political society. The Slavic Linden, which was to become the most active and important group during the twilight of constitutionalism, will be discussed later.

Meanwhile the Petition of March 11, in its final form, had been signed by a large number of Prague citizens; although it was mostly the work of the people of Prague, the inhabitants of a few other Bohemian cities also formally adhered to it. Among the signatories were both Czechs and Germans, with the former, of course, predominating. At the same time the radicals were agitating for demands more extreme than those contained in the diluted version of the petition; the St. Václav Committee was compelled to bow to their pressure, and on March 17 announced publicly that the original version

56. *Bohemia*, March 19, 1848.
57. This name was borrowed from Concordia, an organization of Czech and German artists which had existed during the pre-March period. The closest English equivalent to *Svornost* is "Concord"; I am retaining the Czech original in the text in order to avoid confusion with "Concordia."

of the petition, in the form presented to the assembly on March 11, would be submitted to the emperor along with the "official" text.

In Vienna, a government had been formed after the dismissal of Metternich, with Count Kolowrat as the presiding minister and Pillersdorf as the Minister of the Interior. This was the first "constitutional" cabinet in the history of the Habsburg Monarchy. It was to this cabinet that the Bohemian delegation delivered the two petitions and was received by the emperor himself on March 22. Though the delegation had journeyed to Vienna amid great exuberance and optimism, the answer it brought home was disappointing. The Cabinet Letter of March 23, issued over the name of the emperor in reply to the demands from Bohemia, was evasive and vague and made only limited concessions.[58] A wave of discontent swept Prague after the delegation returned. The city had planned a grand reception for the returning delegates and the day was to be turned into a holiday. When the text of the Cabinet Letter became known the festive mood subsided and the celebration was cancelled.

On the following day, March 28, a major meeting, attended by hundreds of Prague citizens was held to protest the Cabinet Letter. One frightened observer commented later that the assembly presented a picture of "an English meeting or of a French club." Whoever was present "will hardly ever be able to erase from his memory this moment of excitement." There were cries of "Republic!" and "We don't need the nobles anymore!" with "proletarians and youngsters" presuming to express themselves on constitutional questions.[59] Among the regular speakers was Brauner, who, like other speakers, pronounced the Cabinet Letter unsatisfactory.

The St. Václav Committee was charged with the task of drafting another petition for submission to the emperor. In its final form, the new petition was less loyalist in tone, more self-confident, and more emphatic in demanding certain changes.[60] It repeated, in more explicit terms, the demand for the unity of the Lands of the Czech Crown; and, more unequivocally than the first petition, called for a parliament chosen on "the widest possible basis of free elections"; the existing diet was rejected as being based on "medieval" arrangements

58. Černý (ed.), *Boj*, pp. 46-47.
59. *Bohemia*, March 28, 1848. Also, F. J. Schopf (ed.), *Wahre und ausführliche Darstellung der am 11 März 1848 . . . in Prag begonnenen Volks-Bewegung* (Leitmeritz, 1848), I, 36.
60. Černý (ed.), *Boj*, pp. 58-59.

not in keeping with modern constitutional requirements. Inspired by the success of the Magyars, the new petition called for a separate ministry for the Lands of the Czech Crown.

A delegation of the public, accompanied by armed guards, forced its way into the offices of Governor Stadion and compelled him to affix his seal of approval to the petition. This public humiliation only hastened the governor's decision to resign his position.[61]

This time the government in Vienna was compelled to treat the Bohemian demands with more respect. The political climate was becoming more menacing: there was a revolt in Lombardy; a republic had been proclaimed in Venetia; and in Hungary the national movement was generating a momentum that presaged disturbing prospects for the future. All these movements advertised the weakness of Habsburg rule in these regions. In these circumstances, it was imperative that Bohemia be pacified. As a result, some substantial concessions were made in answer to the Second Petition.

The answer took the form of another Cabinet Letter, dated April 8.[62] The first point of the Letter was that the Czech language should be entirely equal to the German in all branches of the administration and education—a significant concession to the Czechs. It also promised to call the Bohemian diet at the earliest possible date, wisely avoiding giving the impression that the new diet would in any sense be a continuation or modification of the estates diet and recommending that all social classes be represented. This was a radical innovation, though its effect was circumscribed by the provision that in rural districts only the taxpaying population, and in the cities only the "burghers" ("citizens," or property-owners and salaried employees) would have the right to vote. In practice both urban and rural laborers were excluded from voting, and also domestic workers and others, but even with the restriction, a majority of the male population was able to vote.

The demand for the unity and autonomy of the Lands of the Czech Crown was not accepted. It was stated that this matter would be dealt with at the forthcoming central parliament in Vienna, at which Bohemia, Moravia, and Silesia would be duly represented. There is no doubt that to make any decision relating to the unity of the Lands of the Czech Crown conditional upon the decision of the central parlia-

61. Kazbunda, *České hnutí*, p. 92.
62. Černý (ed.), *Boj*, pp. 102-4.

ment took the matter entirely out of the hands of these lands; in so ruling, the Cabinet Letter of April 8 departed from the principle set forth in the previous Cabinet Letter, in which it was left to the diets of the three lands to decide upon the course to be taken.

In rather categorically refusing to accept the demand for the union of the Lands of the Czech Crown, the Cabinet Letter of April 8 was probably influenced by the events in Hungary. Vienna had been compelled to accept the formation of a separate ministry for Hungary; Pillersdorf wanted to placate the Czechs, but was unwilling to undermine further the administrative unity of the Habsburg Lands by countenancing a similar institution for Bohemia. Therefore the only concession granted in answer to this demand was a promise to create separate administrative institutions for Bohemia, but only for Bohemia; their jurisdiction would not extend to Moravia and Silesia. At the same time, the pill was sugared by the verbal promise that Francis Josef, a Habsburg prince who was to become emperor at the end of 1848, would take over the administration of Bohemia as viceroy (subsequent events prevented him from ever assuming this post).[63]

Under the impact of official reports concerning unrest in the Bohemian countryside, the government in Vienna decided not to procrastinate on the question of serfdom. The *robot* had been abolished by a decree of March 28, and the Cabinet Letter referred to this. But the Cabinet Letter also sought to calm public opinion in the countryside by stating that the forthcoming Bohemian diet would deal with the questions and problems arising from the abolition of serfdom. In other words, Bohemia would not be required to wait for the appropriate decisions of the forthcoming central parliament, but would deal with serfdom as soon as the diet met; in this respect the Cabinet Letter made another concession to Bohemian autonomy.

The provisions of the Cabinet Letter of April 8 represented the high-point of concessions granted by Vienna to Bohemia during the 1848-49 period. The developments of the ensuing months may be regarded as a steady whittling down of these concessions. In Bohemia the news of the Cabinet Letter was well received and seemed to satisfy even the most radical opinion for the moment. The radicals were gratified by the provision relating to serfdom and by the prospect of a diet unconnected with the estates.

Yet it is interesting to note that even at this apex in the granting

63. Kazbunda, *České hnutí*, p. 102.

of concessions, the objective of the unity of the Lands of the Czech
Crown had eluded the Czechs. As already stated, the Letter authorized
the establishment of supreme administrative offices and departments
for Bohemia only; this was as far as it went in meeting the Czech
political ambitions (the Bohemian *Staatsrecht*), but even this provision was never carried out. Thus, after the issuance of the Letter
of April 8, Czech unity was no closer to realization than it had been
before. In demanding administrative unity of the Czech Lands, the
two petitions only asked for a return to the situation that had existed
before the centralist reforms of Maria Theresa. The petitions also
asked for a common diet for these lands, however, and in this respect,
it must be pointed out that the demand went beyond the situation
that had existed even in the period before the White Mountain: at
that time the common meetings of representatives of the three lands
were irregular and did not exist as a permanent institution (these
were the so-called general diets); after the White Mountain they
ceased almost completely. This shows, of course, that the Czech
leaders, with Brauner as the chief initiator, were vigorous enough
to ask for more than a mere return to the past; they wanted a future
that would be better than the past.

The strength of the Czech demands was considerably reduced by
the failure of two groups to support them. A majority of the Germans
of Bohemia, Moravia, and Silesia were opposed to the constitutional
unity of the three lands. But more damaging still was the failure of
the Czech element in Moravia to support the Bohemian Czechs in
this demand. Czech national consciousness in that province was still
only in its incipient stage; besides, there was a strong sentiment of
provincial Moravian patriotism which was shared by Moravian Czechs
and Germans alike and which would be at odds with any strengthening of constitutional ties with Bohemia. Although Czech voices
favoring union with Bohemia were not wholly lacking, they did not
represent the preponderance of public opinion.

On April 14, the Moravian diet voted overwhelmingly in favor
of its committee report opposing the union with Bohemia; it was
characteristic that a major statement against the union was delivered
by a Czech deputy, Alois Pražák, as rapporteur of the committee.
Only a few Czech deputies sat in this diet, but a reformed diet called
later in which Czech and German deputies were evenly divided also

voted against a union with Bohemia.[64] With such evidence of a lack of support for unity, it was not difficult for the government in Vienna to deny the demands of the Czech national leaders in Prague; it could rightly claim to be acting in accordance with public opinion as far as Moravia was concerned.

Throughout the latter part of March and the early part of April the St. Václav Committee continued to consolidate its position and rapidly assumed the role of spokesman not only for Prague but for Bohemia as a whole. The Committee was the authentic original product of a movement that had prepared the way for the first open breach in the absolutist structure of Bohemia, before the abdication of Metternich. It became associated in the public mind with everything pertaining to the new order, and symbolized all the aspirations for reform and for justice. Its prestige was further enhanced by the cooperation of a number of prominent and respected citizens, Czech and German, some of whom had originally been hostile to it. It filled the administrative vacuum brought about by the collapse of absolutism. There was chaos and uncertainty in the established administrative machinery. The prestige of officials associated with the status quo had been undermined. A host of new issues had arisen for which the existing officialdom was utterly unprepared. In short, a new era had been ushered in and it was quite appropriate that new instruments should be devised to cope with it and to give expression to the new forces. The St. Václav Committee was the logical instrument for this change. It refused to die, as Stadion and others like him had hoped. From a body charged originally with the sole purpose of preparing a petition to the emperor, it evolved into a permanent institution that gradually came to deal with a number of constitutional and other problems. Indeed it seemed on the verge of becoming the unofficial government of Bohemia and was in fact occasionally alluded to as such in the contemporary press.[65]

Those in official circles watched this development with a wary eye. The earlier attempts of Stadion to restrict or variously neutralize the position of the committee had failed. His position thus having been rendered precarious, the governor resigned his post. But since he was not one to give up easily, before the resignation became effective he made one more attempt at undermining the prestige of the

64. J. Macůrek, *Rok 1848 a Morava* (Brno, 1948), p. 48. Text of the statement approved by the diet on April 14, 1848, in Černý (ed.), *Boj,* pp. 129-32.
65. See, for example, *Bohemia,* March 29, 1848.

committee. At the end of March he conceived the idea of creating, on his own authority, a gubernatorial commission that would be charged with the tasks being "usurped" by the St. Václav Committee. The commission was appointed on April 1.[66] It comprised prominent Czechs and Germans, largely of conservative bent, among them Palacký. Some of its members were also members of the St. Václav Committee, but there were no radicals. This transparent stratagem provoked rumblings of discontent in a population already showing unmistakable signs of impatience with repeated bureaucratic sabotage. It is difficult to believe that at a time of general distrust of officialdom Stadion could really have convinced himself that a body so manifestly branded with a stamp of official benignity would have any appreciable chance with the public. There was even less chance that the public would permit the St. Václav Committee to die or be pushed into the background by a government-sponsored body; nor was the committee itself of a mind to allow that to happen.

Stadion's commission met only twice, and in closed sessions. Mounting pressure against it led to the calling of another public assembly on April 10. It met in the same St. Václav's Baths at which the memorable March assembly had met almost exactly a month earlier.[67] At the meeting Stadion's commission was criticized as being unrepresentative of the people, and the confidence of the public in the St. Václav Committee was thunderously expressed. It was proposed that the committee be expanded and merged with Stadion's commission, the new body, on the proposal of Karel Havlíček, to be named the National Committee. These suggestions were adopted, the merger was effected—Stadion was unable to resist the force of events—and the first meeting of the National Committee took place on April 13. Paradoxically, the governor of Bohemia became its chairman.

It is not possible today to reconstruct satisfactorily the circumstances surrounding the assembly of April 10. There are many gaps in the police reports, and no protocol of the meeting itself has survived. It is not known which group was responsible for the distribution of

66. G. Čechová and J. Martínek, "Národní výbor v roce 1848," *SAP*, IV, No. 1 (1954), 10. Text of the relevant documents issued by Stadion in Černý (ed.), *Boj*, pp. 71-72, 82-84.

67. This meeting is described in Heyde's report of April 10, 1848, in *SÚA* Prague, PG 1846-49, 15 c/3, No. 2826/1848 (also in *NN*, April 11, 1848).

posters summoning the people of Prague to the assembly.[68] Some radicals later charged that the assembly itself was a liberal plot designed to cripple the St. Václav Committee by merging it with Stadion's group.[69]

The radicals were correct in charging that the merger constituted another step in the deradicalization of the St. Václav Committee. Yet it was hardly a victory for the government. It was true that the governor of Bohemia had become the official head of the National Committee and that this set certain limits on the extent to which the committee could go in championing reform. But against this fact must be set other facts: the government was compelled to accept the existence of a popularly chosen body, with its highly objectionable name of "National Committee," conveying, rather painfully to the diehards, its popular nature. The committee had intruded upon the sacrosanct structure of the traditional bureaucratic institutions. Composed as it was of the best and most respected minds in the country, at the outset it enjoyed unparalleled esteem among the populace. This unpalatable situation the government had to acknowledge with as much grace as it could muster. It could hardly be called a victory for the government.

The National Committee became the hub of political activity in Prague and in Bohemia for the next two months or so. The Cabinet Letter of April 8, which had just then become known, furnished a long-range *raison d'être* for the committee. It provided for the summoning of the Bohemian diet, but this assembly could not take place without intensive preparation. There was no precedent for the electoral process: for the selection of candidates, for the conduct of elections, or for any of the practices associated with the expression of

68. Copy of the poster in No. 2826, as above. No names of organizers are given.

69. Frič, *Paměti,* I, 441. Frič's account here is highly emotional, and two of his statements are contradictory: He says that the meeting was so carefully organized by a few individuals (he does not name them) that it was impossible for others to express any dissenting points of view. But two paragraphs later he says that he and some others declared at the meeting that Stadion's commission did not enjoy the confidence of the people and that the proposed merger should be rejected.

Udaltsov, in *Aufzeichnungen,* p. 64, accepts Frič's views. He states further that Stadion himself proposed the merger with the St. Václav's Committee, but he does not give any source, and I could find no evidence anywhere for this assertion.

popular will. It was obvious that the National Committee faced a rigorous task.

It is but bare justice to state at this point that the first group in Bohemia stirred into organized action by the Paris events was actually the nobility. In point of time, its action preceded that of the radicals by a few days. As early as March 2 a number of nobles residing in Prague approached the government with an urgent demand for the convocation of the diet, with a view to giving additional representation to the middle class. The nobility had for several years pressed for constitutional reform that would strengthen the diet vis-à-vis the government. The fear of revolutionary changes which the example of Paris might provoke in Bohemia now lent special urgency to the need for reform. As Count Friedrich Deym, one of the originators of this action, related later: "As soon as the first news of the February events arrived here, the majority of members of the estates present here gathered in order to bring about their legal convocation as soon as possible because in this catastrophe they saw correctly a transition to a new age" that had been held back for thirty-three years by the Holy Alliance.[70]

Partly because of hesitation on the part of the government and partly because of a misunderstanding, the request of the nobility was not acted upon and the diet never met. The public did not find out about this action until March 22, from a statement of Count Deym published in the Prague press. The bid of the nobility as a group to gain the initiative and to obtain a determining influence in the reform movement of 1848 thus was frustrated at the outset. It was left to the non-noble element to seize the initiative and set in motion the wheels of change and revolution.

70. Černý (ed.), *Boj*, p. 42.

Chapter 3

The Frankfurt Question

The downfall of absolutism in March was welcomed by Czechs and Germans alike. This was the honeymoon period—all too brief—for the two nationalities of Bohemia. Czechs and Germans appeared to forget past wrongs and animosities, and a millennium of eternal brotherood seemed about to begin. Both Czechs and Germans were members of the National Committee, and the overriding concern was for political reforms, not national exclusiveness.

But it was not long before the first jarring notes were struck. Hitherto, Bohemia had presented a picture of one ethnic group being dominated by another. If any kind of brotherhood and equality was to be instituted between the two ethnic groups, a political and social surgery of major proportions would be required. In the process, the Germans would, almost overnight, be vastly reduced as a group in importance and power, and it was unlikely that such a situation would be acceptable to them either as individuals or as a group. It would affect their social status. It would close to them many economic opportunities and civil service posts, in proportion to the Czech eligibility for positions hitherto available only to Germans. It would produce a wholly new kind of experience, a completely new set of circumstances within which the Germans would be compelled to live.

The first differences appeared at the very beginning of the constitutional period. On March 18, Havlíček published in the *Pražské Noviny* a front-page appeal to his Czech countrymen to "remove German signs" from their stores and businesses and replace them with Czech ones.[1] (This issue of the *Pražské Noviny* was still under partial censorship; the following issue was the first published without any censorship.) Havlíček's appeal to the national sentiment and pride of the Czechs created ill-feeling and anxiety among members of the German community, which compelled the writer to calm them in the next issue by explaining that "this is no war, no enmity; it is

1. K. Havlíček, *Politické spisy,* ed. Z. Tobolka (Prague, 1900-3), I, 234.

not meant the way it may at first glance appear." Havlíček now
asked that the store signs be made bilingual,[2] a significant modification of his earlier announcement.

The mild tiff over the store signs was symptomatic rather than
fundamental, but the Czech-German relationship was about to be
marred seriously and irreparably by the problems arising from the
movement for the unification of Germany. On March 31 there
gathered in Frankfurt-am-Main the so called pre-parliament of some
five hundred prominent Germans whose job was to prepare the way
for the unification of Germany along liberal democratic lines. The
pre-parliament chose a Committee of Fifty to carry out the preparations. The committee decided to broaden its base by inviting six
representatives from those parts of the Habsburg Monarchy that had
belonged to the German Confederation, and earlier to the Holy Roman
Empire, which included the Czech Lands. Among the six chosen
was Palacký. (The text of the letter dated April 6, by which the
invitation was extended, is not extant.)

Without hesitation and in words ringing with national pride
Palacký declined the invitation in a letter dated April 11, which has
since become a classic in Czech history. The letter jolted, not to say
shocked, the Germans (of Germany) into a recognition of the Czechs
as a nationality claiming its own past and hopefully charting its own
future, independently of the Germans. Before publication of Palacký's
letter, the Czech Lands had been regarded in Germany without
question as belonging to the body politic of Germany. On the surface
they appeared entirely German; at best it was vaguely realized that
there was a mass of people of the lower strata who were Slavs.
Though the Slavs had excited the interest of a few German scholars,
chiefly historians and philologists, this interest was purely cultural.
Their political ties with Germany had not been called into question.
Palacký now rudely shattered this complacent view of the Czech substratum, and his words, coming from a man esteemed in German
circles as a historian, at first caused bewilderment, then disbelief, then
dismay. For the Czechs, the greatest significance of Palacký's letter
was that it thrust them onto the European stage for the first time
in modern history.[3] The March petitions had claimed the attention

2. *Pražské Noviny*, March 23, 1848, as quoted in Havlíček, *ibid.*, pp. 236-37.

3. The text of the letter has often been reprinted. It is conveniently available in J. M. Černý (ed.), *Boj za právo: Sborník aktů politických u věcech státu
a národa českého od roku 1848* (Prague, 1893), pp. 112-17. The English trans-

of Austria, but Palacký lifted the Czech cause onto a higher level of recognition; his words threw a gauntlet to the elite of Germany's intellectuals and, through them, to Europe.

In the celebrated letter, the Czech historian offered several reasons for declining the offer. He honored, he vowed, the aspirations of the Germans for unity; but precisely because he honored them, he must dissociate himself from them, for he was a Czech, not a German. There was no honorable place for him in an undertaking the objective of which was to unify Germans. In a famous phrase, he proudly declared, "I am a Czech of Slavic descent." His total commitment was to his people, he said. Moreover, he cautioned the committee to make no mistake about Bohemia's constitutional position in the past; according to Palacký—and he offered historical arguments (not always valid) to buttress his point—Bohemia had never been, in any meaningful sense, a part of Germany's past, and it could be expected even less to desire to form a part of Germany's future, a future in which, more than ever before, nationality would constitute the basis of the state.

Palacký had yet another reason for his stand. He was not merely opposing Czech incorporation into Germany, he was actively favoring a strong Czech role in Austria, and a strengthening and rebuilding of Austria. In his letter he stressed the need for a continued existence of Austria as a multinational state in which the interests of its many nationalities would be properly safeguarded and strengthened through cooperation between them. In contrast, the movement for the unification of Germany as envisioned in Frankfurt, would lead to a fatal weakening, perhaps a complete demise, of Austria as an independent state. This in turn would open the way for Russian domination of the small nationalities of Central and Southeast Europe. He was, he declared, an enemy of neither the Germans nor the Russians as people. But he felt that the Russian state would endanger the integrity of these nationalities and that the only defense against that was the existence of a strong and healthy political structure built upon the interests of the small nationalities.

This was the historic role of Austria; as Palacký expressed it, in another celebrated phrase: "If the Austrian state had not already existed for so long, it would have been in the interests of Europe, in-

lation is in C. and B. Jelavich (eds.), *The Habsburg Monarchy* ("Source Problems in World Civilization" [New York, 1959]), pp. 18-23; the translation appeared originally in *SEER*, XXVI (1948), 303-8.

deed of humanity itself, to endeavor to create it as soon as possible."[4]
Unfortunately, Austria had in the past misunderstood its own mission.
That mission must now begin to be performed, he said, and this would
be accomplished through a transformation of Austria into a state in
which all nationalities would enjoy equality and mutual respect.
This must be done soon: "Metternich fell not only because he had
been the greatest enemy of liberty, but also because he was the most
bitter, the most unyielding enemy of the entire Slavic nationality in
Austria."

Finally, Palacký voiced uncertainty over the political form a
unified Germany would take in the future. He purported to see the
introduction of a republican form of government as the only solution
for the conflicting trends the movement for German unification would
generate. It was not, he said, within his competence to pass judgment
on the suitability of republican institutions for Germany, but Austria
was a different matter; here he felt qualified to judge and that judgment led him "positively and emphatically [to] reject in advance any
idea of a republic."

What can current observation add to his eloquence? The avowed
goal of the Frankfurt intellectuals was the establishment of a unified,
though federal, German state in which the following matters would,
among others, belong to the central government: foreign affairs, war
and peace, the military, and a good deal of legislation in the realm
of both civil and public law. With such prospects before them, if the
Czechs permitted themselves to become a part of this structure ties
and relationships would be established between Germany and the
Czechs that would be far closer than any that had existed before. It
was not to be expected that at a time when their national consciousness
and pride were awakening the Czechs would wish to belong to a
German state that was being born from a rising national consciousness
no less intense than that of the Czechs, a state that would so patently
bear the stamp of Germanism.

The Czech fears in this respect were not diminished by German
pronouncements that the rights of non-German nationalities would be
respected in the new state. Subsequent developments bear out these
fears, judging at least from the fate that befell the Poles of the Duchy
of Poznan. The entire history of the Poles in Poznan in the half-cen-
tury preceding World War I is one of severe Germanization, sys-

4. Černý (ed.), *Boj,* pp. 115-16.

tematically pursued. The rise of German nationalism in the latter half of the nineteenth century would hardly have permitted a scrupulous safeguarding of the ethnic rights of the Czechs in a unified German state. Palacký's answer therefore appears to have been justified.

Palacký's committment to Austria as a state in which the rights of small Slavic nationalities would best be safeguarded is an expression of Austro-Slavism, which became the creed of the Czech national movement in 1848. In its simplest form, Austro-Slavism meant recognition of the common interests and fortunes of the Slavs of Austria. The roots and the first expressions of Austro-Slavism predate Palacký's letter by several decades.[5] Nevertheless, it was with this letter, published as it was at a time of rapid change, by a respected scholar, that Austro-Slavism received full publicity for the first time and was raised to the level of a political program. The letter helped create an atmosphere within which the first Slavic Congress was organized, in Prague in June, 1848, representing the high-point of Austro-Slavism in this revolutionary period. Of course, Palacký's Austro-Slavism was predicated upon a radical transformation of Austria from a centralist into a truly federalist state. This change was never destined to materialize, and years later, in 1872, Palacký publicly expressed his disillusionment with the policy he had championed for so long, allowing that the views he had formulated in 1848 had been erroneous. Throughout 1848-49, however, Austro-Slavism dominated the minds of Czech liberals and exerted great influence upon other Slavs of the monarchy.

Besides being a manifestation of a genuine national feeling, Austro-Slavism was also economically motivated. It reflected Czech fears of the stifling influence of a more highly developed German industry upon a young and still comparatively weak Czech bourgeoisie in the event of Bohemia's incorporation into a unified Germany. This fear was paralleled by hopes of an expanding Czech influence in the less developed economies of the Balkan Slavs.

The advantages of such a southeastern orientation were given what amounted to an ideological basis by the Czech historian and writer Jan Erazim Vocel, in an article entitled "The Future of the Czech Nation." Vocel had some unflattering things to say about Germans, Englishmen, and Frenchmen as economic competitors who were exploiting the markets of Eastern and Southeast Europe—a

5. See notes 67 and 68 in Chapter 1.

region in which Czech businessmen and artisans, as Slavs, would be
more welcome and more successful than the West Europeans. In the
highly developed West, Czech products could not hope to find a
sufficient market. In the underdeveloped East, such markets existed,
and while cultivating them, the Czechs would simultaneously
strengthen the Czech nation and the ties binding that nation to other
Slavs.

Here was a perfect and legitimate blend of national and economic interest. The prominence of the journal in which the article
appeared assured it the best audience.[6] As for the Frankfurt question,
Czech business leaders, on studying the possible impact of Bohemia's
incorporation into Germany upon Bohemia's economy, were unanimous
in their verdict that it would be injurious. With the abolition of
tariff barriers Bohemia would become prey to Germany's competition,
and the consequences for Czech small businessmen (there were almost no Czech big businessmen) could be easily predicted.[7]

Palacký's letter was not devoid of shrewdness. His reference to
German republicanism was a calculated move; though it reflected his
own conservative views and keen distaste for republicanism, it was
at the same time designed to goad the Austrian ruling circles into
making concessions to the Slavs by identifying the Germans with the
republican nightmare and contrasting with them the loyalist Slavs,
far removed from any flirtations with such dangers. Similarly, the
dark hint concerning the Russian menace was a calculated move in
that it echoed the standard fears and charges of the enemies of Slavdom. With Palacký raising the cry of the "Russian danger" as loudly
as the Germans, it was difficult for his critics to accuse him, as was
their wont in such cases, of being the tool of Russian Pan-Slavism.
By using the favorite arguments of the enemies of the Slavs, he beat
the Germans at their own game; yet he was simultaneously advo-
cating a policy (federalism for Austria) that, if carried out, would
greatly fortify the position of the Slavs within the Habsburg Monarchy.

A blend of patriot's ardor and historian's craft, Palacký's letter
was more than a letter: it was a manifesto. It was commented upon

6. Reprinted in *NNM*, II (1962), 329-33. Appeared originally in *Časopis
Českého Musea*, XXI (1847), Part I, 658-63.

7. *NN*, August 5, 1848. For this subject, see V. Vomáčková, "Die Bourgeoisie in Böhmen und der Deutsche Zollverein im Jahre 1848," *Aus 500 Jahren
deutsch-tschechoslowakischer Geschichte,* ed. K. Obermann and J. Polišenský
(Berlin, 1958), pp. 223-48.

editorially in the major newspapers of Austria and Germany, both German and Slavic. It influenced friends and foes with equal cogency. At home Czech liberals adopted it as a guideline for Czech policy to be followed throughout the revolutionary era. Czech radicals were critical of Palacký's conservatism. Nothing could frighten them less than the specter of republicanism in Germany; but they were at one with the historian in averting their gaze from Frankfurt and offering an unqualified rejection of the wooing of German intellectuals.[8]

Palacký's contribution was to crystallize the opinion of the Czech community into a firm stand against Frankfurt. Nor was the imperial government oblivious to the message proclaimed by Palacký. It could not be indifferent to such a manifestation of loyalty from the most influential Czech, and it was no coincidence that a few weeks later it extended to him an invitation to join the government in Vienna as Minister of Education.[9] Regarding Frankfurt, however, the government was in a difficult position. It could not ignore the strong pro-Frankfurt opinion among Austrian Germans. Nor did it wish to abandon its traditional role as a member of the German Confederation. In fact, Austrian and Habsburg influence in Germany had been on the wane, and the Austrian government was prepared to go along with the Great German movement insofar as that waning influence could be restored. On the other hand, it could quite obviously not underwrite any movement or policy—and this was the direction in which the Frankfurt movement seemed to be heading—the result of which would be the slightest loosening of the various parts of the Habsburg realm, or cause the interests of that realm to be subordinated to any outside body. Thus, the imperial government had to walk a tightrope: it was moderately both for and against Frankfurt, with the latter sentiment being somewhat stronger. It was in no small measure the effect of Palacký's letter that in the weeks to come the government slowly but increasingly resisted the lure of Frankfurt, in the knowledge that it had Austria's Slavs on its side.

What was the reaction of the Germans in the Habsburg Monarchy? In the first few months, the majority was undoubtedly in favor of Frankfurt, though it should be noted that some Germans

8. J. V. Frič, *Paměti*, ed. K. Cvejn (Prague, 1957-63), II, 23.
9. K. Kazbunda, *České hnutí roku 1848* (Prague, 1929), p. 165. Palacký declined, largely because he felt that acceptance of such an important post by a Slav would strengthen the hand of those Germans who played on the fear of the Slavic domination of Austria.

had different ideas concerning the constitutional position of Austria in a unified Germany. Some envisioned a unified state with only limited powers for the constituent provinces; others envisioned a loose association of states in which each province, including the provinces of Austria, could still retain its distinctive character and perpetuate its distinctive traditions. It is only fair to add that the Habsburg Germans supported Frankfurt for the same reason, and—from their point of view—with the same degree of justification with which the Czechs opposed it. It appealed to their German sentiment, and they saw it as a means of strengthening the German element.

That the German element needed to be strengthened seemed to them indicated by the almost precipitous emergence of the Slavs as a political force since the March Days. The Slavs' recent assertion of their rights posed a threat to German power; it had caused doubts about relationships that had never been doubted; it had called into question values that had never been questioned. Almost overnight, the Slavs began boldly to pry open the door that had so jealously guarded the German privileges, and they gave every sign of not only wanting to open the door, but to take over the household. The Habsburg Germans were gradually beginning to fear that any transformation of the monarchy into a democratic federation of equal nationalities would have a disastrous effect on their status, and that in such a federation, far from being equal, the Germans might be submerged by the Slavic masses.

Nor were the leaders of the Slavs oblivious to such possibilities. As early as March 19, Havlíček published in *Pražské Noviny* a strongly nationalist article stating that in Austria "we live with our Slavic brethren, Illyrians and Poles . . . here we will always have natural superiority," and that in this state "we, Slavs, shall at last attain glory."[10] Many similar, and some stronger, statements could be read in the Czech press during this period. For example, *Národní Noviny* said in May that the "Rhine and Danube are the two main rivers of Greater Germany. . . . But one artery had been cut by the French and the other must be cut by the Slavs. The Danube is a Slavic river . . . and the Danube will be our Slavic river, Austria will be a Slavic empire."[11] Such pronouncements left little doubt in the

10. Havlíček, *Politické spisy*, I, 240.

11. J. Heidler, "Český sněm ústavodárný 1848," *ČČH*, XIII (1907), 51. In a public address in October, 1848, Sabina stated that "if Austria wants to exist, she must become a Slavic state" (*NLS*, October 30, 1848).

minds of the Germans that the Slavs hoped that in a liberalized Austria they would call the tune and reverse the pattern of centuries.

The Germans in Bohemia found themselves confronting special problems that their brethren in Austria proper (i.e., in what is roughly present-day Austria) did not have to face. The Bohemian Germans lived in a province in which they were in a minority; this made their political future more precarious and their fears correspondingly greater. The first openly hostile German note in Bohemia, introduced by a provincial newspaper, depicted the events in Prague most unfairly and accused the Czechs of causing hardship to the Germans.[12] In the manner in which it was presented the charge was so untenable that a number of Germans from Liberec (Reichenberg) publicly dissociated themselves from it, and several prominent Prague writers, both Czech and German, issued a denial of the charge.[13]

The next step from the German side was the foundation of an organization designed to defend their nationality in the face of Slavic pressure: the League of Germans of Bohemia, Moravia, and Silesia for the Preservation of Their Nationality (*Verein der Deutschen aus Böhmen, Mähren, und Schlesien zur Aufrechterhaltung ihrer Nationalität*). It was perhaps not atypical that this organization was founded by the "Sudeten Germans" residing in Vienna, where the German nationalist movement was strongest. It was brought into life as a reaction to the Second Petition of March 29, and opposed many of its demands in a statement issued on April 9.[14] In the statement, the League opposed the unification of Bohemia, Moravia, and Silesia; it opposed the equality of the Czech and German languages in high schools and at the University of Prague; it demanded the incorporation of Cisleithania into Greater Germany. This was the first public onslaught on the Czech national program, the first anguished cry of a German group, dismayed at the prospect of its nationality's losing

12. Quoted in *NN*, April 5, 1848. The German newspaper in question was *Reichenberger Wochenblatt*, April 1.

13. *Ibid.*

14. *NN*, April 15, 1848. The exact date of the origin of the League is not known, but it was formed during the first days of April. See E. K. Sieber, *Ludwig von Löhner: Ein Vorkämpfer des Deutschtums in Böhmen, Mähren und Schlesien im Jahre 1848-1849* (Munich, 1965), p. 59.

The term "Sudeten Germans" was first used at the beginning of this century. It is used here occasionally to avoid the cumbersome "Germans of Bohemia, Moravia, and Silesia."

its ruling position in Austria. Even the First Petition had caused no negative public reaction from the Germans.

With the publication of Palacký's letter, the gap between the Czech and German points of view widened. On April 18, a number of members of the National Committee issued a statement that, though cautious, was nevertheless negative with respect to Frankfurt; the committee proposed that any decision regarding this question be reserved to the forthcoming Bohemian diet.[15] This in turn induced the Bohemian Germans to found, in Prague, on April 19, yet another organization for the defense of their interests, the so-called Constitutional League (*Constitutioneller Verein*),[16] soon to become a major center of an implacable anti-Czech sentiment. The League's purpose was to serve as a counterweight to the National Committee. At the same time, within the National Committee, German representatives were beginning to feel increasingly uncomfortable, and began withdrawing from it. Their representation in the National Committee was just and equitable, and corresponded to the number of Germans in Bohemia as a whole. But, unfortunately, from their point of view, their representation did not adequately reflect their past historic role and their present social and cultural strength, and they felt that they would, in practice, be outvoted on every important question of interest to the German nationality.

From the very beginning, the Czech weight of numbers gave the National Committee the character of a Czech organization, although this had not been the original intention, but now, with the Germans withdrawing, it was actually becoming a "Czech" National Committee. During the latter part of April, the liberal and radical Germans continued to play a part in the committee's activities, in the hope of averting a complete breach between the two nationalities, but in the end, they too succumbed to the surging power of nationalism and to the magic of Frankfurt. By the middle of May, the last few remaining Germans—including the German radicals—pulled out: the breach between the two ethnic groups was now complete.

The more the Bohemian Germans fell under the spell of Frankfurt, the more the Czechs campaigned against it. At almost exactly the same time as the Germans, they founded their own "League," known as the "Czech-Moravian-Silesian Society" (*Česko-moravsko-*

15. Kazbunda, *České hnutí*, p. 149.
16. An account in *CBB*, April 22, 1848.

slezská jednota);[17] it too was founded in Vienna, by the Czechs residing there. Although its sphere of activity included all the Lands of the Czech Crown, in practice it limited itself largely to Moravia and Silesia, where the Czech element was weak and a considerable propaganda effort was required to match the German influence.

The Czechs campaigned in the press and with popular songs and public speeches. The most aggressive vehicle of the anti-Frankfurt "party" was the daily newspaper *Národní Noviny,* which had been founded on April 5. Its editor,[18] Havlíček, was also the author of the lyrics of the most popular anti-Frankfurt song, entitled "New Song about This German Parliament." The opening stanza ridiculed the Bohemian German Schuselka, who had irritated the Czechs by his tireless efforts to win them over to the Frankfurt cause. Though witty, the lyrics of the song are in poor taste; the last stanza is so coarse as to preclude its being reproduced in these pages.[19] It was a terrible irony that both the author of this song and the man it ridiculed were to spend years in internment and prison during the period of Bach's absolutism. In the refrain of another song, the popularity of which rivaled Havlíček's, was the following: "Forward against the German, forward against the murderer, against Frankfurt."[20]

The Czechs would doubtless have sincerely disclaimed any anti-German hostility, even while singing such songs, which illustrates the difficulties hindering understanding, especially if one realizes that on the German side the abuses were similar, if not greater. A Czech and a German could indeed have genuinely been friends, as individuals, but once each began to think of the other in terms of a national group, he invariably conjured a vision of something undesirable and hostile. And in the vocabulary of each, certain unflattering expressions became

17. R. Maršan, *Čechové a Němci r. 1848 a boj o Frankfurt* (Prague, 1898), p. 96. This organization never became very prominent.

18. Havlíček had been editor of the semi-official *Pražské Noviny* from January 1, 1846, to April 4, 1848. The constitutional era had opened new vistas for journalism and Havlíček did not wish to continue to be associated with this newspaper. He assumed editorship of a new paper, the *Národní Noviny,* with its first issue (April 5), and made it the first great Czech newspaper.

19. Text in J. J. Toužimský, *Na úsvitě nové doby* (Prague, 1898), p. 324. A contemporary text of this song has survived, in which there are three additional stanzas so obscene that they could not be printed in any acceptable medium and are of course not reproduced in Toužimský. See Kazbunda, *České hnutí,* p. 156.

20. Toužimský, *Na úsvitě,* p. 368.

almost synonymous with the other nationality. Thus, one Czech daily could refer to the German language as "babbling,"[21] while another could refer to Germans editorially as "our sworn murderers."[22] One newspaper asked a rhetorical question: "What good has a German ever done for you?"; another spoke of "typical German insolence";[23] and still another went so far as to describe a certain German as being endowed with a "stupid physiognomy" that marked him immediately as a supporter of the Frankfurt movement.[24] With such comments finding their way into print, one may well imagine the force and frequency of those used in daily parlance that were not considered "fit to print." The Czechs had had, of course an unhappy political experience with the Germans, especially since 1620, which explains the bitterness of their comments. At the same time, one may well imagine the effect of these slurs upon the Germans.

If the Czech popular image of the Germans savored of bitterness, the German image of the Czechs or Slavs was at best condescending and at worst contemptuous. The Czechs were regarded as a savage, uncultured mass who required German tutelage in order to be raised to a level of culture. There were appreciable nuances between the intensity with which various German groups expressed their views. The German press in Prague was the most moderate; indeed it was on the whole more guarded in its anti-Czech pronouncements than the Czech press in Prague was in its anti-German pronouncements, for the obvious reason that the German community in Prague was heavily outnumbered by the Czechs and could not match their political vigor. As a result, the German press had to be more circumspect and was more sincerely interested in keeping open the dialogue between nationalities.

Unfortunately, the same could not be said of German opinion outside Prague. It was blatantly anti-Czech in the Sudeten regions and in the German districts of Moravia, and it was particularly un-bridled among the German radicals in Vienna. By every criterion, the German radical press in Vienna was the most brutally and of-fensively anti-Czech and anti-Slavic in the monarchy. Although chauvinism, of greater or lesser degree, dominated the presses of

21. "We hope that the poor [Czech] children won't long be tortured by German babbling, unintelligible to them" (*PVL*, November 14, 1848).

22. *NN*, May 12, 1848.

23. Both in *NN*, May 16, 1848.

24. *NN*, July 4, 1848.

all ethnic groups in the monarchy, the Viennese radical press was by far the most unscrupulous. Its hatred of the Czechs began to rise to appreciable heights with the opening stages of the Frankfurt controversy, and it reached one of its many peaks at the time of the Slavic Congress and the June Uprising in Prague. On the occasion of the uprising, one radical newspaper spoke of "the insane or corrupt Slav party of the Czechs" who want to "turn Austria into a Slav Empire." It commended General Windischgrätz for defeating "the wild, hate-brewing, fear-inspiring doings of the Czech party," and added that "a victory for German concerns in Bohemia and in the monarchy can never be a misfortune, for the Germans bring humanity and freedom to the conquered."[25]

The Bohemian German writer and democrat Alfred Meissner wrote after the defeat of the June Uprising that the Czech movement began "with a lie"; he derided Palacký, who, "as a typical Slovak and son of the country from which the itinerant tinkers originate, thinks that the old broken pot called Austria needs only to be mended with a Slavic wire in order to last into eternity"; and concluded by saying that when the Czechs came to their senses they would willingly agree to "join Germany."[26] Only two years earlier the same Meissner had glorified the Hussite movement in his poetry, particularly in his *Žižka*, written in 1846, and had been a friend of Czech aspirations. He had also belonged to the National Committee but withdrew at the beginning of May, later becoming completely hostile to Czech national efforts.

Another Bohemian German, Ludwig Löhner, published a newspaper in Vienna in which the following homily was presented in the very first issue (July 11): "We believe in the Holy Spirit of humanity which reigns and gives life to all nations of the world, of whatever name and race, and whose realm lasts forever. We believe that this Spirit became incarnate in the German nation whose breath is its breath, in order to awaken all nations, alive and dead, awake and slumbering, so that they may become great. . . ." In the next issue the same newspaper described Germany as being "called to bring and preserve education along the rivers of Austria as far as the shores of

25. *Volksfreund*, June 24, 1848, as quoted in R. J. Rath, *The Viennese Revolution of 1848* (Austin, Tex., 1957), pp. 262-63.

26. *Kölnische Zeitung*, June to August, 1848 (reproduced in V. Žáček and Z. Tobolka [eds.], *Slovanský sjezd v Praze roku 1848: Sbírka dokumentů* [Prague, 1958], pp. 416-17).

the Black and Adriatic Seas," adding that "the banner of humanity, borne by German hands on blessed Magyar soil and the receptive land of the Slavic nations, will blossom. . . ." As Havlíček remarked, in commenting on Löhner's outlook: "There is not a man in the world whom Mr. Löhner does not consider it just to Germanize."[27]

Meanwhile, the Frankfurt question was increasingly thrusting itself upon the political stage in Bohemia. Throughout the territory of the German Confederation elections to the Frankfurt Assembly were to be held, and it was assumed that the Lands of the Czech Crown, as well as other parts of Cisleithania insofar as they belonged to the German Confederation, would participate in the election. Taking their cue from Palacký's letter, however, the Czechs declined to have anything to do with the undertaking, much to the dismay, even fury of the Germans. This placed the government in a most precarious position, the burden of dealing with the matter on a day-to-day basis falling upon Minister Pillersdorf. As mediator between the Germans, clamoring impatiently for an election, and the Czechs, agitating against it, Pillersdorf finally chose a compromise: the government officially authorized an election to be held, but with the explicit proviso that both individual voters and entire electoral districts could abstain from going to the polls if they wished to do so.[28] In circumstances less filled with rancor, such a compromise might have proved acceptable. As it was, it satisfied neither the Czechs nor the Germans.

The Frankfurt Committee, upon being apprised of the Czech opposition, dispatched a delegation to Prague. It consisted of two men: Karl J. Wächter, and Ignaz Kuranda, the latter a prominent liberal journalist born of a German-Jewish family in Prague. They were soon joined in Prague by Dr. Arnold Schilling, a Vienna physician. The delegates were not *au courant* as far as the political situation in Bohemia was concerned. It was not until they arrived in Prague on April 28 that they realized the true importance of the National Committee and also discovered that the committee had already discussed the issue and decided against the elections. Their mission was reduced to a meeting, on April 29, with Section 9 (foreign affairs) of the National Committee. The Frankfurt delegates could entertain no hope of inducing the Czechs to change their minds.

27. Reproduced by Havlíček, in *NN*, August 5, 1848. The newspaper cited is *Schwarz-Roth-Gold*.

28. For the decree of April 22, see Černý (ed.), *Boj*, pp. 144-45; for details, see Kazbunda, *České hnutí*, pp. 147 ff.

The meeting became, in effect, only an exchange of views in which the Czechs flatly opposed any idea of going to Frankfurt; they were seconded by the moderate Bohemian Germans present at the meeting. With restraint Wächter and Kuranda presented the point of view of the Frankfurt Committee. A jarring note was introduced by Schilling, who opined that "the idea of liberty is not to be found among the Slavs" and for that reason he was appealing "to the Czechs to join with Germany." His whole contribution was marked by a display of intolerance and arrogance that ill-fitted the occasion.[29] On May 3, in a meeting of the Frankfurt Committee, this same Schilling declared: "I believe that since Bohemia cannot be held in the German Confederation by conviction, she must be bound to Germany by the sword's edge."[30]

That same evening there was a meeting of the German Constitutional League to discuss the Frankfurt question. It was to be a solemn occasion, with the three Frankfurt envoys present, but a number of Czech nationalists attended the meeting and broke it up. This was the first violent encounter between Czechs and Germans in the revolutionary year 1848; it had taken little more than six weeks for the Czech-German relationship to pass from honeymoon to violent hostility.

On May 5 the Frankfurt Committee issued an appeal to the people of Bohemia asking them to take part in the elections and assuring them that the rights of all nationalities in the new Germany would be safeguarded. This had no appreciable effect on the Czech population; indeed the appeal remained almost unknown to the people, since the Czech press was in no mood to publicize it.

In Bohemia, the elections were set for May 23-24 in Prague, and for May 20 and 22 in the rest of the province. The elections were indirect, with the voters choosing electors, who in turn elected the candidates. It was the first democratic election in the history of Bohemia but, paradoxically, it proved unwelcome and was deliberately ignored by one of the two nationalities. Although the election to Frankfurt was to be based on universal suffrage, in practice, the manner in which this was carried out differed from state to state, and the working classes were in most cases not admitted to the polls. In Bohemia, in particular, a voter, in order to qualify, had to be "inde-

29. Protocols of the meeting in Černý (ed.), *Boj,* pp. 160 ff.
30. Quoted in F. L. Rieger, *Řeči Dra. Frant. Ladisl. Riegra,* ed. J. Kalousek (Prague, 1883), I, 13.

pendent," which of course excluded all those working for a wage.[31]

The Germans, who felt that the date for the election had been set deliberately late in order to prevent their deputies from attending the opening of the Frankfurt Assembly, took matters into their own hands, and in many districts held the election on May 13. In the midst of the campaign the Frankfurt cause received a setback. A radical outbreak in Vienna in the middle of May forced the emperor to flee the imperial capital. Since the radicals behind the outbreak were the most zealous crusaders for Frankfurt, the cause of Frankfurt lost much of its attraction for the German moderates, who had not the slightest sympathy for the political extremism of the radicals and were horrified at the spectacle of the emperor's having to flee for his life. As a result, more than a few Bohemian Germans decided at the last moment to dissociate themselves from the Frankfurt propagandists and to abstain from the polls on election day.

All in all, of sixty-eight electoral districts, only nineteen elected deputies.[32] All Czech-speaking districts, and a few German-speaking ones, abstained. In the whole city of Prague, only three votes were cast—a notable success for the Czechs. One of the reasons for the small turnout was that the Constitutional League announced just on the eve of the elections that it had not pressed for participation in the Prague elections because it was afraid of inciting strife and violence.[33] Then, too, a number of Germans were frightened away from the polls by Czech belligerence. On the eve of the election, Czech chauvinists tore down virtually all official posters in Prague announcing the manner in which the election was to be carried out. Havlíček himself commented upon this with great satisfaction. Also on the eve of the election Czech throngs were marching through the streets of Prague singing anti-Frankfurt songs and staging noisy demonstrations, thus hardly creating an attitude conducive to a free expression of opinion. On election day, much the same display of sentiment could be observed.[34] It was, of course, Havlíček, who, through his newspaper, was responsible, more than any other single Czech person, for making the boycott such a success. He threw himself into the struggle with all the strength and persuasiveness of his

31. Text of the Electoral Regulation in *CBB*, May 23, 1848.
32. J. Pfitzner, "Die Wahlen in die Frankfurter Nationalversammlung und der Sudetenraum," *Zeitschrift für Sudetendeutsche Geschichte*, V (1941), 225.
33. Text of the statement in *CBB*, May 23, 1848.
34. *NN*, May 25, 1848.

satirical pen and struck a responsive chord among the Czech populace. Anti-Semitism was also employed as a weapon against Frankfurt; a notable example was a popular Czech song ridiculing Kuranda, with crassly anti-Semitic overtones.[35] In the rural regions, Czech agitators spread the rumor that Frankfurt would force all good Catholics to become Protestants.[36]

In this doubtful contest of terror and rumor-mongering, the Germans fully matched the Czechs. In areas in which the Germans predominated, Czech voters were subjected to intimidation and propaganda. There were emissaries conducting a campaign throughout the countryside; there were pamphlets addressed to the Czech peasants in Czech, written in a style and language so tortuous and awkward as to readily betray their German origin. The pamphlets repeated endlessly the fiction that it was the order of the emperor that all must vote and that abstention meant disobeying the imperial will. In German districts, the peasants were told that the Czechs would expel them from their homes; this caused the Germans to hold nightly vigils in the expectation of a Czech "invasion." A South German newspaper (*Augsburger Allgemeine Zeitung,* May 11, 1848) called for the sending of an army of ten thousand men to Prague in order to keep Bohemia within Austria and the German Confederation. A pamphlet said that the Slavic movement was a plot of the Bohemian nobility, who wanted to sell Bohemia to Russia in order to be able to maintain serfdom under its aegis![37] German chauvinism was particularly marked in Moravia, in the cities of Brno and Olomouc.

As was expected, the Frankfurt movement was notably more successful in Moravia. In Moravia proper, twenty-three out of twenty-eight districts voted; in Silesia, seven out of seven.[38] The above figures are not wholly accurate, since they do not indicate the

35. For a sample, see F. Roubík, *Český rok 1848* (Prague, 1931), p. 170.
36. H. Lades, *Die Tschechen und die deutsche Frage* (Erlangen, 1938), p. 115.
37. Maršan, *Čechové a Němci,* pp. 97, 125, 130, 132.
38. Pfitzner, "Die Wahlen," pp. 223, 225. In Bohemia and Moravia, a number of deputies, for various reasons, declined to accept the mandate. As a result, the total number of deputies who actually went to Frankfurt was lower than the number of districts in which a valid election had taken place. For Bohemia, Moravia, and Silesia combined, the total number of candidates elected was forty-nine, yet the number who went to Frankfurt was only thirty-three. See Pfitzner, p. 229.

proportion of eligible voters taking part. Thus, in Brno and Olomouc, the election was considered valid, but in fact the number of voters who had come to the polls was very small. In Brno, a city having more than forty thousand people of whom perhaps one fourth might have been eligible, excluding women, minors, and those not "independent," only three hundred people are said to have voted. In Olomouc, the situation was similar.[39] The low turnout was doubtless influenced by the lack of experience with and understanding of the electoral process. It is interesting to note that although the election was supposed to be secret, it was frequently not so in practice.[40] As far as the social composition of deputies is concerned, it goes without saying that the majority were officials, intellectuals, and professional men.

Such opposition to Frankfurt as existed in Moravia drew its strength not only from the Czech element, still politically weak, but also from those Germans who possessed a strong provincial Moravian loyalty. This feeling manifested itself especially at the Moravian diet. The same sentiment that caused a resistance to union with Bohemia also militated against any closer ties with Greater Germany. The Moravian estates diet devoted a whole session (April 26, 1848) to the Frankfurt question and the anti-Frankfurt sentiment prevailed, although all but a handful of the deputies were Germans. After a lengthy debate, the diet voted 45-21 to leave the decision concerning the holding of elections to the reformed diet, which was to meet shortly. In practice, this meant a vote against Frankfurt. This could not, of course, prevent the government in Vienna from authorizing the holding of elections. The new reformed diet that met on May 31, 1848, did not deal with this problem and the question soon lost relevance.[41]

The Czechs may have ignored the Frankfurt Assembly, but the assembly did not ignore the Czechs. The defiance by the Czechs of the august assembly was brought up for consideration, with the German deputies from Bohemia and Moravia naturally playing a significant part in the debates. It was hoped that Czech deputies could be lured to Frankfurt if they received an assurance that in a

39. *NN,* May 19, 1848.

40. H. Ibler, "Die Wahlen zur Frankfurter Nationalversammlung in Österreich . . . ," *MIÖG,* XLVIII (1934), 106.

41. J. Dvořák, *Moravské sněmování roku 1848-49* (Telč, 1898), p. 125. Only several months later did the diet protest against the Frankfurt decisions.

unified Greater Germany the rights of non-German nationalities would be respected. (The Czechs were not the only Slavic truants; Slovene deputies were also absent.) On May 21, a proclamation was accordingly adopted by the plenum recognizing the rights of non-Germans to their full development, and even suggesting that a powerful free Germany would offer them the best protection. The proclamation was adopted with one dissenting vote only, but it was not explicit enough to dispel the fear of the Czechs for their collective future in a new Germany.[42] Since it produced no visible effect, the Czech question reached the floor of the assembly chamber again on June 5. A few moderate speakers cautioned against pressing the issue, but the decision of the majority was to entrust it to an existing committee, which would investigate the situation in the "Slavic-German" regions and make appropriate recommendations.[43]

But before the committee could begin its work, news of the program of the Slavic Congress with its anti-Frankfurt tenor was brought to the attention of the deputies. This added new dimensions and new gravity to the problem. As a result, the work with which the above committee had been entrusted was suspended, and on June 7 a new committee was chosen especially for the purpose of investigating the situation. Yet the Czech question refused to subside; the climax was reached on June 20 when the assembly discussed the Czech situation in the light of reports on the June Uprising (see Chapter 6) that had arrived on the previous day. The assembly labored under the misapprehension that the uprising was a Czech-German struggle. Consequently, it decided to ask the Prussian, Bavarian, and Saxon governments to have troops ready to march into Bohemia if the Austrian government should appeal for help. Two deputies actually advocated dispatching an army into Prague immediately, without awaiting an official request from Austria; the majority, however, decided not to take this extreme course, but to leave the matter to the committee recently appointed.[44] That committee's proposals were discussed in the plenum on July 1. During the debates only a few deputies of the radical left rose above a nationalist bias (notably Alfred Ruge, who had done so on previous

42. Z. Tobolka, "Česká otázka v jednáni frankfurtského parlamentu," *ČMM* XXX (1906), 222.
43. *Stenographischer Bericht über die Verhandlungen . . . zu Frankfurt am Main,* ed. F. Wigard (Frankfurt am Main, 1848-50), I, 217.
44. *Ibid.,* p. 422; Tobolka, "Česká otázka," p. 224.

occasions), and took a point of view sympathetic, on the whole, to the Czechs.

The net result of the debate was a decision, adopted by a majority, to ask the Austrian government to take urgent steps to ensure a Slavic representation in the Frankfurt Assembly.[45] The Austrian government, however, never more than half-hearted in its sympathy for the Frankfurt movement, moved with a calculated slowness; it was more in need of supporters at home than in a far-off German city; and it knew that the surest way to lose the support of the Czechs was to subject them to any kind of official pressure in the matter of elections. No force was ever applied and no Czech deputies ever occupied a seat in the Frankfurt Assembly. By its conduct, the assembly only succeeded in demonstrating its woeful lack of appreciation of political realities in the Habsburg realm.

And so the Czech question dwindled away. But the broader and more fundamental question of Austria's (Cisleithania's) relationship to a unified German state loomed ever larger on the agenda of the assembly, and it was principally this question that wrecked the assembly's work. On October 19, the assembly began the debate about a proposed German constitution, of which Paragraphs II and III had a direct bearing on the Austrian problem. Paragraph II provided that "no part of the German Empire may be united with non-German lands into one state." Paragraph III stated that if a German and a non-German state are ruled by the same person, their relationship must be that of personal union only.[46] If Austria had abided by these two paragraphs, it would have ceased to exist: the existence of Hungary as a constituent part of the monarchy could not be reconciled with the two paragraphs. (It is interesting to note that during the days in which the fate of Austria was being decided in Frankfurt, it was being decided at a different level in Vienna where Windischgrätz was bombarding the city into submission.)

When the votes on Paragraphs II and III were finally counted on October 27, they were adopted by a vast majority of 340-76 (with 6 abstentions) and 316-90, respectively.[47] This was an insult to

45. *Stenographischer Bericht,* I, 660 ff; Tobolka, "Česká otázka," pp. 225-26.

46. W. Schüssler, "Die nationale Politik der österreichischen Abgeordneten im Frankfurter Parliament," *Abhandlungen zur Mittleren und Neueren Geschichte,* No. 51 (1913), pp. 34 ff.

47. H. G. Teller, *Das österreichische Problem im Frankfurter Parlament im Sommer und Herbst 1848* (Marburg, 1933), pp. 142-43.

Austria. After this the Czechs could rightly claim that their past policy of boycotting Frankfurt had been proved correct. The Austrian government, on its part, could henceforth hardly be expected to cooperate even half-heartedly with the German nationalist movement. Several Austrian deputies began to withdraw from Frankfurt and finally, in April, 1849, the government officially recalled all Austrian representatives. At the same time, the Prussian king, to whom the assembly offered the imperial crown in a new state as envisioned by the constitution, declined the offer.

Thus the entire movement for German unification ended in a fiasco. The Czechs could congratulate themselves on their wisdom in having kept aloof from this venture, but there was little cause for smugness, for the venture to which they had made a wholehearted commitment and upon which they had pinned all their hopes, the Imperial Parliament, also ended in a debacle.

Chapter 4

Assemblies and Elections

All through the Frankfurt controversy, and indeed from the very beginning of the March Days, the one hope dominating the Czech national movement was the Bohemian diet. The diet was to be the shining symbol of the integrity of the state and the embodiment of the national aspirations of the Czechs. It was expected to offer a framework within which the Czechs would wield at least a measure of control, would be to some extent the masters of their destinies, and would, by sheer force of numbers, definitely outweigh the Germans in influence. Whatever problems required solution, whatever ailed the country was to be discussed and remedied at the reformed Bohemian diet, democratically elected. The pages of Havlíček's *Národní Noviny* abounded in hopeful allusions to it. The liberals and the radicals, the middle classes, and, insofar as they were politically conscious, the peasants, seemed united in their expectations for it.

For different reasons, Count Thun, the new governor of Bohemia, was almost as anxious as the Czech leaders to see the diet brought to life. Thun was by tradition a "Bohemian" patriot and to that extent was not indifferent to the status of Bohemia as a distinct polity within the Habsburg Monarchy. Also, he felt—and here the public mood was bearing him out more and more—that the best guarantee of the stability of the province was to put an end to the makeshift measures surviving from the March Days and replace them with orderly processes and institutions duly anchored in the new constitutional framework as established by imperial decrees.

Specifically, Thun was becoming uneasy about the National Committee—that, to him, baffling and nagging product of the March Days which the authorities before him had tried in vain to paralyze but which showed every sign of continuing vigor. As chairman of the National Committee, he now found himself in a position of ultimate anomaly and humiliation, presiding over a body which was revolutionary in origin and which he regarded as a nuisance at best and as subversive at worst, a usurper of the traditional powers of the bureaucratic establishment. It is true that as chairman of the National Committee he could keep an eye on the organization and presumably prevent it from going too far in becoming an unofficial government. The reality of the situation gave him no comfort, however; in private he lamented his role as a figurehead who had "almost no influence."[1] But unfortunately for Thun, he could not dispense with the National Committee until it had completed the preparatory work for the diet, as it had been charged to do. He therefore tried to goad Vienna into making whatever concessions to Bohemia he deemed essential for the maintenance of peace, which included convoking a provincial diet. The fact that he saw in a provincial diet elected by commoners an answer to his problems was indicative of the new political climate. Only a few weeks ago, for a governor or anyone else to press for the creation of a representative body would have been unthinkable, but now such a move was regarded almost as a panacea.

The National Committee took its task seriously. It drafted an electoral law, dated May 20, 1848, though prepared much earlier.[2] The lawmakers did not envision a completely unrestricted adult suffrage. In the cities, only the burghers were permitted to vote, which excluded the working class. In the rural areas, suffrage was conferred on everyone "paying a direct tax" (Article XXXVIII)—a provision that excluded farm domestics and agricultural workers but did not exclude the bulk of the peasantry, since even many cottagers paid some direct tax. With some slight modifications, Thun recommended to Vienna the approval of the electoral law, but the imperial government procrastinated. Since public opinion in Bohemia continued to be in a state of ferment, Thun urged swift approval, and, having failed to obtain it, presented Vienna with what amounted to an ultimatum: on May 12 he wired that if approval of the electoral law did not come within three days he would take it upon himself to announce officially the date for the opening of the diet.

The governor's decision to act on his own was hastened by the outbreak of violence in Vienna, which seemed to be pushing the government to the brink of collapse and making it virtually a prisoner of the demonstrating masses. In these circumstances, Thun's conservative conscience, revolted by the thought of having to take orders from a government that was seemingly controlled by a group of rebels,

1. In a submission to the emperor on June 17, 1848 (quoted in K. Kazbunda, *České hnutí roku 1848* [Prague, 1929], p. 199).

2. Text in J. M. Černý (ed.), *Boj za právo: Sborník aktů politických u věcech státu a národa českého od roku 1848* (Prague, 1893), pp. 230-38.

made it easier for him to take the action he deemed necessary, and
on May 17 the governor officially announced that the diet would be
summoned for June 7.[3] On May 19, after the news had reached
Prague that the emperor had fled the capital, Thun went a step
further and announced in a public notice that in view of the critical
situation in Vienna he would "employ the power entrusted to him
by His Majesty for the preservation of the throne as well as the
provincial constitution in whatever manner the extraordinary circumstances will require it."[4] When fresh violent outbreaks were reported
on May 26 and 27, he capped the assertion of his power by an act
truly without precedent in Cisleithania: he appointed a "provisional
governing council" to act, strictly under his powers, of course, as a
kind of provincial cabinet. The council consisted of eight respected
citizens, four Czech and four German. Among the Czech members
were Rieger, Palacký, and Brauner.[5]

For a man who was the epitome of conservatism, this seemed to
be a revolutionary act. Viewed in the light of the events in Vienna,
however, its conservative intent is obvious: with the imperial government tottering, the emperor in flight, and anarchy imminent, this was
a loyalist answer to the Viennese rebels, accompanied as it was by the
most eloquent pronouncements and gestures of devotion to the throne.
The fact that General Windischgrätz himself approved of the move
is evidence enough of its conservative character. Thun's principal
motive, however, was to check any further spread of "popular" rule
in Bohemia. The governor realized that the seeming helplessness and
vacillation of the imperial government in the face of radical pressure
would tend to weaken the gubernatorial powers in the provinces. In
Bohemia, this trend would only stiffen the back of the National Committee and cause it to encroach still further upon gubernatorial powers.

The situation did indeed beckon to the National Committee to
expand its powers had it wanted to do so. Since the March Days a
vast new range of political and social activity had emerged that demanded urgent attention yet could not be easily fitted into the established administrative framework. Often the new type of activity
exceeded the mandate of the *gubernium* as traditionally conceived,
yet did not clearly fall within the purview of the ministry in Vienna.

3. *Ibid.,* p. 219.
4. *Ibid.,* p. 224.
5. *Ibid.,* pp. 267-68. Kazbunda's account in *České hnutí* (pp. 208 ff.) is indispensable.

This "no man's land" was partly invaded by the National Committee, and after the latest events in Vienna Thun was oppressed by a vision of the further corrosion of the traditional fabric of administration by the work of the committee. His anxiety was heightened by a wave of fresh popular discontent that swept Prague in the last days of May, the chief expression of which was a mass rally held on May 27, again in St. Václav's Baths, and another one two days later on the same premises. Both meetings were completely dominated by the radicals, and their aspect could only be described as menacing. At both meetings, the stage was captured by the young Czech student radical Karel Sladkovský; the meetings catapulted him for the first time into fame as a swayer of audiences and one of the leaders of the radical movement.

With the streets of Vienna barricaded by rebels and the specter of revolution casting an ugly shadow over Prague, Thun felt there was not much time to lose. Some members of the National Committee had been pressing for the implementation of the Cabinet Letter of April 8, notably its provision relating to the establishment of a separate administration for Bohemia. Fearing that the National Committee might itself create or impose upon him a "revolutionary cabinet," the governor wished to forestall this possibility by setting up such a "cabinet" on his own initiative and under his own powers. There was no suggestion that the "provisional governing council" should be responsible to any popularly elected body.

Having weathered the storm, the government in Vienna was shocked and scandalized by this display of "disloyalty" on the part of a trusted public servant, and Thun, after a bitter private correspondence with Pillersdorf, gradually retreated from his position. In a public notice on June 4, the governor stated that the provisional council would only begin to function if "unconstitutional events in Vienna" should render it necessary. This was the death-knell of the whole idea. The provisional council never came into existence and was soon discreetly forgotten. But the bitterness between Thun and the government lingered.

The other scheme set into motion by Thun, the calling of the Bohemian diet, proved no more successful. It soon became evident that the date set for the opening of the diet, June 7, could not be met because it was impossible to prepare for an election in such a short time. The opening was therefore postponed. Elections took place during the second week of June and had almost been completed before the outbreak of the June Uprising on June 12. In Prague itself, they were prevented by the uprising, and were never held. At the same time, the uprising furnished the imperial government with a welcome excuse for delaying the convocation of the diet—a delay that dealt the diet a death-blow, for it was destined never to meet during the 1848-49 period. In this respect the Bohemian diet was probably unique among the duly elected representative bodies in Europe in 1848.

This was a most serious and lasting calamity for the Czech community. But in the climate of conflict and jealousy between Czechs and Germans, what caused grief to one group seemed invariably to bring relief to the other. The "Sudeten Germans" shed few tears for the diet; most of them were centralistically oriented, their sights set upon the forthcoming Imperial Parliament in Vienna rather than on the provincial diet. For weeks before the elections, they had been issuing protests against the wrongs, some real, some imaginary, to which the electoral law for the diet had subjected them. In a few cases, they boycotted the election, although this boycott did not at all match in magnitude the Czech boycott of Frankfurt. Because they constituted a minority in Bohemia, they faced the prospect of being outnumbered in the diet by the Czechs.

The total number of deputies in the diet was supposed to be 537, divided as follows: nobility, 210; non-noble landlords, 20; cities, 73; rural communities, 216; and Prague and the University of Prague, 18. Of these, the nobles sat in the diet only by virtue of their status; they were not elected representatives. The other categories were represented by 327 deputies altogether, chosen through the regular process of voting.

The data concerning election results are incomplete, and many of the names of the elected candidates are not known. According to the best-informed source, more than 300 deputies were elected of a total of 327 to be elected. In the rural constituencies, 202 deputies were chosen, of which 126 were Czech and 76 German. In the urban constituencies, 82 were elected, of which 52 were Czech and 30 German.[6] These figures confirm the Germans' apprehensions: in these two most important categories, the Czechs elected 178 deputies, the Germans 106. If the representatives had all been elected, the

6. The sources are the private notes by Alois Pravoslav Trojan, an election commissioner (see J. Heidler, "Český sněm ústavodárný 1848," ČČH, XIII [1907], 48).

Czechs would have clearly dominated the diet, but, discounting the small number of Prague deputies and the non-noble landowners, to the above number must be added the 210 nobles, who were largely German or ethnically neutral. To what extent they would have allied themselves with the Germans, had the diet met, is impossible to say. But one fact is certain: the position of the Germans in the diet would have been vastly more modest than the one to which they had been accustomed throughout many centuries.

The peasants gained an impressive representation in this diet. This is not to say that the representation was fair—it could not have been as long as the nobles held seats as unelected individuals representing only themselves—but it offered a prospect of considerable peasant influence upon the diet's work. About half of the elected deputies belonged to the peasant class. Most were peasants having larger-than-average holdings, but there were also a few cottagers.[7] Havlíček himself had urged his readers to send to the diet deputies noted for their patriotism and courage rather than their education. He asked them, when voting, to "have no regard for social position or learning," but to choose "neighbors" who enjoy public confidence, are "fearless," and have proved themselves to be "good patriots."[8] It was fully expected that serfdom would be one of the important questions discussed at the diet and Havlíček wanted the peasants to be well represented. Peasant interests would doubtless have also been defended by the radical democrats, and a few had been elected, notably Karel Sabina, Emanuel Arnold, Vilém Gauč, and the German Uffo Horn.[9] Together, however, they amounted to only a handful and would have had little influence on the proceedings.

The history of the diet in Moravia was completely different. There, on March 11, the date of the revolutionary assembly in Prague, about twenty members of the nobility gathered in Brno made an urgent request for the calling of the Moravian diet. Whereas in Bohemia a similar request made on March 2, under the impact of the events in Paris, ran into a wall of bureaucratic bungling and inertia, the Moravian estates found the Vienna government more receptive. Chastened by the precipitous events then unfolding throughout the monarchy, the government this time did not turn a deaf ear upon the one class on whose loyalty to tradition and dynasty it could

7. *NN*, July 9, 1848.
8. *NN*, May 30, 1848.
9. *NN*, July 9, 1848.

count. The requisite permission was granted and the diet, still in
its estates form, met on March 30. Among other matters, it went on
record as being opposed to the union with Bohemia and to the elections
to the Frankfurt Assembly. It was, of course, composed almost entirely
of the nobility, which, in turn, was largely German. There were only
five Czech deputies of a total of some seventy, still far from imbued
with a compelling sense of Czech national consciousness. The only
voice that rang out in favor of the Czechs was that of Count Sylva
Taroucca. Sensitive to the popular pressure for a liberal application of
the representative principle, the diet moved swiftly to broaden its
base by increasing to thirty the number of deputies from the cities
(hitherto the cities together had held only one vote), and by adopting
the principle of an increased representation from the rural areas. The
additional city deputies were elected while the estates diet was still
in session, and appeared on April 14, in time to take part in the last
meetings.[10]

The most important subject of the session was the question of
the future provincial diet. Its discussion at the meeting of April 27
resulted in an electoral law (also referred to as a provisional constitution) to govern the elections for the diet that was to be summoned
after the conclusion of the current session. To the astonishment of
many, the diet adopted the principle of a one-chamber body, and in
a manner typical of the time conferred the right to vote on all male
adults of a certain age who were "independent" or paid a direct tax;
laborers, apprentices, and others were excluded.[11] The nobility was
to have a separate representation, which would still be considerably
above the proportion of this class in the population as a whole. Nevertheless, a sharp break with the past had been made in that the
peasantry was to have a large number of deputies.

The estates diet held its last meeting on May 13. A few days
later, elections to the new diet were held under the electoral law just
approved. The new diet opened on May 31, the first "democratic"
diet. It was characterized by a strong peasant flavor, presenting a
spectacle so striking as to be labeled a "peasant parliament" in
popular parlance. Of the total number of 247 deputies who had
assembled by the end of June, 97 came from rural communities. The
Czechs and Germans were divided evenly, with the former having

10. K. Hugelmann, *Die österreichischen Landtage im Jahre 1848,* Part
III, published as *AÖG, CXV,* Part I (1940), 29 ff.

11. Černý (ed.), *Boj,* pp. 152-55.

124 deputies, the latter 123.[12] The proportion of Czech deputies was, of course, far below their proportion in the population as a whole; this was largely because of a lack of national consciousness among the Czech electorate.

The diet was to be a "constituent" one, one of its tasks being to draft a permanent constitution for Moravia. The draft, which was modeled on the Belgian constitution, was completed, approved by a large majority, and published on September 20, 1848.[13] Remarkably liberal and democratic in spirit it recommended the establishment of one chamber, and not only did it make no provision for special representation for the nobility but after a heated debate among the deputies it also abolished noble titles in a celebrated provision (Article IX of the constitution) stating that "in the province of Moravia, the nobility with all its prerogatives, including titles, has forever ceased to exist, and no further noble titles are to be created."

One of the major accomplishments of the diet was the abolition of the *robot,* for compensation, effective July 1, 1848. Following the example of the estates diet, the new diet also reaffirmed the equality of the Czech and German languages, and on August 12 it declared itself overwhelmingly in favor of Moravia as an "independent province, bound only and organically, to the constitutional empire of Austria." Implicit in the latter declaration was opposition to the concept of union with Bohemia; incorporated into the new constitution as Article I, the statement proved to the Czechs that at that stage resistance to the Czech national program was far from being only an affair of Moravian Germans or of "feudal nobles."

The diligent and progressive work of the Moravian diet was ultimately frustrated by the reaction; the constitution never received imperial sanction. But the realistic appreciation by the nobility of the need for change and its readiness to make concessions produced results unique among the legislative bodies of Cisleithania in 1848-49. Without revolution the diet speedily opened its ranks to the lower social classes, and by this measure as well as by many others it swept away the cobwebs of centuries, in a manner unmatched by any other diet in Cisleithania. It may be added that to some extent the diet played the role performed in Bohemia by the National Committee. It did not become an object of such public enthusiasm and esteem as

12. For a list of deputies, see *NN,* July 26, 1848.

13. Text in J. Dvořák, *Moravské sněmování roku 1848-49* (Telč, 1898), pp. 253-56.

the National Committee enjoyed, but peasants, towns, and other groups submitted hundreds of petitions to it seeking redress of grievances in the manner in which Bohemian groups addressed petitions to the National Committee.[14] When the diet finally closed its session on January 24, 1849, it could take satisfaction in a reasonably impressive record.

In Silesia the diet developed in a manner different from the diets of both Bohemia and Moravia. Before 1848, there was no single estates diet, although the estates of each one of the four Silesian principalities were represented in a "Convent" consisting of five members. After March, 1848, the convent was enlarged by the inclusion of representatives of the lower social classes, and earned the displeasure of the Czechs by its proclamation of May 9, 1848, expressing vigorous opposition to any union with Bohemia.[15] At the end of May, elections to a new convent were held, which met on June 19 in Opava. National consciousness in the Czech ethnic group in Silesia was very limited, and this was reflected in the composition of the convent. The convent was wholly German in spirit. Unlike its Moravian counterpart, it did not abolish the *robot,* although the matter was discussed. Unable to arrive at any decision regarding compensation, the convent suspended the discussions of the *robot,* leaving the Imperial Parliament to deal with the issue.

The Imperial Parliament was scheduled to open in Vienna in July. The Constitution of April 25, 1848, provided for the new parliament to have two chambers, one elected by the people and the other consisting of three groups of members: princes of the imperial house; persons appointed by the emperor; and deputies chosen by the "most prominent landlords," to use the wording of the constitution. The upper chamber, which was unmistakably designed to neutralize the effectiveness of the elected chamber, was regarded as an affront to democracy by the Viennese radicals. In addition, the supplementary electoral law required the election to be indirect and to specifically exclude "workers on daily or weekly wage, servants, and persons drawing support from public charities."[16] Such blatant exclusion of an entire social class further infuriated the radicals. After a series

14. J. Radimský and M. Wurmová (eds.), *Petice moravského lidu k sněmu z roku 1848* (Prague, 1955).

15. Text in Hugelmann, *Die österreichischen Landtage,* pp. 241-43.

16. E. Bernatzik (ed.), *Die österreichischen Verfassungsgesetze* (2nd ed., Vienna, 1911), p. 110. Decreed through a patent dated May 8.

of violent protests and demonstrations which threatened to plunge Vienna into civil war, the government was compelled to back down; the two-chamber concept was abandoned and the provision relating to the workers was altered to extend to "independent" workers the right to vote. The term "independent," however, as applied to the working class, was a highly ambiguous one, and there was lingering uncertainty on this point.[17] The indirect election was retained. The balloting took place at various times in June throughout the provinces of Cisleithania (Hungary, which had its own parliament, was not represented). In Bohemia the June Uprising forced a postponement and the balloting was held on July 8 and 9. (The results of the elections to the Imperial Parliament will be analyzed below.)

It is interesting to note that after years of absolutism and apathy during which the very mention of elections was proscribed, the Czech Lands were suddenly plunged into a veritable vortex of elections and election polemics. Within a space of some four weeks, the people in each province were called upon to go to the polls on three different occasions to vote for causes and assemblies as far apart as Frankfurt and Vienna. It augured ill for the future that the first election held was one that occasioned the bitterest controversy and inspired widespread boycott: the election of delegates to the Frankfurt Assembly. Of course, no politically conscious Czech could be expected to take part in it, but it was ironic—even tragic—that the first exercise of the precious principle of a free vote was marred by such serious controversy. The Frankfurt election campaign had left many a peasant, of whatever nationality, confused, and that confusion was often carried into the elections that followed: the election of deputies to the respective provincial diets of Bohemia and Moravia and to the convent of Silesia, and finally the election of members of the parliament in Vienna. In addition, the burghers in several cities were called upon to vote for a municipal council; in Prague, the first such election took place on April 6.

The bafflement of many voters was increased by the haste with which the elections in most cases had to be prepared and carried out. With no precedent, and no previous experience whatsoever with the election process, millions of voters now had to go to the polls at least three times, with only a short time between elections. The elaborate edifice of elections and parliaments had to be constructed

17. *CBB,* June 23, 1848, Supplement One.

from the foundation up. There were no electoral districts. There was no machinery for selecting candidates. Many voters were still unskilled in the difficult art of writing and reading. There were no voters' lists, no political parties. All this had to be devised, sometimes with only a few days' grace, through trial and error, and it had to be accomplished at a time when the burst of political and social activity thrust a score of other issues upon the average man's attention. The secrecy of the ballot was guaranteed in each case, yet it would be utterly false to claim that the ballots were uniformly cast in the privacy of a voting booth.

For many a peasant in particular, the election, for all the exuberance of these first weeks of freedom, must have been somewhat of a nightmare. Accustomed to being badgered, openly derided, and otherwise abused by officials, the peasant suddenly found these same officials often assisting in various capacities at elections. This alone was often enough to render him suspicious of the whole procedure. Sometimes officials, true to form, took pleasure in keeping the peasant in ignorance of his rights as a voter and gloated over his bewilderment. In some districts, peasants refused to vote for fear that the election was merely a trap set for them by officials. Elsewhere, they saw no necessity for casting a ballot, proclaiming disarmingly that "the emperor will take care of it all himself."[18] There was no precedent for a critical evaluation of issues; the new questioning created issues where seemingly none had existed before. There was also a barrage of emotion-packed words, such as "aristocracy," "democracy" and "constitution," on which a peasant was asked to vote, the meaning of which may have eluded him. The indirect election only intensified the puzzlement; the common man could perhaps be pardoned for thinking that voting for an elector who was going to vote for a certain candidate was a curiously roundabout way of making democracy work. Yet the governments and the ruling classes often insisted on the indirect vote as a means of deradicalizing the voice of the still unlettered classes. There was indirect voting in the elections to the Imperial Parliament, to the Frankfurt Assembly, and to the Silesian Convent; the elections to the Bohemian and Moravian diets were direct.

Against this background, many voters, unable to muster the interest or fathom the spectacle, simply stayed home on election day

18. *NN*, June 6, 1848.

(the Czech boycott of the Frankfurt elections was, of course, a different matter). As a result, the turnout at the polls was poor— a circumstance often noted by the daily press. The very first election, for the city council of Prague, revealed an apathy that contrasted strangely with the general excitement aroused by the introduction of constitutional government; according to a police report only one-tenth of the eligible voters cast their ballots.[19] This is the more striking because the eligible voters were the propertied classes, who were more politically conscious than the lower classes. Similarly, in the elections for the Bohemian diet, only 986 voters cast their ballots in Prague, a turnout so low as to cause *Národní Noviny* to lament that "Prague burghers regard the elections as an insignificant matter."[20]

Election regulations were being violated because of a lack of experience, and this led to the contesting of results by disgruntled candidates on purely procedural grounds. In at least one case several communities refused to recognize a properly elected candidate because he "was a traitor and neither a democrat nor an aristocrat but a sworn republican."[21] Some enterprising candidates, going from house to house, obtained a written pledge from voters to vote for them on election day! Should the voter balk later in keeping his word, the candidate could brandish the pledge and make the citizen feel that voting for another candidate was in fact a violation of a written commitment. As these abuses came to light before the elections, the responsible leaders endeavored to explain to the voters that written pledges of this nature were not binding in the eyes of the law.[22] There was also a widespread belief that parliaments would settle disputes between individuals or groups.

In many instances, prominent personalities were elected in several ridings simultaneously. Palacký, Rieger, and Havlíček were all chosen in at least five different constituencies in the elections to the Imperial Parliament.[23] This must have seemed rank injustice to one unfortunate candidate who had earlier run for the Bohemian diet

19. Heyde to Stadion, March 30, 1848 (*SÚA* Prague, PG 1846-49, 15 c/3, No. 2297/1848). See also P. Burian, *Die Nationalitäten in "Cisleithanien" und das Wahlrecht der Märzrevolution 1848-49* (Graz, 1962), p. 36.

20. *NN,* July 9, 1848. This refers also to the voting in Prague.

21. *Verhandlungen des österreichischen Reichstages nach der stenographischen Aufnahme* (Vienna, 1848-49), I, 30.

22. *NN,* June 2, 1848.

23. *NN,* July 14, 1848.

in six constituencies but was elected in none.[24] In one district in
Prague, in the elections to the Imperial Parliament, voters cast their
ballots for an elector who had been dead for some time.[25] A candidate's
election in more than one constituency may have been a gratifying
token of personal popularity, but it slowed down the election machinery, for the candidate could accept election only in the constituency
of his choice, and a new election had to be held in the remaining ones.
In the elections in Bohemia to the Imperial Parliament some twenty
supplementary elections had to be held for this reason, which delayed
the departure to Vienna of the candidates finally and validly chosen.

Certain forms of the electoral process, if not its substance, caught
on remarkably quickly. Thus we see candidates, after elections, reporting to their constituents through the medium of printed pamphlets
on their record in the diet or parliament.[26] In some cases there was
only one candidate for each seat, which meant there was no contest;
this occurred especially in the elections to the Imperial Parliament,
where it was felt that only the most highly qualified and educated
deputies should be chosen. But in the elections to the Bohemian diet,
there was no dearth of candidates: according to incomplete official
figures, 446 candidates presented themselves to the electorate of 72
rural constituencies![27] And already in these incipient stages of constitutionalism, there was a plentiful supply of candidates who, as one
contemporary put it, promised the voters "pie in the sky" in order to
win their precious votes.[28]

Of all the elections that took place in the Lands of the Czech
Crown in the first half of 1848, the one best prepared for was the one
that bore the least fruit. The election for the Bohemian diet was most
diligently planned by the National Committee, yet that diet was destined never to meet. The National Committee regarded the preparation for this election as its most important task and, within the time
available, spared no effort toward that objective. Havlíček considered the political education of his people a number-one priority,

24. Heidler, "Český sněm," *ČČH*, XIII, 48.
25. *Bohemia*, July 10, 1848.
26. See the text of a leaflet (September 5, 1848) distributed to his constituents by a Silesian deputy in the Imperial Parliament, in J. Vochala, *Rok
1848 ve Slezsku a na severovýchodní Moravě* (Opava, 1948), pp. 104-6. It
discusses serfdom.
27. Heidler, "Český sněm," p. 48.
28. "Hory doly . . . slibují" (*NN*, June 2, 1848).

and in his *Národní Noviny* he devoted many columns to instructions and explanations of the issues involved in the elections to the Bohemian diet (and later to the Imperial Parliament) and to other political matters.[29] He was enthusiastically assisted by other Czech leaders, notably Brauner, who enjoyed particular prestige among the peasants. One must pay the highest tribute to the strivings of the Czech leadership, for these efforts were vigorous and impressive enough to elicit reluctant praise from no less a person than the Prague acting police director, who wrote in one of his reports: "Besides, it cannot be denied that the leaders of the Czech party are far superior to their rivals in energy and activity, in that they employ all levers in order to attain their objective."[30]

From the beginning of the March Days until the June Uprising, the most influential body or assembly having a broad popular character was the National Committee. It was the child of the March revolution in Bohemia, and its formation as the St. Václav Committee antedated the outbreak of the March revolution in Vienna. It counted among its members the most illustrious figures of the Czech national movement. Not having to compete with an estates diet, the committee became the logical center of gravity of political life. The fact that its membership included only a few nobles placed it well within the mainstream of political life, which ran strongly against the nobility as a class. And since it was not, legally speaking, either a parliamentary body or an executive one, it did not have to observe in its work and discussions the limits appropriate to either.

The committee's original primary task was to prepare the ground for the Bohemian diet, but it soon passed beyond this goal, not through choice but rather through the sheer weight of the confidence of the public, which tended to entrust to it an astonishing variety of matters. It was asked to arbitrate disputes between management and labor, between peasants and landlords; between Czechs and Germans, and between Jews and Christians. It was asked to protect the Jews against public wrath. It collected and distributed funds for the unem-

29. Havlíček himself wrote a special article intended to explain to the rural voter in simple language what the elections to the diet were all about (see *NN*, May 30, 1848). He also hoped to compile a "political encyclopedia," as he himself says (*NN*, June 28, 1848); his statement suggests that it was in an advanced stage of preparation, but it has never appeared.

30. Heyde to Stadion, April 12, 1848 (*SÚA* Prague, PG 1846-49, 15 c/3, No. 2987/1848).

ployed. Individuals and groups, workers and peasants, villages and cities, began to bring it their grievances. To the peasant especially the National Committee became the incarnation of all his aspirations. In a movement completely without precedent in the history of the Czech Lands, peasants from all over the province addressed petition after petition to the National Committee, spelling out their grievances and their demands.[31] It is as if suddenly the entire countryside had come alive, after centuries of servitude, to speak in one mighty voice, giving vent to the accumulated fears and hopes of generations.

The petitions—the first one was dated March 27, 1848—flowed into Prague in a gathering tide that was halted only by the June Uprising. No less than 580 petitions were recieved from the villages alone (sometimes one from a group of villages), and there were 89 from the towns and cities. The 580 total represents over 1,200 villages in Bohemia, a stunning figure bespeaking the intensity of the sentiment among the rural population. Of the 580, 465 were in Czech and 115 in German.[32] Although all the petitions were bitterly critical of officialdom, they were loyal to the throne and above all permeated by a high esteem for the new post-March Czech national leaders. The National Committee made no attempt to deal with this avalanche; had it wanted to do so, it was simply not physically equipped for the task. The petitions were usually answered in a form letter indicating that all questions relating to the peasantry were to be dealt with at the forthcoming diet, then filed *ad acta* and forgotten. The text of many of the petitions are still extant, and today they provide a unique source for a study of social and economic conditions in the province.

As the business of the National Committee expanded, it was necessary to establish several sections, which, after dealing with each matter assigned to them, reported back to the plenum. The number of sections grew, reaching twelve in the last stages of the committee's existence. The first section was regarded as the most important, being charged with the task of drafting an electoral law and of preparing for the elections for the Bohemian diet. The job of the second section was to write a draft of a constitution for Bohemia for the consideration of the Bohemian diet, and that of Section 7 to deal with the peasant question. Section 10 dealt with internal conditions, a broad

31. F. Roubík (ed.), *Petice venkovského lidu z Čech k Národnímu výboru z roku 1848* (Prague, 1954).

32. *Ibid.*, pp. 511 ff. For a map, see *Atlas československých dějin* (Prague, 1965), p. 20, a.

mandate which brought into its agenda a wide spectrum of business, ranging from the reform of a savings bank to the settling of a labor dispute.[33] Other sections dealt with local government, schools, law courts, the equality of the Czech and German languages in schools and offices, foreign affairs, and religious affairs. Some of these sections were more active than others; some had, for one reason or another, hardly begun to function at all.

From the ethnic point of view, the National Committee contained at the outset Czech and German members in a proportion roughly corresponding to the proportion of the two ethnic groups in the population as a whole. This, of course, as discussed in Chapter 3, placed the Germans in a minority—a role unacceptable to them. Irked increasingly at being forced to play a second-class role, they began to withdraw one by one, and within a little more than two months from the meeting of March 11, most withdrew, leaving the Czechs in possession and making the National Committee for all practical purposes a Czech body.[34] Yet, paradoxically, the discussions in both the plenum and the sections were conducted almost entirely in German, and the surviving protocols are mostly in German.[35]

In its social views, the majority of National Committee members were solidly liberal—liberal according to the nineteenth-century meaning of the term. This was reflected in their attitude to the working classes and to the lowest urban social strata of the population in general. From the very beginning, the committee had been preoccupied with the need to protect the community against the proletariat, but saw no need to protect the proletariat against the employer. In the tradition of a classic laissez-faire liberalism it regarded any legislative protection of the worker by the state as undesirable interference in the "free" relationship between employers and workers. It wrote into its banner the principle of a broad representation of the population but it saw no particular conflict between that principle and the exclusion of the working class from the right to vote, which it favored. During a meeting of the St. Václav Committee, which was still comparatively radical, the German radical democrat Ludwig Ruppert publicly proposed the introduction of universal suffrage, without

33. G. Čechová and J. Martínek, "Národní výbor v roce 1848," *SAP*, IV, No. 1 (1954), 15.

34. The German radical Ludwig Ruppert took part in its discussions as late as June 7. See *NN*, June 10, 1848.

35. I have photocopies of most of the protocols.

property qualifications and similar restrictions. This was the first time such a proposal had ever been made from a public platform in the history of the Czech Lands. Brauner opposed it; he regarded it as impracticable because, as he put it, "the untutored proletariat, led astray by corrupt principles" could cause the newly won freedoms to be destroyed. Suffrage without restriction could not be used "during a transition from the complete state of unfreedom into a state which presupposes long maturity."[36] Eventually, the views of men such as Brauner were adopted by the National Committee and written into the electoral law, which, as noted above, limited the franchise in the cities to "burghers," which in practice meant property-owners or those not living on a wage, and in rural areas to those paying a direct tax. The same provisions were later incorporated into the proposed constitution for Bohemia.[37]

Curiously, the National Committee seemed content at the prospect of a large contingent of nobles taking part in the forthcoming diet. This is surprising since no more than a few nobles were represented in its membership and it displayed a generally anti-aristocratic temper. Yet the fact remains that it accepted without any major opposition the provision of the Cabinet Letter of April 8 (which was to be the basis of the electoral law to be worked out by the National Committee) stating that, in addition to the classes newly enfranchised, those who had in the past enjoyed the privilege of sitting in the estates diet should sit in the reformed future diet. This was a severe restriction upon the principle of democratic representation. It meant that the new diet would include 210 nobles, elected by nobody, occupying their seats merely by virtue of their social status. The total number of deputies was to be 537; the 210 nobles would constitute, of this total, a group of considerable strength, although they represented only a very small proportion of the population as a whole. When the more radically minded people in Prague realized the implications of this, they began to stir. It was in large part against what threatened to be the disproportionate strength of the nobility in the diet that the protest rallies of May 27 and May 29 were organized in which Sladkovský first emerged as a leading radical figure. Having just arrived as a student from Vienna, imbued with radical thought, he not only

36. Quoted in V. Král, "F. A. Brauner za revoluce a reakce 1848-1849," *SAP*, II, No. 1 (1952), 180. See also V. Pokorný, "Volební zákonodárství v Čechách v letech 1848-1849," *PHS*, VI (1960), 97.

37. Černý (ed.), *Boj*, pp. 236, 288.

vehemently opposed this disproportionate representation of the nobility, but suggested on May 29 that the "worker interests" should also be represented in the Bohemian diet.[38]

On the other hand, the influence of the nobility and of officialdom was to be reduced by the provision of the electoral law that excluded public officials from being eligible as deputies in the districts in which they performed their functions. These officials, usually German, were relics of the feudal past, and were frequently either directly employed by or in other ways dependent upon, the nobility. Their exclusion reduced the possibility of undue pressure upon the electorate on the part of the nobles and conservative officials and was therefore of great importance to the peasantry. The original proposal, which was brought up by Brauner, provoked a heated debate. In the final vote a large majority favored Brauner's position.[39]

The committee's second section completed the draft of a constitution for Bohemia and submitted it to the plenum on May 29.[40] The plenum had just begun to debate it when the June Uprising interrupted its work. The proposed constitution was divided into three parts. Each part defined respectively (1) the relationship between the central institutions of the monarchy and those of Bohemia, (2) the provincial legislature (diet), and (3) the provincial executive.

The first part listed the powers reserved for the central institutions. These were powers required by the monarchy in the conduct of its affairs vis-à-vis other states: military affairs, state credit, state and commercial treaties, and foreign affairs. Then there were powers needed for the preservation of a basic unity of the constituent lands of the monarchy; they included, among others, budget, railways and principal highways, postal services, customs, and currency. All those powers not explicitly reserved for the central institutions fell to the province.

The second part of the proposed constitution, that which defined the organization of the diet, provided for a two-chamber legislature: the lower chamber, the Chamber of Deputies, to be elected directly by the voters, and the upper chamber, the Senate, consisting of sixty deputies, to be chosen by the lower chamber. The model for this

38. F. J. Schopf (ed.), *Wahre und ausführliche Darstellung der am 11 März 1848 . . . in Prag begonnenen Volks-Bewegung* (Leitmeritz, 1848), IV, 22, 26.

39. *NN*, May 12, 1848.

40. Text in Černý (ed.), *Boj*, pp. 287-90.

structure was the Norwegian constitution.[41] The proposal of two chambers provoked a heated debate in the plenum on June 7. Among its opponents was Havlíček, who, in this instance, argued against Palacký, who favored it strongly. Havlíček's views were shared by a few other members, but in the final vote the proponents of the two-chamber legislature won.[42]

The electoral provisions in the proposed constitution, like the electoral law adopted earlier (see above), restricted the right to vote to the propertied and tax-paying classes. As far as is known, no objection to it was made in the plenum. In addition, the suggested electoral provisions created a vast inequality in representation by requiring one deputy to represent twenty thousand inhabitants in the rural constituencies and six thousand inhabitants in the cities (Prague and the other largest cities were to have special representation). This proposal, which vastly reduced the voice of the peasantry, was vigorously defended in the plenum by Brauner (though he was generally considered the peasants' tribune) and other proponents, who argued that the cities included the best element in the community, the intelligentsia and the business classes, and that this entitled them to a special consideration and influence in the legislative process. Once again, Havlíček took the more democratic view, by opposing the measure, and once again the majority, including Palacký, Brauner, and Trojan, carried the day.[43] As far as the published accounts of the discussions reveal, it did not occur to any Czech spokesman to point out that this electoral inequality would greatly favor the Germans, reducing the voice of the peasant masses, who were predominantly Czech. The proposed constitution gave no special representation or place to the nobility and to the Roman Catholic hierarchy, both of which had dominated the pre-March estates diet. All deputies were to be elected. This was, of course, a departure from the spirit of the Cabinet Letter of April 8. But the document confirmed the basic anti-aristocratic and anti-clericalist character of the National Committee, thus placing the committee strictly in the mainstream of mid-nineteenth-century liberalism.

The third part of the constitution provided for a provincial executive, under a viceroy, and consisting of five portfolios: (1) political

41. Z. Tobolka, "Národní výbor r. 1848," in *Obzor Národohospodářský*, X (1905), p. 66.
42. *NN*, June 10, 1848.
43. *NN*, June 9 and 10, 1848.

provincial administration, security, and national (provincial) defense; (2) religion, education, and culture; (3) justice; (4) provincial finance and credit; and (5) industry and public works.

Backed by the force of public opinion, the National Committee was presented with a rare opportunity to permanently seize the power hitherto wielded by the bureaucracy. But its leaders seemed at times frightened by the very potential of the instrument they had helped bring into life. From the very beginning the radicals pleaded that the National Committee (or the St. Václav's Committee) should set up branches throughout Bohemia and transform itself into a truly national organization. In this respect, the German radical Ruppert was the most resourceful and among the most active in defending the gains of the March Days. At a meeting of the St. Václav's Committee on April 1, Ruppert proposed that the larger cities in other parts of Bohemia be encouraged to found committees that would be linked with the committee in Prague; thus, he argued, an organization would develop that would represent the whole province. The proposal was rejected for the time being.[44] Similar proposals were advanced from radical quarters later on, but the liberals hedged, showing no desire to assert themselves in this manner. In so doing, they closed an important avenue that might have placed the National Committee on a solid footing and allowed it to successfully challenge the existing state apparatus. Without a nationwide organization and without effective means of control, the democratic forces were engaged in an uneven struggle with the forces of the status quo, which, though temporarily disorganized, retained the important instruments of power and coercion throughout the revolutionary year.

Although the National Committee did not seize the levers of power, it did become an extremely influential body. Originally, it had cast itself voluntarily in the role of an advisory body that was not meant to pre-empt the authority of the existing institutions or of the institutions expected to be formed soon. In practice, however, circumstances caused it to perform many important government functions and to push the bureaucracy into the background, without, of course, stripping the government of its power. The committee assumed the performance of certain functions which were the outgrowth of the new

44. Heyde to Stadion, April 2, 1848 (*SÚA* Prague, PG 1846-49, 15 c/3, No. 2428/1848). The German radical Uffo Horn made the same request at the meeting of April 10 and was applauded, but no decision was made (Heyde to Stadion, April 10, 1848, No. 2826).

constitutional era and for which the cumbersome bureaucracy, frightened for the moment by the specter of public wrath, could not yet devise a proper machinery. It was the only organization enjoying universal public confidence outside the German community at a time when
the prestige of the bureaucracy had reached an all-time low and the
bureaucracy itself seemed paralyzed. It did, in fact, issue regulations
having a legal character.[45] The best evidence of its significance is
the attitude of the governor; as mentioned above, Thun resented the
committee's intrusion into the bureaucratic realm, complained of his
own lack of influence, and made it one of the cardinal objectives of
his policy to get rid of it as soon as circumstances would permit.

In accomplishing this objective, Governor Thun was aided by
the growing lethargy that afflicted the National Committee in the last
weeks before the June Uprising. The members of the National
Committee began to lose the sense of urgency that had motivated
their debates earlier. In the plenum, they tended to indulge in time-
consuming rhetoric, so much so that even the committee's friends and
supporters chided it for this tendency. Havlíček, himself a member,
observed on May 11: "Gentlemen of the National Committee, talk
less and act more, act every day swiftly and vigorously. Time rushes
by; God forbid that it should be said: 'It's too late now'."[46] The
committee, which now had more than 150 members, grew unwieldy;
yet at the same time, many members ceased to participate in its
deliberations with the zeal they had exhibited at the beginning.

Governor Thun could not impose his will on the committee, but
he could at least sabotage its work to some extent by skillfully manag-
ing its agenda. Many years later he wrote that after the end of May,
with the calling of the diet and the appointment of the Provisional
Advisory Council seemingly assured, there was no longer any reason
for the committee's existence.[47] Apparently, only a desire not to
antagonize the public prevented him from dissolving it outright at this
stage. He deliberately obstructed its work, however, by filling the
agenda with unimportant but time-consuming formalities and leaving
the important business for the end of the meeting, at which time so
many members had wearied and left that the required quorum did not
obtain and a vote could not be taken.

45. Pokorný "Volební zákonodárství," *PHS*, VI, 98.
46. *NN*, May 11, 1848.
47. J. A. Helfert, "Graf Leo Thun," Part II, in *Österreichisches Jahrbuch*,
XIX (1895), 223.

Havlíček saw through this stratagem and lamented it in his news-paper on June 9: "The National Committee has at last been gradually 'in a skillful manner' destroyed so that only the name remains."[48] Little did Havlíček realize how prophetic his words would turn out to be; that after the next issue (June 10), his newspaper would be suspended, and that two weeks later (June 26), after a bloody up-rising, Thun would at last be able to realize his wish and abolish the National Committee. With this act, the first and the most con-spicuous symbol of the March movement would pass from the scene —a portent of things to come.

With the extinction of the National Committee, more than a symbol had vanished; with it passed a legacy that no amount of official fiat could erase. The committee had made substantial contri-butions to Bohemia's political life and to the Czech movement. It constituted the first popular forum for a genuine public discussion in the Czech Lands. Its social policies were strictly of the mid-nineteenth century, but its national policies anticipated the twentieth century and were only realized then. It was the first organization to formulate a systematic Czech national program, and that program formed the basis of Czech demands until the dissolution of the Habsburg Mon-archy. One of the committee's chief goals was the unification of Bohemia, Moravia, and Silesia; even to many Moravian Czechs this idea sounded premature and impertinent in 1848, but by 1918 it was not only hardly questioned but also easily accomplished.

During the period of its existence, the committee was the most important of the Czech organizations; nothing comparable was found in Moravia. It offered a preview of Czech leadership and of Czech "official" policy in the next hundred years: a compound of progressiv-ism and caution, at times excessive caution; an ability to look forward without violence and to look backward without reaction; a progress sustained by education; a realism shading off occasionally into undue opportunism. The ardor and thoroughness with which the National Committee, more than any other institution in the Czech Lands, ap-plied itself to the task of educating the masses in the intricate business of choosing candidates and casting ballots, strikes the present-day observer as one of the finest episodes in its short history. The Na-tional Committee revealed to the Germans for the first time how far the Czechs intended to go, and to the Czechs how much the Germans

48. *NN*, June 9, 1848.

were willing to concede. It was the earliest child of the Revolution of 1848 in the Habsburg Lands: the first popular assembly grown into an institution of major influence. Its image and its memory outlasted the generation that had created it: it was resurrected in the "National Committees" that sprang up spontaneously in 1918 after Austria's demise, and again in 1945 in the "National Committees" formed in the wake of another German defeat.

Chapter **5**

The Slavic Congress

The movement for German unification spurred a movement for a close cooperation of the Slavs of Central and Eastern Europe, which found its climax in the Slavic Congress held in Prague during June 2–12, 1848.[1] In the more fundamental sense, the idea of Slavic brotherhood emerged from the Slavic awakening of the decades preceding the congress, having been formulated with particular cogency and poetic charm by the Slovak poet Jan Kollár (1793-1852). The concept of a congress had also been nourished by the concern of the Hungarian Slavs over the impact on their destinies of the flamboyant and intolerant Hungarian nationalist movement.

In its more immediate sense, the idea for such a congress originated in at least three different segments of Slavdom. It was first publicly broached in print by the distinguished Croat Ivan Kukuljevic, in an article published in a Croatian newspaper.[2] A few days later, on April 30, the article appeared in Czech translation in *Národní Noviny*. On the same day on which Kukuljević's article was published in Zagreb, the Slovak national leader Ľudovít Štúr arrived in Prague from Vienna and began to propagate the idea of a Slavic congress.[3] Much the same idea was discussed by Jędrzej Moraczewski, a member of the National Committee in Poznan and a prominent figure in the Polish national movement, in a letter to Brauner dated April 23.[4]

Among the circumstances that stimulated the idea for a congress

1. The Slavic Congress was not directly a part of the Czech Revolution, and only the salient facts are offered here.

Basic collection of documents: V. Žáček and Z. Tobolka (eds.), *Slovanský sjezd v Praze roku 1848: Sbírka dokumentů* (Prague, 1958). The volume by Tobolka (Z. Tobolka, *Slovanský sjezd v Praze roku 1848* [Prague, 1901) is still the only monograph.

2. On April 20, 1848. Reproduced in Croatian in Žáček and Tobolka (eds.), *Slovanský sjezd*, pp. 22-25.

3. J. V. Frič, *Paměti*, ed. K. Cvejn (Prague, 1957-63), II, 24, 27. For other related documents, see Žáček and Tobolka (eds.), *Slovanský sjezd*, pp. 25-26.

4. Text in Žáček and Tobolka (eds.), *Slovanský sjezd*, p. 30.

of Slavs was the intoxicating experience of a number of Slavs from various ethnic groups meeting in Vienna toward the end of March and the beginning of April. As members of delegations coming to Vienna to submit to the emperor petitions expressing the demands of their respective nationalities, they, as well as the many Slavic intellectuals residing in Vienna at the time, met informally in order to become better acquainted with the members of the Slavic "family." These informal meetings gave rise to the conviction that in some form the contacts should be continued and expanded.

A decisive step toward turning the idea from vision into reality was taken in Prague, on April 20: on that day a group of Czech leaders met and chose a committee to begin preparations for a Slavic congress.[5] Among those chosen for the committee were Palacký, Rieger, and many other prominent Czechs. It was generally agreed by all the Slavic leaders that a congress of this kind should take place in Prague, which was something of a Mecca of Slavdom, at least for all but the Poles and eastern Slavs.

The opening date was originally set for May 31—the date of the scheduled opening of the Frankfurt Assembly—and at the beginning of that month, the planning committee issued a proclamation announcing the congress and setting forth its purpose.[6] In order to mollify the Austrian authorities, who were sure to view such an unprecedented gathering with a jaundiced eye, the committee decided to restrict formal participation at the congress to the Habsburg Slavs; the proclamation therefore extended the invitation to "all Slavs of the Austrian Empire." Yet the other members of the great Slavic family seemed to beckon and the committee, which could hardly resist the temptation of encouraging them to take part in the meeting as guests, concluded the proclamation with the statement: "If the Slavs living outside our monarchy desire to honor us with their presence, they will be welcome guests." This presumably also included the Slavs of Russia. The Russian government, however, was hardly sympathetic to the undertaking, and the organizers of the congress seemed unwilling to press the invitation too vigorously upon the Russian Slavs. The proclamation was issued in the Czech, Slovak, Slovene, Croatian, Serbian, Polish, German, and French languages, but no Russian text was ever prepared or issued, although at one time it was apparently being contemplated. There was an incongruity in the fact

5. Protocols of the two meetings that took place on that day, *ibid.*, pp. 32-33.
6. Text, *ibid.*, pp. 48-49.

that a mighty display of Slavic brotherhood was in the offing, with Russia, the largest Slavic nation, conspicuous by its absence. As for the Austrian government, it had reconciled itself to the congress, after assurances that it would have an "Austrian" character, and now viewed the congress as a useful instrument against the pressures of Magyar separatism.

Well before the congress actually met and could be judged on the basis of its work, its policies, and its statements, the Germans and the Magyars were plunged into a fury at the idea of the strengthening of Pan-Slavism in Central Europe. The first announcements and invitations issued at the beginning of May were enough to convince them that their worst nightmares had been realized. To calm the stormy reaction, the planning committee published another proclamation a few days later emphasizing more unequivocally than the first one the Austro-Slavist character of the congress and repudiating "Separatism, Pan-Slavism, Russism."[7] But the enemies of the congress, who were far from satisfied, continued in their denunciations. As might have been expected, the loudest and most virulent in its attacks was the Viennese radical press. One radical Viennese newspaper accused the Slavic leaders of waiting "for an outbreak of a revolutionary movement in Russia, for the disintegration of this enormous empire into states divided by dialects, and then for the foundation of an almost unlimited Slavic republic which would dominate the shores of the Arctic and the banks of the Bosporus." Although the German radicals were fanatics *par excellence,* in both the political and national sense, they found it possible to accuse the Slavs of "national fanaticism stirred by the malevolent and the egotistical."[8] The only Viennese newspaper that did not permit itself to be whipped into a frenzy over the Slavic Congress was the conservative *Wiener Zeitung;* though the *Zeitung* was not friendly to the Slavs by any means, it preserved a degree of objectivity on this occasion.[9] The influential German newspapers of Prague were moderate, though somewhat condescending.

The agenda for the congress as drafted by the preparatory committee posed four principal problems to be discussed:[10] (1) the im-

7. *Ibid.,* pp. 51-52.
8. *Ibid.,* pp. 184, 185; the newspaper was *Der Freimütige,* May 10 and 11, 1848.
9. *Ibid.,* pp. 182-83.
10. *Ibid.,* pp. 220-24.

portance of the Austrian Slavs and the relationship between them (specifically the delegates were asked to decide whether they favored a Slavic association for mutual defense) ; (2) the relationship of the Austrian Slavs to the other peoples of the monarchy; (3) the relationship of the Austrian Slavs to other Slavs; and (4) the relationship of the Austrian Slavs to other European nations (one specific problem mentioned under this heading was how to view the decisions of the Frankfurt Assembly insofar as they affected the Slavs of Austria).

Last-minute delays and complications caused the opening date to be moved to June 2, a Friday, and the delegates began arriving in Prague at the end of May. Without a doubt the Slavic Congress brought together the greatest galaxy of Slavic scholars and leaders that had ever been assembled. It is not possible to say with accuracy how many delegates were actually present because the number fluctuated, with some delegates arriving at a time when others may have already left. According to the official data published by the congress, the number was 340, but in reality the total was higher. The most complete list compiled to date lists 385 names, of whom 317 were full-fledged delegates and 68 were "guests" and "observers."[11] The dividing line between delegates and guests was not always rigidly maintained. The Czechs constituted the largest single body of delegates, and the Poles the second largest. There were no Montenegrins, Bulgarians, or Lusatian Serbs.[12] The absence of the Montenegrins is explained by Montenegro's dependence on Russia, that of the Bulgarians by their isolation under Turkish rule and a retarded national consciousness.

The delegates were grouped into three sections: (1) the South Slavic section, comprising Slovenes, Croats, and Serbs, as well as the southern Slavs, known by their regional designations as Dalmatians and Slavonians; (2) the Polish-Ruthenian section, comprising Poles and Ukrainians; and (3) the Czecho-Slovak section, comprising Czechs, Moravians, Slovaks, and Silesians. According to official (but not quite accurate) data, the above sections numbered 42, 61, and 237 members, respectively. Each of the sections was supposed to deal separately with the appropriate parts of the agenda, whereupon the conclusions reached were to be discussed at plenary sessions, at which

11. *Ibid.*, pp. 544 ff.
12. The Lusatian Serb J. P. Jordan took part in the congress, but not as a representative of the Lusatian Serbs. He was living in Prague at the time.

the final official decision was to be made. The head of the South Slavic section was Pavao Stamatović, the Serbian writer from the Serbian region of southern Hungary (present-day Vojvodina in Yugoslavia) ; of the Polish-Ruthenian section, Karol Libelt, the noted Polish democrat from Poznania; and of the Czecho-Slovak section, Pavel Josef Šafařík. The keynote speech on the opening day was delivered by Šafařík, and the opening address on the same occasion was given by Palacký, who had been chosen chairman of the congress.

German spokesmen later ridiculed the congress—Marx and Engels were second to none in their invective—unkindly spreading the rumor that the Slavic delegates, unable to understand each other, were forced to use "the hated German language, as the only one that was generally understood!"[13] This was quite untrue. Indeed, in July, 1848, Kuranda, who was no friend of the Slavs, declared in the Frankfurt Assembly: "Whereas it may not be true that the proceedings at this congress had to be conducted partly in German, it is nevertheless true that the individual sections had to communicate with each other through interpreters and that only in this manner could they understand each other."[14] Only Slavic languages were employed in all the deliberations, but it was true that the problem of communication was at times difficult. Thus, when at a meeting the Pole Libelt made a speech in Polish it had to be explained in a free translation in Czech and in Serbo-Croat by delegates conversant with the languages in question.[15] The German language was used officially only in one instance, as specifically provided by congress rules: after the plenary session approved a decision, the decision was announced in German.[16] This was good public relations. German was the language of the Habsburg dynasty and of the central government, as well as a world language, and it was appropriate that the important resolutions of the congress should be announced to the world in that

13. F. Engels, *Revolution and Counter-Revolution or Germany in 1848* (Chicago, 1896), p. 93. This edition still ascribed the work to Marx, but the book is now known to have been written by Engels.

14. *Stenographischer Bericht über die Verhandlungen . . . zu Frankfurt am Main,* ed. F. Wigard (Frankfurt am Main, 1848-50), I, 665.

15. See the protocol of this meeting in Žáček and Tobolka (eds.), *Slovanský sjezd,* p. 286. In view of this, Frič's assertion (*Paměti,* II, 93) that the delegates understood each other, speaking their mother tongue only, is not correct.

16. See the rules of procedure (in Polish), in Žáček and Tobolka (eds.), *Slovanský sjezd,* p. 220.

language. According to the surviving protocols, however, none of the discussions were conducted in German.

No sooner had the Slavs settled on an agenda than they discovered that even at the height of sentiment favoring Slavic brotherhood disagreements were occurring. Having lived for centuries under different political, social, and cultural conditions, the Slavic nations had reached widely different stages of development and were confronted with widely different problems. There were differences of opinion between those who attributed to the congress only moral significance and those who hoped to turn it into a permanent institution that would meet regularly and be endowed with a quasi-legislative status within the Habsburg Monarchy. There were those who emphasized loyalty to Austria, along Austro-Slavist lines, and those who wanted the Austrian Slavs to be Slavs first and Austrians second. There were those desiring the congress to take a stand on social issues, and those who wanted to limit its work to national questions. The Slovaks, confronted with the Magyar danger, saw their immediate tasks in a different light from the Czechs, who were preoccupied with the danger of Frankfurt. Ukrainians and Poles did not see eye to eye on questions relating to the status of the Ukrainian element in Galicia.

The Poles occupied a unique position.[17] With the memory of an independent Poland still fresh and the hope for the restoration of that independence as ardent as ever, they viewed the congress as an instrument for Poland's resurrection rather than for Slavdom's millennium. A strong segment of Poles had opposed the congress from the time it had been announced; they could not bring themselves to endorse a movement so manifestly directed against their best friends, the Magyars. At the congress, alone of the delegates, the majority of the Poles were Magyarophiles, and as such tried to mediate between Slavs and Magyars. They could be described as the least enthusiastic Slavs. The fact that millions of Poles chafed under the rule of Slavic Russia was hardly calculated to endear them to the idea of Slavic brotherhood. A considerable proportion of their delegates were exiles. Seasoned by an intimate knowledge of Western Europe, as a group, they surpassed other delegates in the universality and progressiveness of their political and social views; an especially impressive figure was Karol Libelt, the most forceful and imaginative member of the Polish delegation. It may be added, however, that

17. For a most detailed account of the role of the Poles, see V. Žáček, *Čechové a Poláci roku 1848* (Prague, 1947-48), II, Part 3.

though the Polish delegation was the most progressive, it also was the most aristocratic; in other national delegations the nobility was either wholly absent or had only an insignificant representation.

The Poles viewed Austria (or Galicia) as only a small part of their problem. Poland was dominated by Germany, Austria, and Russia, the three largest countries in Europe; its problem was Europe's problem. The Poles therefore, not unnaturally, tried to deflect the congress to a considerable extent from an Austro-Slavist to a European track. In this sense they succeeded in imposing their will upon the Czechs, whose Austro-Slavism had originally set the pace for the congress. Largely through the influence of the Poles, the principle of restricting full-fledged participation at the congress to Austrian Slavs had been completely violated from the very beginning. The official list of the Polish-Ruthenian section includes sixty-four members, of whom about one-fourth came from outside Austria.[18] Indeed, the man chosen to head the section, Libelt, was not an Austrian subject at all, but a Pole from Poznania; it would be difficult to imagine a more serious breach of one of the explicit rules and of the entire concept of the congress as originally envisioned. There were at least nine Poles from Poznania in the section, one Latvian, and two Russians. One of the two Russians was Mikhail Bakunin, an exile from tsarist Russia, well-known in Western Europe as a radical and a revolutionary. The other Russian member was one Miloradov, a clergyman from Bukovina, listed as being "from Galicia, Russian." A few members of the Polish-Ruthenian section were Poles from Russian Poland. There were at least two delegates from Serbia who were accepted as members of the South Slavic section. All of these non-Austrian Slavs had been admitted as full-fledged members, not merely as visitors. And in view of the fact that Libelt was elected to head the Polish-Ruthenian section—a move that, to many, seemed the height of indiscretion—it is little wonder that the congress was accused by the Germans and Magyars of bad faith. The full-fledged participation of Bakunin, expelled from France in 1847 for revolutionary activity, provided further ammunition for the enemies of the Slavs, who were quite prepared to damn all participants on the basis of one name.[19]

18. List in Žáček and Tobolka (eds.), *Slovanský sjezd*, pp. 208-9.
19. Palacký later declared that Bakunin was not really a full-fledged member of the congress. See F. Palacký, *Spisy drobné*, ed. B. Rieger (Prague, 1898), I, 91 (originally in *Prager Zeitung,* January 26, 1849). Actually, Baku-

At the same time, the claims of these enemies that the Slavs wanted to establish a large Slavic-dominated empire could, if one tried hard enough, be read into certain pronouncements of the congress. In Part III of the official program, the final emancipation of Serbs from Turkey was envisioned; the program stated that when the Serbs had won their independence "they they too will be encompassed in the brotherly union of a Slavic federal state."[20] This wording suggests the extension of Austria (as reformed according to the Slavs' wishes) beyond its existing borders. To this may be added the vision of a Slavic future unfolded by Kollár, who may be regarded as the spiritual father of the Slavic Congress. In his celebrated poem, *Slávy dcera (Daughter of Slava)* he wrote that "it is true that we came somewhat late, but so much the younger we are"; in a century, "everywhere the Slavs like a mighty flood will extend their limits; the language which the Germans wrongly consider a mere speech of slaves will resound in places and even in the mouths of its rivals. The sciences will flow through Slav channels; our people's dress, their manners and their song will be fashionable on the Seine and on the Elbe. Oh, that I was not born in that great age of Slav dominion; or that I may not rise from the grave to witness it."[21] This is an expansionist vision, the effect of which is somewhat lessened by the fact that it is a poetic rather than a political vision. But it furnished ample ammunition to the Germans and Magyars in their onslaught on the movement of Slavic awakening. It apparently did not occur to the Germans and Magyars that their spokesmen had made similar, more explicit pronouncements that might justly alarm the Slavs.

The reason for the admission of a large number of non-Austrian Slavs as delegates was not hard to find. The congress opened amid an intoxicating atmosphere of "Slavic nationalism." The Slavs had never before met on any comparable occasion. They had never seen their future so bright and their strength so overwhelming. They were wiping out the shame of centuries. Against this background, it would

---

nin is included in the official list as a full member and was regarded as such throughout the congress.

20. Žáček and Tobolka (eds.), *Slovanský sjezd*, p. 223.

21. H. Kohn, *Pan-Slavism: Its History and Ideology* (2nd ed.; New York, 1960), p. 9.

How deeply Kollár's ideas influenced the climate that produced the congress may be seen from Frič, *Paměti*, II, 90. Kollár himself, not wishing to antagonize the Hungarian authorities unduly, did not attend the congress, but was toasted enthusiastically by the delegates in his absence (*ibid.*, p. 99).

have appeared blasphemous and petty to quibble over the detail of a person's birthright—it was enough that he was a Slav. Besides, of all the Slavic visitors to Prague, the Poles were the most numerous; the sheer number of them made it difficult to wave them aside on the plea that they were not Austrian subjects. Yet their admission into the ranks of delegates was a basic departure from the declared policy, and the more conservative Czech sponsors could not help feeling alarmed at the new trend. In particular, Count J. M. Thun, who had at first supported the idea of the congress and served as chairman of the planning committee, asked to be excused from his duties on the eve of the congress, on a plea of illness; thereafter, he had no further connection with it. The illness may have been genuine, but the main reason for Thun's absence was political: he was dismayed at the opening of the doors to non-Austrian Slavs.[22] In this connection, it may be noted that the Poznan Poles had issued, on their own initiative, a manifesto dated May 9, 1848, exhorting their countrymen "regardless of boundaries and language differences" to attend the Prague congress;[23] this clearly violated the original declared policy of the planning committee.

From the social point of view, the congress was overwhelmingly middle class, with the nobility constituting a small segment. There were no peasants and no workers. Educationally speaking, it was, like its counterpart in Frankfurt, weighted in favor of the educated groups; it represented in the purest sense of the word the intellectual elite of non-Russian Slavdom. Politically, the liberal outlook prevailed, with the radical democrats (chiefly Polish) in a small minority. Through the radical democrats certain proposals and drafts were made placing the congress on record in favor of some social reforms, but none of these were ever approved. As a result, the congress did not approve any programs or measures relating to social issues, such as the peasant question, staying well within the bounds of nationality and related issues. It was characteristic that the "economic committee" set up by the congress had nothing whatever to do with economics as the term is usually understood: its task was to handle the job of accommodating visitors, providing entertainment, and other such functions.[24]

Less than halfway through the congress, Libelt proposed a change

22. Tobolka, Slovanský sjezd, p. 103.
23. Žáček and Tobolka (eds.), Slovanský sjezd, p. 98.
24. See the protocol of a committee session of June 5, ibid., p. 284.

in the program. According to his proposal the congress should set itself three tasks: (1) to prepare a manifesto to the European nations, setting forth the principles and the objectives of the Slavs; (2) to prepare a petition to the emperor containing the demands of the Austrian Slavs; and (3) to conclude a federation of Slavic nations.[25] The first point constituted a radical departure from the original program, and it is noteworthy that there was no major opposition to it, from the Czechs or any other group, as far as can be gathered from the protocols. For with such a manifesto, the congress went far beyond the original Austro-Slavist concept, thrusting the Slavs as a whole deliberately onto the European stage. On the other hand, a manifesto of this kind dovetailed neatly with the plans of the Poles, most of whom had from the beginning chafed at the restricting framework of Austro-Slavism. Libelt justified, and others agreed to, his proposal on the ground that the Slavs, maligned by their enemies for their alleged reactionary views, must proclaim to the Europeans in loud and clear tones their devotion to the cause of freedom and progress.

In his draft of the new program, Libelt suggested, for inclusion in the manifesto, a number of democratic and progressive principles, which, as he saw it, would have improved the image of Slavdom in the eyes of Europe. In addition to emphasizing freedom of speech and of the press, national equality, and trial by jury, he proposed "social reforms, notably the improvement of the conditions of the peasantry"; free education for both sexes; direct suffrage, restricted as little as possible; and the abolition of capital punishment.[26] The final text of the manifesto was written by Palacký, who had at his disposal drafts submitted to him by Libelt, František Zach, and Bakunin, all members of the committee chosen for this purpose. The draft by Libelt and Zach was first published only in 1958.[27] As for Bakunin's draft, all efforts of historians to locate a copy of this document have thus far proved fruitless.[28]

The Manifesto to European Nations, from Palacký's pen, duly

25. *Ibid.*, p. 285.

26. Text, *ibid.*, pp. 289-90.

27. *Ibid.*, pp. 361-68. Zach was a Czech by origin (born in Brno), but spent a lifetime in Serbia, eventually becoming a general in the Serbian army.

28. That Bakunin also submitted a draft is known from a letter addressed by Palacký to Libelt (June 9) in which Palacký states that he is enclosing two drafts, one by himself, another one by Bakunin. Bakunin's draft has never been found. (*Ibid.*, p. 361.)

approved, was destined to become the only public statement the
congress was able to debate and formally approve before being compelled to adjourn.[29] The manifesto reflects the sustaining hopes for
the future as well as the burning resentments of the past. Though
the product of Slavdom's best intellects, it is permeated by a romantic view of the Slavs and is at times disarming in the simplicity
with which it endows the Slavs with a past as immaculate as that of
the Germans is shameful. The "Romance and Germanic nations"
had "secured for a millennium by the sword their political independence" but had also known "how to satisfy their lust for domination." Their statecraft rested "primarily on the right of superior
force . . . limited liberty only to higher estates, governed through
privileges, imposing upon the people nothing but duties." With these
nations are contrasted "the Slavs, with whom liberty has from time
immemorial been loved the more devoutly, the less they manifested a
lust for domination and subjugation." Now new times had brought
new concepts; hence, "We Slavs range ourselves on the side of the
law and reject and hold in contempt every domination of mere force;
we reject all privileges and illegal acts as well as political differences
between estates; we demand without exception equality before the
law." The manifesto was intended to do no more than make Europe
aware of the existence of Slavdom and of the justice of its demands
for equality. The only concrete measure proposed was the calling
of a congress of European nations for the settlement of international
questions. Behind this measure was the hope that "free nations will
find it easier to reach an agreement than paid diplomats." The statement concluded with the words, "In the name of liberty, equality,
and brotherhood of all nations."

The document reflects the romantic bias in favor of the Slavs
which was prevalent in the first half of the nineteenth century and
which even the seasoned historian Palacký was unable to overcome.
It is worth noting that much of this bias stemmed from the writings
of the German philosopher Herder. It completely ignores the fact
that the subjugation of the lower classes by the privileged estates
was a phenomenon of European and world history, a process in which
Polish, Czech, and Serbian nobility had taken part as vigorously as
their German counterparts. The concept of a superior devotion of
Slavdom to liberty has long since been abandoned by both Slavic

29. *Ibid.,* pp. 358-61.

and non-Slavic historians. Palacký's attempt to present the Slavs
in a uniformly favorable light led to some curious omissions. The
Germans and Magyars are saddled with the sin of dominating other
nationalities. Even "the free Briton" is chastized for his failure "to
recognize the Irishman as his equal." But nowhere does the manifesto
even hint that Russia was a conqueror and oppressor of nationalities,
despite the fact that the majority of Poles were living under oppressive Russian rule. Though the fate of "our unhappy Polish brethren
who had by devious force been deprived of their independence" is
lamented, Russia is not mentioned once. Only Prussia is blamed for
the mistreatment of the Poles. Incomprehensibly, the manifesto
states that the "majority" of Slavs live under Austria—an observation that must have been equally puzzling to the Austrian emperor
and the Russian tsar. It is easy to see how such cavalier treatment
of the past and the present would open the Slavs to charges of in-
sincerity.

How did Palacký's text compare with the draft submitted to
him by Libelt and Zach? Libelt's draft was also imbued with a
romantic view of the Slavic past, but it exhibited a profound social
consciousness and contained many specific recommendations of a
social character. Boldly proclaiming the need for "socialism," Libelt
hailed the great new idea "from the West . . . the idea of a Christian
socialism and of a Christian international policy." Libelt's socialism
connoted a system of social justice rather than of true socialism. One
wonders what Palacký thought of such a highly unorthodox way of
advertising the cause of Slavdom to Europe. In any event, not a trace
of "socialism" crept into his manifesto; Palacký's aversion to anything
savoring of socialism was well-known, and the saving epithet "Christian" was not likely to make it more palatable to him. Libelt extolled
the early Slavic village community with its communal property, viewing it as "the core for the broadest foundation of national life, national
representation, and national militia." He referred to the Slavic Congress as a "Slavic Pre-Parliament," a term deliberately chosen to
underline its role as Slavdom's answer to the Frankfurt Assembly.
With respect to Poland, Libelt predictably asked that "the work of
the restoration of Poland . . . begin as soon as possible."[30]

Zach's draft was an even-tempered document, less preoccupied
with social issues than Libelt's and less stridently anti-German than

30. *Ibid.,* pp. 361-65.

Palacký's. The German-Slavic antagonism was implied, but the Germans were never mentioned by name. Social content was not absent; Zach pleaded for the usual liberties and for a broad electoral right, from which "no one should be excluded because he is poor." He also proposed the holding of annual congresses of Slavic scholars in order to facilitate an exchange of ideas and quicken the cultural life of the Slavs.[31]

Palacký's version, as finally endorsed by the congress, bore little resemblance to the drafts of his two colleagues. Limiting himself exclusively to the national theme, Palacký made no single concrete reference to social questions; the lack of social content was, however, more than compensated for by a nationalist fervor directed against both the Germans and the Magyars. As for Libelt's document, it must be admitted that though it was progressive and sensitive to the social needs of the time, it bore an uncomfortable resemblance to a political tract. Palacký's version was considerably shorter and less didactic than that of either of his two colleagues; it was, on the whole, better attuned to the declared purposes of the congress, more suitable as a manifesto, and expressed more faithfully the temper of the liberal middle classes who gave the congress their stamp.

According to the revised program, the congress was also supposed to prepare a petition to be submitted to the Austrian emperor. The petition had been actually completed but was not formally approved before the congress adjourned. In it the nationalities put forward their particular demands, and in addition, three nationalities (Czechs, Moravians, and Slovenes) jointly declared themselves opposed to any policy resulting in their incorporation into a unified Germany.[32]

The third task of the congress was the consideration of an alliance among the Austrian Slavs for the protection of their interests. Several proposals were made, but the work was far from complete at the time the congress was compelled to adjourn.

For the Czechs, the congress constituted a special triumph. It was their beautiful capital city that was chosen to play host to the gathering. It was the Czechs who organized the congress and mobilized every resource in order to ensure its success. The twin lights of Czech scholarship—more accurately Czech-Slovak scholarship—Palacký and Šafařík, illuminated the proceedings; and the third light,

31. *Ibid.*, pp. 365-68.
32. *Ibid.*, pp. 370-75.

the Slovak Kollár, though prevented by the Magyar authorities from attending, was present in spirit through his works. The enthusiasm aroused by the event was infectious. It swept into its path men as conservative as Palacký, as skeptical as Havlíček (who had only two years earlier attacked Pan-Slavic visionaries), as detached from politics as Šafařík. For days before the opening date, the columns of *Národní Noviny* were filled with news about the forthcoming event, dwarfing the significance of all other happenings in Bohemia and in Europe. The atmosphere of the congress caused reserved men to assume an air of belligerence, law-abiding men to wave aside their legal scruples, and unemotional men to shed tears on beholding sights they had never dared to see. Šafařík's keynote address was, according to all testimony, an unforgettably moving experience.[33] At a meeting of the Czecho-Slovak section, Havlíček stated matter-of-factly that "by invading Slovakia we will divert the attention of the Magyars and this will benefit the Croats," and observed that "legally we won't get very far. After all no one acts legally in these times."[34] At the same meeting, Šafařík, even while counseling caution, declared, in a somewhat menacing tone, "If we had an army, we would act differently . . . the day will come when we will be able to speak out."[35] Such statements can be explained only in terms of the unusual emotional climate generated by the congress. Czech radical democrats participated, but the protocols of the meetings show that they contributed little to important discussions.

It has been estimated that about one hundred Czechs from Moravia participated in the congress.[36] The crucial question of the relationship between Bohemia and Moravia came up for discussion, and the fact that even amid the general display of Slavic brotherhood, the Moravian Czechs clung to some of their cherished constitutional traditions speaks eloquently for the strength of Moravian regionalism. In the petition to the emperor, the Moravians presented their own demands, independently from those of the Bohemian Czechs. Referring to the latter as kin and brethren, they demanded concessions similar to those given the Bohemians in the Cabinet Letter of April 8. They proposed that the supreme offices for Bohemia should have

33. F. Roubík, *Český rok 1848* (Prague, 1931), p. 205.
34. Protocol of June 3, in Žáček and Tobolka (eds.), *Slovanský sjezd*, pp. 249, 252.
35. *Ibid.*, p. 255.
36. J. Macůrek, *Rok 1848 a Morava* (Brno, 1948), p. 66.

control over Moravia, although it is impossible to say how much control they had in mind, and that committees of the Bohemian and Moravian diets should meet from time to time. Nevertheless, the Moravians explicitly insisted that their province should "retain its independence." And they had no desire to surrender their separate diet. Even on this point, however, they were still conceding to the Bohemian Czechs less than what the latter had requested in the Second Petition (of March 29).

It may be observed in passing that the Czech element from Austrian Silesia, which included the well-known region of Těšín, or Cieszyn, was wholly without representation at the congress. Only the Poles from this area had arrived, and they had found, to their displeasure, that they had been assigned to the Czecho-Slovak section (the official name of the section was "Czecho-Moravian-Silesian-Slovak" section). The Poles protested, and the Czechs consented to their being shifted to the Polish-Ruthenian section.[37]

The congress was scheduled to last until June 14, but on June 12 the outbreak of the uprising in Prague put a premature end to it, before the agenda was completed. After the uprising, which led to an imposition of martial law in the capital, it was adjourned indefinitely (on June 28), although some Slavic leaders continued to cherish the hope that it would reconvene soon. That hope was not realized, and with the return to absolutism in March, 1849, the last flicker of optimism collapsed.

What was the significance of the congress? It created many illusions—the natural product of a year in which illusions became almost as potent as realities—which were soon dispelled. Its official and unofficial pronouncements tended to gloss over the real differences that separated the Slavic nationalities from one another; but when the first enthusiasm subsided, these differences again came to the fore, as indeed they had to some extent already during the congress. No political federation of any kind resulted from it, although a defensive federation was envisioned both in the original agenda as well as in the proposal introduced by Libelt. The congress did strengthen a certain feeling of kinship among the Slavs, but this did not take any political forms embracing all of Slavdom. There was a drawing together of certain Slavic groups, notably of the Czechs and the southern Slavs, a relationship that has continued to the present

37. Žáček and Tobolka (eds.), *Slovanský sjezd*, pp. 336 ff.

day. The ambivalent position Russia occupied in the world of the Slavs in 1848 remained ambivalent in the decades to come.

The importance of the congress lies not in any concrete measures taken or achieved. Its timeless contribution was to furnish an added impetus to the national development of the various Slavic groups, to facilitate communications between them, and to promote scholarship and culture as a result of the contacts established among the Slavic scholars present. For all the flamboyance exhibited by the Slavs at the congress, for all the pride, and the defiance of the German challenge, the Slavs still required a long period of consolidation within which to nourish their confidence and to ensure permanence and impart greater substance to their achievement. The Slavic Congress, the first in European history, had brought them barely to the threshold of their collective existence, but it had made Europe aware of this existence for the first time. But if Western Europe was now compelled to accept them, it was still on Western Europe's terms, as newcomers, and they would not be fully accepted for at least two more generations. With the exception of France, the knowledge and the image of the Slavs in Western Europe continued to be acquired through the refracting mirror of the German press and German scholarship, a situation that was to last until World War I. But it is not too much to say that after the Slavic Congress in Prague, the spark of national life among the Slavic nationalities could never again be extinguished, and the voice of Slavdom never again stilled. In that sense, the congress was a landmark always to be remembered.

It can and will always be a source of pride to the Czechs that such a landmark is so intimately bound with their own history. It was the high point of their development in 1848. However, if it was a high point, it also constituted the beginning of the ebb of their fortune and Slavdom's. The abrupt termination of the congress was a rude shattering of hopes and a grim reminder of the still fragile nature of democracy's progress against the forces of reaction.

Chapter **6**

Six Days in June:
The Uprising in Prague

The Assembly of March 11 effected a revolution in Prague but it was a peaceful one, and it seemed that the whole political upheaval would take place without violence and without barricades.[1] In Vienna, in contrast, violence flared up at the very beginning of the new regime (March 13), with a bloody battle taking place between the people and the army, claiming more than two score lives. Another outbreak occurred in Vienna on May 15, followed by still another on May 26. Thus, by the end of May, the imperial capital had been rocked by three uprisings, the second of which had forced the emperor to flee to Innsbruck for safety. Compared with Vienna, Prague may have appeared a haven of tranquility, and indeed the Czech leaders, not without a touch of smugness, seriously contemplated inviting the emperor to take refuge in Prague after his escape from Vienna.[2] In retrospect, it must be deemed prudent and fortunate that the emperor went to Innsbruck, for had he gone to Prague, he would probably soon have been exposed to the humiliation of another escape.

Actually, Prague was far from tranquil and was to prove no exception to what seemed like an inexorable march of violence sweeping Europe. The signs could have been observed for some time. The most tangible forms of unrest were those of the working class. The March revolution had brought no solution to unemployment, and, like other social classes, the workers, far from being placated, were only emboldened by the new freedoms to ask for more concessions. There were strikes and protest marches (see Chapter 12); there were attacks on bakers and Jewish merchants, culminating in two days of anti-Jewish rioting on May 1 and 2—the first sign that the underlying mood was grim and serious. At the same time, the police uncovered a revolutionary pamphlet condemning, in highly

1. The main works are A. Bajerová, *Svatodušní bouře v Praze r. 1848 ve světle soundního vyšetřování* (Plzeň, 1920), and J. A. Helfert, *Der Prager Juni-Aufstand 1848* (Prague, 1897).
2. K. Kazbunda, *České hnutí roku 1848* (Prague, 1929), p. 205.

inflammatory language, the governing classes, including the nobility, the Germans, the Jews, and the clergy. This was the most daring pamphlet of the revolutionary era,[3] and the police arrested the foreman of a printing plant in which it had been printed. The arrest was widely taken as an infringement of the freedom of the press, and resulted in a public demonstration on May 10, which forced the foreman's release and caused the newly elected burgomaster of Prague to resign his office. As if to lend further emphasis to the universal unrest, the inmates of a Prague prison attempted a revolt of their own on the following day.[4] On June 3, a group of textile workers staged a protest march through the city, only to be dispersed by the army, with one worker wounded in the clash. For their protests, the Prague City Council charged the workers with "blind stubbornness" and "menacing demonstrations."[5]

In the midst of a rising unrest came the announcement—which seemed at first too wildly implausible to be believed—that General Windischgrätz was about to arrive in Prague as the military commander of the imperial forces in Bohemia. Windischgrätz was first posted to Prague in 1840; his suppression of the textile workers' outbreaks in 1844 earned him a reputation for ruthlessness, and when he left for an extended holiday at the beginning of 1848 (before the March revolution) few people in Prague regretted his departure. Windischgrätz was an autocrat *par excellence,* totally lacking in appreciation of the aspirations of popular movements and an enemy of constitutional government. Few men in the Habsburg Monarchy could have been less enthusiastic over the downfall of absolutism than the general, and fewer still were more consumed with an ambition to recoup the losses sustained by the reaction since March. His hand forever poised at the trigger, General Windischgrätz could answer the voice of the people with the only language he understood, the language of guns and soldiers. This was his element and the year 1848 was to afford him amble opportunity to prove it. A soldier's uncomplicated mind could not be bothered with drawing fine distinctions between moderate and radical constitutionalists; to Windischgrätz they were all equally dangerous subversives. He was on hand in Vienna in March, 1848, answering the call of Metternich to

3. Text, *ibid.,* pp. 382-84.
4. *Ibid.,* p. 176.
5. F. J. Schopf (ed.), *Wahre und ausführliche Darstellung der am 11 März 1848 . . . in Prag begonnenen Volks-Bewegung* (Leitmeritz, 1848), V, 16, 89-90.

help quell the first uprising. Afterward, officials at the highest levels of government, including the governor of Bohemia, were engaged in confidential correspondence designed to prevent his return to Prague, which was sure to inflame public opinion. But General Windischgrätz was nothing less than an institution in himself, with intimate connections with the imperial court, and he could defy the restraining counsel of the highest officials. Apprised of the working-class disturbances in Prague at the beginning of May, he concluded that this was where he was needed.[6]

He arrived in Prague on May 20,[7] and within a few days the public observed an intensified military activity. Soldiers were increasingly patrolling the streets. Special measures were being instituted for the control of working-class districts. These measures had been devised earlier, it is true, but were held in abeyance; Windischgrätz put them into effect, without the slightest regard for the sensitivities of the Prague population.[8] The events of March had thrust the military into the background, to nobody's regret; the army had been too closely associated with absolutism for comfort, and now, its apparent resurgence generated a fear that the reaction was far from dead. Since Windischgrätz' return, almost every day had brought fresh reminders of the presence of the military: there were movements of troops, parades, day and night patrols, and finally the placing of units of artillery at points overlooking the city—a sight at once offensive and alarming to the inhabitants of the capital.

For General Windischgrätz to brandish his guns in so indelicate a manner before the people of Prague was the height of imprudence, and the people reacted strongly against it. No group was more conspicuous and more determined in its reactions than the university students, and with some oversimplification it may be said that the ensuing conflict reduced itself to one between the students (and intellectuals) and the military. The students had been in ferment since the March Days. From the middle of March, they had maintained contact with the students in Vienna, and had been influenced by their actions. A good many Prague students were inspired by the resolve with which the Viennese intellectuals carried on a successful struggle for democratic reforms; they were also fascinated by the ability of the Viennese to virtually dominate the imperial capital and

6. Kazbunda, *České hnutí*, pp. 135-37.
7. For a typical hostile comment, see *NN*, May 25, 1848.
8. Kazbunda, *České hnutí*, pp. 245 ff.

dictate to the central government. The flight of the emperor may have shocked the moderates, but to many radical intellectuals it was a beacon: if the Viennese intellectuals could force the downfall of cabinet ministers and the flight of the emperor, it should be considerably less difficult for the people of Prague to rid themselves of an unpopular general.

At the end of May and the beginning of June, the radicalization of Prague reached impressive proportions. Two rallies took place, both in St. Václav's Baths, on May 27 and May 29, respectively. The mood of both was clearly radical, and both were conducted under the leadership of the radical student Sladkovský, who had just returned from Vienna where he had been a student at the university and had evidently absorbed the leftist ideas of the Viennese students. At the first rally, the immediate removal of Windischgrätz was openly demanded from the speaker's platform, and at both rallies strong attacks were made on the lingering privileges of the nobility.[9] The rebellious atmosphere also created the setting for the founding of a radical newspaper, *Pražský Večerní List* (*Prague Evening Gazette*), the first issue of which appeared on June 1, 1848. The *Večerní List* soon became a popular paper. Championing the cause of the lower social classes, but marred by a strident and sensationalist tone, it competed with the respectable *Národní Noviny*. Also on June 1 a German-language radical newspaper was launched, under the same title (*Prager Abendblatt,* or *Prague Evening Gazette*) and the same publisher as the Czech paper, though under a different editorship.[10]

The radical segment of the student body now set the pace and gave the direction to the movement against Windischgrätz, with the Vienna-trained Sladovský assuming leadership. How the events of a few days transformed Sladovský from a complete unknown into a dominant figure of the revolutionary movement remains one of the more baffling aspects of this period. But even so, he was not a leader in the classic sense of the word, for the June Uprising produced no such figure. Student pressure against Windischgrätz reached a climax on June 11; on that day the famous "red" posters (printed in red letters) were distributed throughout the city. In the posters the students demanded that the military (1) hand over to the academic legion two thousand rifles with eighty thousand live cart-

9. Schopf (ed.), *Wahre Darstellung,* IV, 23, 26.
10. F. Roubík, *Časopisectvo v Čechách v letech 1848-1862* (Prague, 1930), p. 117.

ridges; (2) surrender to the academic legion an entire battery (artillery unit); and (3) remove the batteries recently installed at certain points in the city.[11] With these demands the students opened themselves to the charge that a group of excited young people, without proper training in the handling of arms, were hardly in a position to be entrusted with firearms, let alone a whole artillery unit. The request for a battery of cannons must have struck Windischgrätz and a number of other people as a monstrous presumption. To such a charge the students would have answered, not without plausibility, that ammunition in their hands was less a danger to hard-won constitutional freedoms than in the hands of Windischgrätz' soldiers. It is to be noted, however, that the revolution did evoke among the young people a marked fondness for the wearing of uniforms and for an amateur handling of weapons. Young Frič, one of the principals in these events, was well-known for his love of the uniform and for an ostentatious display of his pistol, which gave rise to the ludicrous rumor that he planned to assassinate General Windischgrätz.[12]

On the same day on which the "red" posters appeared in Prague, the students sent a delegation directly to Windischgrätz; the delegation was joined by the burgomaster and several burghers, but the latter supported only the students' demand for the removal of cannons. To nobody's surprise, least of all the students', the general rejected the demands; he fulfilled only one of them, in ordering the removal of cannons from some points, but even at that he made it quite clear to the students that he was not complying with their wishes. In firm language, the general said that he would not give in to any kind of compulsion.[13]

At this point the conflict reached an impasse that seemed to permit no peaceful solution. The heightened activity of the military of recent days had been paralleled by the feverish preparations of students for what appeared to be an inevitable showdown. According to subsequent investigation, a group of students had set themselves up as a "Ministry of War"; whether this term was used in earnest or merely in ridicule is not known, but there is no doubt that a group had organized as a kind of commanding unit. By June 11

11. Text in Schopf (ed.), *Wahre Darstellung*, V, 91.
12. The rumor is recorded in J. V. Frič, *Paměti*, ed. K. Cvejn (Prague, 1957-63), II, 107.
13. Bajerová, *Svatodušní bouře*, p. 45.

some students had already acquired home-made bullets, and on the morning of this day, at the time the student delegation was meeting with Windischgrätz, bullets were being distributed to students in the lecture hall in which the radicals were meeting, and weapons were being loaded. After the announcement of General Windischgrätz' refusal to meet the demands, there was a surge of excitement, and for the first time the word "barricades" rang through the hall. For the moment, however, violence was averted; instead of mounting the barricades the young people decided to hold a special mass the next morning in front of the statue of St. Václav in what is today St. Václav's Square.[14] The change in plans seemed incongruous, but the mass itself was to be a demonstration of sorts. It was to be a manifestation of the brotherhood of all social classes, including the working class, to prove that the people of Prague were united against the encroachment of reactionary forces. Against this background, a holy mass could become the point of departure for an outbreak of violence.

The ostentatious parades of Windischgrätz' grenadiers and the radical mood of a segment of students were not the only ingredients in the revolutionary situation. Another important factor was the surging wave of Czech and Slavic national sentiment. The tension in the city was heightened by the Slavic Congress, in session since June 2, and by the lingering uncertainty of the Frankfurt question. It was widely believed among the Czechs that the Reich Germans (Germans of Germany) would not shrink from the use of force in order to compel Bohemia to join the new Germany, and a number of belligerent pronouncements from the Frankfurt Assembly lent plausibility to the Czech fears. Three days before the uprising, almost the whole front page of *Národní Noviny* was devoted to a leading article seriously discussing the possibility of German armed intervention. An appeal was made to the Czechs to protect themselves against such an attack, and to canvass all citizens in "every town, every village" without delay in order to determine how many able-bodied men were willing to defend Bohemia and Moravia against foreign aggression. Registers of such men were to be compiled and a "Central Committee for Land Defense" was to be established to coordinate the defense activities.[15] It mattered little that the article in *Národní Noviny* and the many

14. *Ibid.* New facts and perspectives in F. Jílek, "Pražská polytechnika a její studenti v revolučním roce 1848," *Sborník Národního technického muzea,* IV (1965), 323 ff. St. Václav's Square was then known as Horses' Market.

15. *NN,* June 9, 1848.

rumors of an imminent German invasion were not based on sound evidence. In 1848 rumors speedily assumed the status of realities, and both Czechs and Germans preferred to believe the worst about each other's intentions. As a result, on the eve of the uprising, the Czechs expected a foreign invasion momentarily. If one adds to this fear the sight of Windischgrätz' cannons poised menacingly atop the Petřín Hill overlooking Prague, one can appreciate the sentiment of the city's population. Then, too, the oppressive heat on June 11 must have rendered the people more irritable and more easily provoked than they otherwise would have been. In a letter written on June 11, a Moravian delegate to the Slavic Congress complained of a "sultry" atmosphere, both literally and politically, adding prophetically, "In a few days there will be an explosion, and a terrible one!"[16]

The day of the mass was Whitmonday. It is pertinent to observe that the mass was not officially connected with either the Slavic Congress or the National Committee or the Prague City Council. It did have, however, a Slavic character. The attendance was heavy; there were men and women of various social classes, ranging from maidens solemnly dressed in white to workers from industrial districts; of the latter, some twenty-five hundred are estimated to have turned out for the occasion, largely at the instigation of the university students. Most of those attending the mass had come from conviction, some from curiosity. After the mass, a part of the crowd went home, but others, responding to the spontaneous cries of "Let's march past Windischgrätz!" repaired to the military headquarters situated not far from St. Václav's Square, and it was in front of the headquarters that the fateful clash between the soldiers and the marchers took place. Quickly, the news of the clash sped through the city. Within minutes the barricades began to go up and church bells rang in alarm. The stage had been set for the bloodiest episode of the year 1848.[17]

The June Uprising lasted six days, from Monday, June 12, until Saturday, June 17. The rebels had the advantage of controlling the short, narrow streets running in various directions in the heart of the city on the east bank of the river Vltava, for these streets could easily be barricaded and held even against the superior might of the army. The headquarters of the rebels was the Klementinum (Collegium Clementinum), a complex of university buildings in the

16. *NNM*, II (1962), 396.
17. Bajerová, *Svatodušní bouře*, pp. 58 ff.

Old Town of Prague. Shortly after the outbreak of the uprising, Governor Thun hurried to the Old Town to plead personally with the students to desist from violence. The sight of the governor climbing the barricades, impecably clad and wearing a top hat,[18] was a rare one indeed. The impressive countenance and attire did not prevent Thun from being seized as a hostage later in the day, to be used by the rebels as a lever against Windischgrätz. But the governor absolutely refused to be a party to any mediation or negotiation in such circumstances; he showed himself throughout as entirely fearless, and his courageous conduct earned him the esteem of friend and foe alike. On Tuesday the rebels released him after some of the Czech leaders, Palacký among them, interceded on his behalf.

Windischgrätz acquired something of a personal stake in the crushing of the rebels as a result of a tragedy that struck as close as a tragedy could: his wife was killed by a stray bullet on the first day of the fighting.

Alarmed by the news of the uprising, the Vienna government promptly dispatched a two-man commission to Prague to plead for a cessation of hostilities. The two men arrived on June 14,[19] and for a time success appeared in sight. The commissioners realized that the chief obstacle to peace was the presence of Windischgrätz; in retrospect, it seems incredible that they succeeded at one point in actually inducing the general to tender his resignation, and it is tempting to speculate what the results of the uprising would have been had the resignation remained in effect. The commissioners issued an official communiqué announcing the resignation, and the announcement was posted on the streets. But the announcement, as printed, was prefaced by a short statement implying that the army had capitulated to the city. This wounded the general's self-esteem and furnished him with an excuse to withdraw his resignation within a few hours after tendering it. He finally bombarded the city into submission, compelling it to capitulate on June 17. On the next day a state of siege was declared in Prague and the adjacent area, and a roundup of revolutionary suspects began.

General Windischgrätz was totally lacking in appreciation of public opinion and apparently could see no convincing reason why he should have been so unpopular. As a result, only one logical explana-

18. Frič, *Paměti*, II, 128.
19. Kazbunda, *České hnutí*, pp. 257 ff.

tion of the events occurred to him: the rebellion was the result of a plot, executed by a handful of conspirators and carefully prepared in advance. In fact, no conspiracy was ever proved, and, given the electric atmosphere in Prague, none was necessary. Though not all groups were equally zealous in supporting armed resistance, the uprising was a spontaneous outbreak deeply rooted in the mood of the city. And if one were to reduce the emotions of the citizens of Prague to a single common denominator, that denominator would have been a thorough dislike of General Windischgrätz. No man had been more hated in recent memory. He was abhorred by radicals and moderates alike, by men and women, and by young and old.

The guiding and driving force of the June Uprising was the university students, and among these, the majority were probably from the Polytechnic (College of Engineering), despite the fact that they represented a minority of the total student population in Prague. In this connection, it is relevant to point out that the "engineers" came generally from more modest social backgrounds than the other students.[20] Together, the students, both university and polytechnic, constituted the most politically conscious group involved in the uprising.

After the students, the most substantial support came from the workers. It was the students and the workers primarily who manned the barricades and faced enemy fire, the students as leaders and the workers as followers. A segment of the workers consisted of the least educated, the most uprooted, and the most exploited element of the community; thefts and other excesses were committed by some of them.[21] On the other hand, Frič, in his *Memoirs,* calls the workers the "most reliable, obliging" of all the rebels.[22] The majority of contemporary sources agree that the workers conducted themselves, on the whole, with restraint, and that the number of transgressions was less than might have been expected in the circumstances.[23] In view of the fact that only a few weeks earlier some of these same workers must have been involved in the attacks upon the Jews, their

20. Jílek, "Pražská polytechnika," pp. 273-75, 339.
21. See the burgomaster's decree complaining of thefts committed by the proletariat during the uprising (text in *CBB,* June 27, 1848). See also J. Křížek, *Národní gardy v roce 1848* (Prague, 1954), p. 136.
22. Frič, *Paměti,* II, 140. Frič adds that the workers could be trusted "not to touch a pin" in houses in which they were posted for duty.
23. *CBB,* June 28, 1848.

restraint during the June Uprising is surprising. The reason for this was the moderating influence of the students. In the last days of the uprising, however, the students were able to prevent excesses only with the greatest difficulty: "They [the workers] are still following us," they were saying, "but they will not follow much longer."[24] Even so, the workers behaved with more restraint than the soldiers.

Some of the workers demanded pay for the building of the barricades, and others had to be paid for dismantling them,[25] which reflects their straitened economic circumstances as well as a low level of political consciousness. Yet it was the workers who suffered the largest toll as a result of the fighting. The most complete casualty list available shows forty-six dead, of whom forty-three were combatants. Of the forty-three, at least twenty-nine or thirty did manual work of some kind (there were, for example, twelve unskilled workers).[26] This accounting is certainly not complete, since no students are listed among the dead, although the students participated in large numbers. That a number of them perished during the uprising cannot be doubted. It is implied in Frič's account of the event; it is also known that after the uprising, on July 26, a group of students gathered to pay tribute to "the memory of the student dead," and that throughout the late summer several requiems were held for them.[27] The most complete list of the wounded available does include students, eleven out of sixty-three, but workers in manual occupations again predominate, even more than in the list of the dead. Curiously there was only one cotton-printer among the dead and one among the wounded, although the cotton-printers were by far the most numerous group of workers.[28]

The burghers supported the rebels in various ways. According to Frič, "We received ready cash from various burghers and neighboring houses, from collections on the barricades . . . ." Food supplies were

24. *Bohemia,* June 23, 1848.

25. Křížek, *Národní gardy,* p. 123; Frič, *Paměti,* II, 167.

26. "Die Opfer der Prager Pfingsten," *Vierteljahrschrift für praktische Heilkunde,* IV (1848), 144-45.

27. Frič, *Paměti,* II, 173 (Frič places the number of dead at over four hundred—clearly an exaggeration); *NN,* July 27, 1848; *PVL,* August 24, 1848.

28. The General Hospital lists 11 students out of 63 wounded. The total number of the wounded treated in the reporting hospitals was 130, but for only 63 of them (those treated in the General Hospital), a break-down by occupation is available. See "Die Opfer der Prager Pfingsten," pp. 144, 146.

also provided.[29] Most of the burghers were sincere in their offers; a few helped only under compulsion.

The most striking characteristic of the barricade-fighters of whatever social class was their youth. The students were all young, and their youth was matched, in the ranks of the workers, by journeymen, apprentices, and young workers generally. This was also the pattern in uprisings in other cities in Europe.[30] Among the young were not only men but also women. Even a group of students in a girls' school lent an eager hand in the building of the barricades; their teachers were fainting from fright but the intrepid maidens opened the windows of the school and enthusiastically hurled benches and tables out into the street.[31] Frič, ever alert to the romantic and the erotic, said that "the fair sex showed itself particularly sympathetic to us. Ladies, attired for a promenade and holding parasols, gazed at the persevering defenders of the barricades, flirted here and there with the younger ones, hopped over the barricads like chamois . . . ."[32] Girls cared for the wounded and some even carried arms. The sight of young women on the barricades was not easily forgotten, and the courage of these heroines was celebrated in a contemporary popular song. The uprising also produced its "Amazon," whom observers remembered as a girl with short, loose hair, clad in a Slavic costume, sitting on the main barricade and holding a musket in her hand.[33]

What was the role played by Czechs and Germans, respectively, in the uprising? Except for the handful of German merchants, members of the "German casino," the Germans in Prague shared with the Czechs a strong dislike for Windischgrätz. During the uprising, German radicals took an active part in the fighting, but the

29. Frič, *Paměti*, II, 140.
30. For Vienna, see, R. L. Lutz, "Fathers and Sons in the Vienna Revolution of 1848," *JCEA*, XXII (1962), 162-73.
31. J. J. Toužimský, *Na úsvitě nové doby* (Prague, 1898), p. 600.
32. Frič, *Paměti*, II, 153.
33. *Bohemia*, June 25, 1848. Popular memory also extolled the members of the Franciscan order as barricade-fighters and a well-known contemporary drawing immortalized them in that role (reproduced in Toužimský, *Na úsvitě*, p. 545). However, a letter by a Franciscan monk published in *NN*, August 3, 1848, explains that the stories concerning Franciscan barricade-fighters were a fabrication and that the members of the order were compelled to take part in the building of the barricades by public threats. The letter does admit that at least one student cleric walked about with a sword, but alleges that the sword was entrusted to him by a National Guardsman for a while and that he did not have any intention of rising against the government.

majority of Germans, though not fond of the general, assumed a passive attitude. It may be stated in passing that the Jews took a similar attitude; the Jewish quarter in Prague, though barricaded, was neutral, and was ignored by both the insurgents and by the army. It should be noted that since the majority of the inhabitants of Prague were Czech, even had the Czechs and Germans taken part in the uprising in proportions equal to their proportion in the population, the revolt was bound to become very largely a Czech movement.

Since the Germans were proportionately less involved than the Czechs, the Czech character of the struggle was rendered more conspicuous. This is what accounts, in part, for the many rumors that spread throughout Europe depicting the uprising as an attack by Czechs upon Germans, as a Czech-German war. In part, the rumors were the result of the confusion and chaos of the first days of the uprising when nobody, even in close vicinity of Prague, indeed even in Prague itself, knew exactly what was happening. Amid such confusion and a complete blackout of news, it was easy for the imagination to take full reign, conjuring the dramatic vision of a Czech horde charging upon hapless Germans and hacking them to pieces. Many a German was ready to believe this kind of information, and what Europe learned about the uprising during its first days came almost entirely from German sources. The *Times* of London treated its readers to the following news, culled entirely from German reports: "The cases of atrocious cruelties committed by the Czechs, especially during the first days of combat, have a strong family likeness to the horrors of which the Taborites were guilty during the Hussite wars. They cut off the noses and ears of soldiers whom they took alive, and murdered them after having tormented them."[34] This bizarre bit of reporting was followed up by the observation that the insurgents had apparently "made a deep-laid plot to found a Czechish empire, separate from Austria," and that "almost all the Czechish leaders had an eye set on the Bohemian [royal] Crown, and had the sanguinary undertaking succeeded, they would have fought for it among themselves."[35] It is not too much to say that any resemblance between the story and the reality behind the story was purely accidental.

In justice to the *Times* and to other newspapers, it should be added that similar distorted rumors circulated not only abroad but also within Bohemia and Moravia, and not merely among the "Sudeten

34. *Times,* June 23, 1848, p. 8.
35. *Ibid.,* June 26, p. 6, and June 29, p. 5.

Germans";[36] if so much misinformation had built up so close to the scene of the uprising, one may imagine how the rumors were magnified over a distance of several hundred miles encompassed by several different countries. The Viennese radicals had long since made up their minds that whatever came from the Czechs was baneful and reactionary; as far as they were concerned, the June Uprising was just another evidence of the Czechs' reactionary chauvinism. They successfully overcame, for the moment, their dislike of Windischgrätz, and were quite prepared to tolerate him as an avenging angel. What Windischgrätz had done had to be done: that was their verdict.[37] An endorsement from such quarters could hardly have been pleasing to the general. After the uprising he was flooded with messages from various parts of Austria and from abroad congratulating him on his triumph over the Czechs. He himself had never regarded the uprising as a struggle between nationalities and had done nothing to encourage such a view. In reply to the unwanted honors showered upon him, he declared publicly, on June 22, that he "was compelled to employ armed force not in a partisan struggle between nationalities but in order to quell a public insurgency."[38]

It has often been asked why the uprising failed. It is more appropriate to ask whether it ever had any chance of success. The arithmetic of the struggle was unmistakably against the insurgents. Against an army of several thousand well-trained professionals, they could offer but a few hundred ill-equipped volunteers. Only a small proportion of the Prague population actually fought on the barricades. The number of Prague inhabitants at that time was over a hundred thousand (this of course includes all inhabitants, including children, who were obviously not barricade material), while the number of barricade-fighters was about twelve to fifteen hundred. Of these the students accounted for six to eight hundred, the workers perhaps three to four hundred, and the burghers and others the remainder. The student fighters constituted less than one-fourth of the total number of students.[39] The majority had left for a vacation, which

36. *NN,* August 4, 1848.

37. For the relevant quotations, see R. J. Rath, *The Viennese Revolution of 1848* (Austin, Tex., 1957), pp. 262 ff.

38. Text in J. M. Černý (ed.), *Boj za právo: Sborník aktů politických u věcech státu a národa českého od roku 1848* (Prague, 1893), pp. 313-14.

39. Jílek estimates that the size of Windischgrätz' army was twenty thousand and that the number of students who remained in Prague was less than one-fourth ("Pražská polytechnika," pp. 323, 329).

began earlier that year, and some who stayed in Prague did not become involved in the event. As for the workers, it is not possible to offer anything resembling an accurate figure beyond stating that the number of workers on the barricades in proportion to the total number of Prague workers was less than the corresponding figure for the students. Beyond a doubt the students were the most actively engaged of all the groups involved.

In dealing with the insurgents, Windischgrätz could count on his popularity with his officers and on the loyalty of his troops; the forces of revolution had made no significant inroads into the body military: at no time was there a hint of disloyalty or disaffection. On the rebel side, there was simply no organization, no effective leadership. Of the few names that flashed into prominence before and during the uprising—all students—there was none that could be regarded as an effective and thoughtful leader in a time of crisis. The rebels displayed a good deal of enthusiasm, but that could not compensate for all the other deficiencies.[40] Nevertheless, against this background it must be deemed a remarkable achievement that the rebel pressure caused Windischgrätz at one time to submit his resignation; evidently, to the two commissioners and to the Vienna government the crisis must have appeared serious, particularly when taken in conjunction with the symptoms of national and popular ferment in other parts of the monarchy.

It is significant that the enthusiasm that attended the outbreak of the uprising lost its momentum after the first three days. At the beginning, the number of men and women willing to lend a hand in one way or another was large. The first clash with the troops, with its image of innocent civilians being set upon by the soldiery, produced a great hatred of Windischgrätz and reinforced the general feeling that to rid the city of him was not only desirable but also possible. During these hours, many men normally opposed to any form of violence sympathized, at least to some degree, with the rebels.[41] But the sight of the dead and wounded and the ruined buildings induced

40. Jílek draws attention to the startling fact that of the four hundred barricades only fifteen were effective in hampering Windischgrätz' actions (*ibid.*, p. 332). For a map, see *Atlas československých dějin* (Prague, 1965), p. 20, c.

41. That a man as removed from violence and as opposed to the radicals as Palacký wrote a note to his daughter during the uprising in which he uttered not a single word critical of the insurgents illustrates the transformations in-

second thoughts, and soon the initial enthusiasm and confidence began to wane. Without a binding ideology, national, social, or political; and without a clear and overriding purpose capable of mobilizing a sustained willingness to fight, the movement weakened. By June 17—the final day—earlier support had slackened and turned into indifference or opposition. The burghers, particularly, wanted to terminate the hostilities, and the students, too, exhibited signs of fatigue. The workers were probably the most eager to continue, but without leadership this was not possible; they felt themselves betrayed, but did not know who had betrayed them. In the end they submitted to the lure of gold, and for money paid by the burghers proceeded to dismantle the barricades, thus joining the betrayers.

The mood might have developed differently, had support been obtained from outside Prague, particularly from the National Guards and the peasantry. Agitators were dispatched to the countryside pleading the cause of the beleaguered city. Many rural inhabitants were aroused and began to form groups to journey to Prague. One group that came to help met with a terrible tragedy; upon returning from Prague after the uprising, it clashed with the army at a town near Prague and many civilians were killed or wounded.[42] In proportion to the rural population as a whole, however, the amount of help that actually arrived was small. There was no mass response to the urgent call for help, partly because of the confusion surrounding the uprising. Reports reaching the countryside were baffling and contradictory; nobody was quite certain what was happening, who was fighting whom and who was winning. As a result, some groups were formed which never reached their destination.

The principal reason for the lack of mass response, however, was the limited political consciousness of the peasantry. The peasant

---

duced by a sudden crisis. In the letter Palacký expressed his satisfaction at the resignation of Windischgrätz, commended the "common people and the students" for "behaving well," and accused the National Guard of behaving "partly as cowards, partly as traitors." He would probably not have spoken such words publicly, but in a personal communication to his own daughter he could be candid and express what were presumably his innermost thoughts at the time. In his later public comments Palacký was sharply critical of the rebels. For his letter to his daughter Maria (dated June 16), see K. Stloukal (ed.), *Rodinné listy Františka Palackeho dceři Marii a zeti F. L. Riegrovi* (Prague, 1930), pp. 57-58.

42. The town was Běchovice, the date June 17. See Křížek, *Národní gardy*, p. 191.

harbored many grievances against the status quo, as symbolized by the landlord, but he was not so easily persuaded to exert himself for political and constitutional issues transcending his own interests and environment. He had barely begun to emerge from centuries of servitude; no amount of persuasion by agitators, no matter how silvery their tongues, no matter what their skills and slogans and promises, could undo in a few days the scars of centuries and bring about the massive response needed. In the end, Prague found itself isolated, and later, in October, 1848, Vienna, in the midst of its own uprising, found itself similarly isolated. In Bohemia, as in Lower Austria, the peasant remained, by and large, deaf to the lure of radical propaganda. After the uprising, in a leaflet addressed to the peasants, the radical, Emanuel Arnold, who more than any other single man had endeavored to influence the peasantry during the critical June Days, complained that "your friends" advised you to "take up arms, but you paid no heed, indeed you did not even try to come to know those who work for you."[43] The agitators had difficulty in establishing rapport with the peasantry; it was not to be expected that they could goad it into a mass crusade in support of the Prague uprising.

If success among Czech peasants was limited, it will come as no surprise that there was no response at all in the German districts of Bohemia. In this connection, it is noteworthy that the conspicuous role played by the Czech proletariat provoked no answering echoes among the proletarians, most of whom were German, in Liberec, the largest working-class center except for Prague and one in which working-class organization was superior to that of Prague. Similarly, the Viennese revolution in October created some response in Liberec,[44] but none among the Czech workers in Prague. Evidently, national feelings influenced the workers in both cases more than class feelings.

The uprising cost many lives, wrought destruction upon the city, and caused the government to wipe out some of the important gains of the March Days. That it was a tragedy was recognized by liberals and radicals alike. Years later Palacký wrote that he knew of no event in his memory that had "more fateful and harmful consequences for our nation than this 'Whitsuntide uprising,' "[45] while Frič called

43. E. Arnold in *Sebrané spisy* (Prague, 1954), p. 69. The leaflet was not completed and was never actually distributed.

44. J. Belda, *Liberec v revolučním roce 1848* (Liberec, 1959), p. 130.

45. In his political testament (1872), in *Radhost* (Prague, 1873), III, 281.

it "the unfortunately inevitable Whitsuntide catastrophe."[46] Thus two men standing on opposite sides of the political spectrum agreed that the uprising was a catastrophe. But Frič laid the blame for it primarily at the door of Windischgrätz, while Palacký, at least in retrospect, seemed to place a greater blame on the insurgents, or at any rate, to absolve Windischgrätz, who, he says, was not the enemy of the constitution the people took him for.[47]

Among the repressive measures decreed by the government as a result of the uprising was the dissolution of the National Committee and the postponement—indefinite, as it turned out—of the meeting of the Bohemian diet. Although critics of the uprising point to this as evidence of the baneful consequence of the uprising, this view is negated by what is known today about the intentions of the government before the event. As observed in Chapter 4, Thun had long wanted to get rid of the National Committee. As for the Bohemian diet, the central government had concluded as early as June 8 that it was "most desirable" to postpone the meeting of the diet until after the meeting of the parliament in Vienna.[48] In both cases, the June Uprising did no more than furnish an excuse. The whole course of events in Bohemia, in Austria, and in Europe as a whole, is one of the slow recovery of the forces of reaction, after the first shock of the spring revolutions. The representatives of these forces were in no mood to accept defeat and were, despite the first losses, still strong enough to recapture lost ground. With or without the June Uprising, they would have won in the end.

Windischgrätz' triumph was of considerable moment for the history of the Habsburg Monarchy in 1848, in that it raised the stock of the military and re-emphasized its value as a tool of political policy. Amid the multitude of setbacks—in Hungary, in Italy, and in Vienna itself—the forces of reaction could point to the crushing of the June Uprisings as their first major victory, a milestone in leading the people back into the darkness of absolutism.

In the history of the Czechs, the June Uprising occupies a unique position. With it, university students emerged for the first time as a major revolutionary force, and indeed as leaders of a major political action. With it, too, the workers appeared for the first time as an instrument of political (rather than social) change, though they had

46. Frič, *Paměti*, II, 92.
47. Palacký, *Radhost*, III, 282.
48. Kazbunda, *České hnutí*, p. 283.

not yet become very politically conscious. Curiously, more workers perished during the uprising than on any comparable occasion since then; in subsequent decades the working class grew into a powerful force that often clashed with the state, but at no time has the tragedy been so poignant, the toll of life so large.[49] The uprising compelled the daily press to take a searching and anguished look at the emergence of the working class and reflect on its position in society; and just as the sight of the workers standing on the barricades stimulated the discussion of the social question, so the spectacle of feminine barricade-builders stimulated in the first serious discussion in the press of the emancipation of women.[50] The student, the worker, and the woman became the subjects of popular songs praising their courage and devotion to the cause of liberty.[51] The uprising quickened the formation of a Czech radical movement, with ever-sharper lines drawn between it and the liberal movement.[52] It brought forth the first consciously democratic literature, from the pen of the radical Sabina, whose views were frankly influenced by French literary currents.[53] Soon after the uprising a few short and unpretentious literary pieces having proletarian themes were published; as literature they were of limited value, but they represented the first discovery of the worker in the history of Czech literature.[54]

The June Uprising lived on in public memory. It was enshrined in popular songs, and within a few weeks the first sympathetic accounts of it in pamphlet or short-book form appeared. Furthermore, the students, considering themselves custodians of the memory, set out to collect eye-witness material on "Whitsunweek" for publication.[55] And in the ensuing months countless requiems were celebrated throughout Bohemia's churches in remembrance of the victims.[56]

49. Not even during the General Strike in Czechoslovakia in 1920.

50. See Chapter 14.

51. M. Novotný, *Letáky z roku 1848* (Prague, 1948), pp. 232 ff.

52. See the aggressively egalitarian series of articles entitled "Aristocrats," *PVL*, July 7-14, 1848.

53. First printed at the beginning of October, 1848, in a series of newspaper articles, under the title "Democratic Literature." Reprinted in K. Kosík (ed.), *Čeští radikální demokraté (Výbor politických statí)* (Prague, 1953), pp. 194-200.

54. H. Hrzalová, "Jak vznikal a uskutečňoval se ideál demokratické literatury kolem roku 1848," *Česká Literatura*, VII (1959), 54 ff.

55. See the announcement of the Student Committee of August 8, 1848, in *NN*, August 9, 1848. The project was never completed.

56. See, for example, the requiems noted in *NN*, September 6, 8, 16, 22, and 28, 1848.

For weeks thereafter, bodies of victims continued to be uncovered, as the rubble was being cleared away, and the buildings restored. Fourteen weeks after the uprising the body of the last victim was found. It was the body of a man in an advanced state of decay; his mouth was covered with a handkerchief he had applied to protect himself from the smoke rising from a burning mill within whose walls he had been trapped. Typically, he belonged to the working class; he was a mill foreman, who, like many other mill workers, had fought on the side of the insurgents.[57] His body was duly buried on October 1, 1848, the last victim of what was both the first and the last violent "revolution" in modern Czech history.

On June 18, the same day on which Windischgrätz declared the city in a state of siege, he established a mixed military-civilian commission to investigate the causes of the uprising. Although the commission consisted of both military and civilian judges, its character was, and was intended to be, primarily military. The general appointed the commission without previously consulting with the government in Vienna, and the government, more sensitive than Windischgrätz to public sensibilities, compelled him to accept a restriction of the commission's powers in one essential respect: it could investigate and try only members of the military. As far as civilians were concerned, the commission was to have only investigative powers; if the investigation warranted an indictment, the suspects were to be handed over to a civilian court for a regular trial.[58]

From the beginning, the work of the commission was dominated by one objective: to prove that the uprising was the result of a vast, "deep-laid" conspiracy staged by revolutionaries. It was a tempting, and, to a simple mind, plausible, objective. At the time of the outbreak of the uprising, Prague was teeming with foreigners—participants in the Slavic Congress. Among these was Mikhail Bakunin, an indefatigable preacher of revolutions, a homeless wanderer, an international subversive, a wealthy noble turned radical—a figure uttrely unique in the annals of European history. That he played a relatively innocuous, and, for a time, even moderating role in Prague in June, 1848, has since been well-established.[59] But his name could and did occasion the darkest suspicions that were not lessened by the presence in Prague of so many Poles who had more or less elbowed

57. *Bohemia,* October 1, 1848.
58. F. Roubík, *Český rok 1848* (Prague, 1931), p. 307.
59. Frič *Paměti,* II, 163-64; Bajerová, *Svatodušní bouře,* p. 163.

their way into the Congress, among them radical intellectuals, some with a record of outright revolutionary activity. The sinister hand of the Magyars was also suspected, since more than a few Magyars were known to have been in Prague at the time. Bakunin, the Poles, the Magyars, separately or together, were all considered to be evil enough to have hatched any number of plots, and imagination boggled in conjuring their daring schemes. One unofficial public rumor even credited the Jews with causing the uprising,[60] a view doubtless influenced by the prominence of the Jews in Viennese radical circles but hardly borne out by reality, for in Prague the Jews' only concern was to escape, with as few blows as possible, the rising tide of fury and scorn directed against them by a segment of the public.

Of course, seasoned observers, both Czech and German, were unanimous from the start in their belief that there was no suggestion of a conspiracy,[61] but the commission, ceaselessly prodded by General Windischgrätz, elected to believe in it and in the following weeks left no stone unturned in its pursuit of the alleged conspirators. Hundreds of people were investigated: the distinguished and the unknown; the respected and the ill-famed; vagrants, counts, priests, butchers, innkeepers, workers, students. Scores of men were placed in custody.[62] Among the warrants issued was one dated June 30 for "the candidate in philosophy . . . Joseph Frič . . . eighteen to twenty years old, of frail physique, medium height, with pale complexion, slightly acquiline nose, dark eyes, insecure, shifty look, characterized by a swaying walk."[63] But Frič and a few other youthful radicals had fled Prague in time, eluding the clutches of the gendarmes.

The commission had launched a veritable conspiracy to uncover a conspiracy. Houses were searched and privacy violated. Personal papers were seized and scrutinized for invisible writing. Special informants (soldiers disguised as civilians) were employed to eavesdrop on casual talk in taverns and on the street. In a public appeal, Windischgrätz asked all citizens to report anything they might know about the consipracy and those involved in it. The most damning of all of the effects of the investigation was the spectacle of citizens, too numerous for comfort, rushing to inform on their neighbors, peddling

60. *PVL,* July 6, 1848.

61. See, for example, *CBB,* June 21, 1848.

62. For a complete list, with occupations, see Bajerová, *Svatodušní bouře,* Appendix III.

63. Reproduced in Frič, *Paměti,* II, 183.

flimsy evidence and pure fabrications, presumably to settle personal scores or simply to ingratiate themselves with the authorities. The informants produced an avalanche of denunciatory letters, most of them anonymous, which have survived to this day—a pathetic monument to human malignity and cowardice.[64] The letters and verbal reports proved to be an embarrassment of riches; *Národní Noviny* remarked that "people are diligently informing," so much so that the members of the investigating commission" are allegedly themselves annoyed by it."[65]

After it became clear that Windischgrätz was in full control of the city a mass exodus of people from Prague began. According to one estimate, some twenty thousand people left the city, mostly burghers, and for weeks Prague looked like a ghost town.[66] The refugees hid in villages and did not return for months. Furthermore, about seven hundred workers, unemployed and not domiciled in Prague, were expelled from the city,[67] after which activity to provide employment for the remaining jobless was stepped up. At the same time military guards were posted in textile factories to banish from the workers' minds any thoughts of further violence. Students and young people in general were being rendered harmless by the time-honored method of military conscription. The press was somewhat restricted, as was inevitable during a state of siege, but it continued to criticize the government, though its criticism was more circumspect than previously. The National Committee was abolished, on June 26, as was the popular Czech militia, the *Svornost,* on June 14,[68] both on the vague and doubtful ground of complicity in the June Uprising. The National Committee, already afflicted by a languor before June, died a silent death. The dissolution of the *Svornost* loosed a storm of protest and lingering controversy—it was formally a part of the National Guard—lasting for months, and its legal status remained vague. The National Guard itself was permitted to function, after being purged of "undesirable" elements and shorn of much of its power and prestige. It too had shown signs of lassitude before June, and the restrictions

64. Bajerová, *Svatodušní bouře;* O. Odložilík, "Vyšetřovací komize z r. 1848 a jejich registratura," *SAMV,* II (1929), 88.
65. *NN,* July 19, 1848.
66. *PVL,* June 24, 1848.
67. Z. Tobolka, "Počátky dělnického hnutí v Čechách," *Obzor Národohospodářský* (1903), p. 212.
68. Text of the decrees in Černý (ed.), *Boj,* pp. 321, 345-46.

now placed upon it caused it to decline further, a trend that proved irreversible.

The government in Vienna, though grateful enough to Windisch-grätz for "saving" Prague for the monarchy, was not altogether pleased with the conduct of the commission. The manner in which the general and the commission conducted their investigation savored too much of the discredited methods of pre-March absolutism, and the government feared its impact on public opinion. The first democratic parliament in Austria was about to open in Vienna; the dark picture of Prague under siege would provide a chilling contrast to the bright vision of the first parliament, and would constitute an unsettling reminder to critics that constitutional government was far from secure. In Vienna, radical opinion soon experienced second thoughts on the usefulness of Windischgrätz as an ally and was exerting pressure on Pillersdorf's government to settle the conflict. The government in turn pressed the general to lift the state of siege and to terminate the investigation, but he and Thun, who were not ready to give up their pursuit of the revolutionary conspirators, insisted that lifting the siege would only invite anarchy. Finally, on July 2, the government dispatched a high judicial official to Prague to carry out an on-the-spot inquiry, but was unable to induce Windischgrätz to lift the state of siege. The general's intransigence was aided by a petition, since become famous, submitted on July 5 by sixty-seven Prague ultraconservatives who declared themselves satisfied with the state of siege and urged its continuance.[69] Though it was known that the signatories were members of the "German casino," their names were never revealed. The petition scandalized the Prague community and the number "sixty-seven" quickly became a term of ridicule and a byword for reaction; a reactionary was a "sixty-sevener." For the moment, however, Windischgrätz' hand was strengthened and the city continued to chafe under siege.

Meanwhile the investigation itself had reached a blind alley, with no evidence of a far-flung conspiracy materializing. Then, the day after the petition of the "sixty-seven," the commission's labors at last seemed rewarded: evidence was obtained to show that both the Slavic Congress and the June Uprising were the result of a planned conspiracy. This seemingly sensational piece of evidence was supplied in the testimony of one Marcel Turanský, an enigmatic figure

69. Originally published without signatures in *Prager Zeitung*, July 12, 1848; Bajerová, *Svatodušní bouře*, p. 231.

of whom very little was known at the time and concerning whom not much more has come to light since. Turanský attended the Slavic Congress as a Slovak but may have been a Magyar by sentiment; he was only nineteen years old at the time.[70] He was among those arrested by the commission, and on July 6 unfolded before it a hideous vision of a vast conspiracy reaching into all parts of Central Europe. Turanský claimed to have learned the fearful details from Slavic radicals with whom he had been consorting. His story dovetailed neatly—too neatly—with the charges trumpeted by Windischgrätz for weeks. Turanský provided the link between the uprising and the congress, which Windischgrätz had wanted to establish from the beginning. According to this new testimony, the uprising had been planned, but circumstances had caused it to break out prematurely. It was originally scheduled for 1850, as a link in a chain of rebellions that were to flare up simultaneously in the four Slavic cities of the Habsburg Monarchy, Kraków, Prague, Zagreb, and Bratislava. The unexpected February revolution in Paris in 1848 caused the plans to go awry and compelled the plotters to revise their deadly timetable: instead of 1850, the revolution was to take place in 1848. With painstaking detail, the imaginative witness described his role in the movement, naming names, times, and places with an accuracy that could, depending on one's views, excite admiration or suspicion. It is known today that Turanský did attend some of the meetings he claimed to have attended,[71] but taken as a whole the testimony was a daring fabrication. There never was a plan such as he outlined. But the commission chose to accept it, at least with a view to using it as as basis for further inquiry; Turanský had injected new life into the flagging investigation.

Turanský's motives will probably never be fully explained. He has been considered a Hungarian "agent provocateur," planted by Kossuth in the Slavic Congress in order to discredit it; a confused revolutionary; an opportunistic liar who told exactly what he wanted his audience to hear; or simply a publicity-seeking youth who hoped to attract attention but instead succeeded only in attaining notoriety.

As Turanský was spinning his tale in Prague, important changes were taking place in the imperial capital. The Pillersdorf cabinet resigned on July 8 and a new one was formed, under Minister Dobl-

70. Protocols of the commission in V. Žáček and Z. Tobolka (eds.), *Slovanský sjezd v Praze roku 1848: Sbírka dokumentů* (Prague, 1958), pp. 455-59.
71. *Ibid.*, p. 456, n. 16.

hoff. The Imperial Parliament was about to convene amid general excitement. Criticism of Windischgrätz had been mounting and the state of siege had led to some bizarre situations. Police apprehended the journalist Havlíček on July 7 because of an article that had appeared the day before in *Národní Noviny*. While Havlíček was in prison, an election for the Imperial Parliament was held (July 8), and he was elected in no less than five constituencies. A popular candidate locked up behind bars on election day was not a sight to endear Windischgrätz to the public.[72] Nor was Havlíček the only one in this anomalous position. Brauner too had been taken into custody, for suspected complicity in the June Uprising, and was elected to the Imperial Parliament while in prison. Windischgrätz realized that the barrage of criticism would mount, and that he could expect renewed pressure from Vienna after the recent cabinet changes. He had had the satisfaction of not having yielded to the pressure of an all-mighty government in Vienna under Pillersdorf, but this time he chose to take action himself, before pressure was applied, and on July 20 he announced publicly the lifting of the state of siege. Even in his hour of mercy, he coupled the concession with a stern preachment against those who "by rebellious machinations would bring misfortune upon the city and the country," and warned that "even the slightest attempt at a new rebellion will result in an immediate imposition of the most severe military power."[73] Significantly, this move was not accompanied by any major reduction of the strength of the military; the army would still loom large, as a warning to the people of Prague.

Even after the lifting of the siege, however, the investigating commission continued to function, encouraged by Turanský's testimony. This caused growing uneasiness to the new government, which now had to answer for its conduct to Parliament. The experience was a trying one, since Czech deputies, shielded by parliamentary immunity, could ask embarrassing questions and point accusing fingers at Windischgrätz' regime and by implication at the central government. It was embarrassing to be confronted with the reminder that in the parliament, which formally opened on July 22, Brauner's seat was unoccupied because its holder was still in custody. Brauner's case was especially irksome because he was a well-known and well-respected individual, and his expertise on the agrarian question would soon be urgently required as the parliament began its deliberations on

72. Havlíček was released on July 12. See *NN*, July 11 and 14, 1848.
73. Text in Černý (ed.), *Boj*, pp. 347-49.

peasant problems. Also, it did not take the government long to realize that against the pressure of German radical and/or pro-Frankfurt deputies, it would have to rely on the Czech delegation, politically moderate and "pro-Austrian," for parliamentary support. It thus became a matter of survival for the new cabinet to deal firmly with Windischgrätz, or at least as firmly as the general's strong position would allow. Against his better judgment, the general finally had to dissolve the mixed commission and hand over the entire investigation, with all the relevant material, to a regular court in Prague. The appropriate announcement was made by Windischgrätz on August 2, and once more he liberally spiced his remarks with offensive rhetoric, referring again to "rebellious machinations" and again darkly hinting that the uprising had resulted from a "widespread conspiracy" rather than "merely from an accidental clash between the military and the civilians."[74]

Yet even Turanský's gratuitous contribution could not sustain the investigation indefinitely. The central government attached little credance to the conspiracy theory and had little faith in the eventual success of the inquiry. Indeed, it feared acutely that the inquiry would turn into a complete fiasco. It proved impossible to obtain any corroboration for Turanský's testimony. Once the matter was out of Windischgrätz' hands, the overriding objective of the government was to bring the investigation to a close, with as little loss of face as possible. A number of suspects were released from custody, among them Brauner, to the chagrin of Windischgrätz, who regarded him as a "criminal and a democrat."[75] On September 14-15, the government issued an order setting free all those held in custody, other than the originators and leaders of the uprising. The originators and leaders would, if indicted, enjoy the benefit of a free and open trial by jury,[76] but even here the investigation did not yield success. A lengthy confidential report dated October 13, 1848, lent credence to the Turanský testimony but stated that efforts to verify the testimony had "thus far produced no results"; that the suspected objective of the Slavs to break away from Austria "can in no way be definitely established"; that Turanský "did not learn the actual goal of the unrest [in

74. Text in Černý (ed.), *Boj*, pp. 355-59. For details, see Kazbunda, *České hnutí*, pp. 322 ff.

75. Windischgrätz' letter of March 29, 1849, in Kazbunda, *České hnutí*, p. 326.

76. Text in *CBB*, September 15, 1848, Supplement Two.

Prague]"; that the publicity given to the disclosures would make it possible for the culprits to destroy all evidence of their guilt; and that the chaotic conditions in Hungary rendered any investigation difficult.[77] This was an unqualified admission of defeat. Following this report more suspects were released, and warrants for the arrest of those who were still eluding the police were withdrawn. In the second week of December, the last suspect was released. This brought the inquiry to a close, without yielding a single case of conviction.[78]

But if all the suspects escaped punishment, one person, who was not a suspect, did not: Governor Thun. Thun's position had been precarious since the June events. He had, in the pre-March era, been a fair and friendly observer and supporter of Czech and Slovak national aspirations. But his ideal had been a nationalism more cultural than political, and his support of the Czech cause waned as the movement assumed what seemed to him a belligerently political form. From the time of his appointment as governor of Bohemia, he endeavored to play that most difficult of roles, that of arbiter between Czechs and Germans. This role he performed honorably and without partisanship—which explains the mounting hostility against him from both quarters. He staked everything on the maintenance of order, and when the June Uprising shattered that objective, his prestige suffered a blow. His German critics saw the uprising as the outcome of his coddling of the Czech party. German radicals disliked him on principle, regarding him as a man of conservative bent, a spiritual kin of Windischgrätz. Pillersdorf was not disposed to forget Thun's ill-fated formation of the Provisional Governing Council and was irritated by his continued pressure, even after the uprising, in favor of calling the Bohemian diet. The Doblhoff government fell heir to the prejudices of its predecessor and Thun could not expect any sympathy from it.

The animosity of the Czech community was less pronounced but the governor's stock with it had plainly fallen to a dangerous low. The Czechs impugned his honesty—unjustly, as we know today— in dealing with Vienna in the matter of the Provisional Governing Council and the Bohemian diet. They could hardly fail to be antagonized by Thun's role as an ally of Windischgrätz during the weeks of the siege and of the investigation into the alleged conspiracy.

77. Excerpts in Žáček and Tobolka (eds.), *Slovanský sjezd,* pp. 475-83.
78. Bajerová, *Svatodušní bouře,* p. 370.

And Thun, for his part, could never forget that the insurgents had violated his august office and person by taking him hostage.

The lack of support from both ethnic groups rendered it easier for the central government to act. By a decree of July 19 Thun was relieved of his position as governor of Bohemia.[79] The dismissal came without the usual amenities and formalities, and Thun's parting announcement was a bitter farewell to his countrymen, to whom he had been called amid such high hopes and who had rejected him after less than three months. The administration of Bohemia was now entrusted to Baron Karl Mecséry,[80] hitherto deputy governor. In his capacity as governor—at the beginning only acting governor—Mecséry was destined to preside over Bohemia during the remainder of the revolutionary period and then through all the oppressive years of Bach's absolutism.

The dismissal of Thun raised the question of the position of Windischgrätz. To deal with Windischgrätz, however, was not as simple as dealing with Thun. The general had powerful friends in the emperor's entourage. True, the dissolution of the mixed commission weakened his position, but he showed not the slightest desire to leave Prague. To the contrary, he fed the government in Vienna reports of unrest in Bohemia, which he said required the watchful presence of a strong army. Feeling in Prague against him rose to the point where, on August 2, a group of burghers, in a public protest addressed to the Imperial Parliament, alluded to him as "the hated Prince Windischgrätz"—an unprecedented form to be used in a formal declaration. And a later declaration of Czech parliamentary deputies contained an undisguised call for his removal: "A change of the commanding general would under these circumstances in no wise appear as lack of appreciation of the merits of Prince Windischgrätz, but as a necessary sacrifice by which to pacify the capital city and the nation."[81] In seeking to have Windischgrätz removed, the Czechs were not without influential allies: the government hoped to use a part of the military contingent stationed in Prague for the reinforcement of the imperial forces in Italy where there was a serious situation, but Windischgrätz blocked all attempts in this direction. The behind-the-scenes tug-of-war between the general and the government

79. See Thun's announcement in Černý (ed.), *Boj*, pp. 353-54.
80. Kazbunda, *České hnutí*, p. 319.
81. Both documents in Černý (ed.), *Boj*, pp. 367-75, 376-78. The second statement was written on August 25, but not published until September 15.

—now known in detail from archival sources—[82]shows how far from established was the principle of civilian control over the military, although it was inscribed on the banners of liberals and radicals alike in 1848. Windischgrätz was under the control of civilian power only to the extent that he permitted himself to be so. And the fact remains that it was not the government's pressure that finally brought about his departure, but the outbreak of a revolution in Vienna at the beginning of October. He was lured away from the Bohemian capital only by the prospect of duplicating in Vienna his doubtful achievement in Prague.

82. Kazbunda, *České hnutí,* pp. 332 ff.

Chapter 7

The Czechs
and the Viennese Parliament

Having lost the opportunity of expressing their will through the Bohemian diet, the Czechs looked to the Imperial Parliament in Vienna as the one outlet through which to make their opinions felt and through which to help shape the uncertain course of Austrian politics. After preliminary meetings, the parliament—a one-chamber body representing Cisleithania only—opened on July 22, 1848. The electoral law provided for a chamber of 383 deputies, of which Bohemia had 90, Moravia 38, and Silesia 10.[1] On opening day, many deputies were still absent; indeed a few never arrived and were never heard from after their election. At no time during the life of the parliament were all deputies present; this circumstance makes it impossible to offer completely accurate statistics concerning the background of deputies.

A special difficulty attends an attempt to place the deputies in ethnic pigeonholes: some deputies did not identify themselves clearly with any nationality, but rather with the province they represented. As far as Bohemia was concerned, deputies identifying themselves with the Czech national cause were in a majority, having about fifty-five of a total of ninety deputies. In Moravia, the Czechs were favored far less; nominally, twenty-two Moravian deputies—of a total of thirty-eight—were Czech, but only perhaps one-third of these deputies identified themselves actively with the Czech cause. Of the ten Silesian deputies, only one is believed to have been of Czech sentiment, the remainder being German.[2] In the parliament as a whole, the Germans constituted the largest single group, with the Czechs the second-largest. Counting all Slavic groups together—this is the way the Slavs preferred their statistics—the Slavs had a majority, but not

1. Partial list of Bohemian deputies, *NN*, July 14; complete list of Moravian and Silesian deputies, *NN*, July 27; later list of deputies from all provinces, *NN*, January 26, 1849. The election in Bohemia took place on July 8 and 9, elsewhere at various times in June.

2. *NN*, July 14 and 27, 1848. See also J. Vochala, *Rok 1848 ve Slezsku a na severovýchodní Moravě* (Opava, 1948), p. 38.

a very decisive one, over the Germans. Although it is impossible to offer exact figures, for reasons mentioned above, both Slavic and German observers agreed that the Slavs had a little over 190 deputies, which gave them a slight edge, since the chamber never had the total of 383 deputies provided for by the electoral law. As soon as the Slavs' numerical preponderance became known, the Viennese radical newspapers reacted in a manner that was to be characteristic of their conduct in the months to come. The pages of some radical newspapers, such as *The Radical* and *The Proletarian,* were surrounded by black borders to indicate mourning; others contented themselves with a diatribe against the Slavic "barbarians."[3]

From the point of view of social status, the parliament was very much a middle-class body, as might have been expected. From the available lists, it is not always possible to determine a deputy's occupation or fit it into a definite category, and as a result statistics concerning social status differ. However, this much is beyond dispute: for a deputy to have had a university education or degree was so common as not to constitute a mark of distinction at all. A large proportion of lawyers was to be expected in a gathering of this kind, but a striking feature was the presence of a large number of physicians, who were prepared to abandon the practice of medicine for the lure of politics, more often than not radical politics. There were more than sixty peasants,[4] most of them Polish and Ukrainian peasants from Galicia and many of them illiterate. The nobles represented a small minority; there were only about forty of them, the largest single group consisting of Polish nobles from Galicia.

As for the Bohemian and Moravian delegations, they included only a small proportion of peasants; Havlíček had urged his readers to elect educated men to Vienna who would be resourceful enough to defend the Czech nationality in a hostile environment, and the Czech voters took his advice. The Czech (and also German) delegation from Bohemia and Moravia contained a singularly high proportion of university-trained men. From Bohemia, counting Czechs and Germans together, there were least seventeen lawyers; twenty-seven officials, most of whom could be expected to have had some law

3. A. Springer, *Geschichte Österreichs seit dem Wiener Frieden 1809* (Leipzig, 1863-65), II, 404.

4. See the list in *NN,* January 26, 1849, of the occupations of deputies. Springer's figure of ninety-two peasants (*Geschichte Österreichs,* II, 403) is too high.

training; and seven physicians; plus a number of writers, high-school teachers, and university professors. There were only eight peasants, and only two full-fledged aristocrats. Moravia sent not a single aristocrat or clergyman to Vienna. From Bohemia and Moravia (with Silesia) combined, the number of peasant deputies was fifteen.[5] Thus, the representatives from the Lands of the Czech Crown were a solidly middle-class and educated lot. Naturally there were no women or worker deputies from any province.

At the beginning the parliament, the first in the history of the Habsburg Monarchy, was viewed by the public as an engaging spectacle. In a more practical vein, it was viewed by profit-conscious individuals as a means by which channels of commerce could be enlivened. Eager would-be spectators of the new parliamentary game were willing to pay anything to obtain passes to the gallery, and soon a black market in passes was operating. The term "Imperial Parliament" became a magic word, creating a whole new fad in the merchandising of products. Within days of the opening of the parliament, Viennese merchants were selling "parliamentary neckties," "parliamentary gloves," "parliamentary razor-blades," "parliamentary cigars," and "parliamentary candy."[6]

The peasant deputies generated a good deal of interest. During the first weeks public curiosity was stirred by the Galician peasants roaming the city in their peasant attire—a rare sight in a blasé and cosmopolitan city. The parliamentary proceedings were frequently brought to a halt by peasant deputies who had to have explained to them terms that were commonplace to their colleagues.[7] Because of their lack of political sophistication, the Galician peasants proved the most reliable tool of the government, which could, with some exceptions, count on their support.

The language of the discussion was German; this was agreed upon at the outset, with most Slavic deputies concurring, as a way of expediting parliamentary business, although it wrought hardship on the many deputies who were unfamiliar with the language. Only the

5. These figures are based on the list in *NN,* January 26, 1849. Since the occupations of deputies are not always clearly identified, the figures must be regarded as approximations only.

6. "Reichstags-Kravatten," "Reichstags-Handschuhe," etc., *Bohemia,* July 27. As described earlier, similar fads developed in Prague in March when the magic word had been "constitution."

7. Springer, *Geschichte Österreichs,* II, 402-4.

Poles opposed the use of the German language, and they did so partly because, unlike the Czechs and the Slovenes, who had lived for centuries under German rule, they were not as well versed in German, but also because, as Havlíček said, it offended their "Polish pride." In commenting on the decision to use German as the parliamentary language Havlíček observed succinctly: "The Slavs will speak German because the Germans don't speak Slavic."[8]

In time, the deputies formed political groupings known as "right," "left," and "center." The terms were derived from the position each group occupied in the chamber,[9] but they do not entirely correspond to present-day usage. The most conservative position was the center, consisting of die-hard proponents of the status quo, bureaucrats, and members of the Roman Catholic hierarchy. The center was thus the political "right-wing" of modern parlance. Ethnically it was largely German, but its spirit was decidedly pro-Austrian rather than pro-Frankfurt; it was the most reliable supporter of the government and for that reason the Galician peasants could also be counted a part of it.

The right side was occupied by groups that would in present-day terminology be described as moderates or middle-of-the-road groups. It consisted predominantly of Slavs, but included also a number of Germans from Bohemia and Moravia. The dominant and numerically strongest group comprising the right was the Czechs. The right was politically liberal in the nineteenth-century sense of the word: it was committed to the basic gains of the revolutionary era, particularly with regard to democratic liberties and representative institutions. On the national question, it was a vigorous opponent of a militant German nationalism, and was violently anti-Frankfurt.

The left in Vienna was the same as the left in modern parlance, and it was predominantly German, but it also included several Polish democrats and radicals from Galicia. It was dominated by a spirit of German nationalism and was strongly anti-Slavic. The support of a few Poles on the German left did not dull its anti-Slavic edge any more than the support of a few Germans modified the anti-German sentiment of the Slavic right. The left contained the largest proportion of Frankfurt enthusiasts, although this enthusiasm was beginning to wane at the time the parliament opened. The German left had a radical wing which in many ways dominated the course of Viennese politics. It had not succeeded in electing many deputies to

8. *NN*, July 18, 1848.
9. See Havlíček's description in *NN*, August 1, 1848.

the parliament; of the fifteen deputies from Vienna, the radicals' domain, only five had been favored by the electorate. The strength of the radicals lay in their virtual control of the Viennese press, and in their hold over the Viennese workers and students. The German radicals were the most democratic of all political groups; they were also the most chauvinistic, and their anti-Slavic sentiment was imbued with hysterical overtones. The radicals were the only group favoring the rights of the working class and of the low-income classes in general. In the espousal of their causes, they were the most demagogic and the most vituperative in the treatment of their opponents.

Of course, party divisions were not absolute and two groups often combined to vote on a particular issue. The German left and center tended to vote together on some questions concerning German nationality. On the other hand, the German center and the Slavic right both favored (in different degrees) a reorganization of Austria along federal lines, and on this issue they joined hands against the German left, which was centralist, since centralism was seen as a guarantee of a continued German predominance. The Slavs favored federalism quite naturally as a way of transforming the monarchy into a free federation of equal nationalities. The center's support of federalism was borne by a different spirit, deriving as it did from the conservative legacy of the power of the provincial estates. Reducing the three groupings to numbers is not possible, beyond stating that the largest number of deputies belonged to the right, the second-largest to the left, and the smallest number to the center.

What was the position of the central government vis-à-vis the three groupings? The twin objectives of the government's policy were the preservation of the integrity of the Habsburg Monarchy and a pursuit of moderate-to-conservative domestic goals. A government so oriented could not help viewing the German left with serious reservations, and conversely, could not expect from it reliable parliamentary support. The radical leanings of a segment of the left set it upon a collision course with the government. At the same time, the left's flirtation with Magyar separatists and the Frankfurt nationalists lent comfort to the forces threatening to undermine the territorial integrity of the monarchy and jeopardize its status as a great power.

Unable to stake its future on the odious policies of the left, the government was compelled to look elsewhere for support. The center was a dependable force: it was German, but not too offensive in its Germanism; it advocated a strong monarchy, but did not regard moderate federalism as a bar to strength. It was, in short, a sound and logical ally, but it was too weak in numbers to furnish a parliamentary majority. A majority could only be achieved by winning the backing of the right, especially of the Czechs who were its core. As a group, the Czechs were progressive and moderate in their domestic politics, and unequivocally anti-Frankfurt. They harbored in their ranks men of proved abilities and recognized prestige who were equal to the fury of the radicals and who could hold together the Slavic bloc. Their staunch Austro-Slavism was a useful antidote to the menace of Frankfurtism and Magyar separatism. As the parliamentary session progressed, the government and the Czechs "discovered" each other, recognized each other's usefulness, and gradually concluded a marriage of convenience in which the missing element of romance was filled by a persuasive self-interest.[10] This placed the Czechs in the position of key actors in the bitter scenes that dominated the parliamentary chamber in the ensuing weeks. In fact, it might be said without much exaggeration that from the opening date until the outbreak of the October revolution, in Vienna, parliamentary deliberations were reduced to a contest between the Czechs and the German left. The Czechs were confident that their support of the government would bring them important concessions, and the quality of their confidence was rooted in the quantity of their votes.[11] They felt that their votes, combined with those of their allies, were bound to defeat the German left and, equally, to supply the lever with which to exert pressure upon the government. However, in the existing circumstances in which the forces of reaction were still entrenched, this situation was fraught with peril, for too consistent a support of the government would benefit the reaction.

The Czechs sent to Vienna a high-powered delegation. Not one of their political stars was missing. Among the delegates was the historian František Palacký, the best-known Czech (soon equalled only by his future son-in-law Rieger), and the senior, if reluctant, statesman of his nation. The measure of Palacký's esteem may be gauged from the fact that only recently Pillersdorf had offered him the post of Minister of Education.[12] His wisdom was not matched

10. Havlíček's reflections from Vienna, *NN,* July 30, 1848.

11. Havlíček says quite openly that the Slavs with their majority "have a hope of controlling the direction of the whole Parliament" (*NN,* July 30, 1848).

12. K. Kazbunda, *České hnutí roku 1848* (Prague, 1929), pp. 165 ff. Palacký declined the offer.

by his oratory; he spoke seldom on the floor, making his great contribution in the less conspicuous, if not less arduous, committee chores, notably in a committee set up to draft a new constitution. Among the Czechs, František Ladislav Rieger unquestionably captured the spotlight. Of handsome countenance, persuasive oratory, equally at home in the Czech and German languages, he became a veritable tribune of the Czech cause in a hostile territory, which endeared him to his fellow countrymen as much as it earned him the hatred of his German foes. No other Czech deputy was hated by the German liberals and radicals as much as Rieger. Brauner, too, had been elected, though he took his seat somewhat belatedly because of his having been held in custody for his alleged complicity in the June Uprising. Brauner's special knowledge of the agrarian question rendered him eminently qualified and eminently useful once that question had been placed on the agenda. He was perhaps the best expert on this subject in the parliament. The journalist Karel Havlíček was practiced in the use of words, but his unique dexterity lay in the written, not the spoken word. Havlíček loathed the long-winded and sterile rhetorics of many deputies which hindered parliamentary action, and on the few occasions on which he rose to speak, he proposed that the debate be terminated.[13] He resigned his mandate at the end of the year to return to his first love, journalism.[14] Then there was Antonín Strobach, the former Prague burgomaster (the city's first Czech burgomaster), whose acknowledged ability to raise himself above partisan differences led to his election, for periods of time, to the presidency of the parliament.[15] Another Czech deputy, Alois Pravoslav Trojan, was one of the originators of the assembly of March 11. The leading lights and the majority of Czech delegates were politically liberal, in the nineteenth-century meaning of the term; they believed in constitutional principles in politics and in laissez-faire principles in economics. The Czech delegation contained few radicals, and none of a caliber equal to that of the leading liberals. The best-known radical deputy was František Havlíček, but his contribution in Vienna was modest.

The parliament opened on July 22, and on July 26, Hans Kudlich, a German from Silesia and the youngest deputy, tabled the well-

13. For example, see *Verhandlungen des österreichischen Reichstages nach der stenographischen Aufnahme* (Vienna, 1848-49), II, 262.
14. See his statement in *NN*, December 14, 1848.
15. Springer, *Geschichte Österreichs*, II, 405.

known resolution calling for the abolition of the subject status of the peasantry.[16] Brauner had probably been the first in Austria to put forward such a demand since the March Days, in his draft of the petition presented to the assembly at St. Václav's Baths, but, as mentioned above, his imprisonment after the June Uprising delayed his departure for Vienna until after the discussion of the peasant question began. As a result, it is Kudlich's name, rather than Brauner's, that has since become associated with this important measure. With Kudlich's proposal, the debate concerning the whole question of serfdom was opened. No deputy, of course, questioned the principle of the final emancipation of the peasantry. But this emancipation also entailed the cessation of *robot* duties and other obligations and payments to the lord, in money or in kind, and the acquisition by the peasant of the right of ownership, unencumbered by any feudal restrictions, to the land he cultivated. Some deputies therefore insisted that for such duties and obligations as had not resulted from the peasant's subject status the lord should receive some compensation.

In the next weeks, the term "compensation" became something of a shibboleth identifying the partisans in a violent controversy that unfolded: depending on one's point of view, the cry was "abolition for compensation" or "abolition without compensation." Those opposing compensation in any form were radicals, no matter what their nationality; those favoring compensation, albeit a moderate one, were conservatives and liberals. The controversy sent its echoes throughout all of Cisleithania, including the Czech Lands. The leading liberal Czech deputies, Palacký, Rieger, Karel Havlíček, and Brauner, supported the idea of compensation, and their view was disseminated through the liberals' unofficial organ, *Národní Noviny*. Opposed to compensation were the radicals, their chief voice being the *Pražský Večerní List*. In the Czech parliamentary group in Vienna, the majority, being of liberal stamp, favored compensation.

The leading spokesman of the Czech group was Brauner, who delivered the main speech from the Czech side on August 23, 1848, during the deliberations of the peasant question. Faithful to the principle he had advocated in his published works, he supported the idea of compensation, buttressing his plea with the oft-repeated argument that to deny compensation merely because one did not like the surviving relics of feudalism would constitute an illegal violation

16. *Verhandlungen,* I, 159.

of the rights of property.[17] The views of Brauner and like-minded deputies paralleled the views of the imperial court and the central government, and, of course, of the nobility. Earlier, on August 14, Trojan had made another speech in the same vein. After prefacing his speech with the remark that by origin he was of the peasant class and that "for that reason my sympathies are with the oppressed subject population," Trojan proceeded to argue in favor of compensation. With infinite skill, he invested compensation with an aura of honor and heroism, and made it appear an act of sacrifice that no Czech would shrink from undertaking for the sake of the preservation of liberty. Refusing compensation would be an act of injustice and would begin to sap the life from the free institutions that had been won with so much effort. "Let us guard our freedom!" Trojan cried. "Great sacrifices in property and blood are being made; no shadow of a wrong must darken the honor and the fame of our common fatherland." "The world should know," he said, that "we Czechs do not shun sacrifices when it comes to achieving liberty."[18] Trojan's speech seemed to imply that the Czech peasants were *en masse* in favor of compensation. For this presumption the Czech radical organ took Trojan to task, stating that the nation "would certainly in large majority vote that no compensation be given for the centuries-old oppression of the peasants by the lords."[19] Neither Trojan nor Brauner nor the majority of Czech deputies were even willing to accept a compromise solution under which compensation would be given but would be paid by the state rather than directly by the peasant. The compromise was favored by the young and personable Bohemian deputy Karel Klaudy, a German by origin who had become a Czech by choice.[20] It is to be noted that the imperial court and the government stood firmly behind compensation (not to be paid by the state); this was made absolutely clear by a government spokesman on August 26.[21]

The opponents of compensation argued, not without plausibility, that the abolition of these last vestiges of serfdom did no more than redress the injustice of centuries and that this injustice should not now be sanctified by rewarding its perpetrators with compensation.

17. *Verhandlungen*, II, 4-8.
18. *Ibid.*, I, 533-37.
19. *PVL*, August 18, 1848.
20. V. Klimeš, *Česká vesnice v roce 1848* (Most, 1949), p. 371.
21. By Minister Bach (*Verhandlungen*, II, 84).

One of the most impassioned pleas in support of this view came from the Ukrainian-Galician peasant deputy Ivan Kapuszczak, who related how, in his province, a peasant was always obliged to remove his hat three hundred steps from the residence of the noble, and how he was not permitted to enter the noble's residence because he "stunk" and because he was dirty. "For such mistreatment," he asked, "we should now give compensation?"[22] He might have said too that for centuries it was the peasant, in his impoverished condition, not the noble, who had to bear the brunt of taxation; until the eighteenth century, the nobles were subjected only to certain extraordinary taxes, but not to regular ones. In view of past inequities and injustices, it might have been more logical for the noble to pay compensation to the peasant rather than vice versa. From the Czech side, a strong speech favoring the peasant was made by the Roman Catholic priest Jan Sidon, a high-school teacher of religion by profession. Though a believing Catholic, Sidon took a radical stand on several issues, and, having the courage of his convictions, he voted against compensation in the final vote. Earlier, in a speech of August 24, he combined his espousal of the cause of the peasant with a warning of the return of the reaction. He pointed out how in Bohemia the June Uprising had already begun to stiffen the back of the reaction, and how since the uprising landlords and officials were again beginning to exact from the peasants payments and duties they had not dared exact before.[23]

The question finally came to a vote on August 31. "Moderate compensation" received the endorsement of the majority, with 174 deputies for, 144 against, and 36 abstaining.[24] Of the total of 78 deputies in the parliament who could be identified as Czech-speaking, 53 voted for compensation, 14 were against it, and 11 abstained.[25] Among those voting for compensation were most of the leaders of the Czech national movement, including Palacký, Havlíček, Rieger, and Trojan. Curiously, Brauner abstained; perhaps he felt that his renown as the defender and friend of peasants rendered it impossible for him, when the chips were down, to cast his ballot, in a publicly recorded vote, for compensation—a vote that could be regarded as

22. *Ibid.*, I, 586.
23. *Ibid.*, II, 48.
24. For a complete list of names of deputies, grouped according to their vote, see *ibid.*, II, 163-64.
25. Klimeš, *Česká vesnice*, p. 384.

being against the best interest of the peasants. It was one thing to argue in favor of compensation in a learned treatise or even a sophisticated speech on the floor of the parliament. It was quite another for such a friend of the peasants to maintain his stance, in full view of the public, when the issue had passed from the realm of academic discussion into one of political action—or, to put it more bluntly, when the issue had descended to a bread-and-butter level where even the most unsophisticated peasant would be able to read the meaning of his vote. It is most probable that in a voting by balls (the form of voting sometimes employed in the parliament), he would have had his vote follow his heart and cast a ballot in favor of compensation. It was a remarkable display of inconsistency for Brauner not to honor the principle upon which he had expatiated only a week earlier in the parliament. With his abstention Brauner placed himself in a category comprising the majority of the deputies from Bohemia and Moravia, both Czech and German. Of the total of thirty-six abstentions, fully two-thirds (twenty-four) were from Czech and German deputies from Bohemia and Moravia (of these, eleven, as noted, were from Czechs). Whatever their reasons, the Bohemian and Moravian deputies made themselves conspicuous as the largest group that declined to take a stand—a performance that occasioned caustic comment at the time.[26]

What induced the Czech deputies to vote for compensation? One reason for their stand was their rigid legalistic outlook, instilled into them doubtless by the presence of a large number of lawyers in their midst. The law degree, or at least some legal training, was a requirement for many posts in the bureaucracy—a situation that prevailed throughout all of Central Europe until the present century. The Czech national movement, and indeed the whole liberal movement in Central Europe in 1848, was top-heavy with lawyers. The lawyers' legal "bias" made it easy for Czech leaders to convince themselves that the vote for compensation was a vote for the preservation of law. This was curious reasoning. Ever since the March Days, Czech liberals had been decrying, in all sincerity, the absolutism, corruption, and injustices of the pre-March regime; nevertheless, they now chose to regard the most oppressive institution of absolutism, peasant servitude, in some of its parts, as being rooted in the rule of law, and on the strength of this, were prepared to saddle the peasant with financial

26. Springer, *Geschichte Österreichs,* II, 426.

obligations for years. This was the reasoning of the right and center as a whole, and its deputies were only too prone to hurl the epithet "Communist" at those who regarded it as absurd that the peasant should be required to pay for his own emancipation.[27]

The Czech historian Josef Koči has suggested another reason for the Czech attitude. Koči points out that in 1848 a number of cities were landowning corporations, and that in addition a number of estates were individually owned by members of the middle class. It is estimated that more than two-hundred thousand peasants had "middle class" landlords. In all such cases, the burghers—and most deputies were recruited from this class—stood to gain, individually or collectively, from compensation, and this could not have been without influence upon their vote in the parliament.[28]

Still another factor was the fact that the government made the issue of compensation into one of the survival of the government. As noted above, the Czechs had committed themselves to a support of this government, and to vote for compensation was to fulfill their part of the bargain. In this connection however, it should be observed that belief in compensation was part of their basic laissez-faire, liberal philosophy and their vote reflected that philosophy. Brauner, the pace-setter, had advocated compensation in a pamphlet written before the parliament opened.[29] But if their own predilections counseled voting for compensation, their determination to support the government made it a foregone conclusion that they would lend a hand to the government on this issue.

Finally, the question of compensation, like so many others, was influenced by the national issue: by the antagonism between the Czechs and other Slavs of the right and the German left. The left was emphatic in its opposition to compensation, which automatically influenced the Czechs to vote for the opposite point of view. In fact, in the final vote, among the 174 deputies voting for compensation, the Slavs predominated, whereas among the 144 voting against it, the Germans predominated.

Inasmuch as the Czech deputy Trojan implied that the peasants, at least Czech peasants, would support the idea of compensation, it

27. See the speech by Polish deputy Popiel, who ridiculed the charges of communism (*Verhandlungen*, I, 546).

28. J. Koči, "Příspěvek k rolnické otázce v Čechách v r. 1848," *ČSČH*, V (1957), 250-51.

29. F. A. Brauner, *Von der Robot und deren Ablösung* (Prague, 1848).

is pertinent to ask how the peasant deputies in the parliament voted. Here the answer is quite unequivocal: they were opposed to it. In the crucial vote of August 31, a large majority of the peasant deputies voted against compensation. This group included eleven of the fifteen peasant deputies (Czech and German) from Bohemia and Moravia (with Silesia); of the remaining four, three abstained and only one voted in favor of the measure. More significantly, of the thirty Galician peasant deputies actually taking part in the vote, every single one voted against compensation; there was not one abstention.[30] The attitude of the Galician peasants is of particular moment since they constituted the largest peasant block in the parliament. This suggests that the Czech deputies, insofar as they represented peasant communities, as most of them did, and insofar as they did not vote for compensation, as most of them did not, failed to represent the wishes of their constituents. It may be added that the provision regarding compensation was part of a bill by which the last vestiges of serfdom were wiped out. The bill was given final approval on September 7, then promulgated into law by the emperor on the same date. This was the historic "abolition of serfdom," the most memorable achievement of the parliament.

The final stages of approval of the Law of September 7 thrust forward another question on which the deputies had to take a stand: the question of imperial sanction. This was an important question of principle. Should the laws duly approved by the parliament acquire validity only by imperial sanction? At stake here was not merely a matter of form, of the emperor's signature automatically affixed to a bill in order to invest it formally with the force of law, but a matter of substance: Were the laws of the land basically the expression of the will of the people, as voiced through the parliament? Or were they a joint product of popular and imperial will? The question was further complicated by the fact that this was a constituent parliament; if the constitution it was to draw up was to be made dependent on imperial approval, then the sovereignty of the people would be seriously restricted, and once again their liberties would be a matter not of their inherent right but of imperial grace bestowed upon them. Of course, denying imperial sanction was tantamount to saying that imperial will and sovereignty enjoyed no existence independent of popular will—a view totally repugnant to the court. It was Minister Bach

30. *Verhandlungen* II, 163-64.

who injected this issue into the proceedings on September 2 in the form of a tactless reaffirmation of imperial will that offended the deputies of the German left.[31]

A controversy ensued which cost the parliament many precious days. Both sides accepted the principle of the imperial sanction in some form, since not to do so would have smacked of rank republicanism. But the left tended to ascribe to it only formal importance, whereas the right and the center wished to give it more substance. Among the Czechs, Rieger and Trojan took part in the debate, basically supporting the government.[32] The only Czech to speak against the government was a Moravian, Josef Demel, who was close to the German left and not strongly identified with the Czech national movement; Czech opinion labeled him a "colorless" Slav.[33] In the final vote, the side of the government was favored by a vote of 183 to 119,[34] with the majority of Czechs once again boosting the government, in the colorful company of the Galician peasants. At the time, the issue may not have appeared to many deputies as being of vital importance, but in retrospect, Minister Bach's statement of September 2 may be viewed as the voice of an emboldened conservatism, its self-confidence reinforced by Windischgrätz' victory over Prague.

As the parliamentary meetings continued, the chasm between the Slavic right and the German left widened, partisan passions mounted, and the prospect of a political explosion grew. Eventually the explosion took place in the form of the Viennese revolution. Like all revolutions, it was the product of a multitude of forces and influences, external and internal, fundamental and immediate, social and political. In this instance, a major factor that helped trigger the revolution was the parliamentary conflict between the Slavic right and the German left. And as if this ethnic conflict were not enough, the situation was rendered more serious by the intrusion of yet another nationality upon the political scene: the Magyars. No rational observer can reduce the outbreak of the Viennese revolution to the conflict between Slavs and Germans. On the other hand, no rational observer can deny the important role played in the origin of this holocaust by the ever-

31. *Verhandlungen,* II, 212.
32. This was on September 6. Rieger's and Trojan's speeches in *Verhandlungen,* II, 260, 269 respectively.
33. *NN,* July 27, 1848.
34. *Verhandlungen,* II, 277.

sharpening differences between the national interests and prejudices of the two groups.

The relationship between the central government and the Magyars had been deteriorating rapidly. The government and the court had never reconciled themselves to the concessions exacted from them by the Magyars since the onset of the revolution in March. Hungary, which had succeeded in attaining a high degree of self-government, displayed an alarming and arrogant tendency to demand further concessions. For several months, the government, too preoccupied with a multitude of crises at home and abroad, could offer no resistance to this trend. However, in the late summer of 1848 the situation was changing. Everywhere the forces of reaction, or at least conservatism, were beginning to stage a comeback. Abroad, the June insurrection in Paris, which brought about the most fearful massacre Europe experienced in 1848, had been crushed. At home, in a more modest version of what happened in Paris, His Majesty's staunch grenadiers had bombarded Prague into submission during the June Uprising. On the Italian front, after a discouraging series of setbacks and stalemates, the imperial armies at last celebrated a great victory at Custozza on July 25, which heralded the reversal of Austria's fortune. Conservatism was more resilient than its enemies had given it credit for. Viewing the balance sheet, the government resolved that the time had come to deal firmly with the recalcitrant Magyars, to teach them a lesson in humility, and to reforge the links between Pest and Vienna that the Magyar separatists had all but destroyed. With the emperor's acquiescence, a Croatian army under Ban Jelačić crossed the river Drava on September 11, invading Hungary and signaling the beginning of an open war between Hungary and its nationalities. This catastrophy brought down the Hungarian cabinet of Batthyány and propelled Lajos Kossuth into the forefront of events in the Lands of St. Stephen. As disaster loomed, Magyar leaders resorted to an unusual gesture to bolster their cause: they had failed to move an emperor; now they decided to try to move his subjects. A delegation was dispatched to Vienna, but instead of knocking humbly at the gate of the Imperial Palace, it brought its case to the Imperial Parliament.[35]

In seeking to uphold and defend Hungary's autonomy and terri-

35. R. J. Rath, *The Viennese Revolution of 1848* (Austin, Tex., 1957), pp. 318 ff.

torial integrity, the Magyar government was in a vulnerable position. Hungary was a house of nationalities; to the non-Magyars, however, it was a house but not a home. The Magyars were the rulers; the non-Magyars (Croats, Slovaks, Serbs, Rumanians), the ruled.[36] Since the March Days, the non-Magyar leaders had pressed the Magyars for measures that would lift their peoples out of the humiliation of a second-class existence. They had high hopes, but after a very brief initial honeymoon period, they found their demands rebuffed, their expectations thwarted, their sensitivities jarred. Gradually, as their prospects dimmed beyond hope and their patience was exhausted beyond endurance, they drifted into open defiance and opposition. As it became clear that their enemy, the Magyars, was also the enemy of the imperial government, they entered into an informal partnership with the latter, based on that most strongly binding of ties: hatred of a common foe. As a result, at the most critical juncture in their fortunes in 1848, the Magyars discovered that not only could they not count on the support of the subject nationalities (or rather on the politically conscious segment thereof), but that these nationalities had taken refuge in an enemy camp. They would have to fight a war within a war.

Snubbed by the court, and left friendless at home, the Magyars, who had begun to cast about for allies, now looked to the deputies of the left in the Imperial Parliament. The prospects seemed reasonable enough. The left was German par excellence, endowed by an aversion to the Slavs that fully matched that of the Magyars. As for the Poles on the left, their "Slavicity" could, in this instance, be conveniently overlooked, by others as well as by themselves; they were quite simply Poles rather than Slavs. Besides, a peculiar tie of friendship had developed between the Magyars and Poles which characterized their relationship in the decades to come.

The Magyar delegation consisted of twelve members of the Hungarian Parliament and was accompanied by four magnates. Arriving in the imperial capital on September 18, the delegation formally requested leave to enter the parliamentary chamber and address the deputies. To grant such a request would have been a violation of parliamentary rules, as adopted by the parliament at the beginning of the session. It was therefore suggested that the rules be set aside

36. Naturally, the position of the subject nationalities differed. The Croats enjoyed a degree of autonomy.

temporarily, since the situation was one of special urgency. The resulting debate turned upon this question of procedure—whether the rules should be set aside or not—and it left its mark as one of the most bitter and impassioned in the life of the Viennese parliament in 1848-49.

By their stand on this issue and by their vote, the Czechs cut more deeply and more fatefully into the mainstream of political life in Austria in 1848 than on any other occasion. The debate developed into a breath-taking spectacle and trial of strength between the right and the left, the former opposing, the latter favoring, the Magyars. For the right, there were many speakers, including several Czechs, the most eloquent of whom was Rieger. The most eloquent speaker for the left was the German Ludwig Löhner. Rieger and Löhner were the most compelling orators in the chamber, and both were prototypes of the professional groups that were so influential in political life at the time: Rieger was a lawyer, and Löhner a physician. Paradoxically, both represented constituencies from the same province: Bohemia. Both could be regarded as exemplifying the most intense national feelings of their respective ethnic groups. Rieger, unsparing in his exposure of the Germans' arrogance, and mordant in the flailing of their follies, radiated an alert, flamboyant, and belligerent Czech nationalism. Löhner was the parliamentary leader of the German liberals; consumed by an almost pathological hatred of the Slavs (as many Germans themselves recognized),[37] he was filled with an abiding sense of a German mission and in almost every respect concerning nationality stood zealously for those principles which Rieger, with a matching zeal, opposed.

Although the results of the debate were destined to be of decisive importance for the future course of the Habsburg Monarchy, the debate actually lasted only one day (September 19). The galleries were packed from the early morning; as one correspondent reported ruefully, "I came, I saw, I conquered—no seat." A lady reporter was accosted by total strangers on the street, who offered her money for her precious pass to the building.[38] The Czech Strobach presided over the fateful assembly. As far as the Czechs and other Slavs (a segment of Poles always excepted) were concerned, they saw in the Magyars the incorrigible oppressors of their Slavic breth-

37. Springer, no friend of the Slavs in his later days, taxes Löhner with "a blind hatred of the Slavs" (*Geschichte Österreichs*, II, 407).

38. *Bohemia*, September 22, 1848.

ren and the dangerous separatists who were threatening to spring
the bonds holding together the peoples of the monarchy, thereby
completely destroying the foundation of Austro-Slavism, upon which
their policy was predicted. Indeed, the Slavs were here given the
unique opportunity of facing simultaneously their two chief antago-
nists: the Magyars and the German nationalists. It was an irresistible
opportunity, summoning as it did the vision of all the humiliations
and the abuse the Slavs had suffered at the hands of the Magyars in
Hungary and were suffering at the hands of the German radicals in
Vienna. There were of course other reasons, depending on one's
political outlook, for opposing the Magyars. By their separatist policy
the Magyars, abetted by the German left, seemed to symbolize the
supreme challenge to the integrity and the hallowed traditions of the
monarchy; they seemed the quintessence of revolution. This revolutionary halo about the Magyars is what so fascinated the German left;
but the common hatred of the Slavs was stronger than the Germans'
fascination. The revolutionary aura, however, repelled the conservative center and the moderate Germans, who ranged themselves, on
this issue, on the side of the Slavic bloc. The duel on September 19
thus meant different things to different people. Some deputies saw
it as a struggle between conservatism and radicalism, or at its most
extreme form, between reaction and revolution. Others viewed it
primarily as a conflict between the Slavs and the Slavs' oppressors.
For others still it was a mixture of both.

Within that one day, all the leading Czech deputies took the
floor, in addition to Rieger, and most of them unburdened themselves
of their long-felt resentments against the Magyars in speeches of considerable length. Again and again, they charged the Magyars with
national egotism and with a total disregard for the rights of their
subject nationalities. Repeatedly they pointed out, with justice, that
the Magyar delegation spoke only for the Magyars, that it contained
not a single representative of the non-Magyar groups, which constituted half of Hungary's population. And they decried the fact that
even as the Magyars were pleading for the parliament's sympathy,
they gave no indication that they intended to treat the subject nationalities as their equals. "Why did the [Magyar] delegates come?"
cried Rieger. "Did they come in order to declare that they will again
repair the bond of brotherhood which they had broken? No, they did
not. Did they come in order to declare they want to send delegates to
this common parliament of the monarchy? No, they did not. Did

they come to give us an assurance that they will render justice to all the peoples of Hungary, to Germans and Slavs, who have thus far been . . . by the Magyars most terribly oppressed? Did they come in order to declare before this house that these peoples will from now on enjoy a complete equality? No, they did not."[39] It was clever of Rieger to stress the fact that in Hungary the German minority (notably in the district of Spiš or Zips in the present-day north Slovak region of Czechoslovakia) was affected by the Magyar nationality policy as much as the Slavs; indeed the German deputies realized this and some of them criticized the Magyars for it.

Another Czech deputy set out to refute the odious comparisons that were being made by German radicals between the Czechs' alleged reactionism and the Magyars' progressivism. "Do you believe," he asked, "that in Hungary there exists a democratic monarchy, a democratic system, a democratic freedom? I must own that if this is democratic freedom then I want no part of it; in Hungary there is nothing more nor less than an enslavement by an aristocracy."[40]

The case for the Magyars was presented by Löhner. With complete sincerity, he declared, "I swear to you, gentlemen, that I have forgotten in this moment to which nationality I belong, and that I feel and think solely and only as a member of Parliament." His subsequent address bore out his promise. He conceded the faults and mistakes of the Magyars. There were no condescending remarks about a German mission, no slighting references to the Slavs' backwardness. There was instead a genuine anxiety over the growing intervention of the military in the affairs of the monarchy, and over the menacing shadow the generals and their hosts were again casting over the lives and freedoms of the people. To Löhner Jelačić's invasion of Hungary at the head of Croatian troops meant new interventions and new dangers, not merely for the Magyars, but for all the peoples. To him, Jelačić was not only a Croat, but also an imperial "field marshal"; and Löhner did not know, he said, what responsible minister countersigned the credentials conferring on him the right to invade another people's territory. He added that under pre-March absolutism when "the oppressed peoples were united only in the privilege of mute obedience," only the Magyar nation had lit the path "with a modest light of the constitution."[41] Löhner spoke

39. *Verhandlungen*, II, 472.
40. *Ibid.*, p. 496.
41. *Ibid.*, pp. 482-83.

entirely without sarcasm. Though the speech rang with a burning conviction, its passion was muffled and its ardor controlled, lending it the quality of a "dark glow."[42] It was the best speech of the debate and the best performance of Löhner's parliamentary career.

The eloquence of the Slavs' deadliest enemy could not dispel their deepest suspicions. No amount of persuasion, even from a source less stamped with anti-Slavism, could convince them of the need to listen to a Magyar delegation. A considerable number of Germans shared the Slavs' feelings. After what was probably the most exhausting day the deputies had ever undergone, a roll-call vote was taken at eight o'clock that evening. The Magyars' request was rejected by a safe majority of 186 to 108,[43] a much larger majority than had obtained for the question of compensation during the debates concerning serfdom. Significantly, only one deputy abstained this time. Evidently the deputies had more definite convictions on this issue and were less disposed toward compromise. Of the Bohemian deputies taking part in the vote, only ten voted in favor of the Magyars, but this time there was not a single Czech among them; the majority of German deputies from Bohemia ranged themselves on the side of the Czechs.

The vote was the greatest triumph the Czechs ever scored in the Imperial Parliament. This fact was not lost upon the Viennese radicals; it was on this occasion, more than any before or since, that the voices of the radicals, who had cast aside their few remaining inhibitions, rose to a shrill crescendo of abuse, the target of which was the Czech deputies. More than ever before, the Czechs (and other Slavs) became the lackeys of absolutism, the enemies of liberty, the very incarnation of reaction.[44] At home, the Czech radicals did not, of course, take the same view as the Viennese radicals. There were apparently some radical voices who were not pleased with the flat rejection of the Magyars,[45] but in an editorial, the leading radical

42. Springer's comment in *CBB*, Supplement to No. 72, September 22, 1848.

43. *Verhandlungen*, II, 523-24. A Croatian deputation arrived in Vienna in July, 1848, hoping to receive a hearing in the parliament, but it was not admitted. The case was not entirely identical with that of the Magyars, but it strengthened the arguments of those opposing the Magyar request. See J. Šidak, "Poslanstvo hrvatskog sabora austrijskom parlamentu g. 1848," *Radova Filozofskog fakulteta u Zagrebu, Odsjek za povijest*, III (1960), 9 ff.

44. See Havlíček's complaint after the vote in *NN*, September 29, 1848.

45. This emerges from the above article by Havlíček, who complains of

organ in Prague expressed complete agreement with the action of the parliament, adding that the Magyar nation "must be humbled and brought into line with the other nations."[46] Yet it is significant that even while flatly condemning the Magyars, the same editorial voiced uneasiness over the character of Jelečić, noting that some regard him as an instrument of reaction, others as a savior of Slavdom: "It is probable that never have so many terrible doubts existed about a historical figure as about him." The majority of radicals at home accepted the anti-Magyar vote, although with less wholehearted enthusiasm and more mental reservations than the liberal Czech leadership.

In recent years, the conduct of the Czech deputies on September 19 has invited the strictures of some Czech and Slovak historians that are reminiscent of the criticism expressed by the Viennese radicals in 1848. Again the Czech deputies have been accused of having opposed the forces of progress and abetted the forces of reaction.[47] But for any such strictures to carry weight, one must first probe the alternatives open to the Czech deputies and take an appraising look at the Magyar leadership as a force of reaction or progress.

In fact, such an appraisal will reveal that the issue was far from one of reaction versus progress, justice versus inequity, black versus white. The Magyar governing class was both a liberating and an oppressive force. Before 1848, the Magyar nobility, and particularly the gentry, had established an impressive record of challenging absolutism at a time when other nations still slumbered. After 1848, these classes promoted, to a considerable extent, the forces of progress by their continuing challenge of the court and of the central government. However, they helped progress without being themselves progressive; they worked against reaction while being more than lightly tinged with reaction. The supporters of the Hungarian national movement belonged to a gentry that had not effected a complete break with the feudal past. At a time when the Austrian Parliament had only one chamber the Hungarian Parliament still sported the luxury of an upper chamber of magnates. At a time when the nobility in Cisleithania had been shorn of most of its powers its majesty still glittered in Hungary. At a time when the Austrian Parliament

---

some "thoughtless and inexperienced" men "in our midst" who had "not seen through Magyar-German cleverness."

46. *PVL,* September 23, 1848.

47. *Přehled československých dějin* (Prague, 1960), II/1, 69.

was elected on the basis of a liberal suffrage the electoral regulation for the Hungarian Parliament, with its multitude of restrictions, read like a law against rather than about the right to vote.[48] At a time when in Cisleithania serfdom was abolished completely the corresponding law in Hungary left hundreds of thousands of peasants outside its pale.[49] The treatment of non-Magyar nationalities could hardly be called progressive, and is a fact too well-known to require comment. What is less well-known is that many of the leaders of the subject nationalities were politically and socially more progressive than the Magyar leaders, and advocated a more liberal emancipation of the peasantry.[50]

Against this background could the Czech deputies be accused of having opposed the forces of freedom? Could they, in good conscience,

48. Excerpts in *NNM,* II (1962), 364.

49. They were the nonurbarial peasants. See J. Varga, *Typen und Probleme des bäuerlichen Grundbesitzes in Ungarn, 1767-1849* ("Studia Historica 56" [Budapest, 1965]), pp. 137-38.

50. For example, the program issued by Slovak national leaders on May 10-11, 1848, calls for the emancipation of nonurbarial peasants (*NNM,* II, 282, Article 11). Similarly, a Rumanian Assembly in Blaj (Bálazsfalve) approved a program (on May 16, 1848, by Orthodox Calendar May 4, 1848) demanding emancipation without compensation (C. Daicoviciu and M. Constantinescu [eds.], *Brève histoire de la Transylvanie* [Bucharest, 1965], p. 212).

The one feature of the Hungarian emancipation legislation that was more liberal than the one passed by the Imperial Parliament in Vienna was that it provided for compensation to be paid by the state rather than by the peasant directly. In September, 1848, when the situation between Hungary and the imperial government was reaching a crisis point, the Hungarian cabinet prepared a bill to deal with nonurbarial lands, but the war intervened and nothing came of it. Similarly, in mid-1849, with Hungary already on the verge of defeat, the Hungarian cabinet enacted a law to improve the position of non-Magyar nationalities, but it was obviously too late.

For the Hungarian appraisal of the Hungarian Revolution and its implications for the non-Magyar nationalities, see J. Revai, *Marks i vengerskaia revoliutsiia 1848-1849 gg.* ("Studia Historica Academiae Scientiarum Hungaricae 1" [Budapest, 1951]); Z. I. Tóth, *Koshut i natsionalnyi vopros v 1848-1849 gg.* ("Studia Historica Academiae Scientiarum Hungaricae 8" [Budapest, 1954]); and Z. I. Tóth, "The Nationality Problem in Hungary in 1848-49," *Acta Historica,* IV (1955), 235-77.

For the point of view of the non-Magyar nationalities, see D. Rapant, "Štúr a štúrovci v službe národa a pokroku," *Slovenská Literatúra,* XII (1965), 437-57; J. Mésároš, "K niektorým otázkám hodnotenia L'udovíta Štúra," *Slovenská Literatúra,* XII (1965), 458-65; and W. Felczak, "Vplyv národnostnej otázky na spoločenský charakter maďarskej revolúcie r. 1848," *HČ,* XIV (1966), 85-99.

have voted in favor of those who had shown nothing but contempt for Slovak national aspirations and persecuted Slovak leaders, forcing them to leave their homeland? Should they have jeopardized, with their vote, their good relations with the Croats, whom they valued as allies in their struggle for the emancipation of the Slavs of the Habsburg Monarchy? It may also be observed that by the end of September, 1848, the Czechs had reason to fear that the Magyars would separate themselves completely from the monarchy. Were that to happen, the Slovaks, the Croats, and the Serbs would be left wholly at the mercy of the national egotism of the Magyar leadership, and the Czechs would be pushed perilously close to the precipice of incorporation into Germany. The fate of the Slovaks in Hungary after 1867 and of the Poles in Germany after 1871 bear out the fears of the Czech deputies concerning what the Slavs could expect in 1848 in an independent Hungary and unified Germany. It confirms their wisdom in not inviting the risk of national extinction by condoning Magyar separatism and its ally, the nationalism of the German radicals.

It may, of course, be conceded that by their vote the Czechs strengthened the reaction. But it must also be acknowledged that under the circumstances and on the evidence available to them at the time, they had no other choice but to vote as they did. A resurgent reaction was in September, 1848, only a possibility. By contrast, Magyar oppression of the Slovaks was a stark reality, and Magyar separatism, with all its consequences, too dire to contemplate, was a stronger possibility than that of the reaction. Moreover, the still partially feudal character of the Magyar governing class made it plausible to believe that, in a fundamental sense, voting for the Magyars meant also voting for reaction, at least in Hungary. The history of Hungary in the next hundred years confirms that belief; the regime in Transleithania (Hungary), both in the social, political, and national sense, was to be far more reactionary than that in Cisleithania; and even after the collapse of the Habsburg Monarchy, Hungary was unique among European states in preserving much of its feudal legacy well into the twentieth century. In view of the choices that lay before them in 1848 and in view of what has happened since then, it is difficult to fault the Czech deputies for voting as they did on that fateful day of September 19.

With regard to social and political policies, the constellation of forces as it crystallized in the vote of September 19 was a singularly illogical one. The Magyar gentry class was befriended and supported

by radicals who pursued in Vienna social and political policies their
Magyar allies would never have permitted them to pursue in Pest.
Conversely, the Czechs were in their domestic policies a good deal
closer to the German left than the latter was to the Magyar gentry.
But social and political considerations were outweighed by national
prejudices, which drew the German left and the Magyar gentry together through their common dislike of the Slavs and made it
difficult for the German left and the Czech liberals to have a meeting
of minds. It is true that the Viennese radicals were also attracted to
the Magyar gentry by the latter's radical challenge to the Habsburg
regime; nevertheless, it is most unlikely that without the common
hatred of the Slavs, this strange German-radical–Magyar-gentry alliance would have come into being.

The rebuff of the Magyars was a humiliating defeat for the
Viennese radicals. Stepping up their agitation against the Czechs,[51]
and mainly, of course, against the government, they found ready listeners among students and particularly among workers. Unemployment
continued to be an oppressive problem; a number of unemployed
workers found employment in public works, but this again caused a
drain on the treasury, and on August 18 the government ordered a
cut in their wages. As the Magyar issue loomed ever larger, the
proletariat, angered by the vote of September 19, was in ferment and
ready to follow the radicals. After the vote, events followed one
another in quick succession toward the final catastrophe. On September 28, Count Lemberg, who had just been appointed Imperial
Commissioner in Hungary was murdered by a street mob in Pest.
The imperial government responded on October 3 with a decree dissolving the Hungarian Parliament and declaring all its decisions null
and void, and on October 4 with a declaration of martial law over
"entire Hungary." Simultaneously, all military forces in the Lands of
the Hungarian Crown had been placed under the command of the
Croatian Ban Jelačić.[52] This meant open war between Austria and
Hungary.

The spectacle of a Slavic general entrusted with the job of crushing their Magyar allies threw the German radicals into an unparalleled
paroxysm of fury. Their chief target was Count Latour, the Minister
of War. The latter ordered some of the troops stationed in Vienna to

51. *CBB,* Supplement to No. 92, October 16, 1848.
52. *NN,* October 7, 1848.

proceed against Hungary. One of the battalions, the Richter battalion of grenadiers, made up of Germans, showed signs of disaffection. This led to an outbreak of street violence during the course of which a group of proletarians, their emotions for days whipped up by the radicals, lynched and murdered Latour, then hung his already lifeless body on a lamppost and mutilated it (October 6). A physician later counted forty-three wounds and lacerations on Latour's body.[53] On the following day, October 7, a Saturday, Emperor Ferdinand, with his entourage, fled Vienna and took refuge in the Moravian city of Olomouc (Olmütz). At the same time, thousands of Viennese started leaving the city. This was the beginning of the October revolution.

In Prague, the first indication of trouble was the unusual delay in the arrival of the afternoon train on Saturday. Though due at 3:45 p.m., the train did not pull into Prague station until 5:30 p.m., and it failed to bring the standard load of mail and newspapers from the imperial capital. The news was supplied by the passengers, who told of a new revolutionary wave sweeping Vienna. At first, this might have been regarded as one more of the flurries of violence that seemed to rock the capital periodically, but the next report made it clear that the trouble was really serious: the next train arrived late at night, at 3:00 a.m., and its passengers brought the first shocking news about the murder of Minister Latour. The report caused a Prague newspaper to observe ominously: "We stand on the threshold of 1791."[54]

Prague was now holding its breath, uncertain of the future, and concerned about the fate of the Czech deputies, who were known to be a thorn in the flesh of the Viennese radicals. Masses of people, hungry for the latest news, besieged the trains arriving from Vienna. On Sunday, the first Bohemian deputies arrived. The next day Havlíček, Rieger, and more deputies returned. In a short time, most of the Czech deputies had left Vienna. They had incurred the special wrath of the radicals because of their opposition to the Magyars, and some felt their lives endangered. Certainly, the murder of Latour, which even the radical leaders, with their influence over the proletarians, had failed to prevent, although they had tried to do so, made it appear that the lives of those unpopular with the rebels were in jeopardy. There is no doubt that the threat to Rieger and one or two other deputies was real.[55] To the radicals and to their proletarian and student

53. Rath, *The Viennese Revolution,* pp. 323, 329.
54. This account is based on a report in *Bohemia,* October 3, 1848.
55. Brauner stated at the meeting of the Slavic Linden on October 12 that

followers, Rieger was a symbol of all that they hated; he had already been publicly insulted and threatened on the street in Vienna on July 18, a few days after his arrival for the opening of the parliament.[56] Since then radical propaganda had made him one of its favorite targets, and his continued presence in the imperial capital after the outbreak of the October revolution would have been risky.

Vienna's tragedy brought at least one immediate benefit to Prague. General Windischgrätz, whom no amount of pressure or persuasion could previously dislodge, now speedily came to the conclusion that Prague could do without him. The prospect of turning his guns on the Viennese rebels was too much for him to resist. On October 11, the general issued a parting proclamation to the people of Prague that "anarchy and its terrible consequences," which were "developing in Vienna" were imposing on him a "sacred duty" to depart from Prague with his troops in order to protect the person of the sovereign and the "unity of the constitutional [*sic!*] monarchy."[57] Prague was at last rid of Windischgrätz, but the price at which his removal was achieved was heavy, as the future was to show. The general's posture as a defender of the "constitutional monarchy" was deceiving; a constitution was more likely to be smothered than saved by the embrace of such a defender.

In Vienna, the Imperial Parliament continued to function. On the day of Latour's murder, a number of deputies gathered in the late afternoon hours, declared the parliament "permanent," chose a new president (the Pole, Franciszek Smolka), and asked the emperor to dismiss certain unpopular ministers and form a new cabinet that would have the confidence of the people. While the meeting was in progress, armed demonstrators crowded the galleries normally reserved for spectators. With frequent interruptions, the meeting lasted all night, adjourning only at six o'clock in the morning.[58] On October 7, the parliament issued a manifesto emphasizing its role as the representative of the people of the monarchy.[59] By this time, however, the

---

with the exception of Havlíček, Rieger, and Strobach, the Czech deputies were not in danger; the reason for the mass exodus was a matter of "principle." See the Protocols of the Slavic Linden, *LANM*, October 12, 1848. Nevertheless, it seems that Vienna was unsafe for most Czech deputies. This was admitted by the Czech deputies remaining in Vienna, except Sidon (*NN* October 14, 1848).

56. *NN*, July 22, 1848.
57. *NN*, October 13, 1848.
58. *Verhandlungen*, III, 10.
59. *Ibid.*, pp. 18-19; also *NN*, October 11, 1848.

exodus of the Czech deputies had begun. On October 8, in obvious concern over the departure of the Czechs, the parliament adopted a resolution requesting the absentees to return to Vienna within fourteen days. In reply to this and the proclamation of October 7, thirty-six Bohemian deputies (most of them Czech, some German) issued a statement in Prague on October 12 denying the legality of the parliament in its present form, on the ground that the requisite number of deputies was not present. They reaffirmed their faith in a "democratic monarchy" but denied that it was possible for the parliament to conduct its deliberations "under galleries filled with inflamed people turning their weapons on the seats of deputies." They also declared that they would not regard any future decisions of such a parliament as valid.[60] The Bohemian deputies' charge that the parliament in Vienna no longer had the necessary number of deputies was questionable. Only a simple majority was required to constitute a quorum, and the very issue of *Národní Noviny* that printed the appeal just mentioned reported in its parliamentary column that the number of deputies present at the meeting of October 9 was over 200, more than enough for a quorum.[61] As late as October 16, 221 deputies turned up to collect their regular allowance. Technically, the parliament was in a position to legislate.[62]

Among the Czech deputies who had left Vienna and signed the statement of October 12 were all the celebrities. But a few Czechs remained; as of October 13, six of them were still taking part in the work of the parliament.[63] They included, significantly, Sidon, the maverick priest who had, during the debate on the abolition of serfdom, voted against any form of compensation. It would not be correct to say that this "abridged" parliament consisted entirely of radicals, however. Among the deputies who remained were such men as Pillersdorf and Doblhoff. By October 21, the number of Czech deputies in Vienna had been reduced to four.[64]

60. *NN,* October 13, 1848.
61. *Ibid.*
62. Springer, *Geschichte Österreichs,* II, 560. *NN,* on October 26, reported from Vienna (date line October 20) that with every vote the danger was increasing that the parliament would not have a quorum. This suggests that even at this late date a majority was present, but Helfert claims that this quorum was doctored in various ways (see his "Erlebnisse und Erinnerungen," *Die Kultur,* III [1900-5], 7).
63. Sidon, Sadil, Loos, Šembera, Mokrý, Riegel.
64. Šembera, Loos, Sadil, Sidon. Havlíček condemned only Sidon and went

If the Czech deputies, in self-imposed exile from Vienna, hoped that their flat condemnation of the "rump" parliament would be accepted by the Prague public without question, they were soon disappointed. The June Uprising had crystallized the formation of a radical movement, and the radicals no longer accepted the decisions and explanations of the liberals without question, not even when furnished under the weighty auspices of men like Palacký and Rieger. The center of the new radicalism was becoming the Slavic Linden, whose development was favored by the abolition of the National Committee. As soon as the first news of the events in Vienna arrived, the executive committee of the Slavic Linden decided to dispatch a delegation to Vienna immediately in order to make an on-the-spot investigation. The Slavic Linden was joined by the Student Committee—the governing body of the students of the University of Prague—and it also invited the Prague City Council to add its representatives to the group. A municipal election in Prague had just given the city a new City Council in which more than a sprinkling of radicals were represented, and the council complied readily with the Linden's request. Each one of the three groups sent five members; the deputation left on October 8, at 6:00 p.m.[65]

The radicals had for some time felt uneasy about the support given by the Czech deputies to the government, and some were at first inclined to suspect that the struggle in Vienna might be a political one, between the people and the military, between the forces of progress and the forces of reaction. The returning Czech deputies now had to convince the Czech community that in their view this was a misjudgment of the situation and that the struggle was a national one, between the Slavs and their chief foes, the Germans and the

out of his way to assure the other three that he regarded them as good patriots. As for Sidon, he wrote that at one time Czech deputies were considering excluding him from their meetings because they suspected him of betraying their decisions to "our parliamentary and national enemies" (*NN*, October 24, 1848). An unflattering report on Sidon was also presented by Rieger at a meeting of the Slavic Linden (see Protocol of October 12, 1848, in *LAMN*). Because of his radical views on some questions, Sidon, a priest, was persecuted by the Catholic church and by the government during Bach's absolutism.

65. *NLS*, October 9, 1848. For the time being, the Slavic Linden and the Student Committee issued a proclamation expressing opposition to the "rump parliament" (text [undated, but issued on October 8] in J. M. Černý [ed.], *Boj za Právo: Sborník aktů politických u věcech státu a národa českého od roku 1848* [Prague, 1893], pp. 418-19).

Magyars.[66] On October 9, even before its deputation returned from Vienna, the City Council held a session with Palacký and Rieger. The two men succeeded in persuading the council members to accept their view of the situation, and on the same day the council issued a declaration condemning the Viennese revolution, the forces of anarchy, and the "rump" parliament.[67] In simply publishing the text of the declaration, without background comment, *Národní Noviny*, always partial to the liberals, tried to create the impression of unanimity in the council. But in fact the meeting of October 9 was far from clear sailing for Palacký and Rieger; another Prague newspaper said that the declaration was accepted "after a long and heated debate,"[68] indicating that there was strong radical opposition to the liberals in the council and that the radicals were not easily satisfied with the simple description of the Viennese revolution as a struggle between Slavs and the German-Magyar camp. Of this there was not a whisper in *Národní Novniy*.

After condemning the Viennese revolution, the City Council had second thoughts. Though the liberals seemed undisturbed by the prospect of Windischgrätz' being summoned to crush Vienna, the council, mindful of what Windischgrätz had done to Prague, conceived a certain affinity for what it called a "sister city" and was not quite prepared to gloat over Vienna's humiliation at the hands of the general. It voted to dispatch a deputation to the emperor in Olomouc with a plea to treat Vienna leniently. Before this decision was approved, one member of the council suggested that the Czech deputies should first be consulted concerning the advisability of this step, but he was voted down.[69] Evidently, the council was determined to act independently of the deputies in this particular instance. The delegation duly arrived in Olomouc and submitted to the emperor the petition for lenience, which stated that "Prague, having recently endured the horrors of a siege" and viewing the present situation in Vienna as a "danger to the order of the entire Monarchy" wishes to offer its good offices in order to mediate between the emperor and the city. As might have been expected, the offer was politely declined.[70]

66. For an objective presentation of these two views, see *CBB*, Supplement to No. 91, October 14, 1848.
67. *NN*, October 11, 1848.
68. *CBB*, October 10, 1848.
69. *NN*, October 17, 1848.
70. Text of the petition and the emperor's reply in *NN*, October 19, 1848.

The delegates of the Slavic Linden returned from Vienna during the night between October 11 and 12, and on the evening of October 12 submitted their report to the executive committee of the Slavic Linden. They basically endorsed the views of the Czech deputies, but there was nevertheless a grave note of caution. Their final words were: "From the above impartial report everyone will recognize that the whole rebellion bears a German-Magyar character, but there are also enough reasons for us to take a stand against reaction. Therefore, you defenders of the nation and you Czech people, be on your guard! When the insolence of anarchy has been humbled, the insolence of the military must not touch our rights."[71] The concluding sentence reveals clearly the concern of some members of the Slavic Linden over the possible consequences of the crushing of Vienna. This report was followed by the comments of Brauner and Rieger, conspicuous for a complete absence of any concern over the threat from the military. Rieger reduced the events in Vienna to a disarmingly simple formula. To him "the whole uprising was caused by Magyar money." He was "convinced" that "the court wants to preserve the constitution."[72]

On the following day a special meeting of the executive committee of the Slavic Linden took place at which a few radicals voiced their dissent from the policies pursued by the Czech deputies. One member, Ferdinand Viták, went so far as to put forward a proposal that the deputies should be asked to return to Vienna. This was considered utterly unacceptable; Viták was induced to withdraw his proposal, but instead suggested that the Slavic Linden should ask the Czech deputies to intercede on behalf of Vienna in order to prevent it from being placed at the mercy of the military. In the ensuing debate, the radical democrat František Havlíček expressed, more succinctly than anyone else, the dilemma of the Czech radicals and indeed the dilemma inherent in the political cross-currents and conflicts created by the Viennese revolution. "Should Vienna win, the monarchy will collapse, should it fall, . . . our imperial family does not have the will not to succumb in this instance to the will of the military." Little did Havlíček know how prophetic his words would turn out to be. He then expressed his support for the proposal for the Czech deputies to put in a plea for mercy for Vienna. Again Rieger countered with the

71. *NN,* October 14, 1848; also in *NLS,* October 16, 1848.
72. *LANM,* Protocol of the meeting of October 12, 1848.

assurance, which proved as erroneous in retrospect as Havlíček's proved prophetic, that "the imperial family is favorably inclined to freedom" and that the radicals in Vienna must be completely "broken." Rieger's views prevailed, and the executive committee voted down Viták's proposal.[73]

The way had now been cleared for the Slavic Linden to formally offer its support to the deputies. On October 15, in a brief statement, it declared that after "weighing the grave circumstances of our time and for the sake of preserving the spirit of unity of our nation" it was expressing confidence in the Czech members of the parliament.[74] Nevertheless, the persistent pressure of the radicals within the organization caused the Slavic Linden to take a stand more moderate than that of the Czech deputies. A few days after expressing its confidence in the deputies, it issued a major public appeal for unity. Conforming to the line of the liberals, the Linden condemned the Viennese revolution as a German-Magyar manifestation of hostility to the Slavs. At the same time it stated expressly that it endorsed "the step of the Prague City Council, which had pleaded with the emperor not to injure Vienna."[75] It is curious that although the executive council had specifically voted (as observed above) against asking the deputies to plead for mercy for Vienna, the appeal now came out openly in favor of such a mission. It is evident that the Slavic Linden was torn by internal doubts and conflicts. Its public acts reflected the unhappy dilemma of those who, like František Havlíček, feared the consequences of a German-Magyar defeat only a little less than those of a German-Magyar victory, for the first harbored the possibility of a strengthening of the reaction, and the second, the certainty of an unmitigated disaster for Slavdom as an ethnic family.

The City Council and the Slavic Linden had now placed themselves on record as supporting the "official" Czech policy toward the Viennese revolution, but the students of the University of Prague had still to be convinced of its wisdom. The vast majority of university students were Czech, yet not a few of them felt an initial attraction for the revolution in Vienna, partly because it was a radical movement per se and partly because the students were one of the leading elements in it. Contact between the Prague and Vienna students had been lively since the March Days, and the Prague students had been

73. Protocol of October 13, 1848. Also *NLS*, October 19, 1848.
74. Černý (ed.), *Boj*, p. 432.
75. *NLS*, October 23, 1848.

strongly influenced by their Vienna colleagues. As noted above, the
Student Committee dispatched a five-man delegation to Vienna to
gather firsthand information. Upon arrival there, at least two members
of the delegation fell entirely under the spell of the revolution and
gave prompt expression to their sympathies by posting throughout
Vienna placards proclaiming: "We, the delegates of the Prague
Student Committee to Vienna call upon our Slavic brethren to fight
on the side of the Viennese. Prague will stand, win or fall, with
Vienna."[76] This was a gross violation of the mandate the student
delegation had received; its duty was to report back to the student
body and allow that body to debate the report and decide what
policy should be adopted. Instead, two members of the delegation,
without any consultation with their parent organization took it upon
themselves to commit the Prague students as a whole to a course the
students had neither discussed nor voted upon.

News of this act caused a furor in Prague, especially in the pages
of *Národní Noviny*. Immediately upon returning to Prague, the
delegates reported to a student meeting, held on October 12. From
the fragmentary evidence available it appears that the delegation stuck
to its guns and voiced sympathy for the revolution and for the role
played by the Viennese students in it. For this it was attacked by
Karel Havlíček, fresh from Vienna, in his newspaper. Havlíček
told the radical sympathizers to beware lest their names be remembered as those of "blinded men or—traitors."[77] On the following day there was another student meeting to make a final decision
concerning the stand to be taken vis-à-vis the Viennese revolution.
Fearing opposition to their policies, the deputies sent a strong team
to address the student body and defend their actions. Once again,
Rieger was among those chosen to perform the task. He had already
helped sway the Prague City Council and was in the process of swaying the Slavic Linden. Rieger now applied his oratorical skill to
what promised to be the still more arduous task of convincing the
most youthful and restless of the doubting Thomases. With him
had come the Slovaks Ľudovít Štúr and Jozef Miloslav Hurban, both

76. The two students were Jirgl and the polytechnic student Kleinert. Text
in *NN*, October 14, 1848. The same was printed in the *Wiener Zeitung*, October 11, as noted in *NN*, October 15, 1848. For the whole episode, see F.
Jílek, "Pražská polytechnika a její studenti v revolučním roce 1848," *Sborník
Národního technického muzea*, IV (1965), 352 ff.

77. *NN*, October 13, 1848.

very popular with the students. The student delegates repeated their previous assertion that the struggle in Vienna was one between reaction and freedom. Rieger reiterated his opinion that the struggle was one between the Slavs and the Magyar-German coalition, and Štúr and Hurban seconded him. A few dissenting voices were raised from the audience, but on the whole, Rieger and his two fellow-speakers seem to have encountered little serious opposition from the majority of the students. They carried the meeting, and in the final vote the majority repudiated the action of the delegates. The students even decided to bring the chief offender before a "court of honor" where he would answer for exceeding his mandate by his actions in Vienna.[78]

Nevertheless, as in the case of the Slavic Linden, the final proclamation of the Student Committee, dated October 15, took a more moderate stand than the Czech deputies had taken—doubtless as a result of the influence of the radicals among the student leaders. Duly expressing confidence in the Czech leadership, but with qualifications, the committee stated: "We Prague students endeavor to win the most complete freedom in all directions . . . we want a democratic government and we will defend the throne of the dynasty insofar as it will stand at the head of a constitutional democratic monarchy." As for the Viennese revolution, it said that "we consider that it is not a pure struggle for freedom"—a choice of words that could hardly have been considered appropriate by Rieger and Havlíček, for whom the revolution was not in the slightest degree a struggle for freedom. In conclusion, the student proclamation promised to defend the honor of the deputies "to the extent that they will remain faithful to . . . democratic principles . . . the consequences of our trust in them are their responsibility."[79] This was far from a ringing endorsement of Czech official policy, and one wonders whether Rieger's success did not provoke in him more irritation than gratification. Clearly, the student leaders responsible for the proclamation, their youthful minds not yet firmly cast in a nationalist mold, refused to see the Viennese revolution as a simple contest between nationalities, and the circumstances surrounding the revolution caused them to have grave reservations about the future of democracy in Austria.

The most articulate voice of the radicals at the time was the *Pražský Večerní List*. Its attitude resembled that of other Czech

78. *NN,* October 14, 1848. The chief offender was Kleinert.
79. *NN,* October 17, 1848.

radical elements. It basically supported the Czech deputies, but at
times gave vent to fear lest the crushing of Vienna should help the
cause of reaction. The *Večerní List* published a series of articles on
this question from the pen of the radical Karel Sabina. In the first
article, Sabina condemned offhand the "ultra-German radicalism in
Vienna" and described the revolution as a German-Magyar attack
on the Slavs. He was revolted by the brutal murder of Latour:
"What the rabble perpetrated in this uprising was not just a political
terror, but an animal rage."[80] However, in the second article published the very next day, the author had second thoughts; Sabina was
not always noted for consistency and this second article is strikingly
different from the first. This time, he put a lot of blame on the government for exposing Jelačić to the suspicion of "reaction," he criticized
Latour, and he urged the Czech deputies to return to Vienna. "Let
us not be hasty with our judgments," he warned.[81] Incredibly, the
next (third) article differed again in tone from the second one and
reverted to the tone of the first. "Our point of view has changed
since yesterday," proclaimed Sabina, as he now endorsed the withdrawal of the deputies from the parliament. The Viennese revolution
was branded as a "prepared assassination attempt at Slavdom." Yet
the same issue warned in another article that the reaction would
doubtless try to exploit the events in Vienna for its own ends, and
urged the people to be vigilant and to join the National Guard in
order to be able to defend the cause of freedom if necessary. Three
days later, Sabina repeated this call in the leading article; though he
supported the action against Vienna, he stated that what the Czechs
wanted was both "freedom and nationality," not either one alone.
Against anyone touching either, "We shall draw the sword."[82] Thus,
there were recurring reservations about the repercussions the defeat of
Vienna might have on democracy in the Habsburg Monarchy.

In contrast, the Czech parliamentary leaders permitted themselves
few such reservations, at least for the record. To them, the struggle
was one between nationalities, pure and simple. As far as the fate
of Vienna was concerned, they suffered no qualms of conscience.
Whatever their private thoughts, in public, with hardly an exception,
they claimed to see no danger to constitutionalism and freedom in
the reliance upon Windischgrätz. When the delegates of the Slavic

80. *PVL,* October 9, 1848.
81. *PVL,* October 10, 1848.
82. *PVL,* October 11 and 14, 1848.

Linden expressed concern over the danger the "insolence of the military" might present to civil rights, Havlíček boldly editorialized, "Don't fear for your freedom: neither the court nor the army will or will want to disturb our constitution."[83] This was tantamount to giving Windischgrätz a clean bill of health as a champion of constitutional freedoms—something that could hardly have been deduced from his unhappy record in Prague. Havlíček and other Czech deputies had more than once criticized Windischgrätz during his sojourn in Prague for his disregard of constitutional principles. But now they seemed to be accepting him as a defender of constitutional liberties and of the Slavic cause. Again and again they denied and ridiculed the notion that there was any threat to freedom arising from the military intervention. In June Windischgrätz' feat was praised by the Germans and cursed by the Czechs; now it was being praised by the Czechs and cursed by the Germans. Under such circumstances, it was Windischgrätz and all that he stood for who was bound to emerge the winner, with the most ardent help from all those whose objectives he loathed and who, in their hearts, loathed him.

It was only in the later stages of the drama that the first faint note of doubt crept into the belligerence of Havlíček's pronouncements. It was occasioned by an announcement that seemed to come out of the blue that Windischgrätz had been promoted to field marshal, given vast discretionary powers, and appointed commander-in-chief of all imperial forces, with the exception of those commanded in Italy by Radetzky;[84] translated into language understandable to the Slavs, this meant that Jelačíc, the symbol of the Slavic cause, would henceforth be subordinated to Windischgrätz. This augured ill for the Czechs and induced Havlíček to state that "we shall see if the imperial court will be mindful of how we Slavs behaved in perilous times," concluding that "taught by bitter experience, we will rely on nobody but ourselves."[85] Yet even at this moment of concern about the danger to the Slavs Havlíček expressed no concern about the danger to the constitution. After the crushing of Vienna, to his lasting shame, he went so far as to editorially endorse—and not just reluctantly—the execution of a deputy democratically elected and protected by parliamentary immunity, the Frankfurt deputy Robert Blum, who was in Vienna in October and whom Windischgrätz had

83. NN, October 11, 1848.
84. Manifesto of October 16, in NN, October 21, 1848.
85. Ibid.

ordered executed for his activities during the revolution. With obvious satisfaction, Havlíček remarked that "nobody had asked the Frankfurt Parliament whether they would release him."[86]

The Czech leaders may have been stating publicly that there was no danger of a return to reaction, but their private beliefs did not match their public pronouncements. As early as October 8, the Czech deputy Trojan, while fleeing from Vienna, realized that the withdrawal of Czech deputies from the parliament might furnish the court with an excuse to dissolve it; instead of returning directly to Prague, he repaired to Olomouc in order to dissuade the court from any such idea it might entertain.[87] As they arrived in Prague, the deputies must have been surprised to discover that the radicals were expressing such grave concern over the possible danger of reaction arising from a military intervention in Vienna, and that they were being asked to undertake a mission of mercy for Vienna. This must have caused them to re-examine their opinions; also they could not ignore the persistent rumors that the court would exploit the situation in order to do away with the parliament altogether.[88] Palacký himself conceded to a delegation of the Slavic Linden on October 15 that he did "not conceal it from himself that the imperial family will submit to military influence" and that this called for unity in the Czech camp.[89] This is the only example of any such fear being openly expressed by any of the Czech leaders. Nevertheless it must have been privately shared by other leaders, and in the end, they decided to send a two-man delegation (Brauner and the Bohemian German conservative deputy, Josef Alexander Helfert) to the emperor to assure him of the utmost loyalty of Bohemia, but also to dissuade the court circles from any possible plans they might have harbored of dissolving the parliament. The decision to dispatch the delegation was motivated by the Czech deputies' genuine devotion to constitutional principles. It was doubtless hastened by the continued pressure of the radicals, by the fear of radical violence should the reaction show any real signs of reappearing, and by the desire of the deputies to keep the initiative in their own hands and away from the radicals.

When the delegation arrived in Olomouc, the concern over the

86. *NN,* November 14, 1848.
87. J. A. Helfert, "Erlebnisse und Erinnerungen," *Die Kultur,* II (1900-15), 179.
88. *Ibid.,* p. 272.
89. *NLS,* October 19, 1848; *CBB,* Supplement to No. 93, October 17, 1848.

future of the parliament was reinforced by the manifesto of October 16, referred to above, which had just been issued by the emperor. The manifesto conferred on Windischgrätz vast discretionary powers; its complete reticence concerning the future of the parliament and of constitutionalism in Austria in general alarmed all constitutionally minded observers. Their discussions with the responsible government officials in Olomouc convinced the two deputies from Bohemia that although no clear decision had yet been made there was real danger that the parliament might be dissolved. Along with a few deputies from other provinces, Brauner and Helfert endeavored earnestly to dissuade the officials, the court, and the emperor, who also gave them a hearing, from such a course.[90]

In an interview with Prince Felix Schwarzenberg, soon to be appointed Prime Minister of a new cabinet, Brauner decried the powers given to Windischgrätz: "A general is being given unconditional power to institute peace according to his own criteria; in his hands is being placed an unrestricted authority for the restoration of constitutional freedom, the restoration or order, confidence, security. I have all respect for the personal character of Windischgrätz as a soldier, as an honorable man, as a loyal supporter of the dynasty. But I consider it impossible that the qualities required for the work of peace and pacification are to be presupposed in a man who had in Prague for three months pursued the ghost of a widespread conspiracy the threads of which were nowhere to be found. Prince Windischgrätz has shown in Bohemia that he is least suited to gauge properly the public opinion of a country." Helfert, for his part, observed that "the Bohemians are now quiet" but should the government disregard constitutional principles, "it is to be strongly doubted" that they would continue to remain so.[91]

The government officials were not unimpressed with the force of these arguments. Although the first manifesto was not rescinded, another manifesto was issued three days later, on October 19, in which the emperor stated that it was his "unalterable will" that "the rights and liberties granted to our nations, however abused by indi-

90. Helfert, "Erlebnisse und Erinnerungen," *Die Kultur*, II, 272, 367 ff. On October 17 Brauner wrote to Rieger from Olomouc: "That the military and the nobility wanted to dissolve Parliament, by this I swear—we have enough evidence for it" (J. Heidler, *Přípěvky k listáři Dra Frant. Lad. Riegra* [Prague, 1924-26], I, 46).

91. Helfert, "Erlebnisse und Erinnerungen," *Die Kultur*, II, 370, 372.

vidual malefactors" should "remain unabridged in all their extent."
He also directed the Imperial Parliament to complete its appointed
task of drafting a constitution.[92] Thus, the deputies from Bohemia
contributed in no small measure to the preservation of constitutional
government, at least for the time being.

In the long run, of course, they could not avert the reimposition
of absolutism; by October 31 Vienna lay prostrate at Windischgrätz'
feet. The crushing of the Viennese revolution proved indeed a decisive stage on the return road to reaction, contrary to the public
assurances of the Czech leadership. There is little doubt that by their
total condemnation of Vienna in October and by their insistence that
the issue of freedom versus reaction was not at all involved, the Czech
leaders aided the victory of the reaction. It would be unjust to criticize them for not sympathizing with the Viennese revolution and the
Viennese radicals, however. No self-respecting Czech could do that
in the face of the Viennese radicals' repeated abuse of the Czech
nation and of the Slavs. A victory of the German-radical–Magyar
coalition would have been, under the circumstances, a disaster to the
Czechs, Slovaks, and other Slavs. It would have placed them at the
mercy of the two groups in the monarchy—the German Viennese
radicals and the Magyar gentry—that were most chauvinistic in their
anti-Slavic hostility. Even a German newspaper in Prague was compelled to concede that "one cannot blame them [the Czechs] that they
do not sympathize with Vienna . . . because of its Magyar basis,
October 6 has acquired an anti-Slavic hue."[93] The same newspaper
candidly remarked earlier that the Czechs "rightly fear an exclusive
Germanism from the kind of ministerial combination desired by the
Viennese democrats."[94]

Nevertheless, there was a difference between not sympathizing
with the Viennese radicals and demanding, as Rieger and other Czech
leaders did, that they be completely "broken." The Czech leaders
hoped that Windischgrätz would conveniently do for them what they
themselves never dared hope to do: destroy the Viennese radicals. The
downfall of the Viennese radicals would accomplish two goals of the
Czech leaders: (1) it would clear away the most serious obstacle to
the attainment of Czech national emancipation, and (2) it would put
an end to social radicalism in Vienna, with its deliberate appeal to the

92. *NN,* October 21, 1848.
93. *CBB,* Supplement to No. 97, October 21, 1848.
94. *CBB,* September 29, 1848.

working class, the stirring of which the Czech leaders feared. Of the two objectives, the first one doubtless influenced them more. The Czech leaders became so consumed with a desire to strike back at the Viennese radicals that they underestimated the ability of the reaction to strike back at the forces of progress. As the above record demonstrates, they were not oblivious to the threat of reaction. But they encouraged the reaction (1) by their public denials that any such threat existed, even though these denials were at variance with their own private opinions; (2) by their insistence that the struggle in Vienna was purely national and involved no question of political freedom; and (3) by their frequent demands that the Viennese radicals must be absolutely crushed. It may be added that though they were aware of the reaction that threatened, they believed—wrongly, as we can say in retrospect—that it would not be strong enough to assert itself and that the threat could be held in check by the vigilance of constitutionally minded people like themselves. But the collapse of the radical movement in Vienna weakened the constitutional forces and thereby greatly strengthened the reaction.

Bohemian Acting Governor Mecséry feared the effect of the Viennese revolution on public opinion in Bohemia. Particularly concerned lest the revolution should provoke sympathies among the workers, Mecséry instructed the region prefects to exercise special vigilance "in those communities in which there are many workers."[95] His fears proved exaggerated, however; no mass support for the Viennese revolution developed. The attitude of the population toward the Vienna revolution was shaped largely by national sentiment. All sections of the Czech community, as noted above, basically opposed it, even though some did so with reservations. Such support for Vienna as could be found came only from Bohemian Germans. The German students of the University of Prague, who had recently formed their own organization, came out openly in support of Vienna in a statement of October 19. Many German cities and communities sent expressions of sympathy and support to the Viennese.[96] There was a stirring of workers (mostly German) in Liberec; a group of them tried to seize arms and organize an expedition to aid the imperial

95. Instruction dated October 11, 1848, in *SÚA* Prague, PG 1846-49, 15 c/3, No. 9432/1848.

96. *CBB*, October 20, 1848; Helfert, "Erlebnisse und Erinnerungen," *Die Kultur*, III, 204.

capital.[97] In contrast, the Viennese revolution awakened no sympathies among the Czech workers in Prague, in spite of the fact that unemployment was still far from solved and social discontent was still in evidence, although on a much smaller scale than before June. On November 2, the office of the Prague burgomaster reported that "the taking of Vienna [by Windischgrätz] made the best impression among the workers" and that "even should emissaries [from Vienna] appear they would find no agreement with their views."[98]

How did Moravia react to the events in Vienna? In Bohemia's sister province, the situation was quite different. The German influence there was stronger, and so were the echoes provoked by the Viennese revolution. The Moravian diet was in session at the time, and it opened the discussion of the Vienna events on October 9. It heard a report by the German Moravian deputy to the Imperial Parliament, Kajetan Mayer, who had just arrived from the imperial capital. Mayer was among those who continued to sit in the parliament, and his report was favorable to the German left. He was seconded by the Czech Alois Pražák, who was in 1848 far from an ardent champion of the Czech cause. The next day (October 10) the Moravian diet unanimously adopted a proclamation asking the Moravian people to continue to support the movement and the parliament in Vienna.[99] The unanimity meant that all the Czech deputies present—about half of the total number—voted for it. Nothing illustrates more clearly the gap that existed between the Bohemian and Moravian Czechs at that time. Four thousand copies of the proclamation were to be printed and distributed throughout the province.

It turned out that the Moravian diet had spoken too soon. Before the proclamation could be distributed, fresh political developments forced the diet to modify its stand. The emperor had fled Vienna and found refuge, of all places, in Olomouc on Moravian soil. This created an awkward situation, since the diet was on record as favoring the movement that had forced the emperor out of Vienna. As a result, the diet prudently adopted a new proclamation, on Oc-

97. J. Belda, *Liberec v revolučním roce 1848* (Liberec, 1959), p. 191.

98. Report of November 2, 1848, to the Provincial Presidium (*SÚA* Prague, PG 1846-49, 15 c/3, No. 9983/1848).

99. Černý (ed.), *Boj*, 423-25. See H. Traub, "Ohlas říjnové vídeňské revoluce na Moravě," *Časopis Moravského Muzea Zemského*, XIII-XIV (1913-14), 301 ff.

tober 13, which refrained from asking the people to support the parliament in Vienna. It also refused to condemn Vienna in any way, although it did exhort the Moravians to have confidence in "our constitutional emperor." Clearly, the diet both wanted and did not want to sympathize with Vienna. It was drawn to the movement by its German character, but it was repelled from it by its apparent propensity for violence and social radicalism. The new proclamation was adopted, again unanimously!

The German press in Moravia was almost entirely pro-Vienna. The only two Czech newspapers, *Moravské Noviny* (begun only on November 1, 1848) and *Týdenník*, were against Vienna. A group of Czech-speaking Moravian patriots, identified only as "a few patriots," issued a manifesto dated October 8 condemning the revolution. Unlike comparable Czech documents and statements, it refrained entirely from any suggestion that the struggle in Vienna was one between Germans and Slavs. It condemned the revolution as an attempt at anarchy and lawlessness but did not see it as an attack on Slavdom.[100] From this one can see again how much less developed was national consciousness in Moravia than in Bohemia, even among Czechs sympathetic to the Czech national cause.

Considerable sympathies for the revolution were generated in Brno and in the larger cities. Geographically close to Vienna; connected with it by a recently constructed railroad, and more recently, by telegraph; and bound to it by historic traditions, Brno has often shared the moods of the imperial capital. In the mid-nineteenth century, the majority of the population was Czech (according to a census of 1856 there were 35,000 Czechs and 8,900 Germans in Brno), but most of the Czechs lacked a strong national consciousness, and political leadership was in the hands of the Germans. As soon as the first news was received of the events in Vienna, the National Guard and the students organized a public rally for October 7, which, according to a contemporary account, expressed "the most democratic sentiment in favor of freedom and of Vienna."[101] Some five hundred men in a detachment of the National Guard and of the Academic Legion were promptly dispatched to Vienna to help it in its hour of travail; it was of course under German leadership. At the same time, a segment of the working class was caught up in the revolutionary wave. A major demonstration of workers occurred on October 18

100. Černý (ed.), *Boj,* pp. 419-20.
101. Traub, "Ohlas říjnové vídeňské revoluce," p. 297.

and again on October 29 and 30 (see Chapter 12). The majority of Brno workers were Czech, but devoid of national consciousness and therefore more susceptible to the idea of supporting the Viennese workers, regardless of national differences, and to the influence of German radical agitators. The three or four radical intellectuals who agitated among the workers in favor of Vienna were German; there was apparently also a Magyar agitator working toward the same objective.[102]

A genuine revolutionary movement of a mass character also took place at that time in the rural areas of northern Moravia and Silesia. At the end of October, radical propagandists attempted to stir peasant discontent by circulating in these regions a forged imperial manifesto announcing that as of November 3, 1848, all constitutional freedoms would be suspended.[103] In Silesia social discontent was particularly rife, nourished by the fact that the abolition of serfdom, carried out in Moravia proper on July 1, 1848, did not yet apply to Silesia. Yet such discontent was not always in support of Vienna; it was sometimes exclusively, sometimes in part, a reaction to local conditions having no connection with Vienna.

In the end, Brno proved to be the only community to offer active assistance to Vienna. The failure of the Viennese movement to mobilize active mass support in Moravia is the more striking, since the German radical agitators spared no effort in spreading pro-Vienna propaganda throughout the countryside. It is true that there were, here and there, expressions of sympathy for Vienna, more in German-speaking than in Czech-speaking areas; but no mass movement developed in the rural areas, the overwhelming majority of peasants, both Czech and German, remaining puzzled, bewildered, indifferent, or hostile to the Viennese revolution. Half a dozen communities made or announced plans to send help to Vienna, but for one reason or another, they did not materialize (except in Brno). Vienna waited for help, but in vain, as indeed it waited in vain for help from the countryside immediately adjacent to it. It was easy to send expressions of sympathy; it was quite another matter to send arms and men. It goes without saying that the authorities did their best to discourage and frustrate any plans to help the imperial capital.

102. *Ibid.,* p. 131. See also B. Šindelář, "O úloze lidových mas v revolučním dění roku 1848 na Moravě a ve Slezsku," *ČSČH,* IV (1956), 389 ff.
103. Šindelář, "O úloze lidových mas," p. 412.

Chapter **8**

The Shadows of Reaction

The revolution in Vienna rendered the continued session of the Imperial Parliament in that city, in the eyes of the court, impossible—a view shared fully by the Czech deputies and by Czech public opinion. The question was, Where would the parliament be moved? Brno, the capital of Moravia, was at first prominently mentioned, but the pro-Vienna manifestations that were taking place there made the proposition dubious, and the working-class demonstration on October 18 removed it altogether from the list of cities being considered for the honor of playing host to the Imperial Parliament. Yet the decision that was finally made gave the honor to Moravia: the town in which the parliament was to reconvene was Kroměříž (Kremsier), situated in the heart of a fertile region inhabited by the Hanaks (so-called from the river Haná).[1]

The choice of this town was received with mixed feelings. The Czechs were in favor of the move, since it seemed to bestow a unique honor on the Czech Lands, but many Germans, of various political hues, were noticeably less enthusiastic. Their reserve was partly due to national prejudice, but in addition, the thought of being "banished" to a small town—such national significance as Kroměříž possessed derived from the fact that it was the residence of an arch-bishop—frankly appalled the deputies, most of whom were city-bred and did not relish the prospect of working at their jobs as parliamentarians without the support of the redeeming urban amenities. As one contemporary noted, many deputies, even some of the best-educated ones, had to reach for their maps in order to locate the town.[2] The beautiful parks for which it was noted could not compensate for the total absence of urban diversions, and, more importantly, of the library resources required for legislative work.

The Imperial Parliament reconvened on November 22, with the

1. Text of the decree (October 22, 1848) in *NN,* October 27, 1848. The Hanaks spoke a Czech dialect and were noted for certain distinctive customs and characteristics.

2. A. Springer, *Geschichte Österreichs seit dem Wiener Frieden 1809* (Leipzig, 1863-65), II, 587.

political groupings roughly the same as before. Only the mood and the confidence within the groups had undergone a change. The Czechs felt stronger and the left, correspondingly less vigorous. The left was regarded as being responsible for the outbreak of the Viennese revolution because of its violent agitation, which led to the lynching of Latour. With this stigma to live down, the left was considerably subdued and never again regained its former vigor. Indeed the leading deputies of the left lived in terror of arrest and persecution; fear hung like the sword of Damocles over their heads. The right consisted largely of Slavs, as in Vienna, but it was now better organized. The Slavic deputies formed a Slavic Club of some 120 members including the Czechs, the Ukrainians, and the southern Slavs. The Poles as usual stood aside; only a few of them belonged to the club. The Slavic Club was the largest parliamentary club and the Czechs were its determining core; it was a Czech, Strobach, who presided over it. As in Vienna, the Czechs and the right in general (also, of course, the center) basically supported the government, but in Kroměříž this support was less unqualified, and on occasion the Czechs were in opposition to it.

The work of the parliament, after the Viennese revolution, unfolded amid a series of unpleasant surprises and shocks, for the Czechs as well as for all constitutionally minded deputies. The first unpleasant surprise was the composition of the new government, announced at the end of October, before the Imperial Parliament reconvened. Prince Felix Schwarzenberg, a dyed-in-the-wool conservative, became Prime Minister and Minister of Foreign Affairs. Schwarzenberg was a haughty noble in the classic aristocratic tradition who belonged more properly to the age of Metternich than to the age of the constitution. The second most important member of the government was Count Franz Stadion (to be distinguished from Rudolf Stadion, the former governor of Bohemia). A good administrator, more moderate in his conservatism than Schwarzenberg, Stadion had been closely associated with the Metternich regime and was not noted for his enthusiasm for constitutional principles. The entire government bore the dubious stamp of "dynasticism" and its collective attitude toward the Imperial Parliament could be described as indifferent at best and hostile at worst. Schwarzenberg was a brother-in-law of Windischgrätz, which assured the general of an even greater influence on official policy in the future than he had exerted in the past and signified a correspondingly greater danger to democratic institutions. The court viewed Windischgrätz as the savior of the monarchy; to the liberally minded he was the grave-digger of liberty.

The shock of the composition of the new government was miti-gated, for a time, by the cloak of constitutionalism the government donned as it presented its first program to the parliament. It would have been both premature and imprudent to disregard the democratic sentiment of the deputies; accordingly, the program gave every ap-pearance of moderation and ostensibly represented no major de-parture from previous policies. It was greeted with a sigh of relief from both the right and the left. The warning voices of the radicals were stilled again, and the deputies—or those among them who wanted to do so—were once again able to convince themselves that the danger of reaction was not a serious one.

The first important order of business was to decide whether to approve the protocols of the last four sessions of the Vienna Parlia-ment (for October 28, 29, 30, and 31) that had not yet been approved. Approval was vehemently opposed by the right, which regarded it as an endorsement of the Viennese revolution. With Rieger as its chief spokesman, the right won its point, by a vote of 143–124, with 10 abstentions.[3]

It was not long before the government indicated how little was its regard for the parliament. An extraordinary meeting of the parlia-ment was called by the government for December 2. The meeting was called on short notice: a telegram arrived only at 8:00 a.m. on December 2, summoning the deputies to meet at 12:00 noon on the same day. The government did not reveal the purpose of the meeting except to state that an important announcement would be made. The call set off a wave of rumors; some thought, for example, that the parliament was about to be dissolved, others, that the deputies of the left were going to be arrested. The incident shows how far Austria still had to travel on the road to a genuine constitutional system in which the security of the person would be inviolate: a constitutional system under which elected deputies lived in constant fear of being hounded by the police left much to be desired.

After the deputies had gathered at the appointed hour, Schwarzen-berg announced to the stunned audience that Emperor Ferdinand had abdicated the throne and his nephew Francis Joseph had become

3. *Verhandlungen des österreichischen Reichstages nach der stenographis-chen Aufnahme* (Vienna, 1848-49), II, 5 ff.

emperor. The disturbing ingredient in this event was not the change of rulers. Emperor Ferdinand was mentally retarded, and his abdication, in the face of the exacting duties imposed on the ruler by the quickening tempo of political events since March, was not unexpected. But it was a bad omen that the change, when it came, was accomplished entirely without consulting the parliament. Indeed, that body had not even been forewarned, let alone consulted. Furthermore, it was not difficult to read the political message implicit in the change. Ferdinand had been regarded as a good-natured person, and with his name had been associated all the reforms and concessions made since the March Days. His abrupt departure, in the manner in which it was staged, could mean only one thing: an end to the era of concessions and a possible disavowal of the concessions already made. The manner in which the new ruler announced himself to his people gave thoughtful observers a cause for reflection. Francis Joseph styled himself "Emperor by the grace of God"[4]—a usage discontinued by Ferdinand since the March Days. Havlíček expressed cautious disagreement with this formality.[5]

The most important task for the parliament was the drafting of a constitution. The first steps in that direction had been taken in Vienna. As early as July 31, the parliament had authorized a committee for this purpose. The deputies were aware of the pivotal nature of this constitutional committee, and a major controversy developed concerning the manner in which each province was to be represented. Since Bohemia was among the most populous provinces, the Czech deputies insisted that each province should be represented in proportion to the size of its population. To the German deputies it was clear that any such proportional representation would give a stronger voice to the Slavic element, and most of them opposed it; they preferred to see each province represented by an equal number of members (three). In the final vote the Germans carried the day, thereby dealing a major blow to the hopes of the Czechs of being able to decisively influence the committee proposal. In its final form, the constitutional committee was composed of thirty members, three from each of the ten provinces (*Gouvernements*).[6] The Czechs then took

4. J. M. Černý (ed.), *Boj za právo: Sborník aktů politických u věcech státu a národa českého od roku 1848* (Prague, 1893), p. 472

5. *NN*, December 5, 1848.

6. A. Springer (ed.), *Protokolle des Verfassungs-Ausschusses im öesterreichischen Reichstage 1848-1849* (Leipzig, 1885), p. 4.

sweet revenge on the Germans: they did not choose any German to represent Bohemia; all three members elected were Czech: Palacký, Rieger, and Adolf Maria Pinkas. But their victory was offset by their failure to have any Czech represent Moravia: all three Moravian deputies were German. All in all, the constitutional committee was weighted heavily in favor of the centralists, who were not likely to allow a large voice to the provinces. Before tackling the job, the committee set up two subcommittees from its midst: one, consisting of three members, to draft a preamble or Bill of Rights; another consisting of five members, to draft the constitution proper. The Czechs were represented in both subcommittees: Rieger was on the first, Palacký on the second.

In his subcommittee Rieger was entrusted with the task of working out a preliminary draft of the Bill of Rights, to be discussed and modified in the subcommittee and then presented to the full committee. The text of Rieger's proposal (*Urtext*) has not survived in its entirety. It is known to have had thirty-two articles, but of these only ten have survived.[7] The draft bears the unmistakable influence of that "Bible" of mid-nineteenth-century liberalism, the German *Rotteck-Welcker Staatslexikon* (fifteen volumes, 1834-43). Rieger's surviving *Urtext* incorporates some principles and even verbatim passages from the French constitutions of 1791 and 1793, and from the constitution of Texas; his information concerning these documents was drawn from the *Staatslexikon*.[8] It may be added that the whole work of the Imperial Parliament relating to the constitution was strongly influenced and inspired by the Frankfurt Assembly.

As spokesman for the largest non-German nationality in Cisleithania, Rieger incorporated, appropriately enough, into his *Urtext*, the principle of the protection of nationalities. Article XX stated that "the right to the safeguarding of nationality in general and of the national language in particular, is inalienable and guaranteed by the state."[9] It is interesting to note that Rieger's *Urtext* did not speak of the "equality" of nationalities and national languages, but the draft that emerged from the full constitutional committee did. The relevant principle was incorporated into Article XXI, which stated that "the equal rights of languages commonly spoken in a province

7. A. Fischel (ed.), *Die Protokolle des Verfassungsausschusses über die Grundrechte* (Vienna, 1912), pp. 181-82.

8. *Ibid.*, p. xii.

9. *Ibid.*, p. 182.

(*landesübliche Sprachen*), in the school, office, and public life are safeguarded by the state."[10] Since the protocols of the discussions about this article are among those missing, it is not known how the mere "safeguarding" of national language was transformed into an "equality" of national languages. How the Imperial Parliament would have reacted to it will never be known; it was dissolved before reaching Article XXI. It would probably not have encountered much opposition, since even the centralists and opponents of subject nationalities paid at least lip service to the idea of equality. The principle of equality was later introduced into the Constitution of December 21, 1867.

Another important principle enunciated in the *Urtext* was the principle of popular sovereignty. Rieger incorporated it into Article III, which laid down the sovereignty of "popular will" (*Volkswille*), and stated that "the government exists only through the authority [of the people] and for their benefit."[11] The article echoed vividly Rousseau's General Will and, significantly, contained not a word about an "Emperor by the grace of God." During the discussions in the full committee this article was made Article I and was modified to read: "All powers of the state originate from the people and are exercised in a manner prescribed by the constitution."[12]

Meanwhile, in the five-member subcommittee, Palacký was the first to tackle the forbidding job of drafting a constitution for a state which had never enjoyed one and which had an ethnic and administrative structure more complex than any other state in Latin Christendom. Austria's problems were unique and this made it difficult to apply the constitutional experience of other countries to them. Moreover, the decades of rigid absolutism and censorship had left even the educated liberal classes in Austria with a very limited knowledge of the intricacies of the constitutional process. Only a handful of deputies were competent to prepare a constitutional draft. Palacký completed the preliminary draft by the time of the outbreak of the Viennese revolution.[13]

Based on the Belgian constitution, the draft was composed of seventy-two articles and was limited to Cisleithania only. Its chief

10. *Ibid.*, p. 185.
11. *Ibid.*, p. 181.
12. *Ibid.*, p. 187.
13. See his own account in *Spisy drobné*, ed. B. Rieger (Prague, 1898), I, 349 ff. Text of the first sketch, *ibid.*, pp. 59 ff.

interest lies in the administrative and national divisions Palacký envisaged. Cisleithania was divided into four groups: Polish, Czech, German-Austrian, and Illyrian. The Czech group consisted of Bohemia, Moravia, and Silesia. The division into four groups was for the sake of convenience and was without administrative significance. The basic and significant administrative divisions were the same provinces (ten in number) that had existed before 1848, except that the Italian provinces were omitted because the separatist movements in progress there had rendered their status uncertain; for similar reasons Hungary was excluded from the draft altogether. Bohemia and Moravia were to be administered separately, with no institutions in common; this was a departure from the demands of the First and Second Petitions, both of which had called for common institutions for the two provinces. It was an abandonment of the concept of the Lands of the Czech Crown.

Palacký's draft was not accepted by the subcommittee as a basis for discussion. Later Palacký prepared another draft which differed in many fundamental respects from the first. It was finished in January and its provisions must be considered in conjunction with the views expressed by Palacký in the discussions of the full committee in meetings held between January 22 and February 3, 1849.[14] Whereas the first draft retained basically the existing administrative divisions, Palacký now proposed to reorganize the empire along ethnic lines—a truly radical departure from the first draft. The division into ethnic units was not a part of the second draft itself but was proposed by Palacký during discussions in the committee, on January 22, 1849.[15] Another basic change had been introduced: Hungary was included in the scope of the draft—a change no doubt inspired by the heightened prospects of Hungary's reconquest by the imperial armies. The empire was to be divided into eight groups of provinces. One of these would be the German-Austrian Lands; they would include not only the "hereditary lands" in the narrow sense of the word, but also the German-speaking areas of Bohemia, Moravia, and Silesia. The second group would comprise the Czech-speaking regions of Bohemia, Moravia, and Silesia, and the Slovak regions of Hungary.

In other words, Palacký proposed bringing Czechs and Slovaks under one roof. At the same time, he was willing to countenance the

14. Text of the second draft, with the relevant excerpts from the protocols of the committee, *ibid.*, pp. 69-90.

15. *Ibid.*, p. 79.

reduction of the Lands of the Czech Crown by the separation of the German-speaking areas from them. For this he was later much criticized.[16] He must have been uncertain about it himself, for after specifically assigning the "Sudeten German" regions to the German-Austrian group, he proceeded to state that he would propose their separation from the Czech Lands "if only it were practically possible."[17] This was not very consistent; clearly Palacký shrank from the implications of the administrative divisions he envisaged. He was never a fuzzy or hasty thinker, and his inconsistency here only underscores the difficulty of dealing with problems the solution of which no precedents existed.

The flavor of Palacký's draft was a "federalist" one, of the kind that ran against the grain of the German centralists. Actually, Palacký, faithful to the objective proclaimed in his letter to Frankfurt, desired a strong Austria, strong enough to protect the smaller nationalities; this presupposed a large measure of control at the center and Palacký's draft accordingly leaned comparatively mildly in the direction of federalism. For example, though Palacký proposed the formation of ministries for the provinces, he did not make them responsible solely to the provincial diets; he made them responsible to the Imperial Parliament for the carrying out of imperial laws, and to the provincial diet for the carrying out of provincial laws.[18] He was content to leave a good deal of authority to the Imperial Parliament and to the imperial government.

The use of the ethnic principle as a basis for the reorganization of the empire was too radical to command the necessary support, and Palacký's second draft met with the same fate as the first: although it was presented to the full committee, that committee did not accept it as the main basis for discussion, but instead used a more centralist report prepared by another member of the subcommittee. Palacký's draft was, of course, not entirely disregarded, but the attitude of the constitutional committee indicated plainly the committee's preference and the probable results of its work. His efforts thwarted and his pride wounded, Palacký resigned from the committee at the beginning of February, and his place was taken by the Czech Antonín Strobach.[19]

16. J. V. Frič, *Paměti,* ed. K. Cvejn (Prague, 1957-63), II, 334.
17. Palacký, *Spisy drobné,* I, 79.
18. *Ibid.,* Art. LXII, p. 74.
19. Springer, *Protokolle,* p. 121.

The latter was a federalist, but, like Pinkas, less vigorously so than Palacký. Only Rieger continued to carry Palacký's banner.

In these circumstances, the result of the work of the committee could scarcely be expected to hearten the federalists. As approved by the constitutional committee by a unanimous vote, the final draft was a hybrid document—a mixture of federalism and centralism, with the latter preponderant. The Czechs hoped that they would be able to modify it, along federalist lines, in the plenum of the parliament. The federalists could, Rieger complained, be "easily outvoted" in the committee. But "in the chamber it is different, there we will be able to win the necessary concessions. If we don't win them, then we shall see how we will obtain our rights. If you don't satisfy the large provinces, you will not be able to hold Austria together. Austria cannot maintain itself in a centralist form."[20] Three weeks after these words were spoken, however, the Imperial Parliament was dissolved; the Czechs were not given the opportunity of this confrontation of strength.

The conflict between federalists and centralists was one between a predominantly Slavic and a predominantly German camp, between the right and the left. The left claimed that federalism was a danger to Austria in that it would cause the larger provinces to separate themselves from it. But a German conservative deputy, answering a German centralist-radical in the constitutional committee, put his finger correctly on the reasons for centralism: "What [the centralist] ... fears is not the separation of the large provinces from Austria, but ... the overflowing of the non-German element, and that's why he seeks protection in centralization."[21]

How much voice were the three (or four, counting Strobach) Czech members of the constitutional committee willing to give to the lower social classes? Rieger, who was easily the most liberal of the Czech committee members, advocated universal suffrage with no qualifications whatsoever. He opposed the suggestion, made by another member of the committee, that only those who could read and write should be allowed to vote. Pointing to Galicia as an example, he observed that the exclusion of illiterate peasants would produce for the most part "reactionary elections." He was apprehensive about the workers as voters, however; to him "the great mass of the propertyless" was "mostly, without incitement, unjust and communistic."

20. *Ibid.,* p. 223; spoken on February 16, 1849.
21. *Ibid.,* p. 302.

As Rieger saw it, "The proletarians will vote for those who share their views and goals," which would produce instability. "In spite of this," he continued, "I favor their being admitted to the vote."[22] In the final vote in the committee, Rieger was as good as his word and voted against any property qualification; in contrast, Strobach and Pinkas voted for it. The latter point of view received a majority.[23] Had Palacký been there instead of Strobach, he would doubtless have voted the same way. In connection with the right to vote, a few members of the committee spoke jestingly and unflatteringly of the right of women to vote. There is no record of any of the Czech deputies expressing himself on this subject, but since even the radicals in the committee were waving off this right with an amused benevolence, the more moderate Czechs were not likely to espouse it.

At home, the work of the Imperial Parliament was followed with growing impatience by the radicals, who were becoming critical of the failure of the Czech deputies, in many instances, to take a strong stand against a government that was displaying a growing disrespect for parliamentary institutions. The Slavic Linden made itself into a veritable watchdog of constitutional liberties, keeping a critical eye on the Czech deputies and warning of the gathering clouds of reaction. Branches of the Slavic Linden blossomed out all over Bohemia and, to a lesser extent, Moravia, with a lively and steady contact between them and the parent body. The Czech deputies at times resented its vigilance; Rieger complained in a private letter that the Slavic Linden lectured (*kantoruje*) to the deputies and encouraged public distrust against them.[24] The Linden might have been resented, but it could not be ignored, and, in fact, as its influence spread into the countryside, its voice had to be heeded more rather than less. Its influence was measurably strengthened with the founding of its own newspaper, first called *Slavic Linden* and later renamed *Gazette of the Slavic Linden* (*Noviny Lípy Slovanské*), which was run by radicals. As the Slavic Linden kept a vigilant eye on the liberals, the liberals turned a wary eye on the Slavic Linden, watching apprehensively its radicalization and seeking to curb its influence. As it grew more extreme in

22. *Ibid.*, p. 186.
23. *Ibid.*, p. 208.
24. Letter of October 4, 1848, to a member of the Linden executive. Quoted in J. Heidler, *Antonín Springer a česká politika v letech 1848-1850* (Prague, 1914), p. 65.

its views, the Slavic Linden naturally could not escape the biting criticism of Havlíček in his *Národní Noviny*.

Yet in spite of the efforts of the prestigious liberals, the expanding influence of the Slavic Linden could not be checked. This was because radical forces were again on the rise, after a period of inertia occasioned by the martial law imposed upon Prague after the June Uprising. Though this second radical wave was, to be sure, less powerful than the first one, the one that culminated in the June Uprising, it manifested itself in many novel ways. The second wave was directly triggered by the man who quelled the first: General Windischgrätz. On August 2, 1848, Windischgrätz issued a statement on the results of the investigation of the June Uprising. Charging that the uprising had been a planned conspiracy, he hurled unfounded accusations at various groups, impugning the integrity of masses of Prague citizens.[25]

The first group to respond was the Committee of Prague Students, which flatly denied the general's allegations. On August 14 there was a large protest meeting of Prague burghers and intellectuals of more radical leanings, which led to the publication of a protest, dated August 24, in which Windischgrätz' accusations were subjected to a lengthy analysis and rejected.[26] Among those seething with resentment were, most astonishingly, the ladies of Prague; following the example of their menfolk, the angry women organized their own protest meeting for August 16, thereby scoring a notable first: the first political assembly of women in the history of the Czech Lands. Though sympathetic in its coverage, *Národní Noviny* characteristically devoted only eight lines to the meeting, thus overlooking entirely its significance as the first political stirring of a hitherto mute class of citizens. In contrast, *Pražský Večerní List* headlined it eagerly, consigning to it more than two and a half pages of a four-page issue —an unprecedented coverage.[27] In retrospect, the meeting was a milestone, and, as on many other occasions, the radical press proved itself more sensitive than the liberals to the subtle signs of future events. Later the ladies held another meeting, and finally dispatched

25. Černý (ed.), *Boj*, pp. 355-59.
26. *NN*, August 14, 1848; *PVL*, August 15, 1848. Text of the burghers' protest in Černý (ed), *Boj*, pp. 367-75.
27. *NN*, August 18, 1848; *PVL*, August 17, 1848.

a delegation to Vienna with a protest against Windischgrätz, thus adding their voice to that of other groups.[28]

On September 6, after the ladies had had their say, the most unusual meeting of all took place: that of several subalterns and other lower ranks of officers from the Prague garrison, who had gathered to protest against the favoritism of the military toward the nobility in the matter of promotions; they even had the temerity to suggest that they would present their grievances to the government. The officers also voiced concern over the rapidly deteriorating relationship between the military and the civilians.[29] Appropriately, the meeting took place in Karlín, the suburb of Prague inhabited by the lower social strata. The turnout of the military malcontents did not represent any significant proportion of the garrison personnel. The majority were loyal to Windischgrätz, unfriendly to civilians, and positively hostile to the constitutional movement, which to them symbolized a reduction of the power of the military. Nevertheless, the very fact that a group of Windischgrätz' soldiers actually met in order to complain publicly against the military establishment demonstrates the intoxicating effect of the idea of equality, and the depth of resentment awakened by this second radical wave. Never before had the members of the military participated in such a meeting, and never before had the military hierarchy found itself publicly challenged by subordinates.

Against this new kind of rebellion retribution was swift and severe. Windischgrätz could shrug off the collective political voice of the Prague women, but he could not tolerate such open support among his soldiers for the democratic movement. He could not countenance the spread of the 1848 contagion into his army, the last bastion still unsullied by any association with democracy and the only remaining force in the monarchy capable of keeping the dangerous new forces under control. Several members of the military who had spoken at the meeting were promptly arrested. As a result, at the following meeting, on September 9, at which the discussion continued, only a few soldiers turned out, and all but one kept their peace.[30] After this there were no more meetings and there was no petition to the Imperial Parliament. But the matter reached the floor of the parliament anyhow, as the news came to the Prague deputies

28. This is treated in greater detail in Chapter 14.
29. *PVL,* September 7, 1848.
30. *PVL,* September 10, 1848.

of the arrest of the soldiers involved. On September 22, Rieger interceded on their behalf,[31] and in the end the men were released. Of the
culprits, the three who were considered to have committed the most
serious offenses, two corporals and one sergeant-major, were trans-
ferred to other regiments.[32]

In riding and stimulating the wave of discontent, the radicals were
in their element. Both disappointed and aroused by the results of
the vote in the parliament on compensation on August 23, the Slavic
Linden worked tirelessly during the latter part of August and the
early part of September to secure the election of democrats and radicals to the Prague City Council. The Linden prepared a complete
slate of candidates and, when the results were announced, received
the satisfaction of seeing most of its candidates elected. "The
City Council was elected according to the wishes of the radicals," an
enthusiastic Czech radical newspaper commented.[33] Encouraged by
these trends as much as it was alarmed by the growing signs of reaction, *Pražský Večerní List* published, from the pen of Sabina, a
series of articles entitled "A New Confession of Faith." In these
articles Sabina embraced a creed of an aggressive and inflammatory
radicalism, pillorying those "who bow before the false gods of aristocracy, bureaucracy, and bourgeoisie; who esteem more money than
spirit, estate more than person, prejudices more than merits."[34] The
term "bourgeoisie" was a novum even in the arsenal of the radicals.
It had seldom if ever been used by this newspaper before in the
pejorative sense. While Sabina's series was in progress, the same
newspaper published a special editorial announcing its new and firm
devotion to a consistent democracy and proclaiming its intention
to "defend the rich against the poor" and to fight for the "right to
work so that freedom should not be a mere mockery of poverty but its
salvation."[35]

On October 2, the radical camp was bolstered by the founding
of the Slavic Linden's newspaper (see p. 218 above). Soon, however,
the Viennese revolution introduced a jarring note. The radicals could
not in good conscience support the revolution, but they feared the
consequences of a military victory over Vienna and sought to alert

31. *Verhandlungen*, II, 532 ff.
32. *PVL*, September 29, 1848.
33. *PVL*, September 22, 1848; also, *CBB*, September 22, 1848.
34. *PVL*, September 30, 1848.
35. *Ibid.*

public opinion to this danger. Increasingly, the two leading radical newspapers drew the attention of the public to the need for vigilance, sought to inject life into the National Guards, and generally emphasized the need for the populace to be armed. At the end of November, another Czech radical paper entered the field, *Občanské Noviny,* with Emanuel Arnold as the moving spirit.[36] It directed its message primarily to the peasantry.

Now, however, the growing radical movement was confronted with a force with which it had not been confronted before June: a reviving conservatism, emboldened by the victory over Prague in June and over Vienna in October. The conservative bureaucratic hierarchy and the conservative forces in general had, of course, remained entrenched all through the crisis that began with the March Days, but until June they had been paralyzed into inactivity by the fear of the masses and had not dared antagonize public opinion unduly. Windischgrätz' victories gave them a new confidence.

The formation of the Schwarzenberg government and the subsequent accession to the throne of Emperor Francis Joseph were the unmistakable signs of a rally of conservatism. It was no accident that a few days after Francis Joseph became emperor, the government issued a directive stating that government officials must not criticize government policy and must always speak and act strictly in accordance with that policy. A remarkable feature of the directive was that it applied to conduct both "in and out of office," which might make even a casual remark in private conversation the cause of an official's dismissal.[37] The directive was designed to tighten discipline within the bureaucracy and presumably make certain that no softhearted official would be deflected by constitutional qualms from enforcing reactionary laws. Not too many officials were likely to have such qualms, however; officialdom as a whole was basically hostile to constitutionalism and did its best to hamper its growth.[38] After June,

36. F. Roubík, *Časopisectvo v Čechách v letech 1848-1862* (Prague, 1930), p. 155.

37. Text in *NN,* January 6, 1849.

38. Although most bureaucrats of all echelons tended to be arrogant in dealing with the public, this does not mean that they were all satisfied with their employment. The lower-echelon officials were poorly paid and even in the pre-March era there had been considerable dissatisfaction and skepticism among them. The political upheavals since March created a feeling of uncertainty about future employment, a malaise that threatened to undermine their morale seriously. An official report speaks of a feeling of despondency

through their control of the postal channels, the officials began to sabotage the distribution of liberal and radical newspapers. Editors were receiving numerous complaints from subscribers that their copies were arriving either too late or not at all, but because distribution was not in their hands, they were powerless to do anything about it.[39] Also since June, the arrogance of the landlords and their officials in dealing with the peasants had increased markedly.[40] The number of spies and informants, too, had mushroomed. The regular police agents were at one time known to the public; at a student meeting in July, the students, having recognized an agent in their midst, hustled him out of the meeting, to the amusement of those present.[41] In the early months of 1849, however, spies were no longer amusing; they were becoming a curse on innocent citizens and a hideous preview of Bach's police state.

The army of officials was only a little better than the army of soldiers. After Windischgrätz' victory over Prague, the insolence of the military visibly grew, and instances of harassment and arbitrary arrests of civilians multiplied, in violation of constitutional liberties.[42] The favorite target of the soldiers was the university students. The relationship between civilians and soldiers deteriorated to the point where it claimed the attention of the highest levels of government. In the latter part of August, the acting governor of Bohemia invited the editors of the leading newspapers to his office and asked them to work toward a reconciliation between the two groups.[43] Needless to say, the effort never succeeded. The military continued to function as a law unto itself, and the civilians continued to distrust the military, whom they regarded as a symbol of absolutism.

A very real sign of the changing climate was a political revival of the one class that seemed at first to have suffered a complete eclipse: the landowning class, which included the nobility. Claiming the constitutional right of free association, on September 17, a group of land-

---

(*Mutlosigkeit*) (see Heyde's report of April 12, 1848, in *SÚA* Prague, PG 1846-1849, 15 c/3, No. 2938/1848).

39. *Bohemia*, July 9, 1848; *NN*, July 27, 1848.

40. Examples given by Czech deputy Sidon in his speech in the parliament, August 24, 1848; *Verhandlungen*, II, 48.

41. *PVL*, July 26, 1848.

42. One person was seized for wearing trousers mistakenly identified by the soldiers as the costume of the banned organization *Svornost* (*NN*, August 20, 1848).

43. *NN*, August 22, 1848.

owners issued an appeal calling for the formation of a "League of Landowners of Bohemia." The appeal was published as a large spread in the major newspapers, sometimes in several successive issues of the same paper; one of its purposes was the "safeguarding and the furtherance of the political and material interests of the landowning class." Typically, the predominant influence in the League was to be wielded by owners of the large landed domains. This much is clear from the provision, which stated that those possessing more than three hundred jochs of land would each have one individual voice, while those possessing less would have collectively one voice as soon as their total area equaled three hundred jochs.[44] Before June such an announcement could never have been so openly trumpeted through the country, but in the latter part of September it fitted into the process of a regrouping and consolidation of conservative forces taking place in Bohemia and Moravia.

From the beginning of the year 1849, with the new emperor at the helm, laws and other measures designed to curb the opposition followed one another in quickening pace. There could be no mistaking the direction in which the new emperor and the new government intended to lead their people. The very first day of the new year brought a chilling development: an announcement about a new law establishing controls over the press. The government had every reason, from its point of view, to be displeased with the state of newspaper publishing in the realm. The daily press in Bohemia, both Czech and German, was almost entirely in the hands of liberals and radicals. The two existing official newspapers, *Pražské Noviny* and *Prager Zeitung,* for Czech and German readers respectively, were read by officials rather than by the public. Feeling keenly the absence of a popular conservative newspaper, Governor Thun launched a conservative paper, just before the June Uprising, under the highly inappropriate title of *Pokrok* (*Progress*). After five issues had appeared, the uprising put an end to it.[45] It was never revived, and as late as November, 1848, the Prague burgomaster lamented, in an official report, the fact that "there still exists here no conservative newspaper."[46]

44. Text of the appeal in *CBB,* First Supplement to No. 71, September 21, 1848. A *joch* equals 1.44 acres.

45. Roubík, *Časopisectvo v Čechách,* p. 161.

46. Report of November 13, 1848 (*SÚA* Prague, PG 1846-49, 15 c/3, No. 10250/1848). It was not until March 1, 1849, that a conservative popular

Unable to destroy the popularity of the liberal and radical news-papers, the government did the next best thing: it decided to muzzle them or at least to create an atmosphere of uncertainty for the printed word. On January 1, 1849, the acting governor gave the press a sample of what the new year would bring. He summoned to his office the editors of all the political newspapers published in Prague and in-formed them of the contents of a ministerial decree relating to the press that was about to be issued. The decree limited the distribution of political posters and pamphlets and obliged the editors of political newspapers to submit a copy of each issue to an appropriate govern-ment office in advance of publication so that this office could confis-cate the issue if it contained "offensive" material. The acting gover-nor sweetened the pill by stating that the new decree would be en-forced with as much consideration for the freedom of the printed word as possible.[47] The announcement of the decree was an ill omen for the new year. The worst ghosts of the Metternich era were being resur-rected; once again, as in the pre-March era, the censor lurked over the editor's shoulder, and, once again, the editor would have to go through the daily humiliation of having a bureaucrat approve his copy.

A few days later, the government announced the abolition of the Academic Legion, thus wiping out another legacy of the March Days. The main reason given was that the Academic Legion and academic work were incompatible, that the bearing of arms diverted the students from their studies.[48] It is impossible to deny that there was much truth in this allegation, but it is equally impossible to deny that this was not the main reason for abolishing the Legion. The students were regarded as the chief troublemakers, and it was the government's intention to neutralize their influence. It was, in fact, the government's campaign to whittle down, one by one, the achievements—many of them still fragile achievements—of the March Days. Soon the students were hit from another direction: in February a major military re-cruitment drive was begun, authorized by a Law of December 5 (the recruitment was by lot within specified groups); since they were all of draft age, many students would naturally be affected. Claiming an old privilege (from the year 1827), the Committee of Prague

---

newspaper was launched, under the name of *Vlastimil*. It never attained popularity and died in 1850. (Roubík, *Časopisectvo v Čechách*, p. 176.)

47. *NN*, January 2, 1849; *NLS*, January 3, 1849.

48. *PVL*, January 7 and 11, 1849.

Students petitioned the imperial government that students be exempted from military service, but the request was denied.[49]

It is to be noted that the recruitment law was issued without any reference to the Imperial Parliament. That the government, in a supposedly parliamentary state, could bypass the parliament in issuing such an important law shows how self-confident it had come to feel by the beginning of December. Recruitment became an instrument for removing politically undesirable people from civilian status. A subsequent regulation issued on April 24 by the General Command for Bohemia stated quite blatantly that because "often there is not sufficient evidence" on the basis of which political suspects "could be legally prosecuted," such suspects would be inducted into the army; in such cases "minor physical defects" could be "overlooked"![50] For a young man to be recruited was a severe blow, for he was obligated to serve for eight years.

That the government did not trouble to consult the parliament before issuing the recruitment law should not have surprised anyone. When the new emperor, in his first solemn act, styled himself "Emperor by the grace of God," he and the government served notice that they did not have much respect for the collective will of the parliament, presumably because it could not boast the manifest advantage of being favored by divine grace. The government formally expressed its views regarding popular sovereignty during the celebrated debate in the plenum of the parliament concerning Article I of the proposed preamble to the constitution. Article I, read in the plenum on January 4, 1849, proclaimed that "all powers of the state originate from the people." As soon as the reading of the article was completed, Minister Stadion, who had been present as the representative of the government, ascended the rostrum and proceeded to attack it. Article I was either intended to be an abstract principle, he said, in which case it was not fitting to incorporate it in a document designed to determine specific political relations, or it purported to describe an actuality, in which case it was untrue. Under the banner of popular sovereignty, laws had been violated, "streets turned into spectacles of wild excesses, the blood of the noble Count Latour spilled." The concept did not correspond to the legal sentiment of the peoples of the monarchy: "The

49. *NLS,* February 11, 1849. Havlíček also opposed recruitment in the manner in which it was being conducted (see *NN.* February 15 and 22, 1849). For a critical analysis of the recruitment law, see *NN,* February 15.

50. *PVL,* May 2, 1849.

hereditary monarchical right appears in the state form of a constitutional monarchy a sacred and inalienable source of supreme power." Stadion conceded that in a constitutional regime legislative power was shared by the monarch with representatives elected by the people but "the assertion that all power comes from the people is quite irreconcilable with the legal status of our monarchy." The tenor of this remark indicated clearly that even now Stadion and the government regarded constitutional government not as the right of the people but rather as a favor bestowed on the people by His Majesty's generosity.[51]

The minister's words, uttered with an imperious air, were a mixture of impatience and insolence. They were simultaneously a lecture, a reproach, and a warning. The note of threat was but thinly veiled. The statement, which came without any advance notice, created a sensation. The principle of popular sovereignty was the very heart of the Revolution of 1848 and a basis for all the aspirations and reforms of that year. Without it, the whole movement of 1848 was emptied of meaning; it was regarded as one of the least controversial and most self-evident achievements of the March Days. Stadion's words could not have been publicly uttered even two months earlier, but so swift had been the consolidation of conservatism since the defeat of Vienna that a minister of the crown could now flaunt them before the deputies, the majority of whom could not help feeling deeply offended.

Such a challenge could only be met by an even greater challenge, and it seemed at first that the chamber would stand up to the government. Aroused and angered by Stadion, on January 8, 178 deputies affixed their signatures to a protest drafted by the Czech deputy Pinkas accusing the government of exerting unfair pressure upon the deputies and restricting their freedom of conscience by its ill-timed interference in the debate. One hundred and seventy-eight deputies constituted a majority of the 332 deputies present at the meeting at which the protest was submitted.[52] The protest was signed by the deputies of both the right and the left; it was the first time in the short history of the Imperial Parliament that the two sides had joined hands, leaving only the center to support the government. Surprised by the vehemence of the response, Stadion offered a conciliatory statement, without, however, making any concession of principle. Later at

51. *Verhandlungen*, IV, 267.
52. *Ibid.*, p. 277. Text in *NN*, January 9, 1849.

the same meeting, Pinkas' protest was carried by 196 votes against 99, with some abstentions, a seemingly crushing defeat for the government.

A full-fledged debate then unfolded, with spokesmen both for and against Article I. The most prominent speaker in defense of Article I was Rieger, who, in defending the article on January 10, delivered the most famous speech of his life and gave one of the most spell-binding performances ever witnessed in the parliamentary chamber. Rieger held the chamber's attention for almost two hours, earning repeated "stormy applause." Stadion's speech had been an attack on the sovereignty of the people; Rieger's was an attack on the sovereignty of the monarch. Stadion had been imperious and arrogant; Rieger was impassioned and mordant. He explained at the outset that Article I did not deny the hereditary right of the dynasty to the throne, that it merely asserted that sovereignty in a state rests ultimately with the people. As formulated by Stadion, the principle of monarchical sovereignty would inevitably lead to absolutism. Though it was true that popular sovereignty was susceptible to abuse, it was equally true that all principles, no matter how lofty, were susceptible to abuse. Should we, Rieger asked, eat with bare hands merely because a knife may become a murder weapon? Should we leave our homes unheated because fire might destroy them? He then proceeded to question the very idea of monarchical legitimacy. If Cromwell had had an able son, his successor would today be sitting on the English throne, the descendant of a usurper. The Carolingians gained power by overthrowing a legitimate dynasty and becoming themselves a legitimate dynasty. The foundation of sovereignty is the will of the people, and a monarch who wants to challenge it ought to beware, for "the wrath of the people is a powerful hurricane, its breath upsets thrones, causes crowns to fall from anointed heads, and even as a mighty storm lays low an old oak tree, so does a nation's wrath seize an ancient dynastic tree, sever it from the life of a nation and cast it away like a light willow twig."[53]

Rieger's speech was greeted with enthusiasm, and was later reprinted in liberal and radical newspapers. It sounded like the distant rumbling of a revolution. It needed only a firm stand on the part of the deputies to back it up and demonstrate to the government that they could be pushed only so far. But when it came to deeds, the

53. *Verhandlungen,* IV, 354.

wrath of the people proved to be anything but a hurricane. On January 8 a majority of deputies had endorsed Pinkas' resolution. On January 10, a majority applauded Rieger's speech. Then, on the same day, a few minutes after the speech, in an about-face almost beyond belief, a majority voted not to press Article I, but to shelve it for consideration in a later section of the constitution.[54] This was, of course, a complete surrender to the government. The deputies could soothe their collective conscience by arguing that the incorporation of Article I into the constitution had not been abandoned but merely postponed. In fact, Article I had been abandoned: it had not been endorsed; what had been endorsed was only the proposal that the question of sovereignty should be considered later. It was the Czech deputies who committed the about-face and deserted a principle in which they honestly believed, in the face of the government's stand. In the crucial vote, only the German left remained faithful to it and to its convictions. The Czechs and others on the right joined with the center to dispatch the article to oblivion. More than any other single act, the vote on Article I mars the record of the Czech deputies in the Imperial Parliament. The Polish deputy Smolka described their action fittingly in a letter to his wife. Rieger spoke very well, he wrote, "But what good is it when afterwards all Czechs voted in the spirit of the government so that the whole of Rieger's speech looked like sheer comedy?"[55]

In the end, Rieger's speech irritated but did not check the government; after the vote the government could be certain that it could do what it pleased and had nothing to fear from the parliament. One might have expected that the deputies on the left would have hissed and booed as they had done on similar occasions before, or that the center might have rejoiced. But nothing like this happened. No emotions were expressed when the vote was announced, and it is little wonder that such a display of weakness only cemented the resolve of the government to move with its own plans. Within ten days of the vote the government finally decided to dissolve the parliament and put it out of its misery altogether.[56]

At home, Havlíček did not react at all to the vote. By that time he had come to regard his newspaper so much as the voice of the Czech liberals that he did not publish a word of criticism. In con-

54. *Verhandlungen,* IV, 358.
55. V. Žáček, *Čechové a Poláci roku 1848* (Prague, 1947-48), II, 316.
56. *Ibid.,* p. 323.

trast, one radical paper wrote that "the ministry won, the chamber no longer has the strength manfully to resist the government."[57] Another cried that "the idea of the Austrian revolution has been led to the scaffold by those whom it raised up" and warned the Czech deputies: "Your weakness has become proverbial; unwittingly you sink further and further into the tentacles of ministers who will ill-reward you for your devotion."[58]

Yet the parliament was given a few more weeks of a precarious existence. It continued to debate the Bill of Rights. On January 17, it abolished the nobility by an overwhelming vote, with the Czechs voting with the majority; the temper of the chamber had from the beginning been anti-aristocratic and there never was any doubt concerning the results of the vote. It displayed a similar attitude toward the Roman Catholic church. One perceptive observer gave the following description of the religious attitude of the liberal middle classes that dominated the parliament: "A customary participation in the splendid religious ceremonies satisfied entirely the religious needs. The middle strata of the population had Catholic mores, but no Catholic convictions."[59] The Roman Catholic deputies seemed to suffer no inner conflict in voting against their church. Over the protest of the hierarchy, the parliament approved, with the support of the Czech deputies, Article XV, which placed the Roman Catholic church and its property under the supervision of the state.[60]

This article, from the original Bill of Rights, was the last one discussed; the vote on the church question the last business accomplished; the speech made on that occasion by Rieger, criticizing the church, the last great speech to ring through the chamber; and the day, March 6, the last in the life of the parliament. On March 7, Francis Joseph, "by the Grace of God Emperor of Austria"—to use the words of an imperial manifesto issued on that day (though dated March 4)—sent out two infantry companies to occupy the premises of the palace in which the Imperial Parliament was housed. The parliament had thus been officially disbanded, the "will of God" had triumphed over the will of the parliament, and the soldiers were there to prove it to those who might otherwise have been difficult to convince. Within a few hours, the police had begun to hunt down a

57. *PVL,* January 14, 1849.
58. *NLS,* January 14, 1849.
59. Springer, *Geschichte Österreichs,* II, 610.
60. *Verhandlungen,* V, 426.

few deputies of the left; the sword of Damocles, after being suspended over their heads for three months, had fallen. The revolution died an infant, a few days less than a year old.

Since the beginning of the year 1849, hardly a day had passed without a rumor that the parliament was about to be dissolved. The chamber carried on its work entirely in the shadow of the imminence of its dissolution. In fact, it may be said without undue exaggeration that the deputies had learned so well to live with the idea of dissolution that it had virtually bowed to it before it happened. Because of this fear, every next meeting was a welcome reprieve, every sound of the opening gavel a pleasant surprise. It is a melancholy commentary on the spirit of the chamber that although dissolution was daily expected, it was never resisted. No plans were ever made, no action contemplated, no strategy worked out to thwart the government. Therefore, when dissolution finally came on March 7, there was no display of determination to carry on, in the face of the government's autocratic act. The parliament could have strengthened its moral stature by declaring its permanence and placing on the shoulders of the government the responsibility for what might then happen. But nothing of this sort was done. The deputies could justify their inertia, however, by the undeniable truth that the masses of the people were not yet politically conscious, or were, at any rate, not ready to rise in defense of the parliamentary regime.

For the Czech deputies the dissolution was a defeat. In fact, it was a fate worse than defeat; it was a stunning humiliation. After the event, Havlíček feebly wrote: "We confess that . . . the unexpected act of the government startled us so much that we still gaze, as though in a dream, at everything that is happening."[61] A man may be defeated, honorably, after he has resisted and fought to the last of his strength, but the Czech deputies were defeated by a group which they had sought to please and which they had supported to the very eve of dissolution. Through the weeks of siding and voting with the government and enduring the jeers of the left, they had been sustained by the hope that at the end of the painful road was a harvest of political gains and a new strength for their nation. Now the end of

61. *NN*, March 10, 1849. In view of the repeated rumors about dissolution, it is curious that Havlíček refers to "the unexpected act of the government." The explanation is that although dissolution had been feared, many deputies were still shocked when it finally came; they did not expect that the government would resort to such a drastic measure.

the road had been reached, and it proved to be a dead-end street, with no rewards and no laurels. By supporting, far beyond the counsel of prudence—and patience—the reaction, they forefeited the sympathy of the left, but being known by conviction as partisans of constitutionalism, they never gained the confidence of the reaction.

That they needlessly abetted the reaction after the end of 1848 there can be no doubt. Until the formation of the Schwarzenberg government, the cabinets had been reasonably liberal and the Czech leaders could support them in reasonably good conscience. During that period too they opposed the Viennese revolution, and here also they could not have acted otherwise, given the dogmatic centralism and the chauvinistic nationalism of the forces that had unleashed the revolution. But in this latter case they should have been on guard against reaction; instead they continued to publicly assure every anxious and doubting voice that there was no such danger. Then came the Schwarzenberg government, which, from the beginning of December, demonstrated by its almost every action that it was pursuing a reactionary course. Its ministers increasingly ignored the parliament; they gradually ceased attending its sessions and did not deign to appear personally to answer for their conduct in office. After January 8, the ministerial benches remained completely empty in fourteen out of twenty-nine meetings; and by February 26, some twenty-five interpellations remained unanswered.[62] Despite these numerous warning signs, the Czech deputies remained committed to a support of the government. It is probable that a few deputies would have wished to alter this course, but the prestige and the pressure of the leadership, chiefly of Palacký, prevented them from so doing. A few Slavic deputies complained of "a tyrannical pressure exerted on them by the leaders," mainly by Palacký, Strobach, and Brauner.[63]

To say that the Czech deputies basically supported the Schwarzenberg government is not to imply that during this period they neglected the interests of their nation. To the contrary, Havlíček, in his *Národní Noviny,* often subjected the Schwarzenberg government to scathing criticism, and the Czech deputies often criticized it in their speeches and interpellations. On several occasions, they demanded that the government submit to the parliament all the acts relating to the in-

62. J. A. Helfert, *Geschichte Österreichs vom Ausgange des Wiener Oktober-Aufstandes 1848* (Prague, 1869-86), IV/3, 254.

63. *Ibid.,* p. 370.

vestigation of the June Uprising.[64] In response to Slovak complaints that the imperial government was oppressing their nationality, a parliamentary investigating committee consisting of three Czechs was chosen; later, the Slavic Club dispatched on its own a three-man delegation, consisting of two Czechs and one southern Slav, to take up the matter directly with the government, and received assurances that the national rights of the Hungarian Slavs would be respected.[65] Czech deputies applauded the interpellation of a member of the left, the Pole Machalski, asking that the state of siege over Lvov be lifted.[66] The Slavic Club also submitted a memorandum to the government opposing the recruitment law and the manner in which it was being carried out; apart from some of the law's defects, it seemed to the deputies that certain regions, particularly the Czech and South Slavic ones, were bearing a heavier load than others.[67]

In instances of basic importance in which a vote was required, however, the Czech deputies supported the government, once the latter made the matter into a fundamental issue by taking a public stand upon it. Even when, for a time, they appeared to be emancipating themselves from this attitude, their new freedom was of short duration; they initiated, through Pinkas, and supported, the resolution chastizing Stadion for interfering in the debate on Article I, but they dulled its edge immediately by explaining, again through Pinkas, that it was not a "nonconfidence" measure. Through Rieger, they defended Article I in the most eloquent language, but voted within minutes after Rieger's speech to bury the article to satisfy the government.

For all their support, the government showed remarkably little consideration for Czech sensitivities or for specific Czech wishes. The draft of a law on local government submitted to certain deputies at the end of 1848 was, as Havlíček wrote, a "centralist-bureaucratic-aristocratic monster."[68] Apart from the reactionary spirit by which this law was permeated, it hit Czech sensitivities in two directions: (1) by its centralism, and (2) by the provision according to which

64. *Verhandlungen*, IV, 540.
65. Helfert, *Geschichte Österreichs*, IV/3, 252-53.
66. *Verhandlungen*, IV, 475-76.
67. Dated February 28, 1849. Text in Černý, *Boj*, pp. 529-31.
68. *NN*, December 12, 1848; his article includes a sampling of the provisions of the law.

any citizen of the German Confederation would automatically become the citizen of those provinces of Austria belonging formally to the confederation; this included the Czech Lands and meant that Germany and Austria were being treated as one state—a horrifying idea for a Czech patriot. In general, the government pursued centralist rather than federalist policies, in direct opposition to Czech wishes. And as late as February, 1849, it authorized an election to Frankfurt in those constituencies in which no valid election had been held—an affront to the Czechs that provoked a major interpellation from Palacký.[69]

The original "bargain" between the Czechs and the imperial government was prudent and made sense, but it was predicated on the government's respecting the principles of constitutionalism. The Schwarzenberg government belied this respect by every major step it took. In answering their radical critics, the Czech deputies replied that theirs was a policy of wisdom and realism; this was, for example, the answer given by Brauner after the vote on Article I.[70] Actually, the Czech deputies carried their realism to a point at which they lost sight of reality. For if there was one reality as the parliament continued its work, it was that the government was leading the monarchy down the path of constitutional ruin. This the liberals purported not to see. Of the radicals' fears that the parliament would be dissolved, Havlíček—though one can detect a growing note of uncertainty in his articles—wrote as late as February 18 that he did not believe that "the government would dare take such a tyrannical step."[71] Was he expressing a conviction or merely a hope? In any event, the tyrannical step was only two weeks away. In contrast, the radicals warned repeatedly that constitutionalism was in grave danger, and on March 4 saw "reaction virtually over our heads."[72] This struck as close to the truth as any observer could ever hope to come.

It is only fair to note that after the parliament was dissolved the Czech deputies were the only parliamentary group that defended the Imperial Parliament's integrity and record, in a protest statement issued on March 15. Though there were also a few members of other nationalities, the majority of the thirty-four signatories of this docu-

69. *Verhandlungen,* V, 221-23.
70. *NLS,* January 14, 1849.
71. *NN,* February 18, 1849.
72. *PVL,* March 4, 1849.

ment were Czech.[73] It is further to be noted that before the parliament's dissolution, during its weeks of dying agony, it was only from the Czech regions that the parliament received major expressions of confidence and support. The most outstanding of these was the "monster" petition of the Slavic Linden, consisting of messages from 732 cities and villages of Bohemia, with a total number of 40,595 signatures. The petition was received and gratefully acknowledged on March 1, six days before the parliament was disbanded.[74] The Prague Student Committee sent its own message of confidence, to which were added messages from a few individual Moravian communities. A third campaign of this kind was being planned in German Austria, but it failed for lack of support.[75] Thus only the Czechs rallied to the parliament in its hour of crisis. Symbolically, the last official act of the legislative body was a letter written by parliament president Smolka to the Prague Student Committee, thanking it for its message of confidence.[76] After the parliament was dissolved, it was again only in the Czech Lands that some resistance to the government developed.

On the same day on which the emperor dispersed the parliament by an imperial manifesto, he issued three further documents: (1) an "octroyed" constitution (octroi), prepared by the government and thus imposed on Austria from above, by fiat (2) an "octroyed" Bill of Rights; and (3) an imperial patent concerning compensation to the landlords for their losses due to the abolition of serfdom.[77] Though issued on March 7, all four decrees were dated March 4. The patent on compensation, confirming as it did the abolition of serfdom, was a shrewdly timed piece of legislation; while disbanding the parliament, the emperor was in effect telling the peasants that they did not need

73. Černý (ed.), *Boj*, pp. 592-95. Typically, Brauner's name is not among the signatories.

74. *Verhandlungen*, V, 252.

75. The student message, dated February 19, 1849, bore the signatures of two thousand students; it stated that "only that constitution can bring blessing to the peoples of Austria which will spring from the will of the freely elected representatives of the people" (text in *CBB*, February 20, 1849; see also Helfert, *Geschichte Österreichs*, IV/3, 252).

76. *CBB*, March 11, 1849. After March 7, the government invited a few prominent Czech deputies (as well as those of other nationalities), including Palacký, to collaborate with it in preparing new measures. All Czechs except Brauner declined.

77. Text of all four measures in Černý (ed.), *Boj*, pp. 564 ff.

parliaments because he was there to take care of their interests. As for the constitution and the Bill of Rights, the government paid lip service to constitutional principles, but the shaping hand of absolutism and centralism was in evidence. In any event, the dissolution of the parliament constituted only the first stage in the reimposition of absolutism. The parliament envisaged by the octroi was never permitted to meet, and further restrictive laws followed. On December 3, 1851, the emperor abolished the very constitution and Bill of Rights he himself had issued in March, 1849, and in a new fundamental law issued on the same day the word "parliament" was not even mentioned.[78] The nightmare of reaction, in its naked form, had now become a reality in Austria.

78. *Ibid.*, pp. 771 ff.

Chapter **9**

The Plot That Failed:
The May Conspiracy

The promulgation of the octroyed constitution and Bill of Rights was followed by two laws designed to severely restrict the most precious freedoms the 1848 revolution had produced: freedom of the press and freedom of association.

The law concerning the press, dated March 13, 1849, which confirmed the worst fears of the editors,[1] barely concealed its ultimate purpose: the destruction of a free press. It forbade any kind of public sale of newspapers, either door-to-door or at newsstands. The only way in which a person could secure a copy of a newspaper was by subscription, in which case it would be delivered directly to his home, either by mail or by personal delivery. It was evidently hoped that banning the public sale of newspapers would reduce their influence on the people. The provision that aimed the deadliest blow at the press, however, was one requiring publishers to post a bond varying with the frequency of the papers' appearance. All publishers of political newspapers in communities having at least sixty thousand inhabitants—this, of course, included Prague and was aimed primarily at the Prague papers—and appearing three times a week or more were required to post a bond of ten thousand gulden. Since this was a sum many newspapers, particularly the radical ones, could never hope to raise, their publishers would be forced to cease publication, and the provision soon caused many newspapers to go out of business. Of the Czech newspapers, one of the first casualties was the *Noviny Lípy Slovanské,* which published its last issue on April 28, 1849. Within a short time, a half dozen or so other Czech newspapers ceased publication, and the German ones were equally affected. Havlíček's *Národní Noviny* and the radical *Pražský Večerní List* were financially more secure, and both survived for a time, the former until the beginning of 1850, the latter until the beginning of 1851.

After issuing the new press law, the government lost no time in using its provisions to attack the leading voice of Czech journalism,

1. Text in *NN,* March 23, 1849.

Karel Havlíček. The government lodged a suit against Havlíček, charging that in a recent article he defamed and sought to bring into disrepute the octroyed constitution.[2] The trial, held on April 13, attracted the interest of the Czech community and became something of a peaceful demonstration against the regime. Havlíček defended himself with characteristic wit, with the Czech community—liberals and radicals alike—supporting him fully. The decision was in the hands of a jury, elected for press cases by the people, and there never was any doubt about the outcome. This time Havlíček triumphed: it took no more than ten minutes for the jury to announce a verdict of "not guilty," to the thunderous applause of the audience.[3] But in less than a year the voice of *Národní Noviny* was stilled forever, and in 1851 the government placed Havlíček under arrest and deported him.

The law concerning association was put into effect on March 17.[4] It placed all political clubs and societies under close government supervision. Such clubs were forbidden to have any affiliates or branches in other localities. Women were excluded "unconditionally" from any political club. Advance notice of every meeting had to be given to the authorities so that a government official might attend. Without a government official present a meeting could not be held, and the official was given the right, by this law, to terminate the meeting at any time he saw fit. The "law on association" had a particularly crippling effect on the Slavic Linden. It compelled the parent body in Prague to cut all ties with its many branches throughout Bohemia and Moravia, thereby completely destroying its national character. The Slavic Linden fought hard to stay alive, but within a few months it succumbed to official pressure and ceased to exist.

The dissolution of the Imperial Parliament, the imposition of an octroyed constitution, and the many other restrictive measures provoked an attitude of defiant opposition among segments of the population. The disbanding of the parliament coincided with a vigorous military recruitment drive in the Czech Lands, which sharpened the resistance. The return of the deputies from Kroměříž was turned into a manifestation of sympathy for them—and by implication for the cause of constitutionalism to which the government had just dealt a mortal blow. A solemn torchlight procession was organized in the evening hours of March 14 to honor the deputies, and two of them, the

2. The article in question appeared in *NN*, March 14, 1849.
3. *NN*, April 14 and 15, 1849.
4. Text in *NN*, March 23, 1849.

German Alois Borrosch and the Czech Rieger addressed the multitude at some length, vowing their determination to defend the cause of freedom. It was not accidental that a Czech and a German, who had frequently clashed in public in the past, spoke now from the same platform and were equally applauded; the intention was to emphasize harmony between the two nationalities in the face of a common foe.[5]

For some weeks patriotic and liberal-minded groups had been preparing to celebrate March 11, the first anniversary of the revolution. Now their plans were abandoned. There was no mood for merriment; March 11, 1849, became only a grim reminder that the revolution had failed so soon that it did not even survive to see its first anniversary. To help overcome the atmosphere of gloom, the government itself proclaimed a "Constitution Day" on March 12, and everything was done from the official side to make it a festive occasion. The government supplied all the impressive trimmings, including a parade of soldiers and a special mass celebrated in Prague's most famous church, St. Vitus' Cathedral. But the people were not deceived. Nobody came to the mass who did not have to, and even many of those who were expected to attend, such as municipal councilors, did not appear. In a report from Prague to Vienna, an official noted ruefully that participation was poor.[6] To drive the point home even more, the Prague students organized their own version of a Constitution Day on the following day (March 13), to remember "all those who had perished in the last 365 days in the noble struggle for the freedom of peoples." Although the day was rainy, throngs of people turned out to watch the procession, and the church in which the mass was celebrated was packed.[7]

This was a peaceful demonstration, the purpose of which was a display of sentiment, not of force. But a small though determined band of young radicals decided to go beyond this: to the agony of the political dying imposed by the government, they decided to offer the antidote of armed resistance. This was the so-called May Conspiracy. The decision of the radicals was hastened by the intervention of Russia in the Austro-Hungarian conflict; Russia was the very incarnation of

5. *NN*, March 16, 1849.

6. Mecséry to Vienna, March 14, 1849 (*SÚA* Prague, PG 1846-49, 15 c/3, No. 1924/1849).

7. *Ibid.*; also J. A. Helfert, *Geschichte Österreichs vom Ausgange des Wiener Oktober-Aufstandes 1848* (Prague, 1869-86), IV/3, 372.

reaction and its political support of any cause was regarded as the kiss of death.

The conspiracy[8] was to be part of a revolutionary upheaval on a European scale. The scope of this grand holocaust was awesome, if one could believe the many rumors circulating through Europe's capitals among the conspirators themselves. It was to involve radicals from Paris to Prague, and was conceived as a Europe-wide offensive of radicals against the creeping reaction. Authorities in Vienna were told by one of the would-be participants that the revolution would begin with an uprising in Paris on March 25, and from Paris the movement would spread to Berlin, Leipzig, Munich, Breslau, Vienna, and Prague.[9] No single directing center for this revolution is known to have existed, however.

The center of gravity of the revolution was to be Central Europe. About this facet of the movement we are well informed and we know that it had been planned and prepared in advance. A leading role was to be played by the well-known revolutionary Mikhail Bakunin, who was not unknown to Czech radicals, since he had spent a few days in Prague at the time of the June Uprising—his first close encounter with the Czechs. After the uprising Bakunin had followed events in the Habsburg Monarchy with interest. He was concerned about the role of Slavdom in the great struggle between European democracy and reaction, and the product of his reflections was his *Aufruf an die Slaven* (*Appeal to the Slavs*), which was published in Germany at the end of the year 1848 in the form of a brochure. The *Appeal* was aimed especially at the Habsburg Slavs, who were exhorted to stage a revolution and to destroy the Habsburg Monarchy. Though critical of Magyar chauvinism, Bakunin encouraged Slavic support of the Magyar struggle against Austria. He attacked those Slavs who claimed that Austria was indispensable to the small Slavic

8. The only monograph is H. Traub, *Květnové spiknutí v Čechách r. 1849* (Prague, 1929). See also Z. Šamberger, "Die revolutionäre Zusammenarbeit der tschechischen und sächsischen Demokraten im Frühjahr 1849," in *Aus 500 Jahren deutsch-tschechoslowakischer Geschichte,* ed. K. Obermann and J. Polišenský (Berlin, 1958).

9. See letters from Vienna to Mecséry, February 16 and 23, 1849 (the latter from Stadion) in *SÚA* Prague, PGT 1849-52, A/1, 65 B.M. and 265/gp. In the latter part of March, Vienna requested directly information from the region prefect of Mladá Boleslav, Kotz, about alleged preparations for a revolution in his region (see letter from Stadion to Mecséry, March 19, 1849, with enclosure, *SÚA* Prague, PGT 1849-52, R/1, 70/gp).

nations as a shield against their big neighbors in the West and East. Far from being a shield, the Austrian Empire was, according to Bakunin, one of the chief pillars of European reaction, and it was in the interest of freedom-loving peoples, including the Slavs, to overthrow it.

At the time of the appearance of the *Appeal* Czech radicals were becoming increasingly disturbed over the encroaching reaction, and many of them were becoming more reserved in applauding the success (such as there was) of Austrian arms over the Magyars. They were also becoming impatient with the support offered by Czech liberals to the central government. Bakunin's *Appeal* could be regarded as a useful corrective for current liberal policies, which induced the *Noviny Lípy Slovanské*, then in radical hands, to take an unorthodox step: it translated the *Appeal* into Czech and spread it over the front page in several installments.[10] Though some deletions had been made, the revolutionary phraseology remained virtually intact in the Czech version, and the effect on the sophisticated reader, whether he was sympathetic or not, must have been stunning. Here was a naked appeal for the destruction of the Habsburg Monarchy staring at the reader from the front pages of a daily newspaper! The *Appeal* had no appreciable effect on the Czech masses; its whole underlying concept and its compulsive revolutionary verbiage were far removed from the experience of the average Czech.

Although the editors tried to protect themselves by adding to the last installment a note in which they dissociated themselves from the document's more extreme views, their action created a furor among Czech liberals. Bakunin had spoken with disrespect, not to say contempt, of the Czech leaders. He had called into question the one concept upon which the liberals had constructed their policy: Austro-Slavism. He had expressed open sympathy for the Magyar cause. And he had openly called for a violent revolution. In other words, he had committed every sin imaginable in the eyes of the Czech liberals. After a few days of silence, Havlíček launched a front-page attack on the radicals for peddling such propaganda. Labeling the action "puerile" and injurious to the Czech and Slavic cause,[11] he charged—

10. *NLS*, January 2-5, 1849. The second "edition" of the appeal, differing somewhat from the first one, was published in March, 1849. It was prompted by the announcement that tsarist armies had entered Transylvania. Text of the second version in V. Čejchan, *Bakunin v Čechách* (Prague, 1928), pp. 193-200.
11. See Havlíček's attack in *NN*, January 21, 1849.

and the justice of it could not be denied—that the enemies of Slavdom would exploit this incident against the Slavs. Then the venerable Palacký, who normally remained aloof from such polemics, added his voice to the criticism.[12]

The reaction to the *Appeal* was probably much stronger than the radical editors had anticipated. The man responsible for the publication of the *Appeal* was Karel Sabina, one of the two coeditors of the *Noviny Lípy Slovanské*. A few days after Havlíček's attack, Sabina published a lengthy explanation of the editorial policies of the newspaper, with particular reference to Bakunin's *Appeal*. Rejecting Bakunin's plans as "fantastic," he dissociated himself from any support of the Magyar cause; he denounced his critics as ill-willed; and he declared that the sole purpose of the editors, in publishing Bakunin's statement, was informative: to acquaint their readers with the thinking of one of Europe's leading radicals.[13] But the liberals were not disposed to forgive Sabina, and under their pressure he was later forced out of his editorial post.

The center of radical activity in Central Europe in the spring of 1849 was Saxony. It was from this province that the revolution was to spread to other German provinces, and it was Bakunin's hope that an uprising of Central European Slavs might be linked directly with the revolution in Saxony. Bakunin would be the leader of the Slavic movement and the link between it and the movement in Saxony. There would also be a tie with the Magyar revolt. Bakunin specifically selected Bohemia and its capital city as the focus of this uprising. He was, of course, aware of the long-standing distrust between Czechs and Germans, and he took it upon himself to bring Czech and German radicals together in one common endeavor. He wanted to demonstrate to the German radicals that not all Czechs were reactionaries, and to the Czechs that not all Germans were chauvinists. He also hoped to effect a rapprochement between Magyars and Slavs.

Why did Bakunin choose Bohemia rather than another country—Poland, for example—as the center of the planned uprising? In his *Confessions* he says that at the beginning of 1849 Poland seemed to him exhausted and demoralized by her previous ill-fated revolutionary ventures, while Bohemia had at the time not yet been touched by reaction, was enjoying complete liberty, and was "disposed of all the

12. F. Palacký, *Spisy drobné*, ed. B. Rieger (Prague, 1898), I, 90-92.
13. *NLS*, January 25 and 26, 1849.

means necessary to a revolutionary movement."[14] Another reason for his preferring Bohemia to Poland was his fear that the Poles might give the revolution a narrow Polish character. Also, he knew that Prague was a city to which other Austrian Slavs (except the Poles) looked for inspiration and guidance, and that as a consequence, a rising in Prague would set an example that other Slavic nationalities would follow. One of his great hopes, says Bakunin, was the Bohemian peasant, both German and Czech, who, having been the subject of an oppressive feudal regime until 1848, was particularly susceptible to revolutionary agitation.

Bakunin's appraisal of the political possibilities afforded by Bohemia constitutes an astonishing example of wishful thinking. How little he knew of Czech affairs may be seen from his observations that Moravia, according to his information, would "without a doubt follow the Czech movement" and that Slovakia and Austrian Silesia would be drawn into it with Moravia![15] It did not take a very profound observer of the political scene in the Czech Lands in 1849 to know that the stock of Bohemian Czechs in Moravia was not very high and that in Silesia the Czech national movement had barely established a foothold. The Bohemian Czechs themselves had no illusions about their influence in these provinces. Bakunin also misjudged public opinion among the peasantry. As far as is known, he had until then not had any opportunity to acquaint himself with the mood of the Czech peasantry; indeed, he had probably never met a single Bohemian peasant. Yet he confidently constructed an edifice of revolution predicated on the readiness of the Bohemian peasant to be swept off his feet by a cause that would unseat an emperor, destroy a monarchy, and in general create institutions and polities that were totally alien to his experience.

As Bakunin conceived it, Prague would be the seat of a revolutionary government, equipped with unlimited dictatorial powers; the nobility would be driven out, and also the clergy if it were hostile to the revolution; the Austrian administration would be abolished completely; and young people, the poor, the industrial workers, and unemployed artisans would form the core of a revolutionary army. These measures were to be financed by confiscations and in certain other ways; here Bakunin would exploit the fact that the nobility and the

14. M. Bakounine, *Confession,* trans. P. Brupbacher (Paris, 1932), p. 202. This work was written in a tsarist prison and was addressed to the tsar.
15. *Ibid.,* p. 209.

grand proprietors were largely German, and that the Czechs would welcome their expulsion and the confiscation of their property. Part of the proceeds from the confiscations would be distributed among the peasants in order to win them over to the revolution.[16] Out of the ashes of the Habsburg Monarchy there would arise "democratic-social republics," which would choose a state form best suited to each particular nationality. The republics would, in turn, constitute a Slavic federation.

Bakunin's republican vision doubtless appealed to many young radicals, but there seems to have been no consensus of opinion among the radicals as a whole. Frič states explicitly that *"none* of us was against the Austrian Monarchy" (the italics are his own),[17] and it is probable that few Czech radicals would have identified themselves with Bakunin's grand design, which was so utterly removed from the reality of the political situation in Central Europe in May, 1849.

At the end of 1848 Bakunin moved to Saxony, first to Leipzig and later to Dresden. While in Saxony, he entered into intimate contact with German, Polish, and Czech radicals (the Polish radicals were to play a most vital role in the revolution). While in Leipzig, he met the Czech brothers, Adolf and Gustav Straka, both students of protestant theology at the University of Leipzig. The Straka brothers became Bakunin's chief confidants for Czech affairs, and Bakunin used them to establish and maintain contact with Czech radicals in Prague. Through them he invited Sabina and Emanuel Arnold to Leipzig in January, 1849, but only Arnold came. In his talks with Arnold, Bakunin emphasized the need for democrats to spread propaganda within the Slavic Linden, especially among the younger members of this group, and asked Arnold to work for a revolution in Bohemia. Bakunin was not too impressed with Arnold, and the encounter proved disappointing to him.[18]

His hopes were restored, however, by the favorable reports his contact in Bohemia began to send him during the next few weeks on the progress of revolutionary work in that province. But the reports were exaggerated, as he was soon to discover. In order to make an on-

16. *Ibid.*, pp. 207-11; *Přehled československých dějin* (Prague, 1960), II/1, 91.

17. J. V. Frič, *Paměti,* ed. K. Cvejn (Prague, 1957-63), II, 370.

18. See Bakounine, *Confession,* p. 221. See also Bakunin's testimony before an Austrian court, in "Bakunin pred avstriiskim sudom," *Krasnyi Arkhiv,* III (1924), 159.

the-spot examination of the situation in Bohemia, he paid a secret visit to Prague at the end of March, 1849. In his *Confessions* he writes that he was dismayed to discover that "literally nothing" had been done to prepare the ground for a revolution. This visit left Bakunin with very negative impressions. The visit was supposed to be secret, yet he found that it was talked about quite openly in the city, and not only among the radicals. He remembers the Czech radicals as "incorrigible talkers," an appraisal that may well be more indicative of his prejudice than of the radicals' behavior.[19] It seems, however, that nothing could deflect Bakunin from the course he had embarked upon. His review of past progress may have disappointed him, but the work of the revolution had to go on; the Czech radicals may have ill-impressed him, but they would still be his instrument in unleashing a social cataclysm in Bohemia. With nothing but failure in the past, he still saw nothing but success in the future. He still thought that there were "in Bohemia all the elements necessary to a revolution crowned with success."[20]

Bakunin's visit spurred the Prague radicals into more vigorous activity, and concrete preparations for an uprising began. The principal force in the conspiracy were the students of the University of Prague, both Czech and German, but a number of nonstudent radicals was also drawn into it. One of the obstacles to success in the undertaking was the distrust between Czech and German students. This distrust was never completely overcome, but a rapprochement was effected and the two groups were prepared to cooperate for a common objective. On the German side, the students were recruited, for the most part, from the student organization Markomannia, which had been radicalized at the beginning of March by the members of another student body it had absorbed. A similar development took place among the Czech students. On the Czech side, an active organization in the past had been the Slavia (*Slavie*); it had lost most of its vigor after the June Uprising, but in February, 1849, at the initiative of Frič, several Slavia members formed a new group, the Czecho-Moravian Brotherhood (*Českomoravské Bratrstvo*), dedicated to an active pursuit of democracy.[21] Markomannia and the Czecho-Moravian Brotherhood became the two pillars of the conspiracy.

19. Bakounine, *Confession,* p. 234.
20. *Ibid.,* p. 235.
21. Frič, *Paměti,* II, 337. See also J. Pfitzner, *Bakuninstudien* (Prague, 1932), p. 179.

In the middle of April Frič journeyed to Dresden to meet Bakunin, and he later recorded the episode in his *Memoirs*. He claims to have tried to convince the Russian revolutionary that Bohemia was far from ready for a revolution, but in the end Bakunin's well-known persuasiveness overcame Frič's objections and he agreed to work actively toward an uprising.[22] Upon his return, a revolutionary committee was set up in Prague consisting largely but not exclusively of select members of Markomannia and the Czecho-Moravian Brotherhood. Preparations now swung into high gear, and subsequently May 12 and the days immediately following were set as the period during which the uprising would break out, to coincide with an uprising in Dresden. Attempts were made to carry revolutionary propaganda to the peasants and workers, and great reliance was placed upon experienced Polish revolutionaries and officers who were supposed to arrive in Prague and play a prominent part in the uprising. Students began to feverishly manufacture ammunition, and plans were also worked out to seize arms from the National Guard and to attack the military arsenal in Prague. On the day of the revolt a diversionary assault was to be made on the Prague Jews in order to distract the attention of the authorities from the true purpose of the action and to serve as bait for the working class. There was talk of seizing Palacký, not with an intent to harm him but in order to neutralize his influence and use him as hostage if necessary.[23]

None of these plans materialized, however. The position of the conspirators was rendered precarious by a premature outbreak of the uprising in Dresden. The uprising in that city started on May 3, which necessitated prompt action in Prague. The target date for the Prague uprising was now apparently May 12, though even at this late hour there appeared to be uncertainty concerning this point among the members of the revolutionary committee. But the Dresden uprising was brought substantially under control before the action in Prague began. The conspirators were still blissfully unaware of the failure of the movement in Dresden when the police, who had known about the conspiracy for quite a while but had been biding their time, struck during the night from May 9 to May 10. Most of the leaders were apprehended, which sealed the doom of the conspiracy.

The consequences of the conspiracy proved disastrous, both for those directly involved and for Prague and Bohemia as a whole.

22. Frič *Paměti*, II, 362 ff.
23. *Ibid.*, p. 369; Traub, *Květnové spiknutí*, p. 113.

Immediately Prague and four other cities were placed under a state of siege that lasted until August, 1853. A state of siege, of course, meant further restrictions on the already precarious freedoms. A military commission was established to investigate the conspiracy, and as a result of the investigations and trials, a total of 28 persons were sentenced to death by hanging. None of these sentences was carried out, however: all death sentences were commuted to prison terms of varying lengths. In addition, 51 persons received terms totaling 474 years.[24] A number of those sentenced, most of them young men, were thus compelled to spend the most precious years of their lives in prison. During the fifties pardons were granted at various times, and finally, in 1857, the proclamation of a universal amnesty wiped out the last sentence. But many of those released continued to live in the shadow of the omnipresent police for years to come, and a few found the exercise of their civil rights restricted well into the constitutional era that began in 1860.

The conspirators, insofar as they were investigated and sentenced, and their identity known, possessed certain well-defined characteristics. With regard to nationality, they were a mixed Czech-German group, with both nationalities about equally represented. In effect, the Germans, whether they realized it or not, were risking their lives to help the Czechs establish a large Slavic commonwealth in Central Europe; this, at least, was Bakunin's plan. An overwhelming majority of the conspirators were students and intellectuals. Only a few peasants and burghers, and no workers, were among those investigated or sentenced; this is attributable to the fact that proportionately few members of these social groups were involved in the conspiracy, and that the captured leaders did not as a rule betray the identity of those workers, peasants, and burghers who may have been privy to the plot.[25] The majority of the conspirators were young people; in fact, the direction of the movement in the last week was left to nine men, the oldest of whom was twenty-six years old.[26] Among the students involved there were both students of the university and of the polytechnic, and as in the case of the June Uprising, the polytechnic students seem to have constituted the largest group.[27] From

24. Traub, *Květnové spiknutí*, p. 284.

25. *Ibid.*, pp. 320-21.

26. J. Matoušek, *Karel Sladkovský a český radikalismus za revoluce a reakce* (Prague, 1929), p. 56.

27. F. Jílek, "Pražská polytechnika a její studenti v revolučním roce 1848," *Sborník Národního technického muzea*, IV (1965), 268.

the above, one fact emerges clearly: the determining factor in the conspiracy was education and youth rather than social class. The total number of participants cannot be established; estimates range from a few score to several hundred.[28]

The conspiracy must be regarded more as an act of daring than of wisdom, more as an act of enthusiasm than of judgment, and more as an act of faith than of reason. It was, above all, to the majority of the young men involved, a desperate, sincere, and valiant protest against an advancing reaction. But against this reaction it had no chance of success. It had no firm leadership. It had, to the last, no clearly agreed plan. It had no money. It was disposed of no experienced military contingent. True, many promises were made and many assurances given. But in the feverish world of the conspirators, the line between dream and reality, between rumor and fact, was a thin one. In such a world, a promise made was regarded as a promise fulfilled and a pledge of secrecy was viewed as a guarantee that the secret would be kept. The conspirators were often promised money, but the money was seldom delivered. They were assured that experienced Polish officers and revolutionaries would be available when needed, but none came. The preparations were made surreptitiously, yet for weeks before the target date, Prague vibrated with rumors about a conspiracy, some of these rumors even correctly linking Bakunin with it.

As early as March 5, an intoxicated journeyman watchmaker, picked up by the military patrol, spoke of "disturbances that would soon break out," and the story was carried by the press. Three weeks later, Havlíček, obviously concerned about such rumors, warned against those who "want only the revolution to begin, regardless of sound calculation." By the beginning of May, the conspiracy was the subject of more or less open talk in Prague cafés and inns.[29] Shortly before the target date, one indiscreet young conspirator told his landlady all he knew about the plot; from her it ultimately reached the police, furnishing the last piece of evidence on the basis of which the police decided to strike.[30] There was also a girl who, according to one version, found out about the conspiracy from her boyfriend, and

28. Traub, *Květnové spiknutí*, p. 320.

29. *NN*, March 7, March 31, and May 5, 1849. The police had picked up rumors as early as February, as noted earlier.

30. The report from Mecséry to Vienna, May 12, 1849, in *SÚA* Prague, PGT 1849-52, A/1, 177/gp.

according to another, by eavesdropping on the conversation of her brother and his friends, who were involved in the plot; at any rate, she passed the information on, and it, too, reached the police.[31]

Among those who helped denounce the conspiracy to the authorities was none other than Palacký, who harbored an intense dislike for the radicals and seized upon this opportunity to neutralize their influence. A medical student who knew about the plot was eager to pass his information on to the authorities, and he found in Palacký a willing intermediary. As an official report by the Bohemian acting governor put it, "On May 1" there came to him "the ex-deputy Palacký, accompanied by the burgomaster Wanka and the medical student John Hensel," whereupon Palacký "declared that Hensel had made to him disclosures about a general uprising contemplated in Prague and in all Bohemia which was connected with the revolutionary movements in Germany," following which Hensel told all he knew.[32]

How lightly important decisions were made is suggested by the fact that one student was asked, on May 4, to be in charge of the uprising that was to break out about a week later![33]

There are indications that a few participants themselves realized that their endeavor could not succeed, but once seized by the revolutionary fever, they continued with the preparations regardless of other considerations. It was a fever that had to burn itself out or be stopped by the shock of exposure and catastrophe. Frič says that a few days before the deadline he concluded that the uprising could not succeed; afterwards, he continues, "I approved mechanically everything that was being decided in the committee," adding, "I am convinced that even without our arrest on May 10 . . . the uprising would not have materialized; even without the declaration of martial law and the state of siege over Prague, reaction would have marched on in its historic pace."[34]

Others—Bakunin among them—were fascinated by the sheer spectacle of the violence the revolution would provoke. As Bakunin himself later described his emotions: "The revolution which I planned was horrible and without precedent although it was directed more against things than against people. . . . When I recall today with

31. Traub, *Květnové spiknutí*, p. 128.
32. Report from Mecséry to Vienna, May 12, 1849, as above.
33. Matoušek, *Karel Sladkovský*, p. 49.
34. Frič, *Paměti*, II, 369-70.

what poor means I intended to make revolution in Bohemia, it seems to me ridiculous; I cannot understand how I could have believed in success. But nothing could hold me then . . . the genius of destruction seized me."[35] To Bakunin and probably to some others, revolution became not a means to an end, but an end itself, justified in its own right as a grand and magnificent cataclysm that would topple thrones, palaces, and empires.

Some conspirators were prompted by a desire to demonstrate heroism and self-sacrifice. Frič writes that he thought that "my hour has struck—I must sacrifice myself."[36] For most participants, several motives doubtless played a part in their decision to join the conspiracy. It may be said—and it has often been said—that the May Conspiracy was an imprudent act, and because it had no chance of success, should not have been undertaken. But then one of the motives of the conspirators, as Frič observes, was the desire to vindicate the Czech nation, which had been stamped with the fiasco of the policy of the liberal leadership. He had to, he writes, "redeem the honor of the Czech name, even if it cost one hundred and fifty lives as young as my own."[37] The May Conspiracy was rashly conceived, without any regard for reality, and to that extent it was a mistake. But in committing this mistake, the radicals at least offered resistance to the reaction, no matter how futile. The liberals committed the greater mistake of abetting the reaction by supporting the Schwarzenberg government to the last moment. Neither side could have prevented the reaction, no matter what it did, and the soundest course in the circumstances would have been neither a futile conspiracy nor a futile support of a reactionary government. But if one compares the two courses, one cannot deny that the radicals were more courageous and more honorable, for it was clearly more courageous and more honorable to fight the reaction than to abet it. And it did not prove to be any more futile.

For the success of the conspiracy, the crucial question was the degree of discontent among the people, and the amount of resistance they were willing to offer to the government. What was the state of the public mind on the eve of the conspiracy? What was the strength of the determination to offer armed resistance to the reaction, if

35. Bakounine, *Confession,* p. 208.
36. Frič, *Paměti,* II, 364.
37. *Ibid.*

necessary? This is an important consideration, for on this determination was predicated the success of the conspiracy.

It is certain that among some segments of the population there was considerable discontent in Bohemia and that this discontent had been on the rise. (The trends were somewhat different in Moravia.) It is equally certain that among other segments of the population there was considerable apathy by May, 1849, and that this apathy had also been on the rise. Among other segments still, numerically less strong, there was a growth of outright conservatism and a distaste for the constitutional experiment. It is also certain that the first group spoke, through the radicals, in a resonant and courageous (if not always consistent) voice and that this lent it the appearance of strength out of proportion to the degree of active support it enjoyed.

Going back in time, it is possible to distinguish certain phases in the development of radicalism and of popular opposition. The first phase or wave began with the March revolution and climaxed in the June Uprising, the high point of the revolutionary era. Afterwards, feeling subsided for a time. In August, 1848, the second wave of radicalism began, provoked by Windischgrätz' regime in Prague and by his offensive proclamation of August 2.[38] During this period, the radical movement may be said to have crystallized, but public support for radical activity was not as strong as before June, and by the end of the year the wave was losing its momentum. At the same time, conservatism was growing.[39] At the beginning of 1849, the third wave of radicalism was initiated. It was nourished particularly by the intervention of Russia in the war against Hungary, first rumored in January, 1849, and confirmed in mid-February; by the army recruitment drive; and finally by the forcible dissolution of the Kroměříž Parliament. Czech radicals, and, to a lesser extent, liberals, modified their uncompromising anti-German and anti-Magyar stand. The canvassing for funds for the support of the southern Slavs in their struggle with the Magyars ceased,[40] and at the same time a Slovak leader complained that some Czechs in Prague were becoming pro-Magyar and that this attitude resembled "Polishness."[41]

The Slovak leader's lament was not wide of the mark. Police

38. See Chapter 8, Note 25.
39. See Chapter 8.
40. *PVL*, April 2, 1849.
41. Letter from Štúr to Frič, March 29, 1849 (*Listy L'udovíta Štúra*, II [1956] 201).

reports for this period noted that in Prague individuals could be heard openly praising Kossuth and the republic: "Students and journalists are unmitigated republicans.[42] Abuses of the constitution, of the ministry, of the young emperor, are unprecedented: people utter their insults quite undisturbed in the streets, in inns. There are public cries of 'Eljen Kossuth, vládě pereat !' ['Long live Kossuth, government perish']."[43] In one district in Eastern Bohemia, an official reported that pro-Magyar sentiment had reached such proportions that if the Magyar rebels approached his district there was a prospect of "at least two-thirds of the population joining them." According to the same official, the spirit of rebellion in his district "spread into all strata of the population and gripped into its fanaticism not only the entire proletariat, but even the small landed proprietors, spurred by the hope of a communist division of property of the well-to-do."[44] In addition, there was a bitter resentment of the recruitment drive conducted in February and March, 1849; the resentment was especially strong in the rural districts and among students, and caused great anxiety to officials in charge of recruitment. In some cases, it came to a clash between the people and the military, the latter summoned in order to "pacify" a particular district.[45] Also in the early months of 1849, unemployed workers in Prague massed on several occasions, assuming a menacing posture and demanding work or financial support; this too created acute anxiety among officials responsible for the maintenance of order.[46]

The most pessimistic description of the Bohemian scene is given in a report of the Military Commander for Bohemia, General Khevenhüller, for February 28, 1849. With the first anniversary of the March revolution approaching, the general saw the contagion of revo-

42. See various official reports, chiefly gathered from police agents, for example, *SÚA* Prague, PG 1846-49, 15c/3, No. 440 (January 19, 1849), 1314 (February 25, 1849), 2114 (March 19, 1849), 2557 (March 26, 1849), and 2772 (April 2, 1849).

43. *Přehled československých dějin,* II/1, 87.

44. Report of an official in Žamberk, May 26, 1849, reprinted in D. Rapant, *Slovenské povstanie roku 1848-49: Dejiny a dokumenty* (Turčiansky Svätý Martin, 1937-48; Bratislava, 1954-67), II/3, 418-19.

45. A particularly serious clash took place in Příbram (see Helfert, *Geschichte Österreichs,* IV/3, 367). See also F. Roubík, *Český rok 1848* (Prague, 1931), p. 387. For a map, see *Atlas československých dějin,* p. 20, a.

46. See, for example, reports in *SÚA* Prague, PG 1846-49, 15 c/3, No. 1670 (March 5, 1849), 2975 (April 10, 1849), 3209 (April 18, 1849), and 3265 (April 19, 1849).

lution again spreading dangerously. Among the signs were the striking presence of foreigners, especially Poles; the hatred shown by many people for "the party of order"; the attempts to assassinate sentries; resistance to recruitment; the excesses of the Slavic Linden; and the open abuse of His Majesty's government. To combat subversion of this kind, the general urged the closest collaboration of the various organs of the government.[47]

Yet with all the signs and reports of discontent, when the May Conspiracy was exposed and its leaders arrested, there was no movement to rally to the young martyrs. There were no mass protests and no demonstrations among the people of Prague and of Bohemia. Clearly there was a discrepancy between the official reports and the reality the reports purported to describe, but official reports usually exaggerate and almost never underrate the extent of popular opposition. The reports of officials and agents are a compound of fear, prejudice, hatred, and the simple-minded bureaucratic habit of labeling every questioning person a dangerous subversive. An extreme example of this is the above report of the Military Commander for Bohemia. In his report, the general went so far as to base his estimate of the growing forces of revolution on (among others) "the unmistakable hatred for the party of order observable in the physiognomies of many individuals." Little wonder that, watching anxiously for the slightest sign of discontent in the faces of passers-by, the general, wherever he went and wherever he looked, saw himself surrounded and pursued by individuals ready to unleash a rebellion. His report accordingly presents Bohemia as a country seething with revolution.[48]

In fact, Bohemia was not seething with revolution. The revolutionary ambitions of the conspirators were not matched by a revolutionary situation in the country. Even among students radicalism was weakening. In the spring of 1849, the students were still constitutionally minded and still willing to sign petitions, but their fighting zeal had disappeared. When the Academic Legion was formally dissolved by the government in January, 1849, there were protests and petitions, and when the Legion banners were carried through the streets of Prague for the last time on February 4, 1849, there was a profound feeling of melancholy at the passing of an institution so closely bound with the achievements of the revolutionary era.

47. Letter to Mecséry, February 28, 1849, *SÚA* Prague, PGT 1849-52, PGT A/1, 143/g.
    48. *Ibid.*

Thousands turned out to greet the banners for the last time and the occasion was turned into a peaceful demonstration against the government.[49] Nevertheless, the dissolution of the Legion prompted no violence or mass resistance. This would not have happened eight months earlier. By May, 1849, the students, like many other segments of the population, had lost a taste for violence and armed resistance. They had been among the chief martyrs in June, and now they were being martyred again by the army recruitment drive. It was not easy to continue to sacrifice oneself, with the prospects of success dimming with every passing day. An official report on the May Conspiracy, prepared after the event, states that "the participation in it of Prague inhabitants was very small and the project encountered even among students too much opposition, as far as I could ascertain the opinions of law students."[50] Though the law students were among the least radical, the account of the events in Frič's *Memoirs* generally confirms the view that the students, who were supposed to be the main revolutionary force, did not wholeheartedly support the conspiracy. This is why Frič writes, "I am convinced that even without our arrest on May 10 . . . the uprising would not have materialized."[51] The plan also called for the proletarians to participate in the uprising, but after the arrest of the conspirators, the acting governor of Bohemia reported to Vienna that "the proletariat and the working class are quiet."[52] And as for the peasants, they too failed to rally to the cause.[53]

Nobody worked harder than the radicals, through the press and propaganda leaflets, to stir revolutionary sentiment in Bohemia. Nobody was more frustrated by the results and nobody gave vent to disillusionment more poignantly than they. The radical press did not miss an opportunity to give prominent coverage to the revolutionary movements abroad. It was with a view to stirring the public that Sabina reprinted in *Noviny Lípy Slovanské* the revolutionary manifesto by Bakunin in the first days of January, 1849. And it was with the same objective that at the end of March, 1849, a number of radical newspapers reprinted a proclamation of an Italo-Slavic Society in

49. *PVL,* February 5, 1849.

50. *SÚA* Prague, PGT 1849-52, A/1, 363/gp. The report had been prepared for Bach and transmitted by him to Prague with a covering letter of June 10, 1849.

51. Frič, *Paměti,* II, 370.

52. Report of May 20, 1849, *SÚA* Prague, PGT 1849-52, A/1, No. 234. For a detailed treatment, see Chapter 12.

53. See Chapter 11.

Turin. Addressed to the "Czech, Illyrian, Ruthenian, and Bulgarian Slavs," the proclamation appealed for national independence.[54] The radical newspapers urged their readers to be vigilant, to strengthen National Guards, and to be ready to fight, if necessary, for their freedom. Individual radicals deluged all of Bohemia with leaflets asking the people to resist the recruitment drive.

Considering the magnitude of the effort in this particular instance, the results can only be described as disappointing. As noted earlier, in some cases it came to a clash between the military and the people, but this was an exception rather than the rule. This is not to say that the people liked to surrender their sons to the grasping hands of the military. Recruitment was uniformly resented, but resentment was not revolution. In most districts, the families, whatever their reluctance, yielded to and accepted the verdicts of the local recruitment commissions, if only because they were sometimes "persuaded" by the unmistakable presence of a company of soldiers. At other times their opposition was overcome, without a display of force, by the explanations of local officials. And at still other times, no resistance developed, although even then there was resentment. On March 5, the day the names of the Prague recruits were being chosen by lot, a major outbreak was expected, both by the authorities and by the people. On the appointed day, a large number of people turned out for the spectacle in front of the municipal hall, but no display of violence marred the occasion. In reporting the event, a radical newspaper noted curtly that "the drawing of lots today has taken place in peace and order"; on the next day, stung by the quietude of the occasion, the same newspaper discussed the incident at greater length, chastizing its readers for their fearfulness: "Excessive timidity, stifling all political life, is harming us in the same manner as excessive licence."[55] Radical journalists found themselves increasingly lamenting political apathy. Examples to the contrary are exceptions rather than the rule. One local correspondent praised "the political maturity of our people," which "had to be admired"; this was with reference to the resistance to recruitment that had developed in the city of Plzen.[56] But such comments in the radical press were few. The more

54. *NLS*, March 22, 1849. For an exhaustive study, see V. Čejchan, "Italo-slovanský spolek v Turině a radikální hnutí v Čechách na jaře roku 1849," *Slovanské Historické Studie*, III (1960), 313-54.

55. *PVL*, March 5 and 6, 1849.

56. *PVL*, March 1, 1849.

usual complaints were about political apathy, which was even the
subject of editorial comment.[57]

The one institution that showed a consistently rising curve of
radicalism after June, 1848, was the Slavic Linden. As its branches
grew, its membership expanded, and the range of its activity widened,
its voice was becoming ever more articulate, exerting considerable
influence in Bohemia. All the radicals belonged to it, and from the
beginning of 1849, they attained a leading position in the executive
of the Prague parent organization. In April they finally gained an
undisputed majority on this executive. Yet even the Slavic Linden
could not withstand the pressure of the reaction, and after its radical
leaders were arrested for their involvement in the May Conspiracy,
it collapsed without resistance.

Although the radicals had been leaders in Prague since January,
1849, the rank-and-file membership of the parent organization and
of the branches included a large—in many branches probably a predominant—proportion of liberals. The number of those rank-and-file
members willing to join the kind of conspiracy planned by the radicals
for May, 1849, could not have been very large. In any case, the rising
radicalism of the Slavic Linden could not compensate for the absence
of a truly revolutionary sentiment in some other segments of the population, and could not pit itself against the power the reaction had
attained by May, 1849. Indeed, one of the lessons of the year 1848-49
was the weakness of radicalism in the nation as a whole. Some idea of
this weakness may be obtained from the lists of political suspects in Bohemia, based on the attitudes of citizens expressed in 1848-49 and
compiled by the Austrian authorities in the early fifties. For the
whole of Bohemia, which then had about 4.5 million inhabitants, only
1,518 suspects were listed (of whom 1,181 were Czech). For Prague,
the total number, Czechs and Germans included, was 189. The lists
included such names as Palacký, Brauner, and Count V. E. Deym,
who could hardly be counted as radicals. The largest social group included were the members of the intelligentsia and the propertied
classes: together they accounted for 957 people (of whom there
were only 6 nobles). There were also 146 peasants, of whom only
5 were cottagers, and 16 workers. The low number of workers and

57. See editorial in *PVL*, March 29, 1849, on "Blind Faith in Authority,"
and April 25, 1849, on "Why a Great Part of Our People Does Not Understand Freedom." See also *NLS*, February 27, 1849. An editorial in *NLS*,
January 21, 1849, states that "general apathy is spreading."

cottagers reflects in part the difficulty inherent in singling out "subversives" in a class that was not politically articulate; fundamentally, it demonstrates the low level of political consciousness of these groups.[58]

It is true then that in both Bohemia and Moravia in the spring of 1849 there was a great deal of resentment. But it is also true that the step from resentment to revolution was a long one. The loose cries of "Long live Kossuth!" and "Long live the Republic!" and the many spiteful and even threatening remarks against the government cannot be equated with a genuine willingness to make an armed assault on the regime. It was one thing to cry "Long live the Republic!" but quite another to be ready to face a barrage of bullets from His Majesty's grenadiers. It was one thing to be sympathetic to a cause but quite another to be prepared to fight for that cause. One of the unmistakable trends of the early months of 1849 in the Czech Lands and in other parts of Europe was the increasing reluctance of the people, in comparison with the spring and summer of 1848, to resort to violence.

There was a reverse side to this coin which could not please the government and of which the highly placed officials were uncomfortably aware: the average citizen, especially the peasant, may not have been eager to join a rebellion against the government, but neither was he eager to actively help the government to quell a rebellion. The most detailed report on the public mood in Bohemia before the May Conspiracy came from the pen of Acting Governor Mecséry himself. Written on May 3, 1849—a week before the conspiracy was to break out—for the benefit of his superiors in Vienna, the report shows the impact of the rumors and fears concerning the planned conspiracy. Fear guided Mecséry's hand and shaped his words, and to that extent the report magnified the symptoms of discontent. Nevertheless, it comes as close to being realistic as one could hope an official report of this kind to be. According to Mecséry, in Prague the higher strata of the propertied urban classes, normally progovernment, were so passive that they could not be counted on in a conflict. The member of the other urban classes either belonged to the "national Czech party" or was a "proletarian who attaches himself to any movement. . . . The Czech national party—the greatest party—desires as such no revolution, but is in its leading elements democratic and will conse-

58. F. Roubík, "Úřední evidence osob politicky činných v Čechách v letech 1848 až 1849," *Časopis Společnosti přátel starožitností*, LVII (1949), 22-23.

quently under no circumstances join the government, but in the event of an uprising will be certainly drawn into it. This party has sympathies in the masses and sets the pace." The actual "revolutionary party," according to Mecséry, was "still small in numbers, but is the most active, is most clearly aware of its purpose and shrinks from no means" when it could realize its purpose. What about the public mood in the rural districts? Mecséry held that in Bohemia, as in other countries, the peasants "have not yet been won over for an uprising, but the government too can count on no active help from their side." Rather, in the Czech-speaking rural areas, the peasants could put up, under their national leaders, an active resistance to unpopular government measures. The smaller cities mirrored the mood of the capital. The German districts were somewhat quieter than the Czech ones. The radical movement derived its strength from its connections with radicals abroad and hoped to be able to take advantage of any success the revolution might attain in other countries.[59]

The report doubtless exaggerated the intensity of the resistance. This was partly due to fear, but it may also have been partly designing: the description of the public mood is but a prelude to Mecséry's request for troops with which to keep order, a request rendered more dramatic by his offer to resign if any more troops were shifted from Bohemia to foreign battlefields.[60] In order to obtain the troops or at least keep the existing ones, it was in Mecséry's interest to paint the picture in the darkest shades. Some exaggerations are obvious. Mecséry's suggestion that Czech national leaders were willing to be drawn into an uprising should one take place, is belied by all that is known of the attitudes of Palacký, Brauner, and most of the other leaders. The Czech leaders feared a violent revolution more than they feared enything else, including reaction itself—a sentiment that had decisively shaped their attitudes and their actions, especially since the June Uprising. Also, Mecséry believed—or purported to believe—that the peasants might, under propitious circumstances, be driven into strong resistance to the government. This appraisal does not accord with the experience of the one group that tried consistently to stir the countryside into action: the radicals themselves, who, as noted earlier, were profoundly discouraged by the lack of response to their efforts. The fact that the peasants made no move to support the

59. Mecséry to Vienna, May 3, 1849 (*SÚA* Prague, PGT 1849-52, R/1, 133 gp.).
60. *Ibid.*

conspirators when the latter were arrested shows that it was the radicals' rather than Mecséry's estimate that was closer to reality. Indeed, Mecséry himself wrote with obvious satisfaction on May 20, after the arrest of the leaders, that the majority of the people of Prague supported the state of siege and "have confidence in the care of the government"; and that the proletarians were "quiet." He stated that the hostile parties continued in their hostility and that many peasants continued to regard Kossuth as a "freedom-fighter," but he voiced no alarm and saw no serious crisis ahead.[61] It is obvious that had the public mood on May 3 been as he had described it, his report on May 20 would have been very different.

Had the Czechs retained an undiminished taste for revolution in the spring of 1849 as they had had in the spring of 1848 they would have been unique in Europe. Since midsummer of 1848 the reaction had been tightening its deadly grip on all Europeans. In June, 1848, the June Insurrection had been crushed in Paris, in the worst massacre of the revolutionary era. By the beginning of 1849, the French had relapsed into the tedium of absolutism under Louis Napoleon. With France, the mother of revolutions and the cradle of the 1848 movement, having fallen prey to the reaction; with the reaction reasserting itself in one German state after another; with Prague defeated in June, Vienna in October, and Lvov in November, it is no wonder that the Czechs had developed a different feeling about the future of freedom than they had harbored in the spring of 1848.

A year ago there was an easy optimism and an overwhelming hope that a new day was dawning at last. But since then new forces and new experiences had been brought to the surface, and they made a difference. The following year had been a year of shattered dreams; of young men cut down on the barricades in the flower of their youth; of new antagonisms replacing the old; of new problems created by the solution of the old. The comparative unity of outlook prevailing in the spring of 1848 gave way to an ever-growing disunity. The national movement split into radicals and liberals; and the dissention between radicals and moderates also invaded the ranks of the working class, the students, and other groups. Within the rural population a gap had opened between landed and landless peasants. Across the breadth and width of Bohemia, the Czechs and Germans, after a

61. Mecséry to Vienna, May 20, 1849 (*SÚA* Prague, PGT, 1849-52, A/1, 234).

brief honeymoon during which they behaved toward each other like
brothers, began again to act like Czechs and Germans, with all this
implied.

And if the year was too long for unity to survive, it was still too
short for democracy to survive. It required more than a year to establish the habits, the discipline, and the understanding that must ac-
company a functioning constitutional government, but before this could
be accomplished, democracy was cut down. Where in March, 1848,
there existed a bright vision, in March, 1849, there loomed a dark
horizon. The early determination was replaced by wavering, courage
by fear, mutual trust by a crippling suspicion.

In the spring of 1849, the state of the public mind could not be
described in simple terms of resistance to, or sympathy for, the government. It was a mixture of resentment, disenchantment, hope, servility,
scorn, apathy, fear, and many other emotions. With the year's dis-
appointments behind them, with the menacing shadow of reaction
before them, and with many antagonisms dividing them, the people
could not rise to defend the achievements of 1848. As the Czech
radical Emanuel Arnold wrote years later, with reference to the
mood in Bohemia in the spring of 1849: "In my view the liberal
teachings of a single year were not sufficient to educate a nation
only just awakened from a sleep of two and a half centuries toward a
vigorous and bloody resistance to the government."[62]

62. Arnold's memoirs, in his *Sebrané spisy* (Prague, 1954), p. 514.

Part Two

The Groups

Chapter **10**

Czechs and Slovaks

The Czechs and Slovaks shared a wealth of common cultural traditions. The two peoples had been politically separated for almost a thousand years, however; the Slovaks had evolved under Magyar rule and the Czechs under German rule, which created different problems—political, cultural, economic, and social.

The Czech leaders during the pre-March period found it difficult to understand that the Slovaks were in fact a different, if closely related, people, with their own historic traditions and experiences.[1] They had never ceased to regard the Slovaks as little more than an extension of or appurtenance to, the Czech nationality. This caused them to oppose any attempts on the part of the Slovak leaders to establish a Slovak national identity. In this endeavor, they were aided by a number of influential Slovaks of the older generation, who, like Jan Kollár, the celebrated poet, felt that the Slovaks must continue to lean on the Czechs and use the Czech language as their medium of literary expression.

The Czech leaders were at all times genuinely concerned for the fate of their Slovak brethren. It was certainly not illogical for them to assume that, confronted with the overwhelming power of the Magyars and devoid of any tradition of statehood, the Slovaks would perish as a national group without the supporting pillar of the Czech language, which, though still far from strong, was at least showing unmistakable signs of achieving recognition. The Czechs were opposed to the establishment of a separate Slovak national identity for another reason: it conflicted with their Austro-Slavism, which was predicated on a close cooperation of all Austrian Slavs against the Germans and Magyars; the creation of a "new" Slavic nationality was bound to weaken the Slavic front.

Yet the younger generation of Slovak leaders thought otherwise. Led by the writer L'udovít Štúr, the towering figure of the Slovak

1. The great work on the Slovaks is D. Rapant, *Slovenské povstanie roku 1848-49: Dejiny a dokumenty* (Turčiansky Svätý Martin, 1937-48; Bratislava, 1954-67). See also A. Pražák, *Češi a Slováci* (Prague, 1929), and works cited below.

national awakening, at a meeting in 1843, a number of Slovak intellectuals decided to elevate the spoken Middle-Slovak language to a
literary tongue of the Slovak nation.[2] This plan, which was put into
effect without delay, had its climax in 1845, in the launching by Štúr
of a newspaper using the new Slovak language: *Slovenskje Národňje
Novini* (*Slovak National Gazette*), with its supplement *Orol Tatránsky* (*Eagle of Tatra*).[3] Until Štúr's time, there had been chaos in
the use of the written language. The Roman Catholic priest Anton
Bernolák (d. 1813) had sought to introduce into literature a language
based on a West Slovak dialect, but his reform was rejected by
Slovak Protestants, who continued to cling to the Czech as they had
done for centuries. Štúr's reform proved successful and supplanted
both languages. Of course, Štúr did not "create" a brand new
language. Slovak language forms had been appearing in Slovak
literature for a long time; Štúr formalized rather than created a
literary language.

The Czech leaders did not accept Štúr's reform graciously. The
Czech press launched a bitter invective against Štúr and his colleagues,
ridiculing their work and impugning their motives. The major opening shot from the Czech side was fired by Havlíček, in his series of
articles "Slav and Czech," in which he branded Štúr and his colleague
Jozef Miloslav Hurban "two vain, quite insignificant men (when
compared to the famous . . . Slovaks of the earlier era) who are
concerned more for their literary fame than for the welfare of the
nation."[4] Havlíček later repeated his attacks, not infrequently re-
sorting to diatribe, in articles that showed poor taste; in fact, some
weeks before he had referred to the Slovak literature in the new
language as "Tatar literature."[5] At about the same time, other Czech
leaders published, under the auspices of the *Matice česká* (Czech
Foundation), a series of articles and opinions, criticizing the Slovak
action, entitled *Hlasowé o Potřebě Jednoty Spisowného Jazyka
(Voices Concerning the Need for Unity of Literary Language).*[6]

2. J. Butvin, *Slovenské národno-zjednocovacie hnutie (1780-1848)* (Bratislava, 1965), pp. 293-94.

3. Both now available in facsimile editions, published in Bratislava in 1956.

4. K. Havlíček, *Politické spisy,* ed. Z. Tobolka (Prague, 1900-3), I, 39.
Originally published in *Pražské Noviny,* February 15 to March 12, 1846.

5. In *Česká Včela* (*Czech Bee*), January 20, 1846; quoted in J. Tkadlečková, "Názory a činnosť Karla Havlíčka Borovského z hľadiska vývoja
česko-slovenských vztahov," *HČ,* VI (1958), 36.

6. Published in Prague in 1846. This volume also contains contributions by

In the face of the mounting criticism and innuendoes, Štúr exercised a restraint that can only be described as remarkable, patiently explaining and justifying his point of view in many articles and studies. He favored, he argued, close cooperation between Czechs and Slovaks, but the Czech language, which could no longer serve the needs of the Slovaks, could never become the language of the people. Štúr's decision was precipitated in part by a wave of Magyarizing measures introduced at the beginning of the 1840's which made Magyarization a real danger. The Czechs concluded from it that the Slovaks could withstand the Magyar cultural onslaught only by drawing more closely to the Czechs and their language—a language that had a longer tradition of use and experience behind it. But Štúr and his colleagues drew an opposite conclusion: they felt that all the resources of the Slovak nation would be needed for this struggle, that the Slovak masses would have to be mobilized for it, and that this mobilization could only be achieved by giving the Slovak people a literary language that mirrored their spoken language. Also, Štúr and the other young Slovak intellectuals were beginning to be affected by the same "contagion" of national pride that was affecting the Czechs and other awakening European nationalities. They wanted nothing less than their own language and literature.

An overwhelming majority of the Czech national leaders, including the best-known figures, such as Palacký, Havlíček, and Rieger, demonstrated no sympathy for the Slovaks at this juncture. A few lesser-known members of the Czech national movement were sympathetic to the idea of a Slovak literary language in the early forties, but by the mid-forties even they had changed their minds, and in 1846, only one, the printer Jaroslav Pospíšil, continued to support the Slovak efforts. Such sympathy as could be found after that date was limited to a handful of radical students and democrats, who were usually more preoccupied with social than with national issues and could view the Slovaks, if not always with overwhelming sympathy, at least with more detachment and understanding. But such voices were very few indeed and without influence upon the Czech public.[7]

The crises and the hopes stirred by the revolution in March,

---

some Slovaks (e.g., Kollár) who opposed the establishment of a separate Slovak language.

7. J. Novotný, *O bratrské družbě Čechů a Slováků za národního obrození* (Prague, 1959), pp. 238 ff.

1848, brought about a Czecho-Slovak rapprochement.[8] The first stages of this trend may be detected at the beginning of 1848, before the March Days: at that time, the general expectation of an impending crisis had created an atmosphere conducive to concordance among the subject nationalities of the Habsburg Monarchy. The outbreak of the March revolution quickened the contact. The revolution itself brought into sharp relief the differences between the strength of the Czech and the Slovak national movements. The latter was, as might be expected, much weaker. It had no established center comparable to Prague. Its middle class and intelligentsia were not as well-developed as they were among the Czechs. The Magyar rule over the Slovaks was much more firmly established and much less susceptible to successful challenge than the German rule over the Czechs. The Slovaks had no tradition of statehood to which to appeal. Nevertheless there was a stirring in Slovakia also, triggered by the March events, and on May 10-11, 1848, an assembly of Slovak national leaders in Liptovský Mikuláš issued "The Demands of the Slovak Nation"—the first national program in modern Slovak history.[9] A progressive program spelling out both national and social goals, its social objectives went beyond those of any program devised by Magyar leaders at the time.

Štúr's newspaper published a report on the assembly of March 11 in Prague,[10] and the *Orol Tatránsky* subsequently published the full text of the First Petition. Thereafter, with the barriers of censorship removed, both Czech and Slovak newspapers gave full and sympathetic coverage to political events in the Slovak and Czech regions respectively. The first major Czecho-Slovak encounter after the outbreak of the March revolution took place in Vienna, between members of the Czech delegation bearing the First Petition, and the Slovak intellectuals, largely students, residing there. There were lively expressions of mutual esteem and pledges of close cooperation in the future. On March 21, 1848, the Slovaks present asked for Czech help against Magyar oppression, but at the same time pointed out that the Slovaks had not even been mentioned in the First Petition

8. In what follows, I lean heavily on J. Novotný, "Příspěvek k vzájemným vztahům Čechů a Slováků v první etapě revoluce roku 1848," *HČ,* XI (1963), 366-88.

9. Text in *NNM,* II (1962), 379-82.

10. *Slovenskje Národňje Novini,* March 21, 1848, Supplement.

(the same was true of the Second Petition).[11] This seems to have embarrassed the Czech delegates, but it is only fair to state that the Czech leaders based their case on the tradition of Bohemian statehood (*Staatsrecht*), and this could hardly have endeared them to the Slovaks. Besides, the Slovak leaders themselves, as the May Petition was to show, did not envision any basic changes in the territorial integrity of Hungary; they did not ask for any union with the Czechs and could hardly expect the Czechs to do more.

Vienna, which served as an important meeting place for Austrian Slavs in general, became the first important meeting place of Czechs and Slovaks after the outbreak of the revolution. Various Slavic delegations, joined by many Slavs residing in Vienna in various capacities (mostly as students), were given the first great opportunity of meeting each other during the last days of March and the first days of April, 1848. These meetings were one of the sources of the idea of calling a Slavic Congress, as noted in Chapter 5. Štúr was clearly the Slovak's dominant figure, after his arrival in Vienna. At a meeting on April 2, he delivered an impassioned appeal for the cooperation of all Austrian Slavs against their enemies,[12] without implying, however, that the Slovaks should break away from Hungary.[13] At this stage the Slovak leaders, including Štúr, were still seeking the solution of the Slovak problem within the territorial framework of the Hungarian state, a view that had been clearly developed in an article published by one of the Slovak spokesmen in reply to Magyar insinua-

11. Rapant, *Slovenské povstanie roku 1848-49*, I/1, 327-28.

12. In reporting the speech, a Moravian newspaper quotes Štúr as calling specifically for mutual support of Czechs, Croats, and Slovaks. *Národní Noviny*, in reporting the same speech, said that Štúr invited the Czech delegation "to return home with a request to their brethren to join with the Slovak brethren against their killers." Both reports in V. Žáček and Z. Tobolka (eds.), *Slovanský sjezd v Praze roku 1848: Sbírka dokumentů* (Prague, 1958), pp. 16-17.

13. A Czech reported from Vienna that Štúr had indicated to him in private that the Slovaks were ready to break away from Hungary and join the Czechs in one polity. This was printed in *Pražské Noviny* (see Novotný, "Příspěvek k vzájemným," p. 374). It is hard to believe that Štúr either said or seriously meant this and it may well have represented wishful thinking on the part of the informant involved. It is true that a Magyar newspaper leveled the same accusation at Štúr, but it was a hostile source, bent upon discrediting Štúr (text of the Magyar report in Žáček and Tobolka [eds.], *Slovanský sjezd*, p. 18).

tions.[14] Yet the Slovaks, though they did not desire the breakup of Hungary, emphasized their community of interests with the Czechs. The Czech radicals seemed ready to respond to calls for a Czecho-Slovak collaboration, but the liberals were less effusive in their response. It was hard for them to forget Štúr's break with the Czech language, and it was even harder to resist an "I-told-you-so" attitude, in the face of the mounting pressure on the Slovaks after March. It should be recognized, however, that the liberals had their hands full with their own petitions and programs, and could not be expected to devote much attention to the Slovaks. It is probable that Štúr himself felt the Czech response to be one of less than whole-hearted enthusiasm, and this probably contributed to his decision to make a trip to Prague, where he arrived on April 20, 1848. Another reason for his trip was that he was no longer personally safe in Hungary. In Prague he found himself, for the first time since the inauguration of the constitutional regime, squarely in the heart of the Czech national movement. His purpose was to further probe the question of Czecho-Slovak cooperation and also to propagate the idea of a Slavic Congress—an idea of which he had been one of the leading originators, having broached it in Vienna at the beginning of April.

While in Prague Štúr enjoyed great popularity, particularly among the radical democrats, who had for some time chafed at what they regarded as the narrowly nationalist policies of the Czech leadership. On the day following his arrival, he met with the Czech university students who were members of Slavia. The Czech students drank a toast to Slovak goals and to Štúr, and cried "Pereat!" to all "ignoble affronts" that had been hurled by Czechs "out of ignorance and misunderstanding of the Slovaks." One student, his belligerance doubtless heightened by alcohol, pierced a copy of the *Hlasowé o Potřebě* (see p. 264 above) with his sword and burned it.[15] In Prague Štúr was instrumental in the founding of the Slavic Linden on April 30, and apparently chose its name.[16] The significance of the Slavic Linden for the Czechs can scarcely be exaggerated, and Štúr's initiative here contributed greatly to Czech political life during the revolutionary era.

14. Text in Žáček and Tobolka (eds.), *Slovanský sjezd*, pp. 19-22.
15. *NN,* April 25, 1848. Also J. V. Frič, *Paměti*, ed. K. Cvejn (Prague, 1957-63), II, 27.
16. Novotný, "Příspěvek k vzájemným vztahům," p. 379.

Of decisive consequence for the course of Czecho-Slovak relations during 1848 was Štúr's personal rapprochement with Havlíček, who, as editor of *Národní Noviny,* wielded vast influence over the Czech community.[17] After the two men became reconciled, Havlíček made the columns of *Národní Noviny* available to Štúr and other leading Slovak spokesmen, which enabled the Czech community to become familiar with the Slovak cause and the Slovak point of view. How far Havlíček now went to meet the Slovaks can be seen from the fact that only a few days after Štúr's arrival in Prague, *Národní Noviny* carried an article of unusual length (five columns) penned by Štúr and entitled "A Look at the Stirring of Western and Southern Slavs."[18] Though dealing with the problems of western and southern Slavs in general, the article is in fact a vehicle for the presentation of the case for a Slovak literary language; never before had the Czech public had an opportunity to acquaint itself firsthand with all the arguments in favor of a Slovak literary language.

After publishing Štúr's article, Havlíček paid more and more attention to the Slovak cause; throughout 1848 and the early part of 1849 *Národní Noviny* reported faithfully and systematically on events in Slovakia, always seeking to awaken sympathy for the Slovak brethren. After the outbreak of an open conflict between the Magyars and the non-Magyar nationalities in Hungary, it supported the Slovaks to the full and reported in detail on military and other events in Hungary. Havlíček's newspaper was not by any means the only Czech organ to devote sympathetic attention to the Slovaks during this period. The radical *Pražský Večerní List* and other Czech papers, of various political hues, took the same attitude.

In June, at the Slavic Congress, to which Štúr contributed so decisively, the Czecho-Slovak question came under consideration. The Slovaks were represented at the congress by the very best of their leaders, with Štúr himself informally heading the delegation. The congress set up a "Czecho-Slovak section" as one of the three sections into which the delegates were grouped—an unmistakable sign of the affinity that was felt to exist between the two peoples. During the congress the Slovak delegates were most cordially received by the Czech public, the Czech radicals being always more demonstrative and enthusiastic in their expressions of sentiment than other segments of the population. Štúr, as usual, commanded the greatest attention;

17. For this, see Tkadlečková, "Názory a činnost K. Havlíčka Borovského."
18. *NN,* May 2, 1848.

possessed of all the attributes of a man capable of attracting a popular following, he seemed almost to be casting a spell over the delegates. In the feverish climate of the congress, which, to those participating, seemed to be dissolving forever many of the misunderstandings and differences that had divided the Slavs for centuries, the recent bitterness between Czechs and Slovaks was all but forgotten. Nothing mattered now except the future, and the future looked bright. The Slovaks, for their part, were carried away by the beauty and the cultural pulse of Prague. In an appeal to Slovakia published in *Národní Noviny*, Štúr's colleague Hurban wrote: "You cannot actually imagine what kind of a city Prague is, for we Slovaks are so unfortunate as to live only in our valleys—isolated from one another. Like a heart in our body—such a place Prague occupies in the whole country."[19]

Yet even at the height of a genuine sentiment of brotherhood significant differences between the Czech and Slovak delegates began to appear. At a meeting of the Czecho-Slovak section on June 3, the Czech liberals clashed with the Slovaks over the attitude to be taken by the Slavs vis-à-vis Austria. The Czech liberals stood for Austro-Slavism, and to that extent showed themselves to be too "pro-Habsburg" to suit Štúr. To Czech Austro-Slavist arguments that it was important to preserve Austria, Štúr countered that "our goal is to preserve ourselves. First, we must serve ourselves, then others. Thus far, Austria has stood, while we have rotted. . . . If Austria falls, we do not." Štúr did not advocate the dissolution of the monarchy; he was merely being less loyalist in his attitude than most of the Czechs. As he put it: "Let us state that we want, as independent united Slavic communities, to stand under the Austrian Empire. Let us not say that we want to preserve Austria or create a Slavic Austrian Empire."[20] In this connection, it may be pointed out that Štúr had on an earlier occasion accused the Czech leadership of being too loyalist. While Rieger was visiting Slovakia in 1847 he met Štúr, and the latter complained to him of the "servility" of the Czech press.[21] At the June 3 meeting of the Czecho-Slovak section of the Slavic Congress Štúr was supported by Havlíček and one or two other Czechs, while one Slovak opposed him. But the majority of

19. *NN*, May 31, 1848.
20. Žáček and Tobolka (eds.), *Slovanský sjezd*, p. 248.
21. K. Stloukal, "Riegrovy zápisky o Slovensku v r. 1847," *Bratislava*, I (1927), 535.

Czech delegates favored the more explicit Austro-Slavist point of view. (The radical Sabina was also present; only one short utterance of his is recorded and it supports Štúr.)[22]

A more important discussion, from the point of view of the relationship between Czechs and Slovaks, took place in the Czecho-Slovak section on June 7. It concerned the possible political union of the two peoples. From the Czech side, proposals were made for such a union, but were not favored by any one of the Slovaks present. The Slovaks pointed to their difficult position and argued that they were not yet ready to make a complete break with Hungary. They invited the support of the Czechs for the goal of national equality within the Hungarian state, but were not prepared to countenance union with them. One Slovak spokesman stated on this occasion that to advocate such a union was at this time impractical.[23]

The congress was interrupted by the outbreak of the June Uprising in Prague. Štúr and a few other Slovaks remained in Prague as long as there was hope of the rebels winning and took an active part in the uprising. He left the city on June 17.

Meanwhile, Magyar-Slovak tension was mounting rapidly. In the week in which Prague played host to the delegates attending the Slavic Congress, the Slovak cause sustained a serious blow as Štúr's newspaper, with its supplement, was compelled to suspend publication; the last issues of the two organs appeared on June 9 and June 6, 1848, respectively. This was the direct result of a highly restrictive press law issued by the Magyar government, which went into effect on June 11.[24] Thus, the Slovak patriots found themselves in the impossible situation of fostering a national movement without a national newspaper. Soon the Magyar-Slovak conflict was transformed from a battle of words into a battle of arms. In September, 1848, a group of volunteers, either Slovak or sympathetic to the Slovak cause, invaded western Slovakia from Vienna in the hope of inciting anti-Magyar resistance and strengthening the whole anti-Magyar front. This first campaign ended in failure, as did two later ones in November, 1848, and the summer of 1849.

The attitude of the Czech community to the Slovak cause during this crisis was one of warm and active sympathy. Many Czech volun-

22. Žáček and Tobolka (eds.), *Slovanský sjezd*, p. 255.
23. *Ibid.*, p. 297.
24. K. Goláň, *Štúrovské pokolenie (Výber z diela)*, ed. F. Bokes (Bratislava, 1964), p. 213.

teers took an active part in the first Slovak campaign, and its three commanders were all Czech. Among those taking part was young Frič, who received an injury in action.[25] During this period, Czech newspapers followed Slovak developments closely. *Národní Noviny* began to devote an entire column to them, printing blow-by-blow accounts of the military campaigns as well as details of the political struggle. *Národní Noviny* and the Slavic Linden launched a nation-wide campaign to collect funds for the Slovaks as well as the Croats, who had also become involved in an armed conflict with the Magyars.[26]

After the October revolution in Vienna, and particularly after the open break between the imperial government and the Magyars, a cloud again began to darken the Czecho-Slovak relationship. Within the Czech community, notably among the radicals, there were doubts concerning the nature of the struggle in Hungary. The skeptics began to fear that the court harbored ulterior motives in waging war upon the Magyars: it was entirely possible, they reasoned, that its ultimate objective, once the Magyars had been humbled, was the destruction of hard-won constitutional liberties and the reimposition of absolutism. A speaker at the meeting of the Slavic Linden declared, "We know that voices are now being raised against the struggle of the Slovaks with the Magyars which the government exploited for the suppression of freedom."[27] At the same time Štúr, who had earlier chastized the Czechs for being too loyalist, now found himself depending upon a Habsburg army for the success of his efforts. The dissolution of the Kroměříž Parliament confirmed the worst fears of those who questioned the motive of the imperial government; the Czechs became preoccupied with the danger of reaction and their concern for the Slovaks naturally lessened. There were expressions of sympathy for Kossuth and a corresponding decline of sympathy for the non-Magyar nationalities of Hungary. This was deeply disconcerting to Štúr, who complained about the new trends in his letters to Prague. Now the Czechs were calling Štúr servile and loyalist.[28]

Throughout the 1848-49 period, neither on the Czech nor on the

25. Frič, *Paměti*, II, 300.
26. A few receipts survive in Havlíček's papers showing the amounts he transmitted to the Slovaks for this purpose. See Tkadlečková, "Názory a činnost K. Havlíčka Borovského," pp. 41-42.
27. *PVL*, March 14, 1849.
28. Štúr's letter to Frič, March 29, 1849, in *Listy Ľudovíta Štúra*, II (1956), 201-2.

Slovak side was any "official" proposal put forward, as part of a national program, for the union of the two peoples. But proposals for such a union were made by prominent individuals among the Czechs. As noted, a few Czech delegates at the Slavic Congress advocated such a union, and earlier Havlíček had come out openly in favor of it in an article in *Národní Noviny*. Havlíček wrote that "the most important thing for the preservation and dignity of our nationality is the combining of the Czecho-Slavic nation into one union so that we can with all our common strength stand against our foes and against all dangers."[29] Much later, when the question of the Czecho-Slovak union came under consideration in the constitutional committee of the Imperial Parliament, Palacký, in his second constitutional draft, envisioned a union of Czechs and Slovaks as part of a reorganization of the Habsburg Monarchy.[30] This proposal provoked misgivings among Slovak leaders. Štúr and some of his colleagues feared that it would establish a Czech hegemony over the Slovaks and other Slavs of Austria, while others, who felt that even such a basic reorganization would still leave the Slovaks in the Magyar sphere of influence, preferred to see Slovakia directly administered from Vienna.[31] Palacký's last word on the subject was his article, "On Centralization and National Equality in Austria." The article was, in effect, a proposal for a constitution of the monarchy, which was to be reorganized along ethnic lines, with the Czechs and Slovaks forming one of seven groups, each of which would have its own ministry. Thus, this last major constitutional proposal to come from a member of the Czech national movement reaffirmed the Czechs' faith in the union of the two peoples.[32] As the hopes for a solution of the Slovak

29. *NN*, April 18, 1848. As for Kollár, he seems to have envisioned only a cultural union (see his proclamation in *NN*, May 2, 1848).

30. See Chapter 8.

31. In the fifties, Štúr wrote that Austro-Slavism opened to the Czechs "the prospect of a hegemony over the Slavic nations in Austria, indeed, over and above that, the prospect of a transformation of Austria according to their concepts which would have perforce placed power in their hands" (L. Štúr, *Das Slawenthum und die Welt der Zukunft* [Bratislava, 1931] p. 185). For this question, see K. Rebro, "Štátoprávne požiadavky Slovákov v rokoch 1848-1849," in *Slováci a ich národný vývin* (Bratislava, 1966), p. 201, and J. Holák, "Politické snahy slovenské v rokoch 1848-49," *Carpatica*, I, Series A (1936), 85-156.

32. Palacký's article, which appeared in *NN*, December 21, 1849, is reprinted in J. M. Černý (ed.), *Boj za právo: Sborník aktů politických u věcech státu a národa českého od roku 1848* (Prague, 1893), pp. 685-92.

question within the territorial framework of Hungary dimmed, the Slovak leaders were compelled to re-examine their program. This re-examination did not lead to an advocacy of a union with the Czechs, but rather to a demand for the formation of Slovakia as a crownland, completely independent from Hungary and subordinated directly to Vienna.[33]

Later Czech interest in Slovakia lessened, and the Czech leaders, with Havlíček as their chief spokesman, once again embarked on a criticism of the movement for a separate Slovak literary language. In 1850, Havlíček again attacked Štúr for breaking with the Czech language, adding, with a touch a paternalism, that in time "the Slovak nation will elevate itself" and "the ancient good Slavic virtues stifled by the Magyars will reappear"; from the Slovaks, he said, would come "a rejuvenation of the entire Czechoslavic nation."[34] These lines were written under the impact of the restoration of the reaction, which brought with it renewed national oppression. To Havlíček, this trend only confirmed his fears that Štúr's reform would weaken the Slavic front and facilitate the victory of the Slavs' enemies.

The future was on Štúr's side, however. Bach's absolutism of the fifties hampered the national development of all non-German nationalities and for a time the Slovak literary language vegetated. Nevertheless, in the long run, its progress could not be stopped, and the language established by Štúr's generation finally became the accepted medium of literary expression among the Slovaks.

33. Rebro, "Štátoprávne požiadavky Slovákov v rokoch 1848-1849," p. 205.
34. In the article "Slovanská politika," *Slovenskje Národňje Novini,* July 17, 20, and 24, 1850 (see Havlíček, *Politické spisy,* III/1, 179).

Chapter **11**

Peasants

With the downfall of absolutism and the dismissal of Metternich in March, 1848, the peasant question[1] quickly forced itself into the forefront of revolutionary events and became the number-one item on the agenda of public business. Discontent in the countryside was rife, and it was recognized—even in the bureaucracy and the governing circles—that prompt action was called for in order to check the revolutionary tide. Since Bohemia and Moravia passed through somewhat different stages in dealing with the peasant question, it is convenient to separate the two provinces in discussing it.

In Bohemia, the draft of a petition submitted to the popular assembly that met on March 11 contained an article calling for the abolition of the subject status of the peasantry and for the cancellation of all peasant burdens and obligations, for appropriate compensation. Although the article was duly endorsed by the assembly, it was considered too radical by the liberals, who were now gaining control of the revolutionary movement, and the St. Václav's Committee, elected by the assembly to give final form to the petition, dropped the specific demand and replaced it by one asking merely for a "thorough reform in peasant conditions appropriate to the times"—a substantial retreat from the original request. No popular assembly could ask for less. The effect of this modest demand was further lessened by tacking it, almost as an afterthought, onto a series of demands having to do with municipal and village self-government.

The excessive caution of the liberals produced an interesting paradox: with respect to the agrarian problem, their call for reform asked for less than that of the Bohemian nobility. Alarmed by the swelling tide of discontent in the villages and fearing the possible consequences of official inaction, a group of Bohemian nobles residing in Prague addressed a hastily prepared petition of their own to the emperor on March 20, 1848, urging him to deal speedily with the

1. See V. Klimeš, *Česká vesnice v roce 1848* (Most, 1949) ; J. Kočí, "Příspěvek k rolnické otázce v Čechách v r. 1848," *ČSČH*, V (1957), 59-85, 248-66. Many studies were contributed by Roubík (see Bibliography, p. 370).

peasant question. "Speed is now an absolute necessity," the petition
stated, and proceeded to set forth ways whereby the obligations of
the peasantry could be abolished, for compensation.[2] The nobles'
petition demonstrates the sense of urgency that had gripped their class,
which was being increasingly confronted with an open breach of discipline among the peasants, including a widespread refusal to perform
the *robot*. Many nobles doubtless appreciated the humane considerations involved in the emancipation of the peasantry from serfdom; at
the same time, as a group they had concluded that the solution of the
peasant question could be deferred only at the risk of a major upheaval; if the emperor acted quickly, both he and the nobility could
retain a measure of control over the course of events and help shape
the solution to the problem. Also, many nobles felt—this had been
dawning upon them for years—that the *robot* was no longer eco-
nomical and no longer satisfied the requirements of sound agricultural management. The nobles' petition made no mention of the
question of the subject status of the peasantry, but even at that it went
further than the liberals' petition.

This feeling of urgency was shared by the court, and on March
28 an imperial decree was issued providing for the cessation of all
robot duties within a year of the issuance of the decree and not later
than March 31, 1849; the extent of the compensation was to be
determined later.[3] That there was no time to lose and that the
peasants were becoming increasingly impatient could be seen from the
refusal of many peasants to perform the *robot* and to render the
customary obedience to the landlord or his official; it could also be
seen from the petitions that soon began to reach the National Committee in Prague and continued to pour in until the June Uprising.
No less than 580 petitions have survived, representing over 1,200

2. J. M. Černý (ed.), *Boj za právo: Sborník aktů politických u věcech
státu a národa českého od roku 1848* (Prague, 1893), p. 31. On July 25, 1848,
some thirty nobles submitted another petition calling for the immediate abolition
of the *robot*, for compensation; they also very sensibly suggested that the compensation be paid not directly to the recipient, but to the state, which would
then apportion it to the landlords. It was hoped that this latter provision would
reduce the friction between peasants and landlords. The petition was rejected
by the government in Vienna, which did not want to complicate the peasant
question, just beginning to be discussed by the parliament. Text of this petition in F. Roubík, "Na českém venkově roku 1848," *ČDV, XV* (1928), 230-31.

3. Černý (ed.), *Boj*, p. 53. The decree did not mention the subject status
of the peasant.

villages (excluding those from towns and cities). Nothing like this had ever happened before in Czech history.[4] The National Committee did not take any action on the petitions beyond replying with a form letter. It was expected that the peasant question would be dealt with at the Bohemian diet, which was supposed to meet soon, but the diet was never permitted to meet.

In Moravia the peasant question came before the diet in Brno, which was in session for the better part of the 1848-49 period. Spurred by the presence of many peasants in its midst, this "Peasant Parliament" approved in June, 1848, after a heated debate, the abolition of *robot* duties and other obligations. The abolition was to become effective on July 1, 1848—a significant provision in that the *robot* in Moravia was being abolished far ahead of the deadline of March, 1849, set by the imperial decree of March 28. The landlords were to receive compensation, but the question of compensation was to be the subject of separate legislation. The abolition did not apply to Silesia, where a separate legislative body had been formed. Like their Bohemian counterparts, the Moravian peasants were propelled into a petition action of unprecedented magnitude. The recipient of the petitions was the Moravian diet.

A few weeks after the Moravian diet had enacted the agrarian legislation, the long-awaited Imperial Parliament opened in Vienna. The agrarian question, which became the first major item on the agenda, plunged the deputies into some of the fiercest debates ever witnessed in the chamber. The chief point of controversy was whether or not the peasants should be required to pay compensation.[5] In the crucial vote on August 31, the proponents of compensation won. The bill providing for the abolition of serfdom was given final approval on September 7, 1848, and the emperor promulgated it into law in a decree bearing the same date.

The question of compensation aroused heated controversy in Prague between the radicals and the liberals, the latter favoring, the former opposing, compensation. *Pražský Večerní List* complained that "the majority of Czech deputies are in favor of compensation, and, with somewhat excessive anxiety, view the abolition of the *robot* without compensation as an approach to communism . . . our conviction is . . . *that the robot duties, and the burdens arising out of the*

4. For a fuller discussion of the petition movement, see Chapter 4.
5. See Chapter 7.

subject status should be abolished without compensation."[6] To ensure that the reader would not miss the significance of the last sentence, the newspaper printed it in boldface type. Many years later the radical Frič charged the Czech deputies with "having solved" the peasant question "in the interests of the nobility and not of the people."[7]

In contrast, Havlíček's *Národní Noviny* editorially supported compensation. From the very beginning, the paper devoted a great deal of attention to the peasant question, its main objective being to educate the Czech peasant after centuries of neglect, and to acquaint him with his new rights and privileges. It sought to instill into him pride in his newly won status as a free man. Regarding the question of compensation, *Národní Noviny* published a good deal of material arguing the case for it. As one might have expected, it published Brauner's speech of August 23 in the parliament *in toto* (see Chapter 7).[8] In reporting the crucial vote of August 31, it did not hint that most peasant deputies from Bohemia and other provinces voted against compensation; indeed, curiously, most of the newspapers in Prague—Czech and German, liberal and radical—neglected to draw this important fact to the attention of their readers.[9] After the emperor issued the Decree of September 7, *Národní Noviny* published a long letter from an unsigned Czech deputy, summarizing the significance of the new legislation and emphasizing that certain burdens "could not be abolished without compensation because justice must be the first rule of the Imperial Parliament" and that compensation would in any event be so "moderate" and so "facilitated by the state that no one need fear it."[10] Its longest exposition on compensation, in two full octavo pages of small print, appeared on September 14, 1848, from the pen of one Karel Tomíček, lawyer and parliamentary deputy. It seems that some of Tomíček's peasant constituents had addressed to him a petition demanding, among other things, that no compensation be paid to the landlords. *Národní Noviny* elected not to publish the petition, but it did publish a two-page rebuttal presenting once again the whole argument for compensation and con-

6. *PVL,* August 15, 1848.

7. J. V. Frič, *Paměti,* ed. K. Cvejn (Prague, 1957-63), II, 268.

8. *NN,* August 28, 1848.

9. Even *PVL* failed to point this out, in its coverage of the vote, in the issue of September 3, 1848.

10. *NN,* September 10, 1848.

demning the opposite stand as a "denial of law." Another reassuring explanation in the same vein, from the pen of another Czech deputy, followed on September 21, evidently spurred by some manifestations of discontent among his constituents.

The manner in which *Národní Noviny* covered the lengthy debates invited criticism from *Pražský Večerní List,* which accused *Národní Noviny* of having omitted from its account of parliamentary debates two speeches against compensation made on the floor of the parliament.[11] Havlíček countered that the point of view expressed in the two speeches had already been presented in earlier speeches (notably by Hans Kudlich) and duly reported in *Národní Noviny.*[12] This was the first major radical-liberal polemic of a political nature in the Czech-language press since the downfall of absolutism in March and it arose, appropriately, over the peasant question—the most vital question of the time.

Though Havlíček was not above withholding news from his readers, even important news concerning radical activity,[13] the censure by *Pražský Večerní List* was not merited in this case. *Národní Noviny* had reported at length the procompensation speech of deputy Schneider and had given on the whole adequate coverage to other such speeches. It had also published a letter against compensation by a Czech peasant which ended with the flat statement: "I am against any compensation for the *robot* which cannot be effected without hurting the peasant."[14] That *Národní Noviny* gave much greater coverage to the viewpoint it favored was only natural, and in so doing it hardly acted in a manner different from that of other newspapers, whether radical, liberal, or conservative.

In any discussion of the rural population in the Czech Lands in 1848, it is usual and convenient to use the term "peasantry." The term conceals important differences within the peasant class, however. It encompasses: (1) peasants having a medium or large holding of land, (2) peasants having only a dwarf holding or no holding whatever beyond a house (cottagers), and (3) peasants having no house

11. *PVL,* August 14, 1848.

12. *NN,* August 20, 1848.

13. One of the more serious omissions of this kind was the failure of *NN* to make any mention of a mass radical meeting that took place in Prague on May 29, 1848. The meeting is described in F. J. Schopf (ed.), *Wahre und ausführliche Darstellung der am 11 März 1848 . . . in Prag begonnenen Volks-Bewegung* (Leitmeritz, 1848), IV, 27.

14. Both in *NN,* August 18, 1848.

or land, farm domestics, and seasonal agricultural workers. The peasants included in the second and third categories above may be regarded as landless peasants. The Revolution of 1848 effected not only a full emancipation of the peasantry as a whole, but brought in its wake the first stirrings of the landless peasantry, particularly cottagers. As a political force, the influence of cottagers was still limited, but their numbers were large enough to compel attention and to cause the peasants of higher status to feel uneasy at the prospect of this landless army growing and menacing their security. In 1848, the landless peasants already encompassed a large segment of the rural population, their numbers exceeding those of the landed peasants in some regions.

One of the most remarkable and enlightening documents on this question is a report dated April 22, 1848, of an official of a landed estate in western Bohemia, which was preserved in the files of the National Committee. The official sought to draw the attention of the authorities to the existence of the rural "proletarians" (*ländliche Proletarier*) who "view the impending benefits to the peasant for that reason with jealousy because they had been hitherto highly dependent upon him (and) oppressed by him." According to the report, the number of "agricultural proletarians" in the region in question "is far greater than that of the peasants."[15] A cottagers' petition to the National Committee (from eastern Bohemia) offered detailed statistics on the situation in their region and concluded that the number of landless peasants there was three times as large as the number of landed peasants.[16]

In Moravia the problem appears to have been less acute, and it is probable that in Bohemia and Moravia as a whole the landed peasants still held an edge from the point of view of numbers. The number of cottagers' petitions to the National Committee was 156, of a total of 580. In Moravia their number was markedly small—only 23 out of 306—an indication that the number of landless peasants in Moravia was much smaller than in Bohemia and that the social consciousness of these people was less developed.

Whatever the respective proportions of cottagers and peasants, the number of the former was unquestionably large—and growing. The peasants felt uncomfortable in the face of such a multitude; in

15. F. Roubík (ed.), *Petice venkovského lidu z Čech k Národnímu výboru z roku 1848* (Prague, 1954), p. 75.

16. *Ibid.*, p. 181.

some regions they were fearful to the point where they questioned the wisdom of bestowing upon cottagers the right to vote. According to Brauner, "many people, especially peasants, complain that even the taxpaying cottagers enjoy a right to vote; since their numbers in many places exceed that of landed peasants, they will have more votes and will outvote the peasants."[17] On the eve of the election for the Bohemian diet, *Národní Noviny* reported that many candidates were collecting votes from the "little people who also have a right to vote" and that this caused the peasants to fear that they would be "outvoted by cottagers" and "will not find in their matters defenders in the diet."[18] In other words, no sooner did the peasants receive, for the first time in Czech history, the precious right to vote than they sought to exclude the poorer strata of the rural population from the exercise of this same right. Similarly, the urban middle classes, having been fully enfranchised by the Revolution of 1848, and having assumed direction of the revolution, lost no time in barring the working class from suffrage.

It is in connection with the cottager problem that the delicate question of the distribution of land was raised. In the Czech press, attention to this problem was first drawn (during the 1848-49 period) by *Národní Noviny*, with the publication of a cottagers' petition (from the region of Rakovník), in which the cottagers asked that they be permitted to acquire, into permanent tenure, certain types of ecclesiastical land. Havlíček himself added a postscript recommending such a solution and even extending it by suggesting that the poorest peasants be permitted to purchase land outright, the payment to be made in installments spread over a long period of time.[19] Havlíček's views here coincided perfectly with his avowed anti-clericalism to which he—a disillusioned former seminarist—was only too glad to open his columns.

Havlíček always thought in terms of purchasing land, but in the course of 1848 there was also—though rarely—a request for something resembling the confiscation of ecclesiastical property. Among the petitions in Bohemia, only two propose what amounts to confiscation of ecclesiastical lands. One demands that the land of the

17. *NN*, June 2, 1848.
18. *NN*, June 8, 1848.
19. *NN*, September 26, 1848. *NN* attacked the "Peasant Aristocracy" in a scathing indictment on October 21, 1848; this was upheld in an article signed by Havlíček himself on November 16, 1848.

Roman Catholic clergy be taken from them and "returned permanently to the nation"; the other urges that church property "be recognized as state property."[20] A sympathetic and vigorous interest in the cottager problem was maintained by the Slavic Linden, which intended to publish a brochure devoted to an analysis of the agrarian problem but never did.[21]

Next there was a demand for the distribution or confiscation of secular property—a request far too radical even for most radical democrats. During the revolutionary period—and only at the end of it—the radical Emanuel Arnold hinted, in his ultraradical *Občanské Noviny* (April 26, 1849), at the possibility of such an upheaval in property relations. He suggested that "if, for instance, one peasant proprietor had a maximum of 400 *korec* measures of land [roughly 250 acres], then much land would be separated from individual large landed properties and pass into the hands of small proprietors."[22] There is no indication in Arnold's proposal of how the surplus land would actually pass into the hands of the cottagers. What is novel is that Arnold does not specifically limit his proposal to ecclesiastical property, and by refraining from doing so implies that secular property would be affected. With this, the question of land distribution may be said to have reached at once its climax and its point of exhaustion. The article—infused with a demogogue's passion, like many other products of Arnold's pen—failed to elicit any significant response, within or without the peasant class, despite the fact that Arnold was the radicals' outstanding "specialist" on the peasant question, with wider contacts among the peasantry than any other radical. The political events following the publication of his article killed whatever chances Arnold had of striking a responsive chord among his countrymen. The article appeared on April 26, 1849, and a few days later, after the exposure of the May Conspiracy (May 10), the police were

20. Roubík (ed.), *Petice venkovského lidu,* pp. 34, 249.

21. Kočí, "Příspěvek k rolnické otázce," p. 264.

22. E. Arnold, *Sebrané spisy* (Prague, 1954), p. 419. An interesting proposal was submitted in a petition of cottagers from two regions, one in Silesia, another in the adjacent parts of Moravia, to the Moravian diet (an identical one was submitted to the Imperial Parliament) in the second half of 1848. The cottagers demanded that they be permitted to acquire a certain amount of land from the large peasant farms for moderate price. What makes this proposal unusual is that land was demanded not from the nobles but from the more prosperous peasants. Text of the petition in J. Vochala, *Rok 1848 ve Slezsku a na severovýchodní Moravě* (Opava, 1948), pp. 101-4.

spreading a dragnet for Arnold and other radicals. Ultimately he was apprehended and condemned to spend years in prison and exile.

What role did the peasant himself play in the political events of the year 1848? The emancipation had opened new vistas for him and required that he be accommodated within the new constitutional framework instituted after the downfall of absolutism. An emancipated peasant should obviously take part, to some degree, in the constitutional process, the first symbol of such participation being the right to vote. In this respect, the peasant fared much better than the urban worker. The latter had been barred from suffrage by electoral laws enacted in both Bohemia and Moravia within two months after the downfall of absolutism. The middle classes did not relish the impact of the working-class vote upon political institutions, but their attitude toward the other underprivileged mass—the peasantry—was of a different order. The peasantry was regarded in a more generous light, being viewed as a potentially stabilizing force—once its legitimate demands had been satisfied. As a consequence, the bulk of the peasantry was admitted to electoral privilege.

In Bohemia the relevant measure was the electoral law prepared by the National Committee in May, 1848, as a basis upon which the new Bohemian diet was to be elected. This law conferred suffrage, in rural districts, on everyone "paying a direct tax" (Article XXXVIII)[23]—a provision embracing the greater part of the rural population, since even many cottagers paid such a tax; the agricultural workers, farm domestics, and all other nontaxpayers were, through this provision, excluded from suffrage. In Moravia the situation was similar. The provisional constitution for Moravia adopted by the Moravian diet on April 27, 1848, was more explicit than the Bohemian document in that it conferred suffrage only on "independent" persons and excluded specifically "farm domestics, paupers, factory workers, journeymen, and apprentices"; on the other hand, all those paying a direct tax had a right to vote. Thus, in Moravia, too, most peasants (including many cottagers) had been enfranchised. The Moravian constitution approved by the diet on September 20, 1848, retained the substance of these provisions but employed different terminology; Article XV bestowed suffrage on those "owning land, house, or taxable business, or those who have proved their educa-

23. Černý (ed.), *Boj*, p. 236.

tion by the attainment of a public office, academic honor, or by passing a state examination."[24]

The electoral law upon which the Imperial Parliament was to be chosen was the subject of sharp disagreements and provoked violent demonstrations in the imperial capital, staged by the radicals and the workers. The Patent of May 8, 1848, valid for all of Cisleithania, excluded from suffrage "workers on daily or weekly pay, servants, and persons drawing support from public welfare agencies." This was later modified under radical pressure, and, with some ambiguity, "independent" workers were given the right to vote.[25] As far as the peasantry was concerned, the majority were enfranchised by this law, as witnessed by the conspicuous presence of a large group of peasant deputies—some of them illiterate—from Galicia. Only servant personnel and paupers on relief had been barred from franchise, but other rural categories, including all cottagers, were entitled to vote, since there was no requirement of income or direct taxation. This was an extremely liberal law for the times, much more liberal than the electoral provisions issued by the National Committee in Bohemia and the provincial diet in Moravia; the imperial electoral law shows the unmistakable impact of pressure from Viennese radicals.

Not only did the Czech (and German) peasant vote for the first time in 1848, but he joined, for the first time, the representatives of other social classes in framing the laws of his province and of his monarchy. In Bohemia proper, the opportunity of so doing was denied because the government in Vienna vetoed all plans, so elaborately and enthusiastically undertaken, for the meeting of the Bohemian diet. Nevertheless, in most parts of Bohemia elections for the diet had actually been carried out, in June, 1848. It had originally been expected that the diet would deal with the question of serfdom, and the rural districts accordingly elected to the diet a large contingent of peasant deputies. Havlíček himself had appealed to the voters to elect a strong peasant representation.[26]

In Moravia the nobility showed itself keenly responsive to the aspirations of the peasantry, mindful, no doubt, of the dangers inherent in a failure to heed these aspirations. The first diet of that year—still based on the old estates structure—opened on March 30,

24. *Ibid.*, pp. 154-55; J. Dvořák, *Moravské sněmování roku 1848-49* (Telč, 1898), p. 254.
25. *CBB,* June 23, 1848.
26. *NN,* June 27, 1848.

and on the following day enunciated the principle that the diet should be broadened by the inclusion of representatives of the peasantry (and also of the burghers who had until then been only meagerly represented). The manner of effecting this change was to be studied by a committee. This was a memorable decision, signifying as it did the first breach in the ancient estates structure of representation. Proceeding speedily in order not to be overtaken by events, the diet enshrined the principle of peasant representation in a provisional constitution of April 27, which, in effect, extended suffrage to most of the peasants (see above). On May 13, the estates diet met for the last time, having smoothed the transition and ensured continuity for the new diet. An election was held on the basis of the provisional constitution of April 27, and a new "modern" diet was chosen, which convened on May 31, 1848, and sat until January of the following year. The new diet was heavily represented by peasants, presenting a spectacle so striking as to be labeled the "Peasant Parliament" in popular parlance. It consisted of one chamber; of the total of 247 deputies who had assembled by the end of June, rural communities were represented by 97 deputies, of whom a majority were peasants.[27]

As for the elections to the Imperial Parliament, the situation was radically different. It was generally held that the parliament would deal with high-level intricacies of constitutionalism which would require a solid educational background. In deference to this expectation, Havlíček now advised the nation to send to Vienna a delegation strong in intellect rather than muscle. He did not expect that serfdom would be discussed, and his main concern was to have the Czechs represented by men well-versed in constitutional questions who would be able to resist and outwit the German centralists whose implacable hostility to the Czechs was only too well-known. As Havlíček himself wrote: "Just as we advised you to elect as deputies to our Bohemian diet mainly peasants and such men as are independent of the landlords . . . so we advise you again sincerely with regard to the Viennese Parliament to choose men capable of higher political negotiation and learned in every respect."[28] The fact that the election was indirect further precluded the chance of too many peasants being chosen. When the votes were in, it turned out that the Czechs heeded Havlíček's advice. Bohemia and Moravia sent only 15 peasant deputies to Vienna, of a combined total of 138.

27. For a list of Moravian deputies, see *NN*, July 26, 1848.
28. *NN*, June 27, 1848.

The legislation of 1848 had brought the ballot box within the peasant's influence. How much inclined was the peasant to go beyond this instrument of popular will and resort to revolution? Was he revolution-prone? Was the countryside, in fact, a vast teeming reservoir of revolutionary sentiment as it was sometimes depicted to be?

The last major peasant rebellion in Bohemia occurred in 1775, and in Moravia a revolt of more limited scope took place in 1821, both movements having been provoked by exactions of heavy *robot* duties. As a result of Emperor Joseph's measures (1781) the situation improved, but no further substantial ameliorations were effected by Joseph's successors, and the revolt in Moravia in 1821 indicated that the countryside was far from peaceful. There was widespread discontent to the eve of 1848, and the downfall of absolutism in March, 1848, by raising the level of expectations, had the effect of intensifying rather than curbing dissatisfaction. It is probable that had the authorities, at this juncture, tried to perpetuate the *robot* and other ingredients of serfdom, they would have provoked a revolution.

The revolutionary wave crested in mid-1848, after which it began to subside. Among the events contributing to this weakening of the revolutionary movement were the crushing of the June Uprising in Bohemia, the abolition of the *robot* duties in June by the diet in Moravia, and the abolition of serfdom by the Imperial Parliament at the beginning of September. After this a violent revolution in the countryside became a very remote possibility; the basic grievance of the peasantry had been redressed. It is true that several developments continued to nourish peasant discontent. There was the October revolution in Vienna, which had some unsettling effect in Moravia. There was the lingering fear that in the end, in spite of all the laws and decrees, serfdom would not disappear or that the relevant decrees would be rescinded. This fear was fanned by radical agitators who even spread the false text of an imperial manifesto purporting to state that constitutional freedoms would be abolished as of November 3, 1848.[29] There was the leavening effect of the war in Hungary, which created widespread sympathy for Kossuth, more so in Moravia than in Bohemia. There was also the recruitment drive and the forcible dissolution of the Kroměříž Parliament. The recruitment drive in particular produced in several communities open resistance and defiance. On the whole, however, the authorities always remained

29. B. Šindelář, "O úloze lidových mas v revolučním dění roku 1848 na Moravě a ve Slezsku," *ČSČH*, IV (1956), 412.

in control of the situation, though sometimes with the help of a contingent of troops, and the discontent remained local in character. In the early months of 1849, the radical mood was much more widespread in Moravia than in Bohemia, but in neither province did it attain the level it had reached in mid-1848, and neither province could be said to have hovered on the brink of a major revolutionary upheaval; all official fears in this respect proved exaggerated. Only in Silesia and the adjacent parts of northern Moravia, for specific reasons, did a truly revolutionary situation exist during this period, but Silesia was too small a region and situated too far on the fringe of the Czech Lands to exert any appreciable effect on the rest of the country.[30]

The radicals tried as best they could to stir revolutionary sentiment, traveling across the countryside and distributing leaflets, but their efforts met with little response. The revolutionary wave was subsiding, and the feeling of apathy was settling on the rural districts. Moreover, the landed peasants began to fear the cottagers, and this reduced radical sentiment still further. When the May Conspiracy was uncovered and the participants were arrested, the peasantry remained calm.

It is now possible to draw up a peasant's balance sheet of the revolutionary era. The significance of the year 1848 for the Czech peasant can hardly be overestimated. In that year, he cast his first ballot; he first sat in a legislative assembly; and he first became a full-fledged owner of his land. After centuries of servitude, he had at last become a free man. Like other citizens, he was henceforth subject to the regular administrative and judicial powers of the state and its agencies, not to those of the landlord; he had, in fact, become the equal of his lord, at least in the juridical sense of the word. The last vestiges of serfdom had been wiped out, never to be revived, for even after the dissolution of the Kroměříž Parliament and the reimposition of absolutism, no attempt was made to tamper with the peasant's new status. And whatever its shortcomings, the emancipa-

30. Adjacent to the Polish and Prussian centers of an advanced radicalism, this region was more exposed to radical propaganda. The fact that the Moravian decree on serfdom did not apply to Silesia only reinforced a mood of grim resentment and belligerence. There were also in Silesia critical food shortages, and many Silesian landlords showed themselves unusually clumsy in dealing with peasant demands. All this combined to produce in Silesia a truly revolutionary situation, with violent and widespread explosions against the landowning class. See B. Šindelář, "Ohlas maďarské revoluce 1848-49 na Moravě a ve Slezsku," *Rozpravy ČSAV-SV*, LXVII, Fasc. 3 (1957).

tion had put an end, permanently, to an era of revolutions in the countryside. Although there were periods of discontent—at times of a serious nature— in the next hundred years there was to be no peasant rebellion.

As the peasant became a free man capable of influencing political decisions, publishers and editors began to compete for his attention. The year 1848 saw the emergence of the first newspapers of opinion specifically and exclusively directed toward the peasant in the history of Czech journalism. The significance of this is not diminished by the fact that none of these peasant newspapers succeeded permanently and all had to suspend publication after a short time, largely because of a lack of reader interest. It was clear that even after the emancipation the peasantry was far from ready to avail itself of all the levers of influence that emancipation had brought within its reach. The best known of these short-lived newspapers was the *Sedlské Noviny,* edited by J. K. Tyl, which appeared in Prague from April 1 to May 15, 1849.[31] In Moravia a newspaper bearing the same name had been launched much earlier (in March, 1848), under the editorship of the Czech Moravian patriot Jan Helcelet, but it died after publication of the third issue.[32]

Not only did the year 1848 bring decisive benefits to the peasant, but also, by emancipating him, it brought collective benefits to the Czech nation. The Czechs enjoyed a great numerical preponderance among the lower social classes; with the millions of Czech peasants now drawn into the political process, the Czech element was bound to reclaim its rightful place in its own country. Although it was not fully realized at the time, the emancipation had sealed the doom of German overlordship in the Czech Lands. Once the inexorable weight of Czech numbers was translated into the arithmetic of political life, nothing could stand in the way of the emancipation of the Czechs as a nation. This emancipation was supported by the expansion of the Czech element in the schools, factories, and cities, which could now become the instruments with which the Czechs would, with growing success exceeded only by their mounting impatience, pursue their national objectives.

To dispose of all the problems left in the wake of the emanci-

31. Now available in J. K. Tyl, *Spisy,* Vol. XIV, ed. F. Strejček and H. Hrzalová (Prague, 1953).

32. H. Traub, "Moravské časopisectvo v letech 1848-1849," *ČČM,* XCIV (1920), 109.

pation legislation was a task of some magnitude. In many ways the Law of September 7 was a beginning rather than a consummation of the process. The law itself left to further legislation many details of enforcement, which were to be worked out in a constitutional manner by a commission composed of elected deputies from each province. But these meetings were not to take place. The Viennese revolution interrupted the regular flow of constitutional life, and after the revolution any constitutional procedure increasingly fell under a shadow of official suspicion, as savoring of revolution and anarchy. Thus, the next stage in the disposition of the problem of serfdom was already accomplished as fiat, imposed from above: this was the Patent of March 4, 1849,[33] which provided for a government commission to deal with the problems arising from compensation and laid down guidelines for its conduct.

It took until 1853 for all the difficulties to be ironed out and for all the problems to be settled. In the final count, a little under one million peasants in Bohemia and Moravia fell within the scope of the compensation law. The number of estates to which compensation was due was 1,912. The total amount received by the estates was ninety-four million florins, of which about one-fourth went to schools, churches, and similar institutions. From the amount of compensation as finally determined, one-third was deducted as the equivalent of taxes and certain other expenses incurred by the landlord in connection with the administration of the urbarial land. Of the remainder, one-half was to be paid by the state, the other by the peasants.[34] The payment period was twenty years and in Bohemia the average amount an individual peasant was required to pay annually was no more than ten florins (in many, if not most cases, it was less).[35] This was not an unduly prohibitive amount and did not meet with any widespread and intense opposition. But the compensation was a boon to the landowner, making it possible for him to introduce technological improvements and rationalize agricultural production—in itself a desirable objective except that, in the circumstances, it placed the emancipated peasant at a competitive disadvantage.

Considering the many centuries during which the peasant had

33. Černý (ed.), *Boj*, pp. 581-87. The new octroyed constitution and the companion Bill of Rights were also dated March 4, 1849.

34. *Přehled československých dějin* (Prague, 1960), II/1, 66.

35. F. Roubík, "K vyvazení gruntů v Čechách v letech 1848-1853," *SAP*, IX, No. 2 (1959), 209.

chafed in serfdom and had borne the brunt of taxation, this seemed a dubious way of releasing him from that serfdom. Whatever the legal terminology enveloping the 1848 reform legislation, the peasant had, in effect, been made to pay for attaining his freedom. It is true that the landless peasant was not required to pay any compensation, but then he was obliged to struggle with a different, more onerous burden: the lack of land. The main cause of land hunger was over-population, and this no amount of social reform could rectify. But there was also inequality of land ownership, which called for legislative action. With this problem the legislators and the governments of 1848-49 failed to deal. The problem of the landless peasantry was one of the principal items of "unfinished business" left from the revolutionary era—an unhappy legacy bequeathed to the coming generations.

Chapter **12**

Workers

The working class constituted a small segment of the population, but was concentrated in a few centers, which gave it an influence out of proportion to its numbers. This influence was enhanced by the fact that the two largest working-class centers were Prague and Brno, the capitals of Bohemia and Moravia, respectively; as a result, the working class exerted a direct and critical impact on the course of events during 1848-49.

The riots in Brno in 1843 and in Prague in 1844, were the first major labor disturbances in the Czech Lands. In the late forties unemployment kept the workers in a state of restlessness, and by the eve of 1848, fear of this new social class hung like an oppressive shadow over the people of Prague and Brno. The news from Paris concerning the downfall of the French Monarchy inspired in Prague a hope for political reform in the Habsburg lands, but from the very beginning this hope was marred by the fear that the change might trigger another wave of working-class violence.

The burgher families in Prague awaited the results of the assembly of March 11 with a mixture of hope and anxiety; some went as far as to carefully prepare and load weapons for the occasion, and all were expecting the worst. One contemporary wrote that a "fear of the proletariat" had begun to grip the public; that the "propertied classes" lived "in terrible anticipation of what would happen"; and that "disturbing rumors about an imminent communist uprising never ceased."[1] In Brno, the atmosphere was similar. Two weeks after the downfall of absolutism, a Brno newspaper spoke of a "fear that had hung over the city for a fortnight" and appealed to the workers to refrain from the use of force.[2] The appeal fell on deaf ears; on April 1, 1848, the same day on which it appeared, the first outbreak occurred: an agitated mass of workers attacked a factory. In Prague, the assembly of March 11 took place without incident, but the memory

1. J. Malý, *Naše znovuzrození* (Prague, 1880-84), II, 11, 19.
2. Quoted in B. Šindelář, "O úloze lidovych mas v revolučním dění roku 1848 na Moravě a ve Slezsku," *ČSČH*, IV (1956), 217.

of the year 1844 continued to haunt the public; danger seemed to lurk beneath the thin veneer of calm.

One of the purposes of the National Guards, which sprang into being during the March Days, was to control the proletariat.[3] It was also deemed necessary to neutralize the proletariat by excluding it from suffrage. On May 28, 1848, the National Committee adopted the draft of an electoral law for Bohemia restricting suffrage in the cities to "burghers" (Article XXXVIII)—a term which, used in its legal sense, excluded workers, domestics, and others. A similar measure was adopted by the diet in Brno for Moravia on April 27, 1848. Thus, within two months of the inauguration of the constitutional regime the working class in the Czech Lands had found itself barred from participating in the constitutional process.

The First and, by implication, the Second, March Petitions called for the abolition of the food and stamp tax—a proposal primarily intended to benefit the lower social classes. But no proposal relating specifically to the workers' needs was included in either petition; the radicals' proposal for the "organization of work and wages" had been left out. The condition of the workers was critical, however, and several steps were hastily taken to calm them and relieve their social distress. The prices of certain food products and beer were reduced; relief funds were collected; and temporary employment was provided on public works projects.[4] At the same time, direct appeals were made to the workers to be patient and calm. On April 3, 1848, the German newspaper *Bohemia* published an editorial addressed specifically to the workers, under the soothing title "Appeal to Our Working Fellow-Citizens." Nothing like this had ever appeared in any newspaper in Prague, which indicates the concern with which the public viewed the working-class danger. As might be expected, the article was patronizing and contained little of substance. It conceded that the workers might say that "the constitution will bring good to many people, but what will we get out of it?" and assured the workers that after the downfall of absolutism "it is utterly impossible that, with the general improvement of the conditions in the life of the

3. See, for example, Brauner's comments on his draft of the First Petition, in J. M. Černý (ed.), *Boj za právo: Sborník aktů politických u věcech státu a národa českého od roku 1848* (Prague, 1893), p. 15.

4. A placement bureau had existed since the beginning of 1847; see the notice by this bureau in *NN*, April 22, 1849.

people, you would not also fare better."[5] The worker was, in effect, being asked simply to wait and hope for a better future.

The largest and most restless group of workers was the cotton-printers; on March 19 these workers presented to the St. Václav's Committee a petition of demands, the main purpose of which was to reduce unemployment. On the next day (March 20), the committee chose a physician, a Dr. Kampelík, to act as a "supervisor, leader, intermediary" among the cotton-printers. Kampelík was soon accused of being a "Communist" and "Socialist," however, and on March 30 he gave up his duties with the committee. His last act was the publication of the first—and last, as it turned out—issue of *Hlasník* (*Herald*), a newspaper specifically directed to the workers. The *Hlasník* is regarded as the first working-class newspaper in Czech history; it was not, of course, a voice of the workers, but a voice speaking to the workers.[6] For a time, the attempts of the St. Václav's Committee and of the authorities to keep the workers quiet seemed to be successful. On March 24 the cotton-printers issued a statement pledging themselves to maintain order, and on April 18, a declaration expressing a similar intent was issued on behalf of four thousand Prague workers;[7] to what extent the two statements may be regarded as genuine products of working-class thinking or to what extent they were shaped by nonworker elements who were trying to influence the workers is impossible to say.

Inasmuch as unemployment continued to plague the workers the attempts to calm them could not be successful for long. Even as the declaration of April 18 was being issued, there were rumblings of discontent. The workers' impatience was mounting; their mood was becoming grimmer. Their anger was being fed by the anti-Jewish propaganda that deluged the streets of Prague in the form of pamphlets, posters, and cartoons. Finally, after sporadic attacks on baker's shops and on Jewish merchants, the discontent erupted with great violence. On May 1, 1848, a group of workers fell upon the Jewish

5. *Bohemia,* April 3, 1848, extra issue.

6. K. Novotný, "První český časopis pro dělnictvo: Kampelíkův 'Hlasník' z r. 1848," *Novinářský Sborník,* X (1965), 174-79. The first issue is dated March, but the day of its appearance is not given; the indications are that it was around the last day of March. This is the only issue that has survived, but historians have believed that three or four further issues were published, though they have not survived. Novotný demonstrates convincingly that the first issue was the only one ever published.

7. *Ibid.,* p. 177. Also, *NN,* April 25, 1848.

stores in Prague, the storekeepers having been accused of (and sometimes they were actually guilty of) charging exorbitant prices for
their merchandise. The rioting lasted all day May 1 and all day May
2, and its effect was overpowering. The specter of the 1844 riots had
been resurrected; a Prague newspaper commented that this was "a
raging movement the like of which we have not experienced since
the unrest of cotton-printers in 1845 [*sic*]."[8] This was the worst
anti-Jewish outburst of the revolutionary era.

The sweeping away of absolutist barriers raised the level of
expectations, nourishing rather than appeasing dissatisfaction. The
months of April and May were filled with hectic activity on the part
of the workers. There were protests, petitions, strikes, and negotiations between workers and employers. Among the categories of
workers involved were the cotton-printers and other textile workers,
journeymen, tailors, carpenters, masons, and typographical workers.
Never before had Prague seen so much happen in the sphere of
"labor relations." Clearly, the advent of the constitutional era had
awakened, if not yet an articulate class consciousness, at least a fresh
sense of grievance and a new boldness in voicing that grievance. Nor
was the wave of discontent limited to Prague. There was unrest in
some other cities and towns having a larger working-class population.
There was a strike of smelters in the Ostrava region (in present-day
northern Moravia) in May, 1848,[9] and there were strikes and petitions in Brno, involving masons, cabinet-makers, and spinners,[10] to
cite two examples.

In Prague, the best organized, though not the largest and
strongest, group was the typographical workers. Their petition, dated
May 4, demanded, among other things, a raise in wages and a reduction of machines. In the latter part of May they staged a two-day
strike, which forced some newspapers to publish an entire issue in
handwritten, mimeographed form; this was the first strike of Prague
typographical workers on record.[11] A few concessions induced the

8. *CBB*, May 2, 1848; also, *NN*, May 2 and 3, 1848.

9. M. Myška, *Počátky vytváření dělnické třídy v železárnách na Ostravsku*
(Ostrava, 1962), p. 165. There was also a rioting of the "rabble" in Hradec
Králové on April 2 (*NN*, April 7, 1848).

10. K. Novotný and M. Myška (eds.), *První kroky k vítězství: Čtení o
počátcích našeho dělnického hnutí* (Prague, 1966), pp. 54-55.

11. K. Novotný, "Hnutí typografického dělnictva v Praze r. 1848," *Zápisky
katedry čsl. dějin a archivního studia*, III, Nos. 1-2 (1958), 9.

strikers to return to work on the afternoon of the second day, but the conflict was not settled until the beginning of 1849.

It was the movement of the cotton-printers, however, that caused the employers and the authorities the gravest concern. Negotiations between the cotton-printers and their employers for improved working conditions had been under way since the latter part of March. The principal issue was the use of machines, which the workers, of course, opposed and the employers favored. In their resentment of the machines, which were depriving them of employment, the cotton-printers shared the grievance of the typographical workers. Though the employers gave the unemployed cotton-printers some financial support for a period, this was not a basic answer to the continuing problem of unemployment; the financial support extended for a few weeks only while many cotton-printers were unemployed for a much longer time.

Unable to achieve their goals through appealing to their employers, the cotton-printers presented their case to the people; at the end of May they distributed a leaflet entitled "Ardent Entreaty to the Burghers of Prague from the [Cotton-]Printers." The leaflet was a humble and pathetic document, pleading for the sympathy of the public. "We are not rebels," it said; we are only asking the officials "to extend a hand to us in our misery." But it also said that "unfortunately our patience is almost at an end, for we cannot adequately describe to you the woes that pursue us."[12] The patience of these workers had indeed come to an end, for on June 3, a group of them staged a protest march through the city. They camped at a public square, awaiting the arrival of one of the manufacturers, whereupon His Majesty's hussars, who were stationed nearby and were summoned into action, dispersed the throng, wounding one worker.[13]

The Prague City Council sought to mediate in the dispute, but it failed in its attempts, and on June 10 issued an ordinance charging the workers with "blind stubbornness" and castigating them for their "menacing demonstrations." The ordinance served as a stern warning that in the future such conduct would not be tolerated; it told the workers that the textile workers in other parts of Bohemia, though in

12. Text in Novotný and Myška (eds.), *První kroky,* pp. 346-47. At about the same time (March 24, 1848) the cotton-printers issued another leaflet, setting forth their specific demands (text, *ibid.,* pp. 348-50).

13. F. J. Schopf (ed.), *Wahre und ausführliche Darstellung der am 11 März 1848 . . . in Prag begonnenen Volks-Bewegung* (Leitmeritz, 1848), V, 16.

greater distress, had endured their condition "without the slightest breach of the peace, in mute despair."[14]   But the Prague workers were not in a mood for mute despair; the ferment continued and added its share to the June Uprising, which broke out two days after the ordinance had been issued.

The workers, and their leaders, the students, were the most dynamic element in the June Uprising; by far the greatest number of casualties were among the workers. In joining the uprising, the participating workers fought for objectives that few of them fully understood and that transcended the sphere of their own immediate social and economic self-interest. It was the first time that any group of Czech workers had been drawn into a major struggle that was political rather than social in character and that was of importance to the nation as a whole. Although various categories of Prague workers had been engaged in a struggle with their employers over social objectives throughout April and May, these objectives played no part whatsoever in the uprising. There is no record of any group of workers voicing any social objectives during the six days when Prague fought Windischgrätz. After the uprising, hundreds of workers who were not domiciled in the city were expelled.

The spectacle of armed proletarians manning the barricades was a novel one and had an alarming effect on the other social classes. It seemed to herald the advent of a powerful working-class movement such as existed in France, with all its destructive capabilities. The disturbances of 1844 and the anti-Jewish outburst at the beginning of May, frightening though they were, were of a different order, for the authorities had remained basically in control of the situation. The drama of June cast the worker in a different role; for six days he wielded arms, fraternized with university students, and stood entirely beyond the reach of the law. This spectacle raised a whole new complex of issues; with the June Uprising, the middle class, itself still weak and only beginning to enjoy the fruits of a political freedom, had found itself face to face with a new social problem: the "working-class question."

After the uprising, Czech newspapers set about exploring this new problem, producing a veritable avalanche of articles and editorials dealing directly or indirectly with the workers. The liberal *Národní Noviny,* the greatest Czech-language daily, featured a front-page

14. Text of the ordinance, *ibid.,* pp. 89-90.

study of the popular mood under the title "Teaching the Common People." The article drew attention to the alarming growth of "a propertyless class of people who have menaced and are still menacing both the nobles and the burghers" and pointed out that "he who is well off does not revolt." The gist of its recommendations was that it was necessary to educate the lower social classes and to cultivate in them an appreciation of a good "civic life."[15] Another article in the same newspaper bore the title "Short History of the Prague Proletariat."[16] The ambitious title concealed a paucity of ideas, for the article was written in the spirit of unrelieved paternalism. *Národní Noviny,* an excellent newspaper, superior in editorial quality to the radical press, could offer little more than honest puzzlement and homiletics when it endeavored to throw light on the new social problem; it could never shed the intellectual armor of laissez-faire liberalism.

The radical press responded with more lively editorializing and probing. The radicals tended to sympathize with the workers, and unlike the liberals, suggested concrete remedies that today seem more in tune with the twentieth century than the nineteenth. The leading Czech radical organ, *Pražský Večerní List,* published no less than seven articles totaling fifteen installments within a month, all devoted to the working class and the related problems of poverty and class distinction.[17] One of its articles, "How to Raise the Level of the Working Class," was remarkable for its modernity. Placing the responsibility for reform on "statesmen and economists," it suggested that in its social reform Bohemia should be guided by the experience and example of England, France, and Switzerland. One of the curses in a worker's life, it said, was his propensity to "linger in a wretched saloon" and to "dissipate the little he earns through painful labor." To counteract this, the article continued, workers should be provided with adequate housing built in attractive surroundings in a community arrangement; commissary kitchens providing inexpensive and wholesome meals; libraries filled with both educational and enter-

15. *NN,* June 30 and July 1, 1848.
16. *NN,* July 30, 1848.
17. "Events of Recent Days in Prague," June 23; "Concerning the Conditions of Cotton-Printers," June 23; "Concerning Wages," June 27; "How to Raise the Level of the Working Class," June 26 and 27; "Aristocrats," July 7–14 (eight installments); "Voice as to How to Relieve Great Poverty," July 3. See also the issue of July 4.

taining materials; and special magazines devoted entirely to the interests of workers.[18] Like the liberals, the radicals also emphasized the importance of moral education and the cultivation of civic virtues, but, unlike the liberals, they realized that without concrete social and economic reform, moral education was bound to be ineffective.

With the June Uprising the working-class movement had reached its peak, and with the defeat of the uprising its most turbulent period had ended. Afterwards, new waves of discontent surged up from time to time, but none reached the proportion of the discontent that had obtained before the June Uprising. In Brno, there were bread riots on June 13 and 14 at the same time that the June Uprising was in progress in Prague, but no direct connection between the two events has been established. Later the outbreak of the October revolution in Vienna set off a wave of unrest in Brno, which had always maintained close contact with the imperial capital. There was unrest on October 14. Another wave of unrest, more serious, swept the city on October 29-30, bringing it closer to the abyss of revolt than any other movement during the 1848-49 period. The unrest on October 29-30 involved demonstrations of workers who wanted to seize arms and come to the rescue of beleaguered Vienna. Though the majority of the participants were Czech, they were entirely under the influence of German-speaking radical intellectuals. In the bloody clash that ensued between the workers and the authorities, at least three and possibly as many as six workers were killed and a larger number wounded.[19] The demonstrations were accompanied by widespread pillaging, looting, and other excesses. A few days later (November 1), a group of workers, also under the influence of Vienna and almost entirely German, demonstrated in Liberec in northern Bohemia; like the workers in Brno, they wanted to seize arms and organize an expedition to Vienna.[20] These outbreaks were the last major labor disturbances in the Czech Lands.

In the first months of 1849, there was an occasional massing of workers in Prague, but these gatherings could not compare at all with the belligerence of the pre-June period. Though the workers took at times a menacing attitude, there was little violence; in most cases they disbanded peacefully after a demonstration, yielding to the

18. *PVL*, June 26 and 27.
19. Šindelář, "O úloze lidových mas," p. 404.
20. J. Belda, *Liberec v revolučním roce 1848* (Liberec, 1959), p. 190.

threats or the cajoling of officials.[21] The extent to which the revolutionary wave had subsided may be seen in the behavior of the typographical workers and the cotton-printers, the two most active labor groups. The movement of the former had attained its peak with the two-day strike in May, 1848; afterwards protracted negotiations followed, with the workers' opposition weakening steadily, and at the beginning of 1849 the workers accepted a settlement that was hardly significant in relation to their original demands. Similarly, the movement of Prague cotton-printers had reached its high point in May, 1848; almost a year of bargaining followed, with the government called in to assist the parties in arriving at a settlement. Only the government could have issued a decree or proposed a law that would give basic protection to the workers, and such a measure was at first being contemplated. But in the end the government decided to adopt a hands-off policy, which, of course, left the workers completely at the mercy of the employers. This spelled the defeat of their position; yet when they were notified of this decision in March, 1849, there was no mass protest and no violent resistance.[22] A year earlier this would hardly have been their reaction. The revolutionary wave was subsiding despite the continued high level of unemployment. That unemployment continued to pose a serious problem is confirmed by an appeal issued by the Prague burgomaster at the end of March, 1849. The burgomaster stated that as a result of the June Uprising the construction of many houses was interrupted and had not yet been resumed, and that because of this "thousands of people are without income and without a living." He asked the Prague property-owners to hire the unemployed for repair work, cleaning, and other odd jobs in the home so that these workers would have a chance to make a living. This would be humanitarian and would at the same time reduce the "dangerous idleness" of the workers and contribute to the maintenance of public order, he said.[23]

In the history of the Czech working class, the years 1848-49 were of great importance. Like the burghers and the peasantry, but with

21. *SÚA* Prague, PG 1846-49, 15 c/3, No. 3265 (April 19 and 20, 1849); No. 3374 (April 22, 1849); No. 3452 (April 24, 1849). See also *PVL,* January 6, 1849.

22. Z. Tobolka, "Počátky dělnického hnutí v Čechách," *Obzor Národohospodářský,* VIII (1903), 217.

23. Text in *PVL,* March 30, 1849; see also *CBB,* Supplement to No. 77, March 31, 1849.

much greater elemental impact, the working class was swept into the current of revolution. In the course of these events, it was lifted upon the revolutionary stage with a compelling force, causing the other groups for the first time to seriously ponder the consequences of the rise of the working class and to reflect urgently upon its place in society. In short, the years 1848-49 witnessed the emergence of the working-class question. After 1848 that question might still be misunderstood, but it could never again be wholly ignored.

The working class still constituted a small segment of the population. It consisted of many diverse elements, and a large part of it had only recently migrated into the cities and towns from the rural areas. Many workers were still part peasants and part workers; this was true especially of the spinners and weavers in the border regions. The industrial proletariat itself formed only a small part of the working class; the earliest estimate available is for the year 1857, at which time the industrial workers constituted only 7.3 per cent of the total population of the Czech Lands.[24] As in other social classes, so also in the working class, there were differences of outlook in response to current problems—differences determined by age, geographic region, type of skill, nationality, and other factors. With respect to nationality, it is pertinent to observe that in the two most important uprisings affecting the Czech Lands, the June Uprising and the Viennese revolution, the response of the workers was determined largely by nationality. The June Uprising in Prague, in which the Czech workers of Prague played such an important role, evoked no significant friendly response among the German workers in the Czech Lands; in particular, there was no appreciable reaction among the German workers of Liberec. Conversely, the Viennese revolution created no reaction among the Czech workers in Prague but set off a wave of unrest in Brno, where the Czech workers were hardly affected by Czech national consciousness, and in Liberec, where the workers were largely German. As to age, the whole course of the revolutionary era shows the young workers, apprentices, and journeymen to have been the most revolution-prone group within the working-class movement.

It is also interesting to note that the workers possessing higher skills tended to look down on those without skills. According to contemporary accounts, the cotton-printers, who were skilled workers,

24. Novotný and Myška (eds.), *První kroky,* p. 21.

looked down on the day-laborers; this prejudice was so extensive that in some factories the cotton-printers would not allow into their midst any comrade who had once accepted a job as a day-laborer.[25]

All in all, the workers exhibited certain characteristics peculiar to their class, but they also displayed attitudes resembling those of other classes. With the other classes they shared, in addition to the attitudes just mentioned, the propensity to divide into groups of moderates and radicals—a division that may be detected even in the early stages of the 1848-49 era. The Prague masons offer a notable example of this. At the beginning of April, 1848, well over two hundred journeymen masons signed a petition for higher wages and a shorter working day. After signing the petition, they realized that their number was, in the words of a police report, "too small in comparison with the mass of masons" and decided to collect more signatures. They visited several construction sites, but the masons there "hardly listened to them, declaring that they wanted to keep on working in peace, that they were satisfied with their wages"; in one establishment a group of workers "threatened to stone them, if they did not leave."[26] The report indicates that only a minority of masons supported the petition movement. A similar disunity developed among the cotton-printers. Toward the end of 1848, a group of Prague cotton-printers wrote to their comrades in other parts of Bohemia seeking support in their struggle against the machines but their request was refused.[27] Evidently the temper of the workers in smaller towns was more moderate than that of the workers in Prague.

Perhaps the most striking characteristic of the working class during this period and the preceding one was its isolation. It had no leaders and few friends. Apart from enjoying the support of a segment of the radical intellectuals and students, it was distrusted by the other classes, including the peasantry.[28] Unlike the peasantry, it stood wholly outside the pale of accepted social relationships. The most eloquent testimony to this isolation comes from the Prague police director, who on June 7, 1846, complained in a confidential

25. *PVL,* June 23, 1848.

26. Heyde's report of April 3, 1848 (*SÚA* Prague, PG 1846-49, 15 c/3, No. 2466/1848).

27. Police report of November 28, 1848 (*SÚA* Prague, PG 1846-49, 15 c/3, No. 10560/1848).

28. See a letter from a group of "landed peasants" (*gruntovníci*) expressing fear of a "rebellion of the rabble," in *NN,* April 19, 1848.

report that he had no police informants in factories and, to compensate for this, was obliged to engage the services of a physician, for only a physician had access to and contact with the workers. The police director explained that "my personal contact in this matter with so many individuals from the lowest class of people seemed to be highly inexpedient."[29] In other words, he found it impossible to recruit agents from the ranks of the workers because of the social gap separating them from his establishment—and this in a police apparatus that was noted for its reliance on spies and informants! It is not accidental that in March, 1848, the burghers chose a physician, Dr. Kampelík, as their link with the workers. All this explains why the workers are the only social group existing during this period into which there are literally no meaningful insights based on intimate personal accounts. The voice of the peasant, and, more dimly, of the agricultural worker or village weaver, may be heard in chronicles penned by educated peasants, but the city worker had no such voice. Though the radical intellectuals tried to maintain contact with the workers, the relationship was shallow and was limited to certain periods or occasions, such as the June Uprising. Socially the intellectuals and workers were miles apart. An official police protocol describes a student agitator who came to mingle with the workers wearing high riding boots and gloves![30] There is no record of any permanent friendship or tie between a radical and a working-class family, and the radicals' memoirs yield few workers' surnames: they had had no occasion to remember them.[31]

Nevertheless, the radical intellectuals did sympathize with the workers and possessed a very advanced outlook on the working-class question. Indeed, this question was of decisive importance in the rise of the radical movement. It was the radicals' views concerning the working class and, to a lesser extent, the peasantry that set them in opposition to the liberals. Without the working class, the radical movement might have remained insignificant in 1848-49.

In 1848-49, the Czech working class was only on the threshold of class consciousness and was still immune to ideology; it is not possible to find any traces of socialistic, communistic, or Marxist influence among them. But both socialism and communism of the

29. *NNM,* II (1962), 301.

30. Police report of May 9, 1848 (*SÚA* Prague, PGT, R/1, 33/g.).

31. See especially J. V. Frič, *Paměti,* ed. K. Cvejn (Prague, 1957-63), in which few such names are given.

non-Marxian kind were known to the educated classes, to the burghers and the radicals: the former abhorred them,[32] while the latter viewed them with a certain sympathy and were influenced by them.[33] It was the radicals, for example, who wanted to include in the March Petition a demand for the "organization of work and wages," derived from the French socialist Louis Blanc. Yet the first comprehensive exposition of socialism from a Czech pen came from a man who was not a radical but a moderate, not a layman but a priest, and not a Bohemian but a Moravian: F. M. Klácel. The account appeared in the form of a series of letters entitled "Letters from a Friend to a [Lady] Friend [*Přítelkyně*] Concerning the Origin of Socialism and Communism" and published in a Moravian newspaper in the first half of 1849.[34] Klácel's letters are remarkable for their insight, and though he does not favor socialism or communism he writes with moderation and understanding. He is profoundly aware that these new political movements are the product of great social change and a reaction to great social inequities.

The first Czech to formulate what amounted to a class concept of the state was the radical student Karel Sladkovský, in an extraordinary work entitled "On the Origin of All Evil in Human Society." Sladkovský wrote his tract while in prison in 1850 and intended it as a memorandum for Count Leo Thun concerning the social question. Though written in 1850, it is definitely a product of the 1848-49 period.[35] As far as can be established, Sladkovský arrived at his concept without Marx, but his work was never published and he himself later abandoned his views.

It was left to the Marxists to plant the seed of the class concept in Czech soil and make it grow, but before and during the 1848-49

32. The best-known critique of communism from the liberal side is Havlíček's article "Communism," published originally in his *Slovan*, June 26, 1850, and reprinted in K. Havlíček, *Politické spisy*, ed. Z. Tobolka (Prague, 1900-3), III, 100-7.

33. Notably Sabina. See selections from his writings in K. Kosík (ed.), *Čeští radikální demokraté* (*Výbor politických statí*) (Prague, 1953), pp. 171 ff.

34. The newspaper was *Moravské Noviny;* the lady, Božena Němcová. The letters appeared in the same year in book form and have recently been published in F. M. Klácel, *Výbor z díla* (Prague, 1964), pp. 95-229. The work through which, more than through any other, knowledge of West European socialist thought was transmitted to the Czech Lands was L. von Stein's *Socialismus und Communismus des heutigen Frankreichs* (Leipzig, 1842).

35. Reprinted in J. Matoušek, *Karel Sladkovský a český radikalismus za revoluce a reakce* (Prague, 1929), pp. 109-35.

period the influence of Marx and Engels on the Czechs was negligible.
Their writings were known to only a handful of Czechs; in fact,
only two—both philosophers (Augustin Smetana and Ignác Hanuš)
and neither associated politically with the radicals—are positively
known to have had a knowledge of some of the works by Marx and
Engels. The works in question were the earlier ones;[36] the *Communist
Manifesto* was not among them and did not penetrate the Czech Lands
at all during 1848-49 as far as is known. Paradoxically, not a single
radical is known to have been familiar with the writings of Marx and
Engels up to this time. In fact, the very name of Marx seems to have
presented difficulties. In a brief allusion to Marx's conflict with the
authorities in Köln, *Pražský Večerní List* referred to Marx as "Max"
and confused his newspaper, the *Neue Rheinische Zeitung* with the
Kölnische Zeitung.[37]   And as late as 1870, Sabina was still mis-
spelling Marx's name.[38] The first mention of the name of Marx or
Engels in connection with the Czech Lands was in a ban on the
circulation in Bohemia of *Deutsch-Französische Jahrbücher* (1844),
edited by Alfred Ruge and Marx in Paris; the ban was issued by the
Vienna police president, Sedlnitsky, on May 12, 1844.[39] In the
mid-forties, the name of Engels was cited several times in a German-
language commercial journal published in Vienna but read widely in
Prague.[40]

Though the Czechs at that time took little or no interest in Marx
and Engels, the two men took considerable interest in what was happening to the Czechs.[41] Their attention was drawn to Bohemia by
the workers' riots that took place in Prague in 1844; Engels made a
passing allusion to this event in a work published in 1845.[42] The

36. Some earlier writings of Marx were known to the Slovak L'udovít
Štúr and are referred to in his *Das Slawentum und die Welt der Zukunft*
(Bratislava, 1931). Some of Engels' works were known to the Bohemian
German Anton Springer. See I. Dubský, *Pronikání marxismu do českých zemí*
(Prague, 1963), pp. 70 ff.

37. *PVL*, May 22, 1849.

38. Dubský, *Pronikání marxismu*, p. 69.

39. Sedlnitzky's communication, in Novotný and Myška (eds.), *První
kroky*, p. 407.

40. Dubský, *Pronikání marxismu*, p. 83.

41. R. Urban, "Marx und Engels über die tschechische Frage," *Donauraum*,
VII (1962), 21-33.

42. "Die Lage der arbeitender Klasse in England" (originally published in
Leipzig in 1845), in K. Marx and F. Engels, *Werke* (Berlin, 1959), II, 432.
A similar brief allusion to this event may be found in Engels' article in the

serious interest of the two men in the Czech problem was awakened
by the events of the year 1848-49. Although, as later developments
show, they basically shared the anti-Slavic sentiment prevalent in
Germany, they were able to overcome it in the early stages of the
revolutionary era, particularly when they believed that the Czechs
could, through their revolutionary activity, hasten the advent of a
general social upheaval. This is why Engels devoted an entire article
to the June Uprising in Marx's organ, the *Neue Rheinische Zeitung*,
commenting with great sympathy:

> What has revolutionary Germany done? It has completely rati-
> fied the old oppression of Italy, Poland, and now also Bohemia by
> German soldiery. Kaunitz and Metternich have been completely
> vindicated. And then the Germans demand that the Czechs should
> trust them? And we blame the Czechs that they do not want to
> join the nation which, while liberating itself, is oppressing and
> mistreating other nations? . . . The brave Czechs are the ones
> most to be pitied. Whether they win or are defeated, their ruin
> is certain. Through an oppression of four centuries at the hands
> of the Germans, which is now being perpetuated in the Prague
> street-fighting, they are being driven into the arms of the Russians
> . . . an unhappy fate places the Czechs on the side of the Russians,
> on the side of despotism against revolution. The revolution will
> win and the Czechs will be the first to be oppressed by it. The
> Germans again bear the guilt for this ruin of the Czechs.[43]

After the collapse of the June Uprising, the sympathy of Marx
and Engels for the Czechs was quickly exhausted. In the fierce
struggle between Czech liberals and Viennese radicals, they identified
themselves entirely with the viewpoint of the latter, and the *Neue
Rheinische Zeitung* became the vehicle for crude and strident anti-
Czech and anti-Slavic propaganda. Reporting on the Viennese revolution, the paper's Vienna correspondent railed at "the despicable dogs,
the Czechs and the Ruthenians, who hope to be able to make Vienna
into the capital city of Pan-Slavism and surrender it to absolutism."
Other reports from Vienna refer to the Slavs as "Slavic beasts," and
to the activity of the Slavic Linden as the "Czech-Croat so-called

London journal *The Northern Star* (September 13, 1845), as quoted in Marx
and Engels, *Werke*, II, 560.
    43. *Neue Rheinische Zeitung*, June 18, 1848, as quoted in Marx and Engels,
Werke, V, 81-82.

Slavic-democratic stupidity" and "Slavic-democratic asininity" (*Eselei*).[44]

Although these epithets were hurled by *Neue Rheinische Zeitung* correspondents, they were published by Marx and they clearly reflect his and Engels' own feelings. That this is so may be seen from their own pronouncements concerning the Slavs. Of the two men, Engels seemed to write more on the subject, his most comprehensive treatment of it being the article "Democratic Pan-Slavism," published in the *Zeitung* on February 15, 1849. The article is hardly more than a tirade against all Slavs (excepting the Poles); it belittles Slavic national aspirations and vilifies the Czechs and their past. About the Czechs Engels says:

> The Czechs, to whom we may also count the Moravians and the Slovaks although they are different from the linguistic and historical point of view, have never had a history. Since Charles the Great, Bohemia has been tied to Germany. For one moment the Czech nation emancipates itself and forms the Great Moravian Empire, in order to be immediately subjugated and become for fifteen hundred years a plaything between Germany, Hungary, and Poland. Then Bohemia and Moravia fall definitely to Germany, and the Slovaks remain with Hungary. And this "nation" having no historical existence whatsoever claims the right to independence?[45]

Three years later, in 1852, Engels expounded such views for the benefit of North American audiences, in a series of articles published in the *New York Tribune* (over Marx's name). Once again he heaped ridicule on everything a patriotic Slav or Czech would cherish. He repeated the cliché that at the Slavic Congress in Prague the delegates had to use the German language as the only one they could all understand. He glorified the German past with a zeal matched only by his disparagement of that of the Slavs. And he crowned his efforts by calling the Czechs, in the memorable phrase, a "dying nationality."[46]

44. *Neue Rheinische Zeitung,* October 12, 1848; January 4, 1849; and January 11, 1849.

45. "Der demokratische Panslawismus," *Neue Rheinische Zeitung,* February 15, 1849, as quoted in Marx and Engels, *Werke,* VI, 275.

46. F. Engels, *Revolution and Counter-Revolution or Germany in 1848,* ed. E. Marx Aveling (Chicago, 1896), p. 90. The editor ascribes this work to Marx, but it is now known to have been written by Engels, though over Marx's name.

Of the Slavs, only the Poles were exempt from Marx's and Engels' scorn. On the national question, both men identified themselves completely with the Magyars and the German Viennese radicals.

Marx and Engels justified their opposition to the Slavs on the ground that after the collapse of the June Uprising, all Austrian Slavs became allies of the reaction. "From this event," wrote Engels, "all South Slavic nations [elsewhere he includes the Czechs in the same category] placed themselves at the disposal of Austrian reaction."[47] Yet it is not possible to explain the attitude of the two men primarily on such grounds. The main reason for their attitude was an underlying anti-Slavic outlook, a national prejudice of the kind that the Germans had always tended to harbor vis-à-vis the Slavs and the Slavs vis-à-vis the Germans. In their attitude to the Czechs and the Slavs, Marx and Engels were Germans first and Socialists second.

The collapse of the June Uprising and the alliance of the Austrian Slavs with the Schwarzenberg government offered a welcome excuse: Marx and Engels could now give free reign to their anti-Slavic sentiment and rationalize it by the thought that in so doing they were in fact only serving the cause of socialism and revolution. In the second half of 1848, the *Neue Rheinische Zeitung* plunged into its anti-Slavic propaganda with great vim and abandon; it was as if Marx and Engels felt a sudden sense of relief from the cumbersome duty of serving the revolution by being sympathetic to the Slavs. They much preferred to serve the revolution by hating them, as the following statement by Engels makes clear: "To the sentimental phrases about brotherhood that are being offered to us in the name of the most counter-revolutionary nations of Europe, we reply that the hatred of the Russians has been and still is the *first revolutionary passion* (original italics) with the Germans; and that since the revolution, hatred of the Czechs and Croats has been added to it and that we, jointly with Poles and Magyars, can secure the revolution only by the most decisive terrorism against these Slavic nations."[48] Thus Marx and Engels elevated a hatred of all Czechs, including workers and peasants, into a sacred duty and a way of life. But this hatred was not dictated merely by their revolutionary outlook. In his articles in the *New York Tribune* Engels stated specifically that "independently

47. "Der magyarische Kampf," *Neue Rheinische Zeitung,* January 13, 1849, as quoted in Marx and Engels, *Werke,* VI, 173.
48. "Der demokratische Panslawismus," in Marx and Engels, *Werke,* VI, 286.

of all revolutionary considerations," history proved that "Bohemia could only exist, henceforth, as a portion of Germany."[49] Whether they faced a Germany that was revolutionary or one that was not, the Czechs had no choice, for Engels assigned them no place in the European community of nations; their only right was to be engulfed by the Germans.

Had Marx and Engels taken a genuine revolutionary and socialist attitude, they would have phrased their references to the Czechs differently. They would have distinguished between the Czech "bourgeoisie," on the one hand, and the Czech "people" or "working class," on the other. In fact, after the middle of 1848 they seldom, if ever, made the distinction. It is no accident that in the statement quoted above Engels labels the Czechs a "counter-revolutionary nation," without regard to social class. Czech burghers, peasants, workers, radicals, were all doomed, and, on the basis of their past performance as a nation, deserved nothing better. In a similar vein, Marx offered the following editorial observation at the beginning of January, 1849:

> The defeat of the French working class in France, the victory of the French bourgeoisie, was at the same time the victory of the East over the West, the defeat of civilization by barbarism. In Wallachia began the subjugation of the Rumanians by the Russians and their tools, the Turks; in Vienna the Croats . . . the Czechs . . . and similar riffraff strangled the German freedom, and at this moment the Tsar is omnipresent in Europe. The overthrow of the bourgeoisie in France, the triumph of the French working class, the emancipation of the working class in general are the watchwords of the European liberation.[50]

Here Marx carefully separated the French working class from the bourgeoisie. But when he turned to the Slavic nations, he damned them all as "riffraff." It is a curious fact that though Marx and Engels lost sympathy for the Slavic workers, they developed a sympathy for the Magyar gentry. It is true that in the future Marx modified his view of Kossuth, to the latter's disadvantage,[51] but the views of both men concerning the Austrian and Balkan Slavs remained unchanged.

49. Engels, *Revolution and Counter-Revolution*, p. 90.

50. *Neue Rheinische Zeitung*, January 1, 1849, as quoted in Marx and Engels, *Werke*, VI, 149.

51. D. Rapant, "Štúr a štúrovci v službe národa a pokroku," *Slovenská Literatúra*, XII (1965), 438.

Chapter **13**

Students

There were two universities in the Czech Lands, one in Prague and another in Olomouc.[1] The University of Prague, the second largest in the Habsburg Monarchy (after Vienna), had, on the eve of 1848, 2,114 students and 78 professors. The University of Olomouc had 628 students and 25 professors.[2] The University of Prague was a "complete" university in that it was comprised of the Faculties of Philosophy, Medicine, Law, and Theology, including a full range of studies in medicine. Olomouc too was comprised of the four faculties, but its Faculty of Medicine offered only limited training, leading to the degree of Master of Surgery, not Doctor of Medicine. In Prague there was also a polytechnic, founded in 1806 and devoted to technical and engineering subjects; its student body numbered 1,485 in 1848.[3]

The majority of students at both Prague institutions came from Czech-speaking homes, but the professorial staff was almost entirely German-speaking and the lectures, with a few insignificant exceptions, were conducted in German (a few were conducted in Latin). At the University of Olomouc, as in Prague, the professors were almost entirely German, but only a minority of the students, in contrast to Prague, were identified with the Czech national movement. It is impossible to determine the proportion of the two nationalities in the student body in Olomouc; judging from the names—a very rough indication—perhaps one-half of the students were of Czech origin,[4] but this figure is deceiving since only a few of them could be said to have been nationally conscious.

For years spokesmen for the Prague polytechnic had striven to

1. Recent contributions: F. Jílek, "Pražská polytechnika a její studenti v revolučním roce 1848," *Sborník Národního technického muzea,* IV (1965), 268-366; and articles by Trapl (see Bibliography, p. 373).

2. *Uebersichts-Tafeln zur Statistik der österreichischen Monarchie,* Besonderer Abdruck des X. und XI. Heftes der "Statistischen Mittheilungen" (Vienna, 1850), p. 75.

3. Jílek, "Pražská polytechnika," p. 270.

4. M. Trapl, "Olomoucká universita v prvním (vzestupném) období revoluce roku 1848," *SVSPO-H,* IV (1957), 8.

make the polytechnic a part of the university, which had a centuries-long tradition (it was founded in 1348) and enjoyed greater prestige. But opposition to such a merger was strong in university circles and in 1848 the two institutions were still separate and have, indeed, remained separate to the present time. There were significant differences between the students of the two institutions. The students entering the polytechnic were less adequately trained for their studies than those entering the university and came from less affluent backgrounds. They often had behind them years of practical work before entering the polytechnic, and many of them went to work after attending the polytechnic for only a year; in contrast, the university students entered the university directly from secondary school. These differences account for an attitude of superiority displayed by the Prague university students toward the polytechnic students. They also account for the distinctly more radical conduct of the latter during the revolutionary era.[5]

The Prague university and polytechnic students were in the forefront of revolutionary activity throughout the 1848-49 period. Several of them belonged to Repeal and were among the organizers of the March 11 assembly. Although many students took part in the assembly, they did not obtain any representation on the St. Václav's Committee, which was elected by it. They promptly began to organize their own action to further their own interests, however; at the same time they continued to lend support to the political action of the burghers and their petition movement. The first center of the student movement was apparently the polytechnic: as early as March 13, before the news of Metternich's dismissal reached Prague, there was ferment in the lecture halls of the polytechnic as student leaders (both from the polytechnic and the university) addressed their colleagues and discussed student demands with them. On the same day, a message arrived from the Vienna students asking the Prague students to join them in a petition action.[6] In the following months, the more radical segments of Prague students tried to maintain contact with the Viennese students and often followed their example.

On March 14, representatives of the polytechnic and of all the university faculties met to prepare a student petition. It was fully in accordance with the new spirit of equality that the polytechnic spokesmen demanded that their institution be attached to the university, as

5. Jílek, "Pražská polytechnika," pp. 271, 275.
6. See Chapter 2. Also *ibid.*, p. 280.

one of its faculties. In spite of the opposition of the law students, the proposal was approved and incorporated into a student petition adopted at a meeting held on March 15. The Petition of March 15, which was addressed to the emperor, demanded that religion should not bar anyone from holding a university chair or pursuing higher education; that "complete freedom of teaching and learning should be introduced"; that university subjects should be taught in both languages of the province; that students should be permitted to attend foreign universities; that the polytechnic should become a part of the university; that the state should provide facilities for the physical training of students; that there should be freedom to form student clubs according to the example of the University of Munich. Point 5 of this petition demanded that students should be allowed to take their subjects in any order they pleased and that the suitability of the students for the civil service should be judged solely on the basis of one "rigorous" state examination. In practice, this would have meant the abolition of semestral examinations.[7] The plenary meeting at which the petition was approved was the first great meeting of students during the revolutionary era. The petition was signed by hundreds of students and also by many members of the academic senate (professors); not a few of the latter were doubtless not in agreement with it, but the pressure of student opinion was overwhelming and the professors could not afford to ignore it if they were to retain a measure of control over the students.

At this point, the burghers viewed the student movement with sympathy, though perhaps not without some uneasiness at its growing radicalism. The St. Václav's Committee invited the representatives of the university, both professors and students, to join its delegates, who were going to Vienna to present to the emperor the First Petition. The delegates were received by the emperor, and on this occasion the university representatives submitted to him the student petition. The emperor's reply to the First Petition provoked general discontent in Prague, and the students were in the forefront of the protest. In

7. Text in J. M. Černý (ed.), *Boj za právo: Sborník aktů politických u věcech státu a národa českého od roku 1848* (Prague, 1893), pp. 17-18. Detailed report on the meeting in *Bohemia*, March 17, 1848; F. J. Schopf (ed.), *Wahre und ausfürliche Darstellung der am 11 März 1848 ... in Prag begonnenen Volks-Bewegung* (Leitmeritz, 1848), I, 12-14. See also J. V. Frič, *Paměti*, ed. K. Cvejn (Prague, 1957-63), I, 375 ff. The semestral examinations were later abolished. A somewhat similar petition, dated March 21, 1848, was presented by Olomouc university students (text in Černý [ed.], *Boj*, p. 41).

fact, student unrest reached such alarming proportions that on March 28, Governor Stadion, after a hurried consultation with Vienna, issued a statement giving provisional approval to the students' demands; only the question of the relationship of the polytechnic and the university was left to further negotiation, although even here the authorities promised to act with utmost speed. A definitive approval was issued on April 2.[8]

In the ensuing weeks and months the minds of the students were not on their studies, but on many other matters. Following the example of the Viennese students, they formed an Academic Legion within a day after the proclamation of the constitution (March 16). The Legion was divided into cohorts, based on the example of the legions of ancient Rome, with each cohort representing one faculty, except that the polytechnic students formed one of the cohorts and there was no cohort of theology. Technically, the purpose of the Legion was to protect the teaching and arts establishments in the city, but it assumed wider duties, protecting order in general. Formally, it was a part of and subordinated to, the National Guard, but in practice it was more or less independent. The polytechnic students were the most dynamic segment of the Legion.

To the students, the Legion was a symbol of freedom and of the new constitutional era. At the same time, they were attracted to it by the opportunity it afforded them of wearing uniforms, boots, swords, and all the outward trappings of authority and adventure. The fondness of some students for flashy uniforms became a byword; the best example of this idiosyncrasy could be seen in the young radical Frič, who greatly enjoyed going about with a shiny sword hanging from his belt. A newspaper observed that "many regard national defense as a mere toy, as an opportunity to wear the sword and the uniform."[9] The remark was aimed specifically at the National Guard, but the observation doubtless applied even more to the members of the Academic Legion. That the students were not oblivious to the heroic image a uniform might conjure in the eyes of a maiden is

8. Text of the decree granting provisional approval in *Bohemia,* March 29, 1848; definite approval in Černý (ed.), *Boj,* pp. 73-74. The definitive approval did not cover the merging of the university and the polytechnic and was never granted; the two institutions have remained separate to the present time.

9. *PVL,* October 31, 1848. See also J. A. Helfert, *Geschichte Österreichs vom Ausgange des Wiener October-Aufstandes 1848* (Prague, 1869-86), II, 294.

easily understood. As one historian succinctly put it: "The greatest rush for weapons takes place not so much when one goes to battle but to a date with a girl."[10] The conduct of the students angered the military, who felt that the students, in carrying arms and patroling the streets, were infringing upon their realm of activity, and soon there developed, in Prague, as in other cities in Central Europe in 1848, an intense hostility between the students and soldiers. The student represented the two things the soldier (especially the common soldier) hated most: he was an intellectual and he was a defender of the constitution, a word that was anathema to the soldier because it placed him, theoretically, under civilian control. It was, in fact, in large part, the friction between the military and the students that led to the June Uprising. The role of the students in this uprising has been related in Chapter 6 and will not be treated further here, except to say that during the uprising many students proved that their enchantment with the uniform was more than matched by their readiness to sacrifice their lives for constitutional liberty, and their heroism was enshrined in many popular songs.[11] It must be noted, however, that it was particularly the students of the polytechnic who were the most active during the uprising.

The June Uprising represented the high point of student radicalism. Afterwards, radical sentiment ebbed more and more, and although it surged again from time to time during the next ten months, it never again attained the level it had in June. In fact, even before June many students showed signs of tiring of the Academic Legion and of radicalism; like the burghers and other groups, the student body was affected by the inevitable split into liberals and radicals. The students of law and medicine were in the liberal camp, while the students of the polytechnic were the backbone of the radical camp.[12] The students of philosophy were divided, with the majority leaning toward the radicals. The law students in particular were noted for their upper-class mentality; the liberal *Národní Noviny* dubbed them the "student aristocracy," and this censure was fully seconded by the radical *Pražský Večerní List*.[13] The line separating the radicals and liberals corresponded to some extent to the line dividing Czech and

10. Jílek, "Pražská polytechnika," p. 301.
11. Text in J. J. Toužimský, *Na úsvitě nové doby* (Prague, 1898), p. 614.
12. *NN*, May 13, 1848.
13. *NN*, December 12, 1848; *PVL*, January 4, 1849. The law students retained this reputation well into the present century.

German and lower-class and upper-class students. At the polytechnic the students came from poorer families, as noted earlier, and the Czech students were in overwhelming majority. The same holds, to a more limited extent, for the philosophy students. In contrast, most medical and law students came from affluent, German backgrounds, and this was especially pronounced among the law students.

What other outlets or organizations did the students have, besides the Academic Legion? How far did the Czech leaders permit them to participate in the political movement? The students did not obtain any representation on the St. Václav's Committee, but its successor, the National Committee, allowed them to elect representatives; the student members of the committee were not regarded as full-fledged members, however, and in any event did not seem to take an active part in the debates. With the rapid surge of national consciousness and the growing rift between Czech and German students within the Academic Legion, the Czech students felt the need to have a student organization of their own and on April 13 founded the *Slavie* (or Slavia), the strongest and most important Czech student club. According to the founding proclamation, the club was to devote itself to politics, literature, journalism, and similar interests, in the Czech spirit, and was also to promote Slavic mutuality.[14] For the next few weeks the Slavia became the center of Czech student activity. Its members took part in the Slavic Congress, but again, as in the case of the National Committee, did not contribute significantly to the debates; this is surprising, since otherwise the students and their leaders were anything but diffident; perhaps in this case they felt themselves overwhelmed by the wisdom of their elders. The members of Slavia endeavored to establish contact with the peasants in order to bridge the social gap separating them from the countryside.[15]

Later on, as its membership expanded, it organized its work into sections. One of the sections was at first called the "military section," which seems indicative of the mounting tensions in Prague and the growing radicalism of the students; the name was later changed to "public section," presumably in order not to offend the law-abiding citizens.[16] The original program of the founders of the Slavia makes

14. Founding proclamation in *NN*, April 14, 1848. See also Frič, *Paměti*, II, 26 ff. At first the Slavia existed only provisionally; it did not adopt a charter until the beginning of May.

15. *NN*, May 6, 1848.

16. See the protocols of the Slavia, as reprinted (only fragments survive) in

no mention of military affairs as being among the purposes of the club. It was perhaps inevitable that the students of the polytechnic, as in the Academic Legion, played the most active role in the Slavia and eventually formed an absolute majority of its members,[17] which gave the club a radical flavor. The military section of the Slavia, led by young Frič, was busy making plans for military action should it become necessary to defend constitutional freedoms against the reaction.

The conspicuous presence of General Windischgrätz' soldiers in Prague since the end of May only lent greater urgency to the problem of organizing some form of defense. The Slavia was the core of the active opposition to Windischgrätz, and its contacts with the Viennese students were intensified. The Prague students were impressed with the success of the Viennese in wresting concessions from the government and they hoped to be able to emulate their example and match their achievement. The Viennese students were frequent visitors in Prague; most of them were, of course, Slavic students studying in Vienna. And many Prague students made short visits to Vienna. It is believed that some two to three hundred Prague students paid a visit to Vienna at the time of the June Uprising. As one Czech student later put it before an investigating commission: "We believed that we would be able to achieve what the Viennese had achieved, and that we must do what they had done earlier. That is why we demanded arms, munition, and cannons, just as all this had been issued to the Viennese."[18]

The defeat of the June Uprising was a turning point in the history of the student movement; it dealt a decisive blow to student radicalism. The students were no longer allowed to carry arms, and the Academic Legion receded permanently into insignificance. The Slavia too suffered a decline from which it never fully recovered. Both organizations had fallen under official suspicion as the chief culprits in the uprising and this rendered their position precarious. The students as a whole had lost most of their belligerence, and the new surge of radicalism of August, 1848, assumed a more moderate form. The militancy of the Legion and the military plans of the Slavia gave

---

K. Boudová, "Úloha J. V. Friče v revolučním studentském hnutí roku 1848-1849," in *J. V. Frič a demokratické proudy v české politice a literatuře. Sborník statí* (Prague, 1956), pp. 83 ff.

17. Jílek, "Pražská polytechnika," p. 314.

18. *Ibid.*, p. 320.

way to a more peaceful instrument of student policy: the Committee of Prague Students, or Prague Student Committee.

After the uprising student life came to a complete standstill and the students had no effective spokesmen. Yet during this very time they were being subjected to arbitrary recruitment by the military authorities. To defend their interests, the students who were in Prague at the time elected on July 31 a Prague Student Committee consisting of sixteen members. The duty of this committee was to represent the students and to "defend to the last all rights and freedoms of Prague students that have been won thus far."[19] Since this was still vacation time and most students could not be present, the committee was to be regarded as only provisional. A permanent committee, consisting of thirty members, was elected on November 16, 1848.[20]

From the very beginning the Prague Student Committee faced one crisis after another. At the end of August it received an invitation (dated August 27) from the students of Breslau to send delegates to a congress of students representing all German universities, to be held in Wartburg on September 25.[21] This looked very much like the invitation extended by the Frankfurt liberals to Palacký in April to take part in the preparatory work for the German Parliament, and the students considered that any acceptance on the part of the Prague students of the invitation to Wartburg would inevitably be interpreted as their recognition of Bohemia as a part of Germany. Nevertheless the Student Committee decided to brave the wrath of the Czech community and to recommend acceptance of the invitation, subject to its approval by a plenary meeting of students. The moving spirit behind this decision was the first secretary of the Student Committee, the radical Václav Pavel Kleinert, a Czech polytechnic student. Kleinert and his colleagues on the committee defended their decision on the ground that the Czech delegates to the German Student Congress would be able to acquaint the German students with the conditions in Bohemia. In fact, Kleinert's record during this period indicates that he was motivated by a desire to strengthen the radical front against the advancing reaction. The recommendation of the Student Committee created a furor among the Czechs, and it was

19. *PVL*, August 3, 1848.
20. *PVL*, November 19, 1848.
21. *PVL*, August 29, 1848; A. Werner, *Die Studenten-Legionen der Prager Universität vom 30 jährigen Krieg bis 1848* (Prague, 1934), p. 133.

attacked, even before the plenary session, by a group of students themselves. In their attack, published in *Národní Noviny,* the students branded the action as "willful" and as one that could not be regarded as "an expression of the opinion of all Prague students, but only of its small part."[22] Subsequent developments bore out this charge. At the plenary meeting held on September 10, it was decided "unanimously" not to accept the invitation from the German students, with the Student Committee itself apparently withdrawing its own recommendation. Yet curiously, the same students also "unanimously" re-elected the very Student Committee whose recommendation they had just rejected, and ignored all attacks on it.[23] They also agreed to call to Prague a congress of students from Austrian universities. The congress was to take place on October 23 and 24, to coincide with the great celebrations that were to mark the five-hundredth anniversary of the founding of the university.[24] Probably the invitations were duly sent out, but the Viennese revolution made the holding of the congress impossible; it is not known how the other universities reacted to the invitation.

The student plenary meeting may have given the Student Committee a vote of confidence by re-electing it, but the German-speaking Prague students were anything but pleased by the stand the student body had taken regarding the congress at Wartburg. The German students were in a minority, and the Prague Student Committee voiced primarily the interests and opinions of the Czech majority. Since the early days of the Student Committee, the German students tended to keep aloof from it, viewing it, quite rightly, as a "Slavic Committee."[25] The decision not to go to Wartburg was the last straw: on September 27, 1848, the German-speaking students founded their own "Committee of German Students in Prague," which was to be their voice.[26]

Weakened by the boycott of the German students, the Student Committee was soon confronted with another crisis, provoked by the controversy in the Czech community over the attitude to be taken toward the Viennese revolution. The details of this crisis have been

22. *NN,* September 6, 1848. See also a separate, stronger attack by one of the polytechnic students in the same issue.
23. *NN,* September 14, 1848; *PVL,* September 11, 1848.
24. *CBB,* September 15, 1848.
25. The complaint is recorded in *PVL,* February 1, 1849.
26. Werner, *Die Studenten-Legionen,* pp. 133-34.

told in Chapter 7. Here it may only be said that many Czech students were at first skeptical of the claims of the Czech deputies that the struggle in Vienna was one between nationalities; and that Kleinert and at least one other member of the Student Committee saw the struggle as one between freedom and reaction and while in Vienna took an open stand in favor of the Viennese. In the decisive meetings of the students in Prague, however, the majority accepted the view of the Czech deputies, and voted to bring Kleinert before a "court of honor." Kleinert seems not to have relented; many others harbored doubts and reservations about the stand taken by the Czech deputies, but he stood virtually alone among the Czechs in his unqualified support of the Viennese. The German students, as might be expected, supported the Viennese revolution.

The crushing of the Viennese revolution strengthened the hand of the reaction and the students and their organizations became its chief target. The Academic Legions in Prague and in Olomouc were abolished at the beginning of January, 1849, and soon an army recruitment drive took many students away from their homes and into the service. The recruitment drive became a means with which to punish and render harmless those "subversives" who could not be persecuted under any existing laws.[27] A large number of students were still faithful to the ideas of constitutionalism, but there was a growing apathy, as witnessed by the fact that the Legion was abolished without any violent resistance on the part of the students, though the act was deeply regretted and resented. That in spite of this the students continued to support constitutional principles is evident from the message of confidence sent by the Prague Student Committee to the Kroměříž Parliament in its last days.[28] This could not, of course, save the Imperial Parliament, but it was a heartening expression of support. Nor was this the last stand of the Prague students against the reaction. After the dissolution of the Kroměříž Parliament, it was only in Prague that an organized opposition to the reaction developed, in the form of the May Conspiracy; and it was again the students, a small but courageous band of them, that formed the core of this opposition. Thus the Prague students took the last stand in Cisleithania in defense of freedom.

27. This was explicitly stated in an army regulation; see *PVL,* May 2, 1849.
28. See Chapter 8, Note 75.

Chapter 14

Women

Though they constituted one-half of the population, before 1848, women had been excluded from public life altogether. Middle- and upper-class women worked in charities and were busy with social events, but beyond that they were not expected to go. The March revolution brought in its wake the first awakening of women, the first attempts, still hesitant on their part, to share to at least a small degree in the exciting events of that year.

There were two main obstacles to their full participation in the political developments of the revolutionary era. First, the vast majority of women were themselves still far from "awakened"; indeed they were hardly touched by any ideas of equality with men. Second, the walls of prejudice on the part of men were truly formidable and would have made any serious bid for emancipation impossible. On July 19, 1848, a women's rights convention in Seneca Falls, New York, issued a declaration demanding political, legal, and educational equality for women; but in Europe the woman was much less disposed to demand, and the man still less disposed to give, any such equality.

Even in Western Europe the cause of emancipation for women, in spite of the previous impetus given to it by the French Revolution of 1789, was far from won. Even the radical, Pierre Joseph Proudhon, was opposed to political equality for women. In April, 1849, his newspaper *Le Peuple* protested against the candidacy of a French woman for a seat in the National Assembly, on the illogical ground that though women were equal to men, they should not aspire to political office.[1] In the Habsburg Monarchy, in the Constitutional Committee of the Imperial Parliament, a progressive-minded deputy came out in favor of suffrage for workers, but did not extend that privilege to women. Another deputy argued in all seriousness that if women should be admitted to suffrage on the ground that they help bear the expenses of the state, one should also admit "children and madmen."[2] A prominent conservative participant in the events of

1. Quoted in *NN,* April 22, 1849.
2. They were Fischhof (February 13, 1849) and Brestel (February 12,

1848-49 wrote years later that in the "upside-down world" of 1848 "a woman mixed herself up in the business of the man, against the destiny assigned to her by nature and custom" and talked about matters for the understanding of which she "lacked detachment and maturity."[3]

In Western Europe in 1848, in many German states, and in Vienna, women were forming political and radical clubs. In the Czech Lands this did not happen, but the women of Prague nevertheless began to take an interest in public life and at times helped shape it to some extent. Soon after the collapse of absolutism, a group of Prague women submitted an appeal to the emperor asking him to grant unconditional amnesty to all Polish political prisoners then languishing in Czech prisons.[4] A few days later, an anonymous Czech writer appealed to the "Maidens and Women of Prague" to devote themselves to patriotic work. Recognizing that during the period of absolutism "you were much less free than we . . . the old system forced you completely out of public life," he said the time had now come to follow actively all that was happening in the fatherland, with particular attention to the cultivation of the Czech language. The writer made it clear, however, that he did not favor political equality for women.[5]

It was the June Uprising that brought women into the limelight for the first time. Young women helped with the building of the barricades, and some even guarded the barricades and carried weapons.[6] Observers agreed that one of the most memorable sights during the uprising was a girl, popularly dubbed the "Amazon," sitting on one of the main barricades, holding a musket in her hands.[7] The June Uprising took its toll of women's lives, and as in the case of the men, most of the victims belonged to the lower social strata. There were five women among the forty-three dead: two day-laborers

1849), respectively (A. Springer [ed.], *Protokolle des Verfassungs-Ausschusses im oesterreichischen Reichstage 1848-1849* [Leipzig, 1885], pp. 187, 189).

3. Helfert's judgment, in his *Geschichte Österreichs vom Ausgange des Wiener October-Aufstandes 1848* (Prague, 1869-86), II, 310.

4. *Bohemia*, March 24, 1848.

5. *Bohemia*, April 2, 1848.

6. "In street-fighting women particularly distinguished themselves in the building of barricades" (letter from Staněk to Čelakovský written from Prague in the midst of the June Uprising, on June 16, 1848, as reprinted in *ČČM*, XLVI [1872], 332).

7. *Bohemia*, June 25, 1848.

(*nádenice*), one cook, one maid, and one innkeeper. As for the wounded, a detailed breakdown for all of them is not available, but it is known that among the eighty-eight wounded, who were treated in the two largest hospitals, nine were women, and for seven of these nine the hospitals listed the occupations: four were day-laborers and three were maids.[8] After the uprising, several women were subjected to a police investigation and ten were imprisoned; thus the June Uprising had given the Czechs their first women political prisoners.[9]

For their part in the uprising, women were honored in popular songs depicting them as freedom-fighters and fearless Czech and Slavic patriots. But if the spectacle of women on the barricades was a source of inspiration to some, it proved to be a source of alarm to others. To the alarmists, the idea of political equality for women was a *reductio ad absurdum*. Shortly after the uprising, a Prague newspaper published a feature article on the "Emancipation of Women." The article is a confused and rambling discussion, liberally punctured with references to the "gentle sex"; the writer treats the woman with utmost gallantry and pays the loftiest compliments to "feminine beauty," only to remind her that emancipation does not mean that she should "elevate herself to a professorial chair or seat in Parliament." These reflections, coming as they did ten days after the uprising, were obviously caused by the event; this was the first full-length discussion of the emancipation of women in Prague after the downfall of absolutism. But it took a long time for the shock of June to wear off, and two months later the same newspaper still railed against those wanting to "summon back the women of the barricades."[10]

There was no need to tell the Czech women that it was not their business to sit in the parliament; such an office was still far removed from the aspirations of the most ambitious. Nevertheless the revolutionary atmosphere could not fail to have a leavening effect on the "gentle sex." In the new wave of radicalism that began to surge

8. See hospital report in "Die Opfer der Prager Pfingsten," *Vierteljahrschrift für die praktische Heilkunde,* IV (1848), 144-46.

9. Among the barricade fighters was also a "beautiful girl" called "Slovanka" (Slavic woman). She was Theofila Dittrichová, a waitress, and she was arrested and held in custody for three months. See A. Bajerová, *Svatodušní bouře v Praze r. 1848 ve světle soudního vyšetřování* (Plzeň, 1920), pp. 74-75. Bajerová gives a complete list of those investigated or held in custody (pp. 389-96).

10. *Bohemia,* June 28 and August 20, 1848.

forth in August, 1848, women were once again swept into the current, and this time they mounted not the barricades but the speaker's platform: on August 16 a group of Prague women held a meeting in protest against General Windischgrätz—the first political meeting of women in Czech history. The purpose of the meeting was to issue a protest against Windischgrätz' statement of August 2, which seemed to indict Prague citizens indiscriminately for their responsibility in the June Uprising and which charged that the uprising was the result of a "plot." The meeting was attended by both Czech and German women, but the Czechs dominated the discussions. The women realized that they were taking an unusual action and went out of their way to assure the public that they harbored no ulterior political motives: "We are not gathered here," declared the opening speaker, "to struggle for our emancipation, we only want that our voice, as that of the citizens of the state, should also be heeded."[11] The women present recalled their part in the June Uprising and emphasized that the outbreak was quite spontaneous: "We built the barricades without any plans," said one of the freedom-fighters. The villain was Windischgrätz and his grenadiers. One of the speakers even urged the ladies of Prague "not to tolerate in service any maid having a grenadier as a lover."[12] Before adjourning, a committee was elected to draft a protest against Windischgrätz; later a delegation was to be dispatched to Vienna to submit the protest to the emperor, the cost of the trip to be defrayed from funds collected by door-to-door canvassers. Before departing for their homes, the women decided to meet again two days later.

The first meeting seems only to have whetted their appetites, for the second meeting was more heavily attended than the first. The protest to the emperor was approved, and a proposal was put forward to found a women's organization along the lines of the Slavic Linden, with its own offices and reading rooms. There was also a proposal for the founding of a truly national Czech school for girls, since, it was asserted, there were no existing girls' schools dedicated specifically to the education of girls in the Czech national spirit.[13] The news-

11. This and the following statements are taken from *PVL*, August 17, 1848. *PVL* says that "the discussions were almost entirely in Czech."

12. The grenadiers were an élite corps distinguished for their height and physical prowess; they were the traditional dating partners of Prague servant girls.

paper accounts of the meeting are far from satisfactory, but it appears that both of the above proposals were accepted.

The first meeting had taken place without incident. But when the public realized that the women meant business and that the first meeting was only a beginning, the reaction was hostile. Windischgrätz' grenadiers attempted to foil the second meeting by a noisy demonstration, but were unsuccessful, and after the meeting the departing women were greeted with a barrage of insults and obscenities from a hostile crowd standing outside the building.[14] On the following day, *Bohemia,* evidently believing that there was not a moment to lose, delivered a scathing attack at the would-be politicians among the fair sex. It did so in a full-length article entitled "On the Right of Women to Politics," its second full-length article on the role of women in society. This time, to strengthen its case, it chose a woman writer to brandish the hostile pen. A woman may reflect on politics in private, sermonized the writer, "but to make demonstrations in the market place of public life" is a "crude aberration." "When you [women] hold public meetings . . . that is a profaning of woman's nature, that is an image in a distorting mirror, that is a parody of cultural history." Insofar as women wish to contribute to political debate, she continued, they should do it "through men."[15]

In the face of mounting hostility, the women remained undaunted and eventually carried out their purpose. There were some delays in dispatching the delegation to Vienna—the reasons are not always clear from the published accounts—but at the beginning of September, the delegates arrived at their destination with the protest against Windischgrätz. When they asked to see the empress, they were told at first that she did not receive women delegations whose business was political, but in the end the empress did receive them and lent a sympathetic ear to their complaints.[16] They were also received by one or two of the ministers, who assured them that everything was being done to speed up the investigation of the June Uprising and granted them an informal ministerial approval of the idea of founding a school

13. *Bohemia,* August 19, 1848; *PVL,* August 19, 1848. The proposal for a girls' school inspired an approving letter (anonymous) from a woman in Moravia, published in *NN,* August 26, 1848. It drew particular attention to the education of women servant personnel.

14. *PVL,* August 19, 1848.

15. *Bohemia,* August 20, 1848.

16. *PVL,* September 12, 1848.

for girls in Prague. All in all, this first political venture of Prague women was more than a moderate success. As if to confirm this success thousands of Czechs and Slavs residing in Vienna came to greet the delegates at the railway station on their departure. It was symbolic that the public greeting on this occasion was offered by Vojta Náprstek, a Czech patriot who was in Vienna at the time.[17] Within a few weeks Náprstek emigrated to North America where he became imbued with egalitarian ideas; later he returned and made a name for himself as the initiator of many progressive causes and as a pioneer of the movement for the emancipation of women.

Before the delegation returned to Prague, a number of political prisoners who were being held in custody in connection with the June Uprising were released, and soon more of them received their freedom. The delegation must have contributed in no small measure to this release. *Pražský Večerní List* recognized this and rendered thanks to "Our Women Delegates" who, it said, acted in Vienna with courage and made it possible for many prisoners to be cleared and gain their freedom sooner than otherwise might have been the case.[18]

Though this movement was an entirely peaceful one, in this eventful year it was not to be expected that women would be wholly immune to the temptations of violence. They had, of course, taken part in the June Uprising, but in that case they did not act as a separate force. There are, however, one or two incidents of street demonstrations that are known to have involved women primarily. On the eve of the June Uprising, the wives of the cotton-printers gathered one afternoon in front of the house of a hated factory owner, with the obvious intent of attacking him. Their action spurred their menfolk into joining them, which forced the factory owner to flee the house through the back door.[19] And after the June Uprising, sometime in August, 1848, a group of burgher women staged a street demonstration in a town in eastern Bohemia. The women there were angered by the persecution of a progressive-minded merchant at the hands of a reactionary municipal councilor. The councilor impugned the integrity of the merchant and when this became known, "a multi-

17. *PVL,* September 13, 1848. Náprstek's original name was Fingerhut and he was often referred to by that name in 1848. He later became well-known as the founder of an ethnographical museum (Náprstek Museum) in Prague, which still exists.

18. *PVL,* September 23, 1848.

19. *PVL,* June 9, 1848.

tude of burgher women gathered in front of the municipal hall" and shouted at him. Taking "this to be a rebellion," the councilor summoned "eighteen lancers" to restore order.[20] This was apparently the only street demonstration involving women that called forth military intervention.

The protest movement of Prague women against Windischgrätz led eventually to the founding of a Club of Slavic Women (*Spolek Slovanek*), the first Czech women's club. The main purposes of the club were to promote the education of women and girls generally and to found a Czech school for girls, but the obstacles to the realization of these purposes were many. There was internal bickering and jealousy among the club's leaders. There were financial and other difficulties, the magnitude of which was not foreseen at the time the club was founded. And to cope with these obstacles there was too little experience. This first women's club therefore was unsuccessful; it ceased to function for all practical purposes at the end of 1849 and was formally dissolved at the end of 1850, its demise hastened by the advancing reaction.[21] The school for girls was not permanently realized until after 1860.

Few women in 1848-49 took an avowed interest in politics to the extent of identifying themselves openly with any political party. But the revolutionary era did produce one woman agitator: a German-speaking actress of radical leanings, who spoke to the workers in Brno in October, endeavoring to stir them into action to aid the Viennese revolution. She was instrumental in fanning unrest during both outbreaks of that month, on October 18 and again on October 29-30.[22] The only instance of Czech women expressing a political preference was that in which a financial contribution was donated

20. *PVL*, September 16, 1848.
21. For this topic, see C. Zíbrt, " 'Sestry slovanské' čili 'Spolek Slovanek' r. 1848 v Praze," *Květy*, Part I, XXIX (1907), 25-38, 203-15, 375-88. The reasons for the internal squabbles between the leaders are not clear. See the founding appeal in *NLS*, October 9, 1848, and the enigmatic notice in *NN*, December 10, 1848. The need for a national school for girls is explained in *NN*, September 19, 1848.

The author of an article in *NN* (January 2, 1849), dealing with the Club of Slavic Women, said that a Czech encyclopedia for women had been in preparation for some time and expressed the hope that the club would complete it. I could not find any further information about this project and what happened to it.

22. B. Šindelář, "O úloze lidových mas v revolučním dění roku 1848 na Moravě a ve Slezsku," *ČSČH*, IV (1956), 401. Her name was Karolina Waser.

to the Academic Legion by two women who identified themselves as "two radical-democratically minded friends (*přítelkyně*) of the Academic Legion."[23]

The most politically conscious Czech woman of the year 1848-49 was one who did not openly identify herself with any political party but whose comments and interests have unmistakably democratic overtones. She was Božena Němcová, the first great authoress of Czech literature and the first Czech feminist. As early as 1846, a critic accused Němcová of giving her stories a bias in favor of "emancipation."[24] Soon after the proclamation of the constitutional era she published a series of articles on "Peasant Politics" in which she commented on the relevance of the constitution to immediate social problems. She expressed dismay at the fact that a poor worker was being compelled to celebrate the inauguration of the constitutional era by purchasing and burning candles—a luxury he could ill afford. "What do we profit from freedom?" she has one worker complain to another; "it will give us neither bread nor work."[25] At a time when the burghers could behold only the noble vision of constitutional liberty, Němcová probed further and beheld a nightmare of destitution that she knew the constitution would not banish; she confessed herself not fully satisfied by the revolution's promise.

Němcová was a restless woman, striving vainly for personal happiness and plagued by poor health and financial want, which gave her an understanding of social problems that others were denied. She was religious without being clericalist, and opposed to violence without being opposed to social change. In her letters and articles written in 1848 she criticized anti-Semitism; commented intelligently on the elections to Frankfurt (which she opposed); defended a Czech patriot against the hatred of all "reactionaries" (*zpátečníci*); observed the friction between peasants and cottagers; opposed the use of titles such as "Gracious Lady" and "Your Grace" as not being in accordance with the new concepts of equality; urged burgher women to treat their maids as their equals, not as slaves;[26] and in general

23. *NN,* November 3, 1848, Supplement, listing donors. The two women gave only their initials.

24. *Květy,* May 30, 1846 (see photo-reproduction of the page in *Božena Němcová v obrazech a dokumentech* (Prague, 1951), p. 50.

25. *Božena Němcová,* p. 155 (originally in *Včela,* April 8, 12, and 15, 1848).

26. These letters and articles are reprinted in B. Němcová, *Vybrané spisy, IV: Básně-stati-dopisy,* ed. F. Vodička (Prague, 1957), pp. 125 ff., 162 ff.

demonstrated a degree of political awareness that was remarkable for a woman whose education had not even included the secondary school. Naturally, her criticism antagonized many of her acquaintances and friends. And her fondness for the company of male students made her an easy target for gossip; there were even sinister rumors that she had tried to smoke![27]

The new atmosphere of freedom induced in Němcová serious reflections on the need for emancipation. "We women have remained far behind the age, behind the banner of freedom and culture," she complained. "Let us confess this, let us not be ashamed, for the fault was not with us, but with those who have completely neglected the education of people, and left the guidance of the female sex utterly to chance." This reproach, addressed to men as much as to women, was uttered openly and published in a Moravian newspaper edited by the Moravian Czech patriot F. M. Klácel.[28] The concluding exclamation of that article, "Freedom, equality, and brotherhood!" in the context in which it appeared, rang with the distinct overtones of political emancipation. In fact, unlike other public pronouncements made by women in that year, Němcová's statement contained no explicit disavowal of feminist aspirations. In a private letter to Klácel, she again raised the question of why a woman should not be equal to a man. She realized that she would be accused of demanding the "emancipation of women"; "I blush" at the thought, she wrote.[29] But she did not shrink from thinking the thought and putting it into words. During this same period, in her exchanges with Klácel, she went still further: she probed deeper into the concepts of equality, asking her friend for explanations of strange new terms such as "socialism" and "communism"—terms that would hardly be spoken by other women. And in answer to her gropings for a political creed with which to help reshape the world that had made her melancholy, Klácel published a series of articles in his newspaper;[30] thus a woman had inspired the first treatise in the Czech language on socialism. Němcová traveled further on the road to political consciousness and came closer to seeking emancipation as an explicit goal than any of her Czech woman contemporaries.

27. V. Tille, *Božena Němcová* (Prague, 1947), p. 111.

28. Němcová, *Vybrané spisy,* p. 163.

29. This letter survived only in a fragment written sometime before September 20, 1849 (*ibid.,* p. 340).

30. See Chapter 12, Note 34.

The condition of women in the mid-nineteenth century was truly pathetic. The appeal of the Club of Slavic Women of October 3 declared that because of educational neglect "the woman stands so far below the man that he cannot carry on any discussion with her about matters going beyond the realm of the most ordinary domestic life," and that as a result of this "there is in the conduct of our men toward women as little gentleness and courtesy as nowhere else."[31] One of the founders of this club conceded that a mother usually could not keep up with the education of her son after he reached the age of ten![32] The prejudices against women playing an active role in society were so deep-seated that even at the height of the revolutionary wave in 1848 no Czech writer or spokesmen, the radicals included, suggested at any time that women should be given the right to vote. In the electoral laws of the revolutionary era the exclusion of women is never spelled out; it is simply taken for granted. The women themselves, even as they began to "awaken," were extremely modest in the objectives they sought. In pleading for the improvement of their condition, they shrank from the use of the word "emancipation," except to assure the men that emancipation was not what they wanted. The opening speaker at the first meeting of the Prague women (see above) felt compelled to announce that "we are not gathered here to struggle for emancipation." The appeal of the Club of Slavic Women similarly stated that "we don't believe we should mix in politics."[33] Women were barred from universities, but the goal of university education for women was so remote that no one ever suggested in 1848-49 that this barrier should be removed.

The advancing reaction after the dissolution of the Kroměříž Parliament put an end to whatever small progress might have been made in expanding the woman's role in society. The reaction had found it distasteful enough to have to tolerate the participation of men of common birth in public life. It could not allow the aspirations of women to a public role to go unchallenged and, having disposed of the Kroměříž Parliament, lost no time in unceremoniously and explicitly banning, in the Law on Association issued on March 17, 1849, all political activity of women; women were not even permitted to be present at political meetings as listeners (Paragraphs X,

31. *NLS,* October 9, 1848, Supplement.
32. "Ženská emancipace," *Ottův slovník naučný,* XXVII (1908), 809.
33. *NLS,* October 9, 1848, Supplement.

XXI, and XXII).[34] In addition, the Law on Communities, relating to local government, specifically excluded women from the right to vote; a wife could exercise her right to vote "through her husband," and widows, unmarried women, and wives separated from their husbands could do so "through plenipotentiaries."[35] Thus the revolutionary experience of 1848-49 now caused the reaction to write the inferior status of the woman into law more thoroughly than it had ever been done before. It may be added that if the revolution brought a meager harvest to all women, it brought still less to the woman of the working class. Though laws were passed to "protect" society against the hazards of a woman's vote, not a single law had been passed to protect the woman worker against the hazards of factory work.

The struggle for emancipation could only begin in earnest after the downfall of Bach in 1860. During the sixties the fresh breeze of emancipation again began to blow across the Czech Lands from North American shores, with Náprstek's return from exile. At Náprstek's initiative the American Club of Women was founded in Prague (made up, in spite of the name, of Czech women) in 1865 and became the focus of an emancipation movement in the years to come.[36]

34. Text in *NN,* March 23, 1849.
35. Par. 30 (text in *NN,* March 22, 1849).
36. S. Kodým, *Dům u Halánků: Vzpomínky na Vojtu Náprstka* (Prague, 1955), p. 81.

Part Three

Conclusion

Chapter 15

Reflections on the Saga of '48

The year 1848 was a year of wonder, of excitement, and of suspense: a year of hopes conceived and abandoned, of hatreds laid to rest and reawakened, of experiments never before attempted, of freedoms never before savored, of illusions never before entertained. It was Year One in the political life of the Czechs. Into that year were telescoped virtually all the significant political issues that have been stamped upon Czech history during the last hundred years.

It was a year of many "firsts" in modern Czech history. The year brought the first Czech political program, the first constitutions, the first elections and election campaigns, the first political parties, the first popular assembly, the first great Czech daily newspaper, the first exercise of the freedom of speech, and the first jury trial.[1]

It was, above all, a year in which large groups hitherto submerged were drawn into the maelstrom of politics, thus imparting to the events of that year that overpowering and feverish quality for which it will always be remembered. The watchwards and objectives were equality, emancipation, freedom, reform; there was hardly a group that remained unaffected by the irresistible power of these concepts. Czechs demanded equality with Germans, burghers with nobles, peasants with landlords, cottagers with peasants, Protestants with Catholics, Jews with Christians, priests with bishops,[2] and the young

1. Began in Prague, February 12, 1849 (*NN*, February 14, 1849).
2. Some Roman Catholic parish priests demanded radical changes, along democratic lines, in the government of the church, changes that would raise their status and influence vis-à-vis the hierarchy. Thus there were calls from the clergy for vicarial, diocesan, and provincial synods which would be attended by priests of various ranks and at which important ecclesiastical matters would be discussed; there were also calls for the representation of the lower, non-privileged clergy at the Bohemian diet (see a letter from an anonymous clergyman in *NN*, April 22, 1848). The parish priests who had raised their voices against the power of the hierarchy were in turn opposed by those still lower on the hierarchical ladder: the chaplains, assistants of the parish priests. In one district of Bohemia, a group of chaplains met in a solemn gathering and adopted an eleven-point resolution calling for the improvement of their lot

with the old. Every tradition, no matter how venerable; every tie, no matter how sacred; every institution, no matter how much hallowed by time, was called into question. Universities wanted to be freed from the stifling grip of officialdom. Students wanted to be freed from the ordeal of semestral examinations (and succeeded). Women, though not yet demanding political equality, wanted to be freed from the shame of educational backwardness. Priests wanted to be freed from the burdens of celibacy,[3] while the "Moroccans" wanted to be freed from the institution of marriage itself.[4] There was a general and insistent demand for reform in all walks of life: for the reform of university education, of medical studies at universities, of secondary education, of taxation, of the armed forces, of church music.[5]

If the observer were to select one group that lent to that year its characteristic revolutionary flavor, that group would be the young:[6]

---

vis-à-vis the parish priests; they also demanded that bishops be elected by the clergy of their diocese (*NN,* September 8, 1848).

3. See an article from the pen of a Roman Catholic priest demanding the abolition of celibacy in *NN,* May 28, 1848.

4. The year 1848 inevitably produced its share of communist ideas, with radical sexual overtones, in the form of a group known as the Adamites, a curious relic of the Adamites of the Hussite period of the fifteenth century. The fifteenth-century Adamites were not entirely wiped out, but lingered on here and there in parts of Bohemia, especially in the eastern regions, as a small and nearly forgotten group that seemed only to reach public notice or intensify its activity during periods of social or religious upheaval. The last time the Adamites had been active was in the last decades of the eighteenth century (A. Helfert, "O tak řečených blouznivcích náboženských v Čechách a na Moravě . . .," *ČČM,* LI and LIII [1877 and 1879]). After this they went "underground" again, to reappear in 1848 in several districts of eastern Bohemia. According to official reports, the Adamites refused to pay taxes, fulfill their civic duties, or recognize the state or any kind of constituted authority. They expected a universal extermination of the Catholics, at the hands of an enemy, a messiah from Morocco; hence they were also called "Moroccans." They believed that once the Catholics had been exterminated, they, the Adamites, would remain as the sole occupants of the country and divide all property among themselves. The Adamites also practiced a sexual communism (see a detailed account in *NN,* March 16 and 18, 1849). The origin of the concept of a messiah from Morocco has not yet been satisfactorily explained. The "Moroccans" held their meetings in some communities in eastern Bohemia as late as the end of the nineteenth century and even today a few still remember those who used to attend these meetings (see M. Machovcová and M. Machovec, *Utopie blouznivců a sektářů* [Prague, 1960], p. 462).

5. *NN,* April 28, 1848.

6. Compare the article by R. R. Lutz, Jr., "Fathers and Sons in the Vienna

the young workers, the journeymen, the apprentices, and, primarily, the students and the young intellectuals. They were responsible for some of the year's follies and for most of its heroism. It was largely the young who manned the barricades, marched in the streets, and languished in prisons. It was the young who tried to lead the peasant out of his lethargy, the worker out of his sordid status, and both into some form of self-respect. Without the young, the political movement of the year would have run a vastly different course. It was on the initiative of the young (Repeal) that the revolution was launched (the March Assembly); and it was on the initiative of the young that the last attempt to save the revolution was made (the May Conspiracy): quite appropriately, young people presided over both the revolution's birth and its demise. When they failed, in May 1849, to save the movement, there was no group that could seize the torch and bear it forward. With their defeat, the constitutional era was defeated; with their martyrdom, political freedom too was martyred. With their will broken and their ranks dispersed and decimated, the ugly hand of the police state could reach for and destroy, though only for a time, most of the fruits of the 1848 era. The university students were, of course, the leading and the most prominent of the young rebels. In 1848, they exerted a greater influence on political developments than any time before or since.

What were the results of that short but eventful period of freedom? First and foremost, the year 1848 constituted a landmark in the history of the Czechs as a nationality; it brought the beginning of their recognition as one of Europe's own children, and it saw them emerge as a political force. Before 1848, the terms "Bohemia" and "Moravia" conjured a vision of a German land, or at least of a land that could never be thought of apart from the German ethnic complex. The existence of a Slavic population there had been recognized but dimly, if at all.[7] Foreign travelers visited either the luxurious spas in western Bohemia or Prague; the spas were German-speaking entirely, and Prague had a German facade below which a foreigner seldom peered. The existence of a Czech-speaking substratum in

Revolution of 1848," *JCEA*, XXII (July, 1962), 161-73. See also K. Kosík (ed.), *Česká radikální demokracie* (Prague, 1958), pp. 279-99.

7. See, for example, an anonymous travelogue, "A Walk Across Bohemia," in *Fraser's Magazine*, XXIX (1844), 290-301. The author complains of unpronounceable names, but from reading the article one would never suspect the presence of a Czech or Slavic mass in the country.

these two provinces was of interest only to a few enthusiasts, notably scholars.

The year 1848 put an end to this humiliation. In that single year the Czech national movement was transformed from a cultural (or quasi-political) movement into a full-fledged political one; and the Czechs, through their leaders, compelled others to listen to their catalogue of frustrations, grievances, and ambitions. Above all, they compelled others to accept them as a nationality that had had its own past and that would not be deprived of its own future. As William H. Stiles, the United States chargé d'affaires in Vienna at the time put it: "Previous to that period," the Czechs and other Slavs possessed "no proper individuality, their political nationality was unacknowledged, and for centuries, consequently, they exercised no influence in the political councils of Europe. The storms of 1848 and 1849 raised them to consideration, and even power."[8]

It was Palacký's letter of April 11 that made Central Europe aware, almost overnight, of the Czechs' existence. In Palacký, the Czechs had a prestigious spokesman; when he declared publicly that he was a "Czech of Slavonic blood" and that he wanted always to serve his nation, his voice had to be taken seriously. But the Czechs emerged as a political force not only by virtue of being recognized by others, but also by virtue of recognizing themselves; Palacký's letter was therefore of great significance in creating in masses of Czechs a heightened awareness of their own nationality. The letter to the Frankfurt Assembly, according to a contemporary, "was a banner around which rallied the Slavs just awakened from a slumber of two centuries, in order to ward off the first attack of a power that had always been inimical to them."[9] This statement shows how well the importance of Palacký's letter was realized by contemporaries; today, in retrospect, it assumes the character of a milestone in the growth of Czech national consciousness. It was the good fortune of the Czech leaders that the new freedom of the press and assembly allowed the voice of Palacký and of others of like views to be heard. The magic of the printed word, the impact of the word addressed to a multitude at a public meeting, the power of a patriotic song chanted by an excited throng marching through the streets—all this produced, in a matter of weeks, a surge of national consciousness such as had never existed before.

8. W. H. Stiles, *Austria in 1848-49* (New York, 1852), I, 388.
9. *NLS,* February 27, 1849.

Soon the language of the new national awareness took on a flamboyant, at times, belligerent tone. And as it did so, it clashed with the belligerence of the Germans: the year brought the Czechs not only the benefit of international recognition, but also the first unwelcome harvest of open conflict with the Germans. To the Germans, the confrontation with the Czechs was a truly traumatic experience. Until 1848, most Germans had not regarded, and had no reason to regard, the Czechs as a political force. Now, they were compelled to include them in their political calculations. From being a submerged nation, the Czechs, in a few weeks, were transformed into a force that had acquired a crucial influence in the Imperial Parliament, concluded a marriage of convenience with the imperial government, and seemed determined to scrutinize and challenge every political act of the monarchy in the light of its self-interest. Above all, it threatened the privileged position of the Germans in all walks of life. It was possible for the Germans to come to terms with Palacký as a scholar, but it was most trying to have to deal with him as a political spokesman of the Czech nation. Engels voiced the anger and despair of many Germans when he wrote that "the chief champion of the Tschechian nationality, Professor Palacký, is himself nothing but a learned German run mad, who even now cannot speak the Tschechian language correctly and without foreign accent," and that the "dying Tschechian nationality . . . made in 1848 a last effort to regain its former vitality."[10] In referring to the Czechs as a dying nationality, Engels was perhaps expressing more hope than conviction. The year in which the Czechs and Germans first clashed in open political combat was merely a prelude to a troubled century of misunderstanding and conflict. After the experience of 1848, the Czechs could never again be permanently submerged. The Czech nationality refused to die, and the year 1848 proved to be not the last but the first chapter in a long and victorious saga.

It was the presence of national conflict that distinguished the Czech (and Austrian) revolution in 1848 from the revolutions in Western Europe. Conflict between nations, more than between classes, shaped the revolution and its final outcome. The need to safeguard the national integrity of the Czech nation and give it a place in the sun confronted the Czech liberal leadership with problems different from those that confronted the liberal leaders in Western Europe,

10. F. Engels, *Revolution and Counter-Revolution or Germany in 1848*, ed. E. Marx Aveling (Chicago, 1896), p. 90.

or the leaders of "ruling" nationalities in Central and Eastern Europe. The Czech leaders were engaged in a struggle in which there seemed to be no rules, only exceptions. They had to grope for precedents where no precedents existed; they endeavored to derive lessons from a past that too often had no lessons to give; they looked for answers in the West, where political realities were different.

Only if one understands how bewildering the problems were can one realize how difficult it was to cope with them. The Czechs felt overwhelmed by their enemies, and were puzzled by their friends. The Bohemian Czechs had reason to wonder if the Czechs of Moravia were with them or against them; if Russia was not to be feared more for its despotism than valued for its role as a possible Slavic ally; if the Poles, with their pro-Magyar sympathies, had any sympathy left for the Slavic underdogs of the Magyars. Their own legitimate homeland was dominated by a German minority from within and by an elaborate German bureaucratic apparatus from without. Their German foes had many faces, even when they answered the same ethnic description. The Czechs had to struggle with the Germans of Bohemia-Moravia, with the Germans of the original Habsburg hereditary lands, and with the Germans of the German Confederation. The Czechs would have gladly been separated from the Germans of Bohemia-Moravia, but this could not be accomplished without severing from these two provinces territory that had been historically their integral part. To surrender territory in exchange for ethnic peace, or to preserve historic boundaries for the price of continued ethnic strife: these were the alternatives, and the choice was difficult, which accounts for the uncertainties that characterized Czech "official" policy in this regard. The Czechs were literally trapped. If they had succeeded in cutting their links with the Germans of the Habsburg Monarchy, they would have fallen into the embrace of the Germans of the Reich; this would have left them a margin of survival too narrow for comfort. In the end, to avoid the Scylla of the Reich Germans, they chose the Charybdis of the Habsburg Germans, about whose mercies, on the basis of their past performance, they felt far from reassured.

In charting the future of the Czechs alongside the Habsburg Germans, the Czech leaders had to substitute strength for trust and calculation for sentiment. They could find their strength by finding allies within the monarchy, and they also hoped to use the monarchy as a springboard for the expansion of Czech commercial influence in Southeast Europe. The product of this chemistry of motives was

Austro-Slavism. It is possible to criticize the concept of Austro-Slavism from the vantage point of the present, but it is not easy to question it as a policy for 1848. Confident enough of the ability of their nation to survive, the Czech leaders were not, and could not, be confident of the ability of their nation to survive alone. They could only perceive their nation for what it was: a nation small in numbers and weak in political power. To safeguard its immediate future, they had to ally themselves closely with other Austrian Slavs, and with them bend the Habsburg Monarchy to their will and purpose. On the evidence then available, Austro-Slavism was the only realistic policy. In 1848-49, no Czech liberal—and no Czech radical either—demanded the destruction of the Habsburg Monarchy or a complete independence of the Czech nation. This would have been pure fantasy, and if attempted, would have spelled pure disaster. The Austro-Slavism of the Czech leaders was not rooted in any sentimental adherence to tradition; for that the past offered too little encouragement. Their Austro-Slavism was calculating; it was rooted in an awareness of the existing geopolitical situation, which left room only for choices that could be applauded not for their closeness to what was ideal but for their distance from what was ruinous.

In pursuing Austro-Slavism the Czech leaders pursued the best policy—indeed the only possible policy—in the circumstances. But in translating their Austro-Slavism into a support of the reactionary Schwarzenberg government, beyond all prudence, to the very eve of the destruction of the Imperial Parliament, the Czech leaders over-reached themselves and committed a signal blunder—their most conspicuous blunder of the revolutionary era. It is undeniable that with or without their support of the Schwarzenberg government, reaction would have triumphed. It is equally undeniable that it would have been better for their collective reputation and wisdom, if reaction had triumphed without their abetting it. They were driven into this position in part by their fear of radicalism, but primarily by their hope that their policy would win them the confidence of the government and bring tangible benefits to the Czech nation. This desire to win the confidence of the government was certainly carried too far: they seemed overanxious to show to a thoroughly undependable government that they were a dependable group. They continued to play this part even when it became clear that the government was leading Austria down the path of reaction. It was a policy of excessive opportunism—which is one of the criticisms that may be leveled at the Czech liberal policy during the revolutionary period. Instead of wanting to show the court circles that they were resolute, they were eager to show that they were loyal. This emphasis proved a misjudgment, for the Czechs' loyalty was calculating, and this did not escape the court circles. In the end, they reaped no rewards for their professions of loyalty, and invited only arrogance and abuse by their excessive caution. Their policy did not in the least improve their image in the eyes of the conservatives. At the beginning of May, 1849, the Bohemian acting governor described the Czech leaders as "democratic"—an opprobrious term in official parlance—and even suspected them of a willingness to be drawn into an uprising against the government.[11] After the restoration of absolutism, Palacký, Havlíček, Brauner, and many other Czech liberals (and radicals) were placed under police surveillance and continued to be subjected to it for years.[12] It is not surprising that the Czech leaders did not succeed in convincing the ruling circles that they were a reliable group: by the criteria of the mid-nineteenth century, they were enlightened and progressive men, sincerely devoted to constitutional principles and to the welfare of their nation; not even their opportunism could obscure this.

The pressure exerted by the Czechs, combined with the sudden burst of the egalitarian spirit, induced the government to give formal recognition to the principle of the equality of the Czech and German nationalities, and of the Czech and German languages in public life, especially in education. Through the force of their numbers as the largest of the subject nationalities, and through the persistence of their spokesmen, the Czechs contributed decisively to the recognition of the principle of national equality in the Habsburg Monarchy in general and thereby aided other subject nationalities; Rieger included the safeguarding of national rights in his first draft of the Bill of Rights (*Urtext*), and the principle of equality was enshrined in the final draft prepared by the constitutional committee of the Imperial Parliament.

Apart from the question of principle, some gains along the lines of equality were made in practice. The year 1848-49 brought the first formal recognition of the equality of the Czech and German languages at the universities of Prague and Olomouc; in a few sub-

11. See Chapter 9.
12. F. Roubík, "Ke vzniku úředních soupisů účastníků hnutí v letech 1848-1849," *Časopis Společnosti přátel starožitností*, LXX (1962), 155.

jects, Czech lectures were actually introduced (or revived, as the case may be) at both institutions of higher learning, although nothing like complete equality was attained, partly because of a lack of qualified Czech candidates for academic positions and partly because of a lack of enthusiasm on the part of the government. Similarly, the Czech language was introduced as a compulsory subject in several secondary schools, and in some it was introduced as a medium of instruction in certain subjects but not all of them. This may appear to be a modest achievement, but it must be measured against the total absence of the Czech language (except as an optional subject) in the secondary schools of the pre-March period.

Some very hesitant steps toward language equality were taken in government service in 1848-49, in the dealing of the officials with the public. The official correspondence within the bureaucracy, however, remained entirely German throughout the 1848-49 period; the German language was used not only, as might be expected, between provincial governors and Vienna, but also in communications passing between the governors and the region prefects. During the fifties, the use of the Czech language in official dealings with the public was reduced; at the same time, the use of the Czech language at universities and secondary schools also declined. By the end of the fifties, the Czech language vanished again almost completely from public life. Nevertheless, during 1848-49 the ice had been broken and the idea of national equality proved so compelling that not even Bach dared abrogate it as a principle, although he did not honor it in practice. With the revival of constitutionalism in 1860, the principle was appealed to by the Czech leaders and used as a basis for forcing concessions from a reluctant government. Progress was slow and painful, but long before 1914 the Czech language had become solidly established in schools and had become a fully recognized medium of cultural expression.

Having become a new political force, the Czechs produced their first political program: the First and Second March Petitions. In their final form, the petitions were shaped by Czech liberal leaders, who placed in the forefront those articles that called for the equality of nationalities, for the union of Bohemia and Moravia, and for autonomy for the two provinces. Although the demands for the union of Bohemia and Moravia, and for their autonomy, had been expressed before, this was the first time that they had appeared as part of an "official" policy of the Czech national movement, voiced in a formal public statement. The proposal for the union of the two provinces was hardly acceptable to the Germans and to the ruling circles, and it found only scant approval among the Czechs of Moravia. Against that opposition, the Bohemian Czechs did not press the issue strongly; they accepted the provisions of the Cabinet Letter of April 8, which promised autonomy to Bohemia only (not to the Lands of the Czech Crown as a whole, as originally requested) and which made the union of the two provinces conditional upon a decision of the Imperial Parliament.

In accepting this, the Czech leaders in effect tacitly abandoned, at least for the time being, the basis of historical tradition and permitted the issue of union to be taken out of their hands. Even the promise of autonomy for Bohemia only was never put into effect; before any progress was made, absolutism, with its ruthless centralism, buried whatever hopes the Czech leaders may have harbored for obtaining autonomy for their province. Demands for the union and autonomy of Bohemia and Moravia were raised again in the 1860's and the ensuing years, but they fell on deaf ears, and continued to fall on deaf ears as long as the Habsburg Monarchy lasted. The two provinces remained separate, and neither received any meaningful autonomy until 1918, when this vital aspect of the Czech program of 1848 was finally realized. In this respect, the year 1848 was memorable not so much for what it attained, but for the goal it placed before the nation. In putting forward this particular goal, the liberal architects of the March Petitions read the future correctly. The goal was a call not merely for the restoration of conditions as they had once existed, but for a union closer than anything warranted by precedent. The vision of the Czech leaders proved a sound one: it was fully vindicated exactly seventy years later.

Whereas the union of the Czechs of Bohemia and Moravia was part of the official political program, the union of Czechs and Slovaks was never so clearly and forcefully formulated. The Slovaks formed part of the state of Hungary, with its own administrative system, and this made the question of the union of the two peoples a highly delicate one. It undoubtedly accounts (along with some other reasons) for the failure of the Czech leaders to include the demand for such a union in the First and Second March Petitions; in fact, the Slovaks were not even mentioned in either petition. Nor did the Slovak leaders put forward any such proposal in their program of May 11. The Czechs were not oblivious to this question, however, and though no official Czech program during the 1848-49 period called for a Czech-Slovak union, proposals for such a union came from influential individuals among the Czechs. Thus, in June, 1848, some Czech delegates at the Slavic Congress suggested a union of the two peoples, but the Slovaks at the congress resisted them, on the plea that their problems and traditions were dissimilar. In January, 1849, Palacký, in his constitutional proposals, included the Czechs and Slovaks in one administrative group, but nothing came of his proposal.[13] On the whole, it may be said that the Slovak leaders sincerely desired the friendship and the support of the Czechs, but preferred, until the end of 1848, to solve their national problem within the legal and territorial framework of the Hungarian state. When the prospects for such a solution dimmed, they began to advocate the establishment of Slovakia as an autonomous crownland; even at this stage, however, they did not advocate a union with the Czechs. Nevertheless, a number of Czechs participated actively in the military campaigns of the Slovaks against the Magyars.

The chief contribution of the Czech liberals was that they gave their people a national program and brought the Czechs to the attention of Europe. But it was the radicals who broadened the vision of the nation's objectives in order to encompass the "have-nots," the poor peasants and the workers. In the political world of the liberals, property rights tended to overshadow civil rights. A member of the lowest social classes was often regarded more as an enemy than as a compatriot and potential ally in the struggle for national emancipation. The radicals opposed this view. They demanded a more consistent democracy; they favored universal suffrage without property restrictions, and they advocated a more militant social reform which would render the benefits of constitutional government meaningful to the working class and the poor peasantry. They formed the "party of opposition" to the Czech official policy as represented by the liberals. The impatience and, on occasion, the demagoguery, with which some radicals voiced their views tended to obscure their insights into the social problems of the times; the liberals in general failed to appreciate the true significance of these problems, but the future was to show that sooner or later they would have to be faced.

13. A later, similar proposal from Palacký's pen appeared in *NN*, December 21, 1849 (reprinted in J. M. Černý, *Boj za právo: Sborník aktů politických u věcech státu a národa českého od roku 1848* [Prague, 1893], pp. 685-92).

The radicals wanted to face them here and now; against the hands-off policy of the liberals they emphasized the moral duty of the state to assist the "have-nots" and stressed the regulatory functions of the state as an instrument of social policy. They were the first group that consciously tried to establish a link with the working class and promote its interests. They reflected seriously on socialism rather than rejecting it a priori as the liberals usually did. It was from the ranks of the radicals (Arnold) that the first proposal—it would be more accurate to call it a hint—came for the distribution of land as a means of improving the condition of the landless peasant; this view represented a most extreme form of radicalism in Central Europe in 1848, but in a few decades it was to become respectable and was to be recognized as one of the essential ingredients of the nation's social program.

It is pertinent to add, however, that for all their social concerns, the radicals were still only spokesmen for, rather than of, the working class and the poor peasantry. They were still only friendly outsiders looking in, and indeed at times a few radicals felt as uneasy as the liberals about the potential violence of the lowest social classes. Since they were educated men, they could not help feeling alarmed and even repelled by the spectacle of a mass of people who had been deprived of the benefits of education and abused by ruthless exploitation, and whose grievances could be easily misued by unscrupulous leaders. Sabina himself voiced this uneasiness: "The will of the people often yields to prejudices," he wrote; "the will of the people, however, sometimes also succumbs to passion—and that is dangerous. It is bad if the people have no will of their own, and allow themselves to be used as an instrument."[14]

The radicals were more determined in what they wanted, though they showed less sense of political responsibility and could not boast the intellectual eminence the liberals collectively possessed; their qualities of leadership were not as high as those of the liberals. On the other hand, the liberals lacked the sense of social responsibility the radicals displayed. For the Czech nation, the ideal leadership would have been a compound of liberals and radicals. In fact, this compound did exist and it did attain, to a degree, a position of leadership in the Slavic Linden. In the ranks of the Slavic Linden liberals and radicals lived at first in an uneasy partnership and later in open

14. *PVL,* October 15, 1848. Sabina is commenting here on the Viennese revolution.

strife. But the presence of both liberals and radicals, with their respective virtues, gave the Slavic Linden its unique blend of vigor and wisdom, of drive and discipline. Although the radicals were gaining the upper hand in the organization as the revolutionary era progressed, and eventually captured its leadership, the liberals were influential in it until the very end. The Slavic Linden was the first political organization of the Czechs—and the finest political-institutional product of the revolutionary era. It emphasized a whole range of needs—political, educational, economic, and cultural. It was also an excellent organizer. It submitted to the Kroměříž Parliament the well-known "monster petition," bearing more signatures than any petition presented anywhere in the Habsburg Monarchy during the revolutionary period. It prepared slates of candidates for public office; few candidates not endorsed by it were successful at the polls. It founded a newspaper. It set up numerous branches in Bohemia and Moravia and inspired the formation of a few branches among other Austrian Slavs, notably among the southern Slavs.

Even apart from the Slavic Linden, the Czechs collectively showed themselves to be able organizers. They staged an effective boycott of the Frankfurt election. They organized the Slavic Congress. They organized (with the Slavic Linden playing an active part) a successful campaign to collect funds for the support of the Hungarian Slavs. They formed the best-disciplined club of parliamentary deputies in Kroměříž. They exerted a profound influence on Slavdom in general; the Slavic Congress was an especially important event in the development of the national consciousness of the Slavic nations. The strength of their numbers and the intellectual eminence of their leaders caused them to exert a particularly strong influence on the Habsburg Slavs. Their geopolitical position gave them certain unique advantages which few nations in Europe enjoyed. Their membership in the Slavic family gave them interests and concerns reaching into Russia in the East and into the Turkish Empire in the Balkans. On the other hand, their historical association with the Germans linked them with Western Europe. They were probably the only group in Europe equally able to speak to the Germans and the Slavs, to the West Europeans and East Europeans.

What benefit did various social groups derive from the year 1848? The most obvious beneficiary was the Czech middle class, insofar as it is possible to use the term "class" with reference to a group that was still very small. The events of 1848 had effected the final emancipation of the middle class and had thrust it into a position of political leadership in the nation. Inasmuch there was no strong Czech nobility, the Czech middle class became a more or less exclusive leader in the decades to come. In this respect, the Czech situation differed from that of their neighbors, the Poles, the Magyars, and the Austrian Germans, where the nobility had been the principal bearer of the national idea in previous centuries, and had survived the year 1848 in considerable strength, which gave it a strong influence in shaping the destinies of their respective nations in the future. In contrast, the influence of the nobility on the subsequent history of the Czechs was limited, and this enabled the Czech movement to acquire a more democratic character. In this connection, it is interesting to note that the period 1848-49 produced a liberal and radical movement of vigor, but that the conservative movement gained virtually no following among the people; insofar as conservatism existed, it was largely associated with the German or ethnically neutral element. It is significant that no Czech conservative newspaper succeeded, despite the wholehearted support of the government; *Pokrok,* for example, ceased publication after less than a half dozen issues. The leadership of the middle class was strengthened in the second half of the nineteenth century by its growing economic power. In this respect, the year 1848 was also important. At that time the last obstacles to industrial expansion were wiped out, which made possible the rise of a powerful Czech industrial and commercial bourgeoisie.

To the peasant, the year brought the final emancipation from centuries of serfdom. The peasant had been freed from all legal dependence on his lord; the *robot,* the hated mark of serfdom, had been abolished. Henceforth, the peasant was no longer subject to the jurisdiction of the lord, but both peasant and lord were equally subject to the jurisdiction of the state. Patrimonial courts had been swept away and replaced by state courts. The state took over all administrative and judicial powers previously exercised by the landlord. These were achievements that even the ruthless regime of Minister Bach in the 1850's did not dare touch. The emancipation of the peasantry had far-reaching consequences for the development of the Czech nationality. With the millions of Czech peasants drawn into the political process, the Czech nation was bound to be strengthened politically vis-à-vis the Germans. The emancipation of the peasants could only result in the emancipation of the Czech nation.

In one respect, the peasant emerged from the emancipation with a handicap. The pertinent emancipation legislation called for his paying compensation to the lord in return for the abolition of certain duties and obligations. Although the sum the peasant was required to pay was not forbiddingly high, it was nevertheless a burden; above all, the total amount of compensation payments supplied the powerful landlords with extensive capital, which made it possible for them to solidify their economic position, to the disadvantage of the peasantry. It was ironic that among the recipients of large compensation payments from Bohemia were two men who more than any other symbolized absolutism: Metternich and Windischgrätz, both of whom held estates in Bohemia.[15]

There was, of course, much unfinished business left when the curtain rang down on the revolution: the worker, the cottager, and the woman, had more or less been bypassed in the distribution of rewards. The workers fought and died on the barricades, but the revolution bestowed no immediate benefits on them. Not a single law had been passed and not a single decree had been issued in 1848-49 that would in any way improve their condition. They were still a class without tradition, without self-image, and without any political organization or ideology. We encounter no names of workers recurring from time to time in connection with different working-class outbreaks or movements, which means there was no one even approaching leadership status from the ranks of the workers. The radical students and intellectuals led the working class during the revolutionary era, but their leadership role was limited almost entirely to a few occasions, such as the June Uprising; outside that, there was nothing like permanent contact between these classes, although both the radical students and the intellectuals endeavored to maintain such a contact. A few names of workers were known, but they were forgotten almost as soon as they appeared. It goes without saying that there were as yet no Czech thinkers and no public figures whose exclusive concern was with the working class and its problems, as was the case in France at the time.

As for the poor peasant, he had been freed from serfdom and had not been required to pay compensation; but he emerged from the revolution as poor, or as landless, as he had been before. There was

15. F. Červinka, *Přehled dějin Československa v epoše kapitalismu* (Prague, 1958), II, 12.

no solution for him in sight and none contemplated. The problem of the poor and landless peasantry was to plague the country for decades to come. This was perhaps the most serious "unfinished business" of the revolutionary era.

Finally, the status of the woman did not undergo any change. At a time when suffrage was almost universal, she was still denied the right to vote. The peasant who may not have been able to read and write had acquired the right to vote, but the cultured woman could not vote merely because she was a woman. The denial of the the right to vote to women was considered so self-evident that most electoral laws did not specifically mention it. The woman had no defenders; not even the radicals thought her worthy of many of the rights she lacked. Like the peasant, she was admired and praised for her pristine virtues, but praise was a poor substitute for equality. Women themselves did not believe themselves entitled to any political rights; in fact, the few pronouncements from women we have on this subject seem to go out of the way to make it clear that Czech women did not demand "emancipation." What the women did demand was improved education, yet even in this respect they were very modest: women were not permitted to attend universities, yet no demand is known to have been made by Czech women asking that they be given equal access to higher education.

Although there were some problems left from the year 1848-49 that took decades to solve, there were also achievements that took decades to match. The Imperial Parliament of 1848-49 was based on a suffrage that excluded only those who were not "independent"; this exclusion affected domestics, agricultural workers, and factory workers, but it did not affect the large majority of the male population. The absolutism of the fifties put an end to this liberality, and for the next fifty years the scope of the electoral law of 1848 was not to be equaled. Only the introduction of universal suffrage in 1907 exceeded the electoral achievement of 1848.

The parliament in 1848 was a one-chamber body consisting entirely of elected deputies, whereas the Imperial Council (*Reichs-rath*) introduced in the 1860's had two chambers consisting of an elected Lower House, and an Upper House consisting of princes of the imperial family, nobles, ecclesiastical dignitaries, and appointed members. In this form the Imperial Council existed until the monarchy's dissolution; the very use of the word "parliament" was considered to be too radical for this institution. Even after the introduction of universal suffrage, the existence of the Upper House prevented the Imperial Council from being as representative as the Imperial Parliament was in 1848. Much the same can be said of the provincial assemblies of Bohemia and Moravia: those that existed between 1860 and 1918 were never as representative as those of 1848. In 1848, the Bohemian diet (which was elected but never met) and the Moravian diet had one chamber only. Although suffrage in both cases was restricted mainly to taxpayers, and although in addition to elected deputies each diet also included unelected nobles, the final outcome was still an impressive gain for the popular element, as evidenced by a large number of peasants in each diet and by the progressive legislation the Moravian diet enacted. In contrast, the diets introduced in the 1860's in Bohemia and Moravia, and in other parts of the monarchy, consisted of *curiae* corresponding to economic and social interest groups; the whole system was heavily weighted in favor of power of wealth and birth. In 1848, the Moravian diet included so many peasants that it was dubbed the "Peasant Parliament," and the Bohemian diet would also have included many peasants, had it been allowed to meet. The diets from 1860 to 1918 never came close to giving this much influence to the popular element.

Thus, in many fundamental respects, the regime of the revolutionary era of 1848-49 was much more liberal than the regime that existed on the eve of World War I. The reason for this is, of course, that the liberal regime of 1848 was the product of a revolution that literally forced the authorities into concessions they would normally never have made, while the constitutional regime of the 1860's was the product of a peaceful change and of concessions made by a government that was at all times strong enough to concede less than the public demanded.

That the revolution was, in the end, bound to be defeated by the forces of reaction there can be no doubt. In retrospect, it can be seen that in spite of the successes achieved by the liberal forces in the first stages of the 1848 movement, the reaction did not relinquish any of its basic positions. The bureaucracy, saturated with a pre-1848 outlook and permeated by an uninhibited contempt for the common man, survived the havoc of uprisings and tumults with hardly a scar. For a time, after the collapse of absolutism, fear compelled the official to display a more congenial countenance to the people. Though the personnel remained, the bureaucracy was paralyzed and the administrative system suffered a partial eclipse. In the absence of a genuine tradition of local government and of any "grass-roots democracy," however, nothing was done by the people to fill the void. The people seemed willing only to follow instructions and orders that came from above; perhaps had the National Committee given instructions for the setting up of local National Committees, there might have been some success, at least for a time, in wresting the apparatus from the bureaucracy. As it was, there was little or no display of local initiative along these lines. Even with the revolutionary momentum generated in the first weeks following the downfall of absolutism and with the widespread discontent, people at the local level were unable or unwilling to take over the bureaucrat's job. The bureaucrat inspired hate and fear, but he also inspired a strange awe and submissiveness. The absence of any tradition of local initiative and the presence of a deep-seated and exaggerated respect for authority were among the important factors accounting for the failure of the revolutionary movement. As *Pražský Večerní List* editorialized, after the dissolution of the Kroměříž Parliament: "One of the greatest weaknesses of our nation is its blind faith in authority."[16] The weakness was not one that could be charged specifically to the Czech nation, however, as *Pražský Večerní List* seems to imply, but to all nations in which feudalism had had a long history and had lingered until comparatively recent times. The present-day observer will note, with some astonishment, that throughout the whole 1848-49 period the bureaucracy remained virtually intact, both in spirit and, to a large extent, in personnel. Some of the most reactionary region prefects, such as Kotz in Mladá Boleslav (Jungbunzlau) in Bohemia, were allowed to remain in their posts all through 1848-49, and had the satisfaction of welcoming back the reaction while still in office.

Of far greater importance to the success of the reaction was the army. With the introduction of constitutional government, the army was supposed to become the instrument of the will of the people and be loyal to the constitution. In practice, it never ceased to be the instrument of the reaction; no group collectively hated the constitution more than the army, and no group despised the people more openly than the army. The army retained its *ésprit de corps* and remained throughout the revolutionary period the chief pillar and hope of the enemies of constitutional government. It was responsible for a far greater destruction of human lives than any of the insurgent elements.

16. *PVL,* March 29, 1849.

The defeat of the revolutionary movement was due not only to the army and the bureaucracy, but also to the growing disunity and the waning enthusiasm of the movement itself. After an initial period of enthusiasm and comparative unity of purpose that transcended the lines between ethnic, social, and other groups, the spirit of particularism reasserted itself; old suspicions were revived, and some new ones were added. Czechs and Germans, landed peasants and cottagers, and burghers and workers again began to eye each other with distrust, even outright fear. Within groups, significant segments soon tired of radicalism and revolution, and the groups split into moderates and radicals. The burghers, the students, and the workers each developed their moderate and radical wings. All this naturally weakened the revolutionary movement. An important factor in the ebbing of the tide was the Decree of September 7, 1848, wiping out the last vestiges of serfdom. The peasant's most serious grievances had been removed by it and he could henceforth not be counted on as a reliable ally of the revolution. This does not mean that afterwards no discontent existed in the countryside. There were new irritations and new frustrations; indeed from the beginning of 1849 we may observe again a growth of radical sentiment among a segment of the population, both in the countryside and in the cities. The radical sentiment assumed much greater proportions in Moravia than in Bohemia, but in neither province did it attain the intensity it had reached during the first months of the constitutional era, and in neither province did it acquire the dimensions of a mass movement. The radical segment remained in a minority, and though this minority was becoming more articulate and vigorous, the nonradical majority was becoming more apathetic. Only in Silesia did a genuine revolutionary situation exist in the first months of 1849. In the rest of the country, there was a certain fatigue, a definite lessening of a willingness to resort to violence even where grievances existed—a disenchantment with revolution. This may be observed among all classes—burghers, students, peasants, and workers. More and more people began to feel that a violent revolution was too high a price to pay for progress.[17] They concluded that violent revolution has its ugliness as well as its glory; that it destroyed the innocent as well as the guilty; that it caused men to sink to the depth of hatred as well as soar to the heights of selfless heroism; that it enabled a minority to impose its views on a majority; that it in-

17. In his report of October 14, 1849, region prefect Kotz speaks of "revolution-weary popular classes" (*SÚA* Prague, PGT 1849-52, R/1, 796/gp.).

duced men to behave, in a group, as they would not behave as individuals.[18] Whatever the significance of the fact, it is worth noting that the June Uprising was the last violent uprising in Czech history.

Although the government defeated the revolution and wiped out many of its gains in the 1850's, the years 1848-49 nevertheless stand out in sharp relief as a dividing line, and as the beginning of a new era. Between the March victory of the revolution in 1848 and the March victory of the reaction in 1849, men beheld and experienced events and movements and institutions that could not be easily erased from their memories. During 1848-49 they went to the polls to elect deputies, public officials, mayors, and members of juries. They were deluged with newspapers speaking an intoxicating new language of political defiance. They listened to public speakers voicing opinions that had never been voiced before. They witnessed a proliferation of clubs and societies devoted to every conceivable whim and purpose. Their intellectual horizon and their daily lives were transformed in that single year more radically than in any other year either before or since.

The meaning of the year was at once simple and profound: it was the first year of freedom and the first year in which the "common man" was forced to recognize himself as a human being endowed with intrinsic worth and capable of playing a part in shaping his own destiny. In that year, man—the "common man"—realized, sometimes still only dimly, that poverty, social and national oppression, and autocratic government are institutions that need not be passively accepted or endured; that man's condition may be changed by man's action; that the lot of the common man should consist of more than rendering unquestioning obedience to those in power; and that, conversely, political power is more than an exercise in despotism or demeaning paternalism. This was a legacy that could never be wholly fulfilled, but more importantly, it was a legacy that could never be wholly forgotten. The revolution generated such a momentum that even the reaction partially succumbed to it. Even Bach did not dare tamper with the peasant's newly won personal freedom. The absolutist government continued to pay lip service to the principle of national equality. It continued and completed the

18. Kotz himself argued in 1852 that some men who had uttered anti-government statements or participated in anti-government demonstrations in 1848 had since become loyal citizens and therefore should not be persecuted (see Roubík, "Ke vzniku úředních soupisů," p. 152).

modernization of universities and secondary schools begun in 1848, thus giving the educational system a form it retained until the mid-twentieth century. It upheld the abolition of feudalism; the personal subjugation of one man to another had been wiped out once and for all. The era of feudalism had come to an end, and nobody could—or tried—to bring it back.

In the 1850's, it seemed that the reaction had succeeded in enveloping the nation permanently in its tentacles. Once again, as before 1848, the eyes and ears of the police kept the citizen in a state of perpetual discomfort and fear. The resounding noise of the revolution was replaced by the nightmarish stillness of reaction. No one, not even cabinet ministers, were exempt from the inquisitive eyes of the police.[19] During the 1850's all the prominent Czech liberals and radicals of 1848 either withdrew from public life, went into exile, or suffered persecution and imprisonment. Palacký, the scholar, returned to his learned dialogue with the muse Clio. The ringing voice of Rieger too was stilled, prudence having dictated his safety as an exile in Western Europe. Brauner, alone of the leading liberals, compromised himself by a temporary collaboration with the government; some others, for example, Palacký, were invited to collaborate, but declined. The fate of Karel Havlíček was the most tragic of all. Havlíček continued to voice as much dissent as the absolutist regime would permit, and after a year of official chicanery, on January 18, 1850, his *Národní Noviny* was forbidden to appear. The indomitable journalist then launched another venture, a magazine entitled *Slovan* (Slav), published twice a week. Now thoroughly repenting his previous support of the government, he more than redeemed himself by turning the biting edge of his satire on the absolutist regime; more chicanery followed, after which Havlíček decided, in August, 1851, to suspend the magazine himself so that the police would not have the pleasure of forbidding it. Later in that year he was arrested and deported to Tyrol. Released in 1855, he died in the following year of tuberculosis, his life undermined by exile and by the despondency he suffered upon returning from exile and finding the political life of his nation at a complete standstill.[20]

19. J. Goll, *Rozdělení pražské university Karlo-Ferdinandovy roku 1882* (Prague, 1908), p. 7.

20. It should be added that Havlíček's wife had for years suffered from tuberculosis (see E. Chalupný, *Havlíček: Prostředí, osobnost a dílo* [Prague, 1929], pp. 42 ff.

Of the prominent radicals, most found themselves in prison during the fifties, for varying periods of time. Sabina, Frič, Sladkovský, Arnold, Gauč, František Havlíček—all faced, at one time or another, the bleak walls of the prison cell.

But of all the men mentioned above, Karel Havlíček was the only one who did not live to see the horizon light up again after 1860. That light would never have appeared had it not been for the work of the men of '48. For even during the darkest days of Bach's absolutism, men would never forget the experience and the magic of that year. There were recesses of their minds that even Bach's police could not reach.

Bibliography and Index

Bibliography

1. ARCHIVAL SOURCES

Literární Archiv Národního Musea. Prague: Slovanská Lípa, 1848-49.

Státní Ústřední Archiv. Prague: Presidium Českého gubernia, 1846-49, 15 c/3.

————. Prague: Presidium guberniální tajné, 1849-52, A/1; R/1.

2. NEWSPAPERS

[The files used cover 1848 and the first half of 1849.]

Bohemia. Prague. Began under this name in 1830; transformed into a political newspaper on April 1, 1848. Survived the period of Bach's absolutism.

Constitutionelles Blatt aus Böhmen. Prague. First issue, April 2, 1848. From January 4, 1852, continued as *Correspondenzblatt aus und für Böhmen;* last issue, June 30, 1852.

Národní Noviny. Prague, April 5, 1848–January 17, 1850.

Noviny Lípy Slovanské. Prague, October 2, 1848–April 28, 1849. From October 2, 1848, to the end of 1848 the title was *Lípa Slovanská.*

Pražský Večerní List. Prague, June 1, 1848–February 1, 1851.

Sedlské Noviny. Prague, April 1, 1849–May 15, 1849. Now reprinted in its entirety in: J. K. Tyl. *Spisy,* Vol. XIV, ed. F. Strejček and H. Hrzalová. Prague, 1953.

Slovenskje Národňje Novini. Bratislava, August 1, 1845–June 9, 1848. Literary supplement, *Orol Tatránski,* during the same period. Facsimile edition in four volumes, Bratislava, 1956.

3. MEMOIRS, DOCUMENTS, AND CORRESPONDENCE

Arnold, E. *Sebrané spisy.* Prague, 1954.

Bakounine, M. *Confession.* Translated by P. Brupbacher. Paris, 1932.

Beneš, K. J. (ed.). *Rok 1848 v projevech současníků.* Prague, 1948.

Bokes, F. (ed.). *Dokumenty k slovenskému národnému hnutiu v rokoch 1848-1914,* Vol. I (1848-67). Bratislava, 1962.

Brauner, F. A. *Von der Robot und deren Ablösung.* Prague, 1848.

Černý, J. M. (ed.). *Boj za právo: Sborník aktů politických u věcech státu a národa českého od roku 1848.* Prague, 1893.

Dlouhý, J. "Dr. Josef Frič," *Osvěta,* VI (1876), 557-73, 727-39.

Engels, F. *Revolution and Counter-Revolution or Germany in 1848,* ed. E. Marx Aveling. Chicago, 1896. (Ascribed by the editor to Marx; now known to have been written by Engels.)

Ernst, W. *Gefängniserlebnisse von Prager Studenten 1848-54.* Vienna, 1913.

Fischel, A. (ed.). *Materialien zur Sprachenfrage in Österreich.* Brünn, 1902.

————. *Das österreichische Sprachenrecht: Eine Quellensammlung.* 2nd ed. Brünn, 1910.

————. *Die Protokolle des Verfassungsausschusses über die Grundrechte.* Vienna, 1912.

Frič, J. V. *Paměti,* ed. K. Cvejn. 3 vols. Prague, 1957-63.

————. *Spisy, I: Politické články z let 1847-1864,* ed. O. Šimáček and B. Šimáčková. Prague, 1956.

Havlíček-Borovský, K. *Politické spisy,* Vols. I, II/1-2, and III/1-2, ed. Z. Tobolka. Prague, 1900-3.

Helfert, J. A. *Aufzeichnungen und Erinnerungen aus jungen Jahren: Im Wiener konstituierenden Reichstag Juli bis Oktober 1848.* Vienna, 1904.

————. "Erlebnisse und Erinnerungen," Parts I-VII, *Die Kultur,* II-VI (1900-5). (Parts I-IV deal with 1848-49.)

————. "Vlastní zkušenosti a paměti," *Osvěta,* XX (1890); XXI (1891); XXIV (1894); XXVI (1896); XXVII (1897).

Hlasowé o potřebě jednoty spisowného jazyka pro Česhy, Morawany, a Slowáky. Prague, 1846.

Hurban, J. M. *Ľudovít Štúr* and *Rozpomienky.* 1 vol. Bratislava, 1959.

Klácel, F. M. *Výbor z díla.* Prague, 1964.

Kolmer, G. *Parlament und Verfassung in Oesterreich,* Vol. I. Vienna, 1902.

Kopp, F. *Die Ereignisse der Pfingstwoche des Jahres 1848 in Prag und in dessen nächster Umbebung.* Prague, 1848.

Kosík, K. (ed.). *Čeští radikální demokraté (Výbor politických statí).* Prague, 1953.

Kübeck, C. F. *Tagebücher,* Vols. I/1-2, and II. Vienna, 1909.

Malý, J. *Naše znovuzrození.* Prague, 1880-84.

Mareš, F. "Nové příspěvky k památnému roku 1848," *ČČH,* XXX (1924), 249-78.

Marx, K., and F. Engels. *Werke,* Vols. V and VI. Berlin, 1959. (Covers the period March, 1848, to July, 1849).

Meissner, A. *Geschichte meines Lebens.* 2 vols. Vienna, 1884.

Menčik, F. "Ein Prager Polizist über die Junitage 1848," *MVGDB,* LIV (1916), 320-45.

Naše národní minulost v dokumentech, Vol. II, ed. F. Kutnar *et al.* Prague, 1962.

Němcová, B. *Vybrané spisy, IV: Básně-stati-dopisy,* ed. F. Vodička. Prague, 1957.

Novotný, K., and M. Myška (eds.). *První kroky k vítězství: Čtení o počátcích našeho dělnického hnutí.* Prague, 1966.

Novotný, M. (ed.). *Letáky z roku 1848.* Prague, 1948.

"Opfer der Prager Pfingsten, Die," *Vierteljahrschrift für die praktische Heilkunde,* IV (1848), 141-54.

Palacký, F. *Radhost,* Vol. III. Prague, 1873.

——. *Spisy drobné,* Vol. I, ed. B. Rieger. Prague, 1898.

Pillersdorf, F. X. *Handschriftlicher Nachlass des Freiherrn von Pillersdorf.* Vienna, 1863.

Polonskii, V. (ed.). "Bakunin pred avstriiskim sudom (materialy iz arkhiva b. III otdeleniia)," *Krasnyi Arkhiv,* III (1923), 173-98.

——. *Materialy dlia biografii M. Bakunina.* 3 vols. Moscow-Leningrad, 1923-33.

Postgate, R. W. (ed.). *Revolution from 1789 to 1906.* New York, 1962. (Originally published in 1920.)

Pražák, A. *Paměti a listář Dra Aloise Pražáka,* ed. F. Kameníček. 2 vols. Prague, 1926-27.

Radimský, J. "Deník Veroniky Vrbíkové z roku 1848," *ČMM,* LXVIII (1948), 97-113.

Radimský, J., and M. Wurmová (eds.). *Petice moravského lidu k sněmu z roku 1848.* Prague, 1955.

Rapant, D. *Slovenské povstanie roku 1848-49: Dejiny a dokumenty.* [See following section.]

Rieger, F. L. *Příspěvky k listáři Dra. Frant. Lad. Riegra,* ed. J. Heidler. 2 vols. Prague, 1924-26.

——. *Řeči Dra. Frant. Ladisl. Riegra,* Vol. I, ed. J. Kalousek. Prague, 1883.

Roubík, F. (ed.). *Petice venkovského lidu z Čech k Národnímu výboru z roku 1848.* Prague, 1954.

Schopf, F. J. (ed.). *Wahre und ausführliche Darstellung der am 11 März 1848 . . . in Prag begonnenen Volks-Bewegung.* Leitmeritz, 1848.

Sojka, J. E. *Naši mužové: Bibliografie a charakteristiky.* Prague, 1953. (Originally published in 1862.)

Springer, A. *Aus meinem Leben.* Berlin, 1892.

——— (ed.). *Protokolle des Verfassungs-Ausschusses im oester- reichischen Reichstage 1848-1849.* Leipzig, 1885.

Stenographischer Bericht über die Verhandlungen der deutschen constituirenden Nationalversammlung, ed. F. Wigard. 9 vols. + index. Frankfurt am Main, 1848-50.

Stloukal, K. "Riegrovy zápisky o Slovensku v r. 1847," *Bratislava,* I (1927), 532-37.

——— (ed.). *Rodinné listy Frant. Palackého dceři Marii a zeti F. L. Riegrovi.* Prague, 1930.

Štúr, L. *Listy L'udovíta Štúra,* Vol. II (1844-55). Bratislava, 1956.

Thun, J. M. *Der Slawismus in Böhmen.* Prague, 1845.

Tyl, J. K. *Pražský posel 1848,* ed. A. Stich. Prague, 1967.

Uebersichts-Tafeln zur Statistik der österreichischen Monarchie. Be- sonderer Abdruck des X. und XI. Heftes der "Statistischen Mittheilungen." Vienna, 1850.

Václavková, J. (ed.). *Písně roku 1848.* Prague, 1948.

Verhandlungen des österreichischen Reichstages nach der stenograph- ischen Aufnahme. 5 vols. Vienna, 1848-49.

"Vzájemné dopisy Frant. Lad. Čelakovského a Václava Staňka," *ČČM,* XLVI (1872), 17-40, 165-87, 313-34, 369-84.

Žáček, V., and Z. Tobolka (eds.). *Slovanský sjezd v Praze roku 1848: Sbírka dokumentů.* Prague, 1958.

4. SECONDARY WORKS

Actes du Congrès Historique du Centenaire de la Revolution de 1848. Paris, 1948.

Andich, E. "Sleduyet li podvergat revizii vzglady Marksa i Engelsa na vengerskuiu revoliutsiiu 1848-1849 godov?" *Acta His- torica,* XII (1966), 373-93.

Atlas československých dějin. Prague, 1965.

Averbukh, R. A. *Revoliutsiia i natsionalno-osvoboditelnaia borba v Vengrii 1848-1849.* Moscow, 1965.

Bajerová, A. *Svatodušni bouře v Praze r. 1848 ve světle soudního vyšetřování.* Plzeň, 1920.

Bartocha, J. *Čeština na bývalé universitě a stavovské akademii v Olomouci.* Olomouc, 1905.

Bass, E. *Čtení o roce osmačtyřicátém,* Vol. I. Prague, 1940.

Batowski, H. "Adam Mickiewicz a Čechové v revolučních letech 1848 a 1849," *ČSČH,* VI (1958), 32-46.

―――. "The Poles and Their Fellow Slavs, 1848-1849," *SEER*, XXVII (1948-49), 404-13.

Belda, J. *Liberec v revolučním roce 1848*. Liberec, 1959.

Bělohlávek, M. "Plzeň v čtyřicátých letech devatenáctého století," *Minulostí Západočeského Kraje*, I (1962), 189-204.

Beneš, V. L. "Bakunin and Palacký's Concept of Austroslavism," *Indiana Slavic Studies*, II (1958), 79-111.

Blum, J. *Noble Landowners and Agriculture in Austria, 1815-1848*. Baltimore, 1948.

Bohmann, A. "Bevölkerungsbewegungen in Böhmen bis zur Mitte des 19. Jahrhunderts," *ZfO*, XIV (1965), 249-65.

―――. "Böhmen und Mähren-Schlesien in Bevölkerungspolitik," *ZfO, XIV* (1965), 39-93.

Bokes F. "Slovenská Národná rada z rokov 1848-1849," *HČ*, XIII (1965), 200-29.

Brandl, V. "Bedřich hrabě Sylva Tarouca," *ČMM*, XIII (1881), 121-62.

―――. "Příspěvky k životopisu Matouše Frant. Klácela," *ČMM*, XII (1881), 71-120.

Burian, P. *Die Nationalitäten in 'Cisleithanien' und das Wahlrecht der Märzrevolution 1848-49*. Graz, 1962.

Butvin, J. *Slovenské národno-zjednocovacie hnutie (1780-1848)*. Bratislava, 1965.

Capek, T. *The First Czech Society in America*. Chicago, 1950.

Čechová, G., and J. Martínek. "Národní výbor v roce 1848," *SAP*, IV, No. 1 (1954), 3-81.

Čejchan, V. *Bakunin v Čechách*. Prague, 1928.

―――. "Italo-slovanský spolek v Turině a radikální hnutí v Čechách na jaře roku 1849," *Slovanské Historické Studie*, III (1960), 313-54.

―――. "M. Bakunin v Praze roku 1848," *ČČH*, XXXVIII (1932), 564-69.

Čelakovský, J. "Stav městský na sněmě českém od léta 1794-1847," Part IV, *ČČM*, XLIV (1870), 3-42.

Černý, V. "Jednání říšského sněmu r. 1848 o zrušení poddanství," *ČDV*, XV (1928), 232-49.

Červinka, F. *Český nacionalismus v XIX století*. Prague, 1964.

―――. *Přehled dějin Československa v epoše kapitalismu*, Vol. I (1848-49), Vol. II (1849-1918). Prague, 1959, 1958.

Československá vlastivěda, Doplněk I, Dějiny 1, by J. Prokeš. Prague, 1933.

Chaloupecký, V. "Hrabě Josef Matyáš Thun a slovanský sjezd v Praze r. 1848," *ČČH*, XIX (1913), 84-91.

Chalupný, E. *Havlíček: Prostředí, osobnost a dílo.* Prague, 1929.

Chlebowczyk, J. *Wybory do organów przedstawicielskich na Ślasku cieszyńskim w 1848 r.* Katowice, 1964.

Dějiny české literatury, Vol. II, ed. F. Vodička. Prague, 1960.

Dějiny Prahy. Prague, 1964.

Dubský, I. *Pronikání marxismu do českých zemí.* Prague, 1963.

Duroselle, J.-B. *L'Europe de 1815 à nos jours: Vie politique et relations internationales.* ("Nouvelle Clio," No. 38.) Paris, 1964.

Dvořák, J. *Moravské sněmování roku 1848-49.* Telč, 1898.

Fejtö, F. (ed.). *The Opening of an Era: 1848.* London, 1948.

Felczak, W. "Vplyv národnostnej otázky na spoločenský charakter maďarskej revolúcie r. 1848," *HČ,* XIV (1966), 85-99. (Appeared originally in Polish in *Przeglad Historyczny,* LIV [1963], 572-91.)

————. *Wegierska polityka narodowościowa przed wybuchem powstania 1848 roku.* Wroclaw-Warszawa, 1964.

Fellner, F. *Franz Schuselka: Ein Lebensbild.* Unpublished doctor's dissertation, University of Vienna, 1948.

Fischer, E. *Österreich 1848.* Vienna, 1946.

Fischer, J. *Myšlenka a dílo Františka Palackého.* 2 vols. Prague, 1926-27.

Fischer, K. "Prager Studenten und Legionäre im J. 1848," *MVGDB,* XLV (1907), 556-61.

Formánek, M. *Myšlenkový odkaz Karla Havlíčka Borovského.* Prague, 1961.

Franz, E. G. *Das Amerikabild der deutschen Revolution von 1848-49.* Heidelberg, 1958.

Friedjung, H. *Österreich von 1848 bis 1860.* 2nd ed. 2 vols. Stuttgart, 1908-12.

Frommelt, K. *Die Sprachenfrage im österreichischen Unterrichtswesen 1848-1859.* Graz-Köln, 1963.

Geist-Lányi, P. *Das Nationalitätenproblem auf dem Reichstag zu Kremsier 1848-49.* Munich, 1920.

Goláň, K. *Štúrovské pokolenie (Výber z diela),* ed. F. Bokeš. Bratislava, 1964.

Goll, J. *Rozdělení pražské university Karlo-Ferdinandovy roku 1882.* Prague, 1908.

Grobelný, A. *Češi a Poláci ve Slezsku v letech 1848-1867.* Ostrava, 1958.

Grünberg, K. *Die Bauernbefreiung und die Auflösung des gutsherrlich-bäuerlichen Verhältnisses in Böhmen, Mähren und Schlesien,* Vols. I and II. Leipzig, 1894, 1893.

Hafner, S. "Das austro-slawische Konzept in der ersten Hälfte des 19 Jahrhunderts," *ÖO*, V (1963), 435-44.

Hanák, P. *Ugnetennye narody Avstriiskoi Imperii i Vengerskaia revoliutsiia 1848-1849 gg.* ("Studia Historica Academiae Scientiarum Hungaricae 5.") Budapest, 1953.

Heidler, J. *Antonín Springer a česká politika v letech 1848-1850.* Prague, 1914.

———. *Čechy a Rakousko v politických brožurách předbřeznových.* Prague, 1920.

———. "Český sněm ústavodárný 1848," *ČČH*, XIII (1907), 36-59.

Helfert, J. A. *Geschichte der österreichischen Revolution im Zusammenhange mit der mitteleuropäischen Bewegung der Jahre 1848-1849.* 2 vols. Freiburg im Breisgau, 1907-9.

———. *Geschichte Österreichs vom Ausgange des Wiener Oktober-Aufstandes 1848,* Vols. I, II, III, and IV/1-3. Prague, 1869-86.

———. "Graf Leo Thun," in four parts, in *Österreichisches Jahrbuch,* XVIII (1894), 93-158; XIX (1895), 137-224; XX (1896), 179-254; XXI (1897), 1-271.

———. *Der Prager Juni-Aufstand 1848.* Prague, 1897. (Originally published in *Österreichesches Jahrbuch,* XXI [1897], as Part IV of "Graf Leo Thun.")

Historický atlas revolučního hnutí. Prague, 1956.

Hobsbawm, E. J. *The Age of Revolution, 1789-1848.* New York, 1964. (Originally published in 1962.)

Hoch, K. "Sociálně-politické poměry v Čechách před r. 1848," *ČČH,* XXXVIII (1932), 113-25.

Horáček, C. *Počátky českého hnutí dělnického.* 2nd ed. Prague, 1933. (1st ed., 1896).

Hostička, V. "Spolupráce Čechů a haličských Ukrainců v letech 1848-1849," *Rozpravy ČSAV-SV,* LXXV, Fasc. 12 (1965).

Hroch, M. "K problematice formování buržoazního národa v Evropě," *ČSČH,* IX (1961), 374-95.

Hrzalová, H. "Jak vznikal a uskutečňoval se ideál demokratické literatury kolem roku 1848," *Česká Literatura,* VII (1959), 40-60.

———. "Rozmach českého novinářství v letech 1848-1849 a jeho význam pro vývoj české literatury," *Česká Literatura,* V (1957), 409-40.

Hugelmann, K. *Die österreichischen Landtage im Jahre 1848,* Part III, published as *AÖG,* CXV, Part I (1940).

Ibler, H. "Die Wahlen zur Frankfurter Nationalversammlung in Österreich 1848 . . . ," *MIÖG,* XLVIII (1934), 103-12.

Istoriia Chekhoslovakii, Vol. II. Moscow, 1959.

Jetmarová, M. *František Palacký.* Prague, 1961.

Jílek, F. "Pražská polytechnika a její studenti v revolučním roce 1848," *Sborník Národního technického muzea,* IV (1965), 268-366.

J. V. Frič a demokratické proudy v české politice a kultuře: Sborník statí. Prague, 1956.

Kameníček, F. "Protokoly ústavního výboru říšského sněmu rakouského 1848-49," in *Pekařův Sborník,* Vol. II. Prague, 1930.

Kan, S. B. *Revoliutsiia 1848 goda v Avstrii i Germanii.* Moscow, 1948.

Kann, R. A. *The Multinational Empire: Nationalism and National Reform in the Habsburg Monarchy, 1848-1918.* 2 vols. New York, 1950. (Revised edition available only in German as: *Das Nationalitätenproblem der Habsburgermonarchie.* 2 vols. Graz-Köln, 1964.)

Karníková, L. *Vývoj obyvatelstva v českých zemích 1754-1914.* Prague, 1965.

Kazbunda, K. *České hnutí roku 1848.* Prague, 1929. (Part I appeared separately in *ČČH,* XXXIV [1928], 25-121.)

————. *Stolice dějin na pražské universitě.* 2 vols. Prague, 1964-65.

Kimball, S. B. *Czech Nationalism: A Study of the National Theatre Movement, 1845-83.* Urbana, Ill., 1964.

Kiszling, R. *Die Revolution im Kaisertum Österreich 1848-1849.* 2 vols. Vienna, 1948.

Klíma, A. "Ein Beitrag zur Agrarfrage in der Revolution von 1848 in Böhmen," in *Studien zur Geschichte der österreichisch-ungarischen Monarchie.* Budapest, 1961. Pp. 15-26.

————. *Počátky českého dělnického hnutí.* Prague, 1950.

————. *Příručka k dějinám Československa v letech 1648 až 1848.* Prague, 1963.

————. *Rok 1848 v Čechách.* Prague, 1948.

Klimeš, V. *Česká vesnice v roce 1848.* Most, 1949.

Kočí, J. *Emanuel Arnold.* Prague, 1964.

————. "Havlíček a austroslavismus," *Dějiny a Současnost,* VII, No. 3 (1966), 9-12.

————. *Naše národní obrození.* Prague, 1960.

————. "Příspěvek k rolnické otázce v Čechách v r. 1848," *ČSČH,* V (1957), 59-85, 248-66.

Kohn, H. *Pan-Slavism: Its History and Ideology.* 2nd ed. New York, 1960. (Paperback.)

Kořalka, J. "Das Nationalitätenproblem in den böhmischen Ländern 1848-1918," *ÖO,* V (1963), 1-12.

———. "K některým problémům národní a národnostní otázky v českých zemích v období kapitalismu," *ČSČH,* III (1962), 376-91.

———. "Über die Anfänge der sozialistichen Arbeiterbewegung in der Tschechoslowakei," *ZfG,* IX (1961), 111-43.

———. "Über die Anfänge der Zusammenarbeit zwischen der Arbeiterbewegung in Deutschland und in den böhmischen Ländern," in *Aus 500 Jahren deutsch-tschechoslowakischer Geschichte,* ed. K. Obermann and J. Polišenský. Berlin, 1958.

———. *Vznik socialistického dělnického hnutí na Liberecku. Liberec,* 1956.

Kosík, K. *Česká radikální demokracie.* Prague, 1958.

———. "Politické názory Emanuela Arnolda," *Filosofický Časopis,* I (1953), 184-202.

Král, V. "F. A. Brauner za revoluce a reakce 1848-1849," *SAP,* II, No. 1 (1952), 123-90.

Kranzberg, M. (ed.). *1848, A Turning Point?* ("Problems in European Civilization.") Boston, 1949.

Křížek, J. *Národní gardy v roce 1848.* Prague, 1954.

Krofta, K. *Byli jsme za Rakouska* . . . . Prague, 1936.

Kutnar, F. "Krise českého bramborářství a sociální situace lidu v době před březnem a po březnu roku 1848," *SH,* X (1962), 229-72.

———. "Počátky hromadného vystěhovalectví z Čech v období Bachova absolutismu," *Rozpravy ČSAV-SV,* LXXIV, Fasc. 15 (1964).

———. *Přehled dějin Československa v epoše feudalismu,* Vol. IV (1740-1848). Prague, 1963.

———. "Sociální otázka tkalcovská v polovině 19. století," *SH,* II (1954), 186-232.

Lades, H. *Die Tschechen und die deutsche Frage.* Erlangen, 1938.

Laiske, M. *Časopisectví v Čechách 1650-1847.* Bibliografický katalog ČSR—České knihy, 1959, Spec. No. 6. Prague, 1959.

Lepšík, J. "Stavy obležení v Čechách v letech 1848-1853," *Rozpravy ČSAV-SV,* LXX, Fasc. 12 (1960).

Lešniewski, A. *Bakunin a sprawy polskie w okresie wiosńy ludów i powstania styczniowego 1863 roku.* Lódź, 1962.

Link, E. M. *The Emancipation of the Austrian Peasant 1740-1798.* New York, 1949.

Lubasz, H. (ed.). *Revolutions in Modern European History.* New York, 1966.

Machovcová, M., and M. Machovec. *Utopie blouznivců a sektářů.* Prague, 1960.

Macůrek, J. "The Achievements of the Slavonic Congress," *SEER,* XXVI (1947-48), 329-40.

——. *Rok 1848 a Morava.* Brno, 1948.

Mann, S. E. "Karel Havlíček: A Slav Pragmatist," *SEER,* XXXIX (1961), 413-22.

Maršan, R. *Čechové a Němci r. 1848 a boj o Frankfurt.* Prague, 1898.

——. "Příspěvky k zjištění vlivu cizích ústav na ústavní zákonodárství rakouské let 1848-1849," *Sborník Věd Právních a Státních,* X (1910), 305-56.

Marx, J. "Die ämtlichen Verbotslisten," *MÖSA,* IX (1956), 151-85.

——. *Die österreichische Zensur im Vormärz.* Vienna, 1959.

——. "Vormärzliches Schedenwesen," *MÖSA,* XVI (1963), 453-68.

——. *Die wirtschaftlichen Ursachen der Revolution von 1848 in Österreich.* Graz-Köln, 1965.

——. "Die Wirtschaftslage im deutschen Österreich vor Ausbruch der Revolution 1848," *Vierteljahrschrift für Sozial-und Wirtschaftsgeschichte,* XXXI (1938), 242-82.

Masaryk, T. G. *Česká otázka.* Prague, 1948. (Published in one volume with *Naše nynější krise.*)

——. *Karel Havlíček.* 3rd ed. Prague, 1920.

Matoušek, J. *Karel Sladkovský a český radikalismus za revoluce a reakce.* Prague, 1929.

Matula, V. "Slovanská vzájomnosť—národnooslobodzovacia ideológia slovenského národného hnutia (1835-1849)," *HČ,* VII (1960), 248-64.

Mésároš, J. "K niektorým otázkám hodnotenia Ľudovíta Štúra," *Slovenská Literatura,* XII (1965), 458-65.

——. "Súčasný stav badania štúrovskej problematiky," *HČ,* XIV (1966), 270-80.

Mokrý, A. *Karel Havlíček Borovský po sto letech.* Lund, 1956.

——. *První kroky: K historii roku 1848.* Lund, 1957.

Molisch, P. "Die Wiener akademische Legion und ihr Anteil an den Verfassungskämpfen des Jahres 1848," *AÖG,* CX (1924).

Mommsen, W. *Grosse und Versagen des deutschen Bürgertums: Ein Beitrag zur politischen Bewegung des 19. Jahrhunderts, insbesondere zur Revolution 1848-49.* 2nd ed. Munich, 1964.

Mylnikov, A. S. "Mesto i znachenie cheshskikh radikalnykh demokratov v cheshskoi istoriografii XIX v.," *Novaia i Noveishaia Istoriia,* No. 2 (1964), 37-47.

Myška, M. *Počátky vytváření dělnické třídy v železárnách na Ostravsku*. Ostrava, 1962.

Nachtmann, E. "Die wirtschaftliche und soziale Lage Brünns im Revolutionsjahr 1848-49," in *Heimat und Volk: Festschrift für . . . W. Wostry*, ed. A. Ernstberger. Brünn, 1937. Pp. 523-45.

Namier, L. B. *1848: The Revolution of the Intellectuals*. London, 1944. (From the Proceedings of the British Academy, Vol. 30, 1944).

Nespor, V. *Dějiny university olomoucké*. Olomouc, 1947.

Novák, M. "Austroslavismus: Příspěvek k jeho pojetí v době předbřeznové," *SAP*, VI, No. 1 (1956), 26-51.

———. "Rakouská policie a politický vývoj v Čechách před r. 1848," *SAP*, III, Nos. 1-2 (1953), 43-167.

Novotny, A. *1848: Österreichs Ringen um Freiheit und Völkerfrieden vor hundert Jahren*. Graz, 1948.

Novotný, J. *Češi a Slováci za národního obrození a do vzniku československého státu*. Prague, 1968.

———. "K některým problémům slovanské myšlenky v českém národním hnutí v době předbřeznové," *HČ*, VIII (1960), 265-90.

———. *O. bratrské družbě Čechů a Slováků za národního obrození*.

———. "Příspěvek k vzájemným vztahům Čechů a Slováků v první etapě revoluce roku 1848," *HČ*, XI (1963), 366-88.

———. "Prispevok k otázke bratských vzťahov Čechov a Slovákov v období národneho obrodenia (do roku 1848)," *Historické Štúdie*, III (1957), 7-72.

Novotný, K. "Hnutí typografického dělnictva v Praze r. 1848," *Zápisky katedry čsl. dějin a archivního studia*, III, Nos. 1-2 (1958), 7-19.

———. "První český časopis pro dělnictvo: Kampelíkův 'Hlasník' z r. 1848," *Novinářský Sborník*, X (1965), 173-79.

Obermann, K. *Deutschland von 1815 bis 1849*. Berlin, 1961.

———, and J. Polišenský (ed.). *Aus 500 Jahren deutsch-tschechoslowakischer Geschichte*. Berlin, 1958.

Odložilík, O. "A Czech plan for a Danube Federation in 1848," *JCEA*, I (1941), 253-74.

———. "The Czechs on the Eve of the 1848 Revolution," *Harvard Slavic Studies* I (1953), 179-217.

———. *Na kroměřížském sněmu 1848 a 1849*. Prague, 1947.

———. "The Slavic Congress of 1848," *Polish Review*, IV (1959), 3-15.

————. "Vyšetřovací komise z r. 1848 a jejich registratura," *SAMV*, II (1929), 3-90.

Österreichisches Biographisches Lexikon, 1815-1950. Vols. I-III, and IV. Graz-Köln, 1957-66.

Okáč, A. *Český sněm a vláda před březnem 1848.* Prague, 1947.

Olesker, I. *Der Anteil der Juden an den Nationalitätenkämpfen in Böhmen im 19. Jahrhundert.* Unpublished doctor's dissertation, University of Vienna, 1934.

Owsińska, A. *Powstanie palatynacko-badeńskie 1849 roku.* Wroclaw-Warszawa-Kraków, 1965.

Palacký, F. *Popis králowství českého.* Prague, 1848.

Pech, S. Z. "The Czech Working Class in 1848," *Canadian Slavonic Papers,* IX (1967), 60-73.

————. "The June Uprising in Prague in 1848," *The East European Quarterly,* I (January, 1968), 341-70.

Pešková, J. "Ideologická emancipace společenských tříd v buržoazní revoluci," *AUC, Philosophica et Historica* No. 2 (1963), 157-85.

————. *Utopický socialismus v Čechách v XIX. století.* Prague, 1965.

Pfitzner, J. *Bakuninstudien.* Prague, 1932.

————. *Das Erwachen der Sudetendeutschen im Spiegel ihrer Schrifttums bis zum Jahre 1848.* Augsburg, 1926.

————. "Die Wahlen in die Frankfurter Nationalversammlung und der Sudetenraum," *Zeitschrift für Sudetendeutsche Geschichte,* V (1941), 199-240.

————. "Zur nationalen Politik der Sudetendeutschen in den Jahren 1848-1849," *Jahrbuch des Vereins für die Geschichte der Deutschen in Böhmen,* III (1933), 210-43.

Plaschka, R. G. "Zur Einberufung des Slawenkongresses 1848," *Bausteine zur Geschichte Österreichs,* published as *AÖG,* CXXV (1966), 196-207.

Pokorný, V. "Příspěvek ke kritice Springerova vydání protokolů ústavního výboru rakouského říšského sněmu 1848-1849," *PHS,* II (1956), 32-42.

————. "Volební zákonodárství v Čechách v letech 1848-1849," *PHS,* VI (1960) 95-110.

Polišenský, J. "Obor historie na pražské universitě kolem roku 1848," *AUC, Philosophica et Historica,* II (1958), 113-30.

Postgate, R. W. *Story of a Year: 1848* New York, 1956.

Potemkin, F. V., and A. I. Molok (eds.). *Revoliutsii 1848-1849.* 2 vols. Moscow, 1952.

Pražák, A. *Češi a Slováci.* Prague, 1929.

————. "Czechs and Slovaks after 1848," *SEER, VI* (1927-28), 119-29.

————. "Czechs and Slovaks in 1848," *SEER,* V (1926-27), 565-79.

————. "The Slavonic Congress of 1848 and the Slovaks," *SEER,* VII (1928-29), 141-59.

Přehled československých dějin, Vol. II/1. Prague, 1960.

Prelog, M. *Slavenska renesansa 1780-1848.* Zagreb, 1924.

Prinz, F. "Die Sudetendeutschen im Frankfurter Parlament," in *Zwischen Frankfurt und Prag.* Munich, 1963. Pp. 103-32.

————. *Prag und Wien 1848* (Munich, 1968).

————. "Revolution und Neoabsolutismus," in *Handbuch der Geschichte der böhmischen Länder,* Vol. III, Fasc. 1, ed. K. Bosl. Stuttgart, 1967. Pp. 13-64.

Procházka, V. *Karel Havlíček Borovský.* Prague, 1961.

Purš, J. "Die Aufhebung der Hörigkeit und die Grundentlastung in den böhmischen Ländern," in *Deuxième conférence internationale d'histoire économique, Aix-en-Provence, 1962.* Paris, 1965. Pp. 247-57.

————. "The Industrial Revolution in the Czech Lands," *Historica,* II (1960), 183-272.

————. "K problematice průmyslové revoluce v ČSR," *ČSČH,* IV (1956), 1-27.

————. "K případu Karla Sabiny," *Rozpravy ČSAV-SV,* LXIX, Fasc. 8 (1959).

Radimský, J. "Dělnické bouře v Brně roku 1843," *Český Lid,* XXXVI (1949), 9-13.

————. "Zemědělská krise před sto lety," *ČMM,* LXVII (1948), 328-51.

Rapant, D. *Slovenské povstanie roku 1848-49: Dejiny a dokumenty,* Vols. I/1-2, II/1-3, III/1-3, IV/1-3, and V/1. Turčiansky Sväty Martin, 1937-48; Bratislava, 1954-67.

————. "Slovak Politics in 1848-1849," *SEER,* XXVII (1948-49), 67-90, 381-403.

————. "Štúr a štúrovci v službe národa a pokroku," *Slovenská Literatúra,* XII (1965), 437-57.

Rath, R. J. "The Viennese Liberals of 1848 and the Nationality Problem," *JCEA,* XV (1955), 227-39.

————. *The Viennese Revolution of 1848.* Austin, Tex., 1957.

Raupach, H. *Der tschechische Frühnationalismus.* Essen, 1939.

Rechcígl, M., Jr. (ed.). *The Czechoslovak Contribution to World Culture.* The Hague, 1964.

Redlich, J. *Das österreichische Staats-und Reichsproblem.* 2 vols. Vienna, 1920-26.

Revai, J. *Marks i vengerskaia revoliutsiia 1848-1849 gg.* ("Studia Historica Academiae Scientiarum Hungaricae 1.") Budapest, 1951.

Revolution von 1848-49 und die Sudetendeutschen, Die," *Archiv für Politik und Geschichte,* VII (1926), 430-70.

Rieger, B. "Náš ústavní vývoj od r. 1848," *Osvěta,* XXVII-XXVIII (1897-98).

———. "O snaze spojiti země koruny české v r. 1848," *Osvěta,* XXVII (1898), 861-72.

———. "Ústava Rakouská dle Františka Palackého v letech 1848-49," in *Památník na oslavu stých narozenin Františka Palackého.* Prague, 1898.

Říha, O. "O národním hnutí a národnostní otázce 1848-1918," *ČSČH,* II (1954), 47-68.

Robertson, P. *Revolutions of 1848: A Social History.* Princeton, N. J., 1952.

Roubík, F. *Časopisectvo v Čechách v letech 1848-1862.* Pague, 1930.

———. *Český rok 1848.* Prague, 1931, 1948.

———. "Český venkov a zrušení roboty v redakční korespondenci Karla Havlíčka z r. 1848," *ČDV,* XXV (1938), 185-98.

———. "Ke vzniku úředních soupisů účastníků hnutí v letech 1848-1849," *Časopis Společnosti přátel starožitností,* LXX (1962), 150-56.

———. "K vyvazení gruntů v Čechách v letech 1848-1853," *SAP,* IX, No. 2 (1959), 160-219.

———. "Na českém venkově roku 1848," *ČDV,* XV (1928), 161-231.

———. "Registratura Národního výboru," *Časopis Archivní školy,* VI (1928), 126-53.

———. "Úřední evidence osob politicky činných v Čechách v letech 1848 až 1849," *Časopis Společnosti přátel starožitností,* LVII (1949), 21-26.

Rudé, G. *The Crowd in History, 1730-1848.* New York, 1964.

Šafařík, P. J. "Myšlenky o prowedení stejného práwa českého i německého jazyka na školách českých," *ČČM,* XXII (1848), 171-97.

Šafránek, J. *Školy české.* 2 vols. Prague, 1913-18.

Šamberger, Z. "Emanuel Arnold, radikální demokrat roku 1848," *SAP,* I, No. 1 (1951), 17-164.

———. "Die revolutionäre Zusammenarbeit der tschechischen und sächsischen Demokraten im Frühjahr 1849," in *Aus 500 Jahren deutsch-tschechoslowakischer Geschichte,* ed. K. Obermann and J. Polišenský. Berlin, 1958.

Schilfert, G. *Sieg und Niederlage des demokratischen Wahlrechts in der deutschen Revolution 1848-49*. Berlin, 1952.

Schüssler, W. *Die nationale Politik der österreichischen Abgeordneten im Frankfurter Parlament*. ("Abh. zur Mittleren und Neueren Geschichte, Heft 51.")

Schwarzenberg, A. *Prince Felix zu Schwarzenberg, Prime Minister of Austria 1848-1852*. New York, 1946.

Seton-Watson, R. W. *A History of the Czechs and Slovaks*. London, 1943.

Šidak, J. "Austroslavizam i Slavenski kongres u Pragu 1848," *Historijski Pregled*, VI (1960), 204-18.

————. "Češki narodni pokret 1848-49," *Historijski Pregled*, VII (1961), 188-200.

————. "Listopadska revolucija u Beču," *Historijski Pregled*, V (1959), 325-29.

————. "Poslanstvo hrvatskog sabora austrijskom parlamentu g. 1848," *Radova Filozofskog fakulteta u Zagrebu, Odsjek za povijest*, III (1960), 1-33.

Sieber, E. K. *Ludwig von Löhner: Ein Vorkämpfer des Deutschtums in Böhmen, Mähren und Schlesien im Jahre 1848-1849*. Munich, 1965.

Šindelář, B. "Ohlas maďarské revoluce 1848/49 na Moravě a ve Slezsku," *Rozpravy ČSAV-SV*, LXVII, Fasc. 3 (1957).

————. "O úloze lidových mas v revolučním dění roku 1848 na Moravě a ve Slezsku," *ČSČH*, IV (1956), 207-31, 388-417.

————. "Přehled dějin dělnického hnutí na Moravě do hainfeldského sjezdu," *ČMM*, LXXIII (1954), 3-57.

Slavíček, K. *Tajná politická společnost Český Repeal v roce 1848*. Prague, 1947.

Slováci a ich národný vývin. Bratislava, 1966.

Slovanský sjezd v Praze 1848. Prague, 1948.

Sobotík, B. "Bouře lidu na Hlučínsku v září 1848," *Slezský Sborník*, LXIV (1966), 341-47.

Šolle, V. "Civilní soudnictví předbřeznové v českých zemích," *SAP*, X, No. 1 (1960), 11-145.

Šolle, Z. "K počátkům dělnického hnutí v Praze," *ČSČH*, V (1957), 664-87; VI (1958), 266-310; VII (1959), 49-70.

Spáčil, J. *Veškerá moc ve státě vychází z lidu; kronika o kroměřížském sněmu 1848-1849*. Kroměříž, 1948.

Springer, A. *Geschichte des Revolutionszeitalters 1789-1848*. Prague, 1849.

————. *Geschichte Oesterreichs seit dem Wiener Frieden 1809*. 2 vols. Leipzig, 1863-65.

Springer, J. *Statistik des österreichischen Kaiserstaates.* 2 vols. Vienna, 1840.

Stanislav, B. *Karel Havlíček Borovský.* Prague, 1954.

Starčevič, V. "Vilém Dušan Lambl a Jihoslované v letech 1848-1850," in *Česká společnost a balkánské národy.* ("Slovanské Historické Studie VI.") Prague, 1966. Pp. 93-125.

Stiles, W. H. *Austria in 1848-49.* 2 vols. New York, 1852.

Šubrtová, A. "Zápisky Karla Červeného o svatodušních bouřích v Praze roku 1848," *Sborník Národního Muzea v Praze,* Series "A," XX, No. 4 (1966), 269-79.

Sudentendeutscher Atlas, ed. E. Meynen. 2nd ed. Munich, 1955.

Svobodová, D., and Z. Svoboda. "Neznámý židovský deník z roku 1848," *Sborník Narodního Muzea v Praze,* Series "A," XX, No. 4 (1966), 281-311.

Szilassy, S. "America and the Hungarian Revolution of 1848-49," *SEER,* XLIV (1966), 180-96.

Teller, H. G. *Das österreichische Problem im Frankfurter Parlament im Sommer und Herbst 1848.* Marburg, 1933.

Thomson, S. H. *Czechoslovakia in European History.* 2nd ed. Princeton, 1953.

Tichý, J. *Rok 1848 v obrazech.* Prague, 1948.

Tille, V. *Božena Němcové.* Prague, 1947.

Tkadlečková, J. "Názory a činnosť Karla Havlíčka Borovského z hľadiska vývoja česko-slovenských vzťahov," *HČ,* VI (1958), 32-47.

Tobolka, Z. "Česká otázka v jednání frankfurtského parlamentu," *ČMM,* XXX (1906), 155-62, 220-28.

———— (ed.). *Česká politika.* 5 vols. Prague, 1906-13.

————. "Národní výbor r. 1848," *Obzor Národohospodářský,* X (1905), 13-25, 66-73, 112-23, 165-72.

————. "Počátky dělnického hnutí v Čechách," *Obzor Národohospodářský,* VIII (1903), 1-7, 57-62, 113-21, 159-68, 208-19.

————. *Počátky konstitučního života v Čechách.* Prague, 1898.

————. *Politické dějiny československého národa od 1848 až do dnešní doby,* Vol. I. Prague, 1932.

————. *Slovanský sjezd v Praze roku 1848.* Prague, 1901.

Tomek, V. V. *Paměti z mého života.* 2 vols. Prague, 1904-5.

Tóth, Z. I. *Koshut i natsionalnyi vopros v 1848-1849 gg.* ("Studia Historica Academiae Scientiarum Hungaricae 8.") Budapest, 1954.

————. "The Nationality Problem in Hungary in 1848-49," *Acta Historica,* IV (1955), 235-77.

Toužimský, J. J. *Na úsvitě nové doby.* Prague, 1898.

Trapl, M. "Klácelovy politické listy z roku 1849," *AUPO-H, III* (1962), 197-229.

――. "Olomoucká universita v době počínajícího odlivu revoluce od června do konce října 1848," *SVSPO-H, V* (1958), 5-33.

――. "Olomoucká universita v obodobí nástupu reakce," *AUPO-H, II* (1961), 5-54.

――. "Olomoucká universita v prvním (vzestupném) období revoluce roku 1848," *SVSPO-H, IV* (1957), 5-54.

Traub, H. *Květnové spiknutí v Čechách r. 1849.* Prague, 1929.

――. "Moravané r. 1848 po říšský sněm ve Vídni, se zvláštním zřetelem na poměr k Čechám," *ČMM,* XXXI (1907), 67-81, 176-92, 325-37, 428-39.

――. "Moravské časopisectvo v letech 1848-1849," *ČČM,* XCIV (1920), 103-16, 203-17.

――. "Ohlas říjnové revoluce vídeňské na Moravě," *Časopis Moravského Muzea Zemského,* XIII (1913), 293-315; XIV (1914), 97-138, 380-413.

Udalzow [Udalzov], I. I. *Aufzeichnungen über die Geschichte des nationalen und politischen Kampfes in Böhmen im Jahre 1848.* Berlin, 1953. (Translated from the Russian.)

Urban, R. "Marx und Engels über die tschechische Frage," *Donauraum,* VII (1962), 21-33.

Urfus, V. "Průmyslový liberalismus a české měšťanstvo v období národního obrození," *PHS, X* (1964), 5-32.

Vochala, J. *Rok 1848 ve Slezsku a na severovýchodní Moravě.* Opava, 1948.

Volf, J. "Agitace Em. Arnolda na českém venkově na jaře roku 1849," *ČDV, IX* (1922), 215-32.

――. "Vyšetřování E. Arnolda pro vydávání Občanských novin r. 1849," *ČČM, XLIII* (1919), 140-49.

Vomáčková, V. "Die Bourgeoisie in Böhmen und der Deutsche Zollverein im Jahre 1848," in *Aus 500 Jahren deutsch-tschechoslowakischer Geschichte,* ed. K. Obermann and J. Polišenský. Berlin, 1958. Pp. 223-48.

――. "K národnostní otázce v buržoazní revoluci 1848 v Českých zemích," *ČSČH, IX* (1961), 1-16.

――. "Österreich und der Deutsche Zollverein," *Historica, V* (1963), 109-46.

Walter, F. "Äusserungen führender österreichischer Personlichkeiten des Jahres 1848 zum Problem des Nationalismus," *Ostdeutsche Wissenschaft,* X (1963), 55-66.

Weinzierl-Fischer, E. "Die Kirchenfrage auf dem Österreichischen Reichstag 1848-49," *MÖSA, VIII* (1955), 160-90.

Werner, A. *Die Studenten-Legionen der Prager Universität vom 30 jährigen Krieg bis 1848.* Prague, 1934.

Whitridge, A. *Men in Crisis: The Revolutions of 1848.* New York, 1949.

Wierer, R. *Der Föderalismus im Donauraum.* Graz-Köln, 1960.

———. "F. Palacký's staatspolitisches Programm," *ZfO,* VI (1957), 246-58.

Winter, E. "Eine grundlegende Urkunde des Austroslavismus," *Zeitschrift für Slawistik,* III (1958), 107-24.

Wolfgramm, E. "Böhmen im Widerstreit der Nationalitäten; zum tschechisch-deutschen Verhältnis um 1848," in *Wissenschaftliche Zeitschrift der Karl-Marx-Universität Leipzig, Gesellschaftliche und Sprachwissenschaftliche Reihe,* XVI, Fasc. 1/2 (1967), 137-41.

———. "Der böhmische Vormärz, im besonderen die böhmischen Arbeitsunruhen des Jahres 1844 in ihren sozialen und politischen Zusammenhängen," in *Aus 500 Jahren deutsch-tschechoslowakischer Geschichte,* ed. K. Obermann and J. Polišenský. Berlin, 1958.

Wright, W. E. "The Initiation of *Robota* Abolition in Bohemia," *JCEA,* XVIII (1958), 239-53.

———. *Serf, Seigneur, and Sovereign.* Minneapolis, 1966.

W Stulecie Wiosny Ludów 1848-1948, ed. N. Gasiorowska. 5 vols. Warszawa, 1948-53.

Wurzbach, C. *Biographisches Lexikon des Kaisertums Oesterreich.* 60 vols. Vienna, 1856-91.

Zacek, J. F. "Palacký and His History of the Czech Nation," *JCEA,* XXII (1964), 412-23.

———. "Palacký and the Marxists," *Slavic Review,* XXIV (1965), 297-306.

Žáček, V. *Čechové a Poláci roku 1848.* 2 vols. Prague, 1947-48.

———. "Revoluční spolupráce Čechů a Poláků v Italii roku 1848," *ČČH,* XLVIII-XLIX (1947-48), 172-80.

———. "Zahraniční náboženská propaganda v Čechách v předvečer revoluce 1848," *Rozpravy České akademie věd a umění,* No. 98. Prague, 1945.

———. "Ze styků Čechů a západních Ukrajinců v revolučních letech 1848-1849," *Z dějin československo-ukrajinských vzťahov.* ("Slovanské Štúdie I.") Bratislava, 1957.

Zíbrt, C. " 'Sestry slovanské' čili 'Spolek Slovanek' r. 1848 v Praze," *Květy,* Part I, XXIX (1907), 25-38, 203-15, 375-88.

Index

A

Academic Legion: founding and functions of, 70; decline and demise of, 225, 253, 313, 315, 318; structure of, 312; Czechs and Germans in, 314

Adamites, 334n

American Club of Women: founded in Prague, 329

Andrian-Werburg, Baron [Victor]: as author of *Österreich und dessen Zukunft,* 43; wants to modernize Austrian institutions, 43; profound effect of critique of, 44

Anti-Semitism. *See* Jews

Archbishop of Prague. *See* Prague, Archbishop of

Army. *See* Windischgrätz, General Alfred

Arnold, Emanuel: agitates among peasants, 154; as editor of radical newspaper, 222; meeting of, with Bakunin, 244; comments on Czech resistance to government, 260; and peasant question, 282-83, 344; imprisoned, 354

Augsburger Allgemeine Zeitung: as main source of information about foreign countries, 35; would send army to Bohemia, 95

Austrian Silesia: as part of Czech Lands, 7n; Czech element weak in, 89, 108; Frankfurt elections in, 95; legislative body in, 108; provincial elections in, 108; serfdom in, 108; and Slavic Congress, 137; deputies of, in Imperial Parliament, 167; social unrest in, 287

Austro-Slavism: early history of, 37-38; advocated by Havlíček, 38; and Palacký, 81-85; economic motivation of, 83-84; at Slavic Congress, 124-32; and Slovaks, 270-71; as realistic policy for Czechs, 338-39

Awakeners, Czech national: achievements of, 23-29, 37

B

Bach, [Alexander]: on imperial sanction, 179-80; does not dare abrogate principle of national equality, 341; does not tamper with peasants' freedom, 346

Bakunin, Mikhail: at Slavic Congress, 129, 132; in June Uprising, 157; opposes Austro-Slavism, 240-41; as author of *Appeal to the Slavs,* 240-42; organizes May Conspiracy, 240-50; reasons of, for choosing Bohemia as center of May Conspiracy, 242-43; visits Prague, 245

Ball, Czech (1840): as milestone in development of Czech national consciousness, 27

Běchovice: bloody clash near, 153n

Bernolák, Anton, 264

Blanc, Louis: inspires Repeal demands for "organization of work and wages," 50; distrusted by Czech liberals, 51

Bohemia: number of inhabitants in, 7; ethnic structure of, 8n; administrative system of, 8-9; Czech national awakening in, 23-29; early Czech newspapers in, 34; autonomy for, demanded, 52, 62, 341-42; Cabinet Letter of April 8 promises autonomy for, 73; relationship of, to Germany, 77-99 *passim;* and elections to Frankfurt Assembly, 92-95; "provisional governing council" appointed for, 102; deputies of, in Imperial Parliament, 167; place of, in proposed imperial constitution, 215; viewed as German land, 335. *See also* Moravia

Bohemian diet: impotence of, under pre-March absolutism, 8-9; divided into four estates, 9; begins to reassert itself, 9, 44; proceedings of, could not be published, 36; plans to convoke, 102; elections to, 103-

of confidence to Imperial Parliament, 318

Pražák, Alois: opposed to union of Bohemia and Moravia, 74

Pražský Večerní List: founding of, 142, opposes compensation to landlords, 174; as the most articulate voice of radicals, 199; and Viennese revolution, 200; issues "A New Confession of Faith," 221

Prefect: as administrative head of region, 8; exercises police authority in his region, 10

Proletariat: used as pejorative term for workers, 20; public fears of, 20. *See also* Working class

R

Radical democrats. *See* Radicals

Radicals, Czech: elected to St. Václav Committee, 59; resist diluted version of March Petition, 62; accept Austro-Slavism, 85; dominate two mass rallies, 103; elected to Bohemian diet, 105; and Slavic Congress, 131, 136; newspaper of, 142; in Imperial Parliament, 173; oppose compensation to landlords, 174; and Viennese revolution, 194-200; and "A New Confession of Faith," 221; and Slovaks, 265; and peasants, 277-78; and workers, 297-98; and women, 324; compared with liberals, 344. *See also* Repeal; May Conspiracy

Railroad workers: riot of, in 1844, 19

Regions: as administrative divisions, 8

Reichenberger Wochenblatt: introduces first note of German opposition to Czechs, 87n

Reichsrat, 348

Repeal: origin and radical program of, 45; sympathy of, for Irish cause, 45; and workers, 45, 48; initiates call for public assembly, 47, 49; appeal of, to public, 48; Czechs and Germans cooperate in, 49; radicalism of, modified by liberals, 49-50; petition of, redrafted by Brauner, 50-53

Rieger, František Ladislav: helps organize first Czech ball, 27; joins Society for the Promotion of In-

dustry, 28; helps Polish revolutionaries, 41; in Italy, 56; in Imperial Parliament, 173; parliamentary speech of, on Magyar question, 184-85; drafts proposed Bill of Rights, 213-14, 340; and universal suffrage, 217-18; speech of, on Article I in Imperial Parliament, 228-29; and Slovaks, 265; forced into exile, 353

Right (political grouping): in Imperial Parliament, 170-72

Robot: during pre-1848 period, 14-15; abolished, 73, 107, 276, 277, 346; and Silesian Convent, 108; and Moravian diet, 277. *See also* Peasants; Serfdom

Roman Catholic Church: radical priests demand democratization of, 333n; call for introduction of synods in, 333n; call for abolition of celibacy in, 334

Royal Bohemian Society of Sciences: origin of, 30; Dobrovský as member of, 30; contributions of, to Czech awakening, 31; publishes early works of Palacký, 31

Ruge, Alfred: regards Czechs with sympathy, 97-98

Ruppert, Ludwig: as member of Repeal, 45, 47; elected to St. Václav Committee, 59; proposes introduction of universal suffrage, 115-16; proposes branches of National Committee in larger cities, 119

Russia: role of, in Slavdom, 37; treatment of Poles and Ukrainians by, 37; as threat to small nations, 38; danger of, stressed by Palacký in letter to Frankfurt, 84; and Slavic Congress, 124, 138

S

Sabina, Karel: at March Assembly, 59; and democratic literature, 156; and Viennese revolution, 200; as author of "A New Confession of Faith," 221; and Bakunin's *Appeal to the Slavs,* 241-42; role of, in May Conspiracy, 244; and Marxism, 304; on workers, 344; imprisoned, 354

Šafařík, Pavel Josef: as author of